Bad Arguments

Edited by
Robert Arp, Steven Barbone, and Michael Bruce

BAD ARGUMENTS

100
of the Most Important Fallacies in Western Philosophy

WILEY Blackwell

This edition first published 2019
© 2019 John Wiley & Sons Ltd

The right of Robert Arp, Steven Barbone, and Michael Bruce to be identified as the authors of the editorial material in this work has been asserted in accordance with law.

Registered Offices
John Wiley & Sons, Inc., 111 River Street, Hoboken, NJ 07030, USA
John Wiley & Sons Ltd, The Atrium, Southern Gate, Chichester, West Sussex, PO19 8SQ, UK

Editorial Office
9600 Garsington Road, Oxford, OX4 2DQ, UK

For details of our global editorial offices, customer services, and more information about Wiley products visit us at www.wiley.com.

Wiley also publishes its books in a variety of electronic formats and by print-on-demand. Some content that appears in standard print versions of this book may not be available in other formats.

Library of Congress Cataloging-in-Publication data applied for

Hardback ISBN: 9781119165781
Paperback ISBN: 9781119167907

Cover image: Wiley
Cover design by Wiley

Set in 10/12pt Sabon by SPi Global, Pondicherry, India

Printed and bound by CPI Group (UK) Ltd, Croydon, CR0 4YY

10 9 8 7 6 5 4 3

Contents

Notes on Contributors   xiii

    Introduction   1

Part I   Formal Fallacies   35

Propositional Logic   37

  1   Affirming a Disjunct   39
     Jason Iuliano

  2   Affirming the Consequent   42
     Brett Gaul

  3   Denying the Antecedent   46
     Brett Gaul

Categorical Logic   49

  4   Exclusive Premises   51
     Charlene Elsby

  5   Four Terms   55
     Charlene Elsby

  6   Illicit Major and Minor Terms   60
     Charlene Elsby

  7   Undistributed Middle   63
     Charlene Elsby

Part II   Informal Fallacies   67

Fallacies of Relevance   69

  8   *Ad Hominem:* Bias   71
     George Wrisley

9 *Ad Hominem:* Circumstantial   77
   George Wrisley

10 *Ad Hominem:* Direct   83
    George Wrisley

11 *Ad Hominem: Tu Quoque*   88
    George Wrisley

12 Adverse Consequences   94
    David Vander Laan

13 Appeal to Emotion: Force or Fear   98
    George Wrisley

14 Appeal to Emotion: Pity   102
    George Wrisley

15 Appeal to Ignorance   106
    Benjamin W. McCraw

16 Appeal to the People   112
    Benjamin W. McCraw

17 Appeal to Personal Incredulity   115
    Tuomas W. Manninen

18 Appeal to Ridicule   118
    Gregory L. Bock

19 Appeal to Tradition   121
    Nicolas Michaud

20 Argument from Fallacy   125
    Christian Cotton

21 Availability Error   128
    David Kyle Johnson

22 Base Rate   133
    Tuomas W. Manninen

23 Burden of Proof   137
    Andrew Russo

24 Countless Counterfeits   140
    David Kyle Johnson

25 Diminished Responsibility   145
    Tuomas W. Manninen

26 Essentializing   149
    Jack Bowen

27 Galileo Gambit   152
    David Kyle Johnson

28 Gambler's Fallacy   157
    Grant Sterling

29 Genetic Fallacy   160
    Frank Scalambrino

30 Historian's Fallacy   163
    Heather Rivera

31 Homunculus   165
    Kimberly Baltzer-Jaray

32 Inappropriate Appeal to Authority   168
    Nicolas Michaud

33 Irrelevant Conclusion   172
    Steven Barbone

34 Kettle Logic   174
    Andy Wible

35 Line Drawing   177
    Alexander E. Hooke

36 Mistaking the Relevance of Proximate Causation   181
    David Kyle Johnson

37 Moving the Goalposts   185
    Tuomas W. Manninen

38 Mystery, Therefore Magic   189
    David Kyle Johnson

39 Naturalistic Fallacy   193
    Benjamin W. McCraw

40 Poisoning the Well   196
    Roberto Ruiz

41 Proving Too Much   201
    Kimberly Baltzer-Jaray

42 Psychologist's Fallacy   204
    Frank Scalambrino

43 Red Herring   208
    Heather Rivera

44 *Reductio ad Hitlerum*   212
    Frank Scalambrino

45 Argument by Repetition   215
    Leigh Kolb

46 Special Pleading   219
    Dan Yim

47 Straw Man   223
    Scott Aikin and John Casey

48 Sunk Cost   227
    Robert Arp

49 Two Wrongs Make a Right   230
    David LaRocca

50 Weak Analogy   234
    Bertha Alvarez Manninen

Fallacies of Ambiguity   239

51 Accent   241
    Roberto Ruiz

52 Amphiboly   246
    Roberto Ruiz

53 Composition   250
    Jason Waller

54 Confusing an Explanation for an Excuse   252
    Kimberly Baltzer-Jaray

55 Definist Fallacy   255
    Christian Cotton

56 Division   259
    Jason Waller

57 Equivocation   261
    Bertha Alvarez Manninen

58 Etymological Fallacy   266
    Leigh Kolb

59 Euphemism   270
    Kimberly Baltzer-Jaray

60 Hedging   273
    Christian Cotton

61 If by Whiskey   277
    Christian Cotton

62 Inflation of Conflict   280
    Andy Wible

63 Legalistic Mistake   282
    Marco Antonio Azevedo

64 Oversimplification   286
    Dan Burkett

65 Proof by Verbosity   289
    Phil Smolenski

66 Sorites Fallacy   293
    Jack Bowen

Fallacies of Presumption   297

67 Accident   299
    Steven Barbone

68 All or Nothing   301
    David Kyle Johnson

69 Anthropomorphic Bias   305
    David Kyle Johnson

70 Begging the Question   308
    Heather Rivera

71 Chronological Snobbery   311
    A.G. Holdier

72 Complex Question   314
    A.G. Holdier

73 Confirmation Bias   317
    David Kyle Johnson

74 Conjunction   321
    Jason Iuliano

75 Constructive Nature of Perception   324
    David Kyle Johnson

76 Converse Accident   330
    Steven Barbone

77   Existential Fallacy   332
     Frank Scalambrino

78   False Cause: *Cum Hoc Ergo Propter Hoc*   ***335***
     Bertha Alvarez Manninen

79   False Cause: Ignoring Common Cause   338
     Bertha Alvarez Manninen

80   False Cause: *Post Hoc Ergo Propter Hoc*   342
     Bertha Alvarez Manninen

81   False Dilemma   346
     Jennifer Culver

82   Free Speech   348
     Scott Aikin and John Casey

83   Guilt by Association   351
     Leigh Kolb

84   Hasty Generalization   354
     Michael J. Muniz

85   Intentional Fallacy   357
     Nicolas Michaud

86   Is/Ought Fallacy   360
     Mark T. Nelson

87   Masked Man   364
     Charles Taliaferro

88   Middle Ground   367
     Grant Sterling

89   Mind Projection   369
     Charles Taliaferro

90   Moralistic Fallacy   371
     Galen Foresman

91   No True Scotsman   374
     Tuomas W. Manninen

92   Reification   378
     Robert Sinclair

93   Representative Heuristic   382
     David Kyle Johnson

94	Slippery Slope *Michael J. Muniz*	385
95	Stolen Concept *Rory E. Kraft, Jr.*	388
96	Subjective Validation *David Kyle Johnson*	392
97	Subjectivist Fallacy *Frank Scalambrino*	396
98	Suppressed Evidence *David Kyle Johnson*	399
99	Unfalsifiability *Jack Bowen*	403
100	Unwarranted Assumption *Kimberly Baltzer-Jaray*	407

Index   410

Notes on Contributors

Scott F. Aikin is Assistant Professor of Philosophy at Vanderbilt University. He works primarily in epistemology and pragmatism. Aikin is author of two books: *Epistemology and the Regress Problem* (Routledge, 2011) and *Evidentialism and the Will to Believe* (Bloomsbury, 2014). He and John Casey have co-authored a number of articles on fallacy theory.

Robert Arp is a researcher for the US Army and has interests in the history of Western philosophy. With Jamie Watson, he treats fallacies in the 2nd edition of his book, *Critical Thinking: An Introduction to Reasoning Well* (Bloomsbury, 2015). See robertarp.com.

Marco Antonio Azevedo is a physician and doctor in philosophy, and teaches in the Graduate Program in Philosophy at Unisinos (University of Vale do Rio dos Sinos, Brazil). He is interested in issues in metaethics, bioethics, and philosophy of medicine. His students know well how much he is bothered by the lack of appreciation for argument in any field.

Kimberly Baltzer is a lecturer at King's University College (at Western) for the departments of Philosophy and Social Justice & Peace Studies. Although her expertise lies in Munich Phenomenology and Existentialism, her interests are vast: metaphysics, epistemology, hermeneutics, Dadaism, WWI history, and tattoo aesthetics and culture.

Steven Barbone is an associate professor of philosophy at San Diego State University. He enjoyed working on this volume as well as on *Just the Arguments: 100 of the Most Important Arguments in Western Philosophy* (Wiley-Blackwell, 2011) with Michael Bruce.

Gregory L. Bock is Senior Lecturer of Philosophy and Religion at The University of Texas at Tyler, where he teaches logic, among other things. His research interests include ethics and philosophy of religion.

Jack Bowen teaches philosophy at Menlo School in Atherton, California. He is the author of four books in philosophy including *The Dream Weaver: One Boy's Journey through The Landscape of Reality* (Pearson, 2006), *If You Can Read This: The Philosophy of Bumper Stickers* (Random House,

2010) and *Sport, Ethics, and Leadership* (co-authored, Routledge, 2017). He has written on fallacies in his book *A Journey through the Landscape of Philosophy* (Pearson, 2007).

Michael Bruce is a software consultant in San Francisco and specializes in the history of Western philosophy. Along with Steven Barbone, he was a contributing editor to Wiley-Blackwell's *Just the Arguments: 100 of the Most Important Arguments in Western Philosophy* (2011).

Dan Burkett is a doctoral student in philosophy at Rice University. He specializes in social and political philosophy, morality, freedom, and the philosophy of time. He has recently contributed chapters to *Futurama and Philosophy* (Open Court, 2013), *Homeland and Philosophy* (Open Court, 2014), and *The Ultimate Star Wars and Philosophy* (Wiley-Blackwell, 2016).

John Casey is Associate Professor of Philosophy at Northeastern Illinois University. Trained as a medievalist, he now works primarily in argumentation theory. He and Scott F. Aikin have co-authored a number of articles on fallacy theory and are currently working on a book on the straw man fallacy.

Christian Cotton is an independent scholar, author, and game developer who has published in the areas of moral and political philosophy. His current interests lie in the philosophies of anarchism and primitivism and the critique of civilization.

Jennifer Culver is an instructional tech specialist at the UNT Health Science Center in Fort Worth, Texas. Her main interests lie in the intersections of rhetoric, story (particularly pop culture), and ritual.

Charlene Elsby is an assistant professor at Indiana University-Purdue University Fort Wayne, specializing in ancient philosophy and realist phenomenology. She is the editor of *Essays on Aesthetic Genesis* (UPA, 2016) and co-author of *Clear and Present Thinking* (Northwest Passage Books, 2013) with Brendan Myers and Kimberly Baltzer-Jaray.

Galen Foresman is an associate professor of philosophy at North Carolina Agricultural and Technical State University. He is a co-author of *The Critical Thinking Toolkit* (Wiley-Blackwell, 2016) with Peter Fosl and Jamie Watson.

Brett Gaul is an associate professor of philosophy at Southwest Minnesota State University in Marshall, Minnesota. His philosophical interests include ethics, philosophy of sport, and popular culture and philosophy. He does his best to avoid committing the fallacies explained in this book.

A.G. Holdier holds an MA in the philosophy of religion from Denver Seminary and currently teaches both ethics courses for Colorado Technical University and theology courses for a local high school. His research interests lie at the intersection of philosophy, theology, and aesthetics with a focus on the ontology of creativity and the imagination and the function of stories as cultural artifacts. His latest work concerns the construction of a phenomenological model of the afterlife.

Alexander E. Hooke is a professor of philosophy at Stevenson University. He is editor of *Virtuous Persons, Vicious Deeds* and co-editor of *Encounters with Alphonso Lingis*. In addition to writing occasional op-ed essays for *The Baltimore Sun*, he has several contributions to the forthcoming *Perry Mason and Philosophy* book.

Jason Iuliano is currently a fellow at the University of Pennsylvania Law School and a PhD candidate in the Politics Department at Princeton University. His research interests are in empirical constitutional law and consumer bankruptcy. Some of his recent articles have appeared in the *University of Pennsylvania Law Review, Vanderbilt Law Review, Michigan Law Review,* and *Indiana Law Journal*. Previously, he earned a JD from Harvard Law School where he was a co-founder and editor-in-chief of the *Harvard Business Law Review*.

David Kyle Johnson is Professor of Philosophy at King's College in Wilkes-Barre, Pennsylvania. He has three courses for *The Great Courses (Exploring Metaphysics, The Big Questions of Philosophy and Sci-Phi: Science Fiction as Philosophy)* and is the author of *The Myths That Stole Christmas* (Humanist Press, 2015). Most of his professional and popular work is available (for free) on his academia.edu page.

Leigh Kolb is an instructor at East Central College in rural Missouri, where she teaches English, journalism, and mass media. Her film and TV criticism has appeared in various publications, and her chapters on feminist philosophy have appeared in the texts *Sons of Anarchy and Philosophy: Brains Before Bullets* (Wiley, 2013) and *Philosophy and Breaking Bad* (Palgrave Macmillan, 2016). She also has chapters in the upcoming *Amy Schumer and Philosophy* and *Twin Peaks and Philosophy* (Wiley, 2018).

Rory E. Kraft, Jr. is an assistant professor of philosophy at York College of Pennsylvania. Most of his work is in ethics and pre-college philosophy. He is co-editor-in-chief of the journal *American Association of Philosophy Teachers Studies in Pedagogy* and Editor Emeritus of *Questions: Philosophy for Young People*.

David Vander Laan is Professor of Philosophy at Westmont College. He has research interests in metaphysics and philosophy of religion. His publications include articles in *Australasian Journal of Philosophy, Faith and Philosophy, Religious Studies, Philosophical Studies,* and *Notre Dame Journal of Formal Logic*.

David LaRocca is Visiting Assistant Professor in the Cinema Department at Binghamton University and previously was Visiting Assistant Professor in the Department of Philosophy at the State University of New York College at Cortland. Educated at Buffalo, Berkeley, Vanderbilt, and Harvard, he is the author and editor of several books, including *Emerson's English Traits and the Natural History of Metaphor*, Stanley Cavell's *Emerson's Transcendental Etudes*, *The Bloomsbury Anthology of Transcendental Thought*, and *The Philosophy of Documentary Film: Image, Sound, Fiction, Truth*. More details at www.davidlarocca.org.

Bertha Alvarez Manninen is an associate professor of philosophy at Arizona State University. Her primary areas of research and teaching are applied ethics and philosophy of religion.

Tuomas W. Manninen is a senior lecturer at the New College of Inter-disciplinary Arts and Sciences at Arizona State University. He regularly teaches courses that address issues in social/political philosophy, metaphysics, and critical thinking, with a particular focus on overlapping issues. His recent publications have focused on metaphysical topics as portrayed in popular culture. He earned his PhD in Philosophy in 2007 from the University of Iowa; his dissertation focused on the social ontology of personhood.

Benjamin W. McCraw teaches philosophy at the University of South Carolina Upstate. His research focuses primarily on epistemology and philosophy of religion – especially their intersection in religious epistemology. He has published articles in the *International Journal for Philosophy of Religion, Philosophy and Theology, Social Epistemology*, and *Logos and Episteme*. He is also co-editor of *The Concept of Hell* (Palgrave Macmillan, 2015), *Philosophical Approaches to the Devil* (Routledge, 2015), and *The Problem of Evil: New Philosophical Directions* (Lexington Books, 2015).

Nicolas Michaud teaches philosophy in Jacksonville, Florida. He is interested in philosophy of education, critical theory, and ethics.

Michael Muniz is a pre-college philosophy instructor at Doral Academy and is a part-time professor of philosophy at Doral College in Miami, Florida. His interests are logic, ethics, and history of philosophy. He is currently developing a program for high school students to engage in active philosophical discourse with undergraduate and graduate philosophy students.

Mark T. Nelson holds the Monroe Endowed Chair in Philosophy at Westmont College in Santa Barbara, California. His research interests lie primarily in ethics, epistemology, and philosophy of religion, and he has published papers in journals such as *Analysis, Mind, American Philosophical Quarterly, Australasian Journal of Philosophy, Religious Studies, Ratio*, and

Journal of Medicine and Philosophy. See http://www.westmont.edu/_
academics/departments/philosophy/MarkNelson.html.

Heather Rivera is an independent writer on philosophy. She has interests in
metaphysics and philosophy of the mind, concentrating her writings on the
philosophy of evil. She has given lectures yearly at the Long Island
Philosophical Society Conference and has published articles in *Philosophy
Now* magazine.

Roberto Ruiz is an adjunct lecturer at LaGuardia Community College and
the New York Institute of Technology. He has contributed chapters to *The
Onion and Philosophy* (Open Court, 2010) and *Psych and Philosophy*
(Open Court, 2013). See http://berto-meister.blogspot.com.

Andrew Russo is an adjunct professor of philosophy at the University of
Central Oklahoma and has interests in the metaphysics of mind, philosophy
of language, and the history of modern philosophy. Recently, he has had a
paper published in *Synthese* on the exclusion problem, entitled "Kim's
Dilemma: Why Mental Causation Is not Productive."

Frank Scalambrino is Senior Lecturer in Philosophy at the University of
Akron, Ohio's Polytechnic University, and has interests in philosophical
psychology, social epistemology, existentialism, and the history of Western
philosophy.

Robert Sinclair is an associate professor of philosophy in the Faculty of
International Liberal Arts, Soka University, Tokyo. He studies aspects of
American Pragmatism, focusing especially on the work of John Dewey and
W.V. Quine. Recent work includes "Vision and Technique in Pragmatist
Philosophy" forthcoming in *The Pluralist*. Other work can be found at
https://suj. academia.edu/RobertSinclair.

Phil Smolenski is a PhD candidate at Queen's University (Canada) in philosophy, where his research focuses on liberalism. Smolenski's work has appeared
in *Journal of Moral Philosophy*, *Dialogue*, and various Philosophy and Pop
Culture volumes, including *Louis CK and Philosophy*.

Grant Sterling is an associate professor of philosophy at Eastern Illinois
University, specializing in ethics and medieval philosophy. He is the author
of *Ethical Intuitionism and Its Critics* (Peter Lang, 1994) as well as various
articles and reviews. His research currently focuses on issues related to free
will and moral responsibility.

Charles Taliaferro, Chair of the Department of Philosophy, St. Olaf College,
is the author or editor of 24 books, most recently *Contemporary Philosophical
Theology* (Routledge, 2016), co-authored with Chad Meister.

Jason Waller is an assistant professor of philosophy at Eastern Illinois University. He is the author of the *Routledge Philosophy Guidebook to Spinoza on Politics* (2015, with Daniel Frank), *Persistence Through Time in Spinoza* (Lexington Books, 2012), and numerous scholarly articles. He regularly teaches courses in formal and informal logic.

Andy Wible is a full time instructor of philosophy at Muskegon Community College. His academic interests are in business and biomedical ethics as well LGBTQ studies. His interest in the *post hoc* fallacy and others occurred soon after his newfound love of politics.

George Wrisley is an associate professor of philosophy at the University of North Georgia. While his past work has focused primarily on the later Wittgenstein, his recent work applies aspects of Wittgenstein's philosophy to the elucidation of the philosophy of thirteenth-century Japanese Zen Master Dōgen. In particular, he uses Wittgensteinian views of language to spell out the way in which for Dōgen language and enlightenment are entwined – counter to the view that enlightenment is a special kind of ineffable experience.

Dan Yim is a Professor of Philosophy at Bethel University in St. Paul, Minnesota. He has interests in early modern philosophy, the intersections of race-gender-sexuality, the philosophy of popular culture, and the epistemology of self-deception.

Introduction

This introduction provides a context for understanding the nature and purpose of fallacies, to include brief descriptions and discussions of claims, evidence, inference, argument, persuasion, and critical thinking, as well as deductive vs. inductive reasoning and what constitutes a good argument, part of which is recognizing a fallacy and avoiding it.

Claims

We all have thoughts, opinions, and beliefs about ourselves, the world around us, and reality, as we perceive it – John thinks himself to be an honest, hard-working person; Judy is of the opinion that the State of Palestine should be granted full membership in the United Nations (UN); Jim believes that when people die, their souls go to a heavenly place, and so on. We make our thoughts, opinions, and beliefs known in spoken or written form through *claims*, which are statements, propositions, or declarative sentences (or parts of declarative sentences) composed of at least one subject noun phrase and a finite verb. Here are some examples of claims:

This cake tastes really good to me.
Some spiders are orange in color.
Most children are born with two hands.
The moon appears to be small, but in actuality its radius is over 1,000 miles (1,600 km) across.

Bad Arguments: 100 of the Most Important Fallacies in Western Philosophy, First Edition.
Edited by Robert Arp, Steven Barbone, and Michael Bruce.
© 2019 John Wiley & Sons Ltd. Published 2019 by John Wiley & Sons Ltd.

Margaret Thatcher was the first female Prime Minister of the United Kingdom.

Margaret Thatcher was the best Prime Minister of the United Kingdom.

The love of money is the root of human-perpetuated evils in this world.

Welfare programs actually create more poverty and should be abolished altogether.

Abortion is immoral.

There is an all-powerful, knowledgeable, and good God who cares deeply for humanity.

Claims are either true or false – either *it is* the case or *it is not* the case that John is an honest, hard-working person, or that the State of Palestine should be granted full membership in the UN, or that when people die, their souls go to a heavenly place, and so on. Unless you're deranged or unaware for some reason, everyone agrees that the following claims are true:

(A)   Some spiders are orange in color.
(B)   Most children are born with two hands.
(C)   Margaret Thatcher was the first female Prime Minister of the United Kingdom.
(D)   There are craters on the moon.

On the other hand, everyone agrees that the following claims are false:

(A)   The sun is a cube-shaped star.
(B)   The cells in an animal's body have little versions of that particular animal inside them.
(C)   Bill Gates wrote *War and Peace*.
(D)   A person can stand and sit at the same time, in the same respect.

Evidence

A claim is shown to be true or false with *evidence*, which is a fact or concept (or set of facts or concepts) that provides support (affirmation, confirmation, corroboration, proof, substantiation, verification) for the truth or falsity of a claim. The most common way that evidence is utilized is in a court of law where the prosecution has to provide proof for the truth of the claim, "The defendant is guilty of the crime" for example. However, you have probably heard someone make a claim and someone else ask, "What's the evidence for that claim?" or "Where's the proof for that claim?" Evidence comes in a number of forms:

Direct sense evidence of spatiotemporal entities using sight, sound, touch, taste, or smell.

   For example, you go to Paris and see the Eiffel Tower for yourself, and this gives support for the truth of the claim, "The Eiffel Tower exists in Paris, France."

Sense evidence of spatiotemporal entities that is indirect through a device, machine, or instrument that is reliably calibrated, such as a magnifying glass, periscope, camera, video recorder, binoculars, microscope, telescope, or meter.

   For example, you've never been to France, and you see pictures and videos of the Eiffel Tower, and this gives support for the truth of the claim, "The Eiffel Tower exists in Paris, France."

The testimony of others whom we trust.

   For example, you've never been to France, but your parents go to France and tell you that they saw the Eiffel Tower, and you believe them. Once again, this gives support for the truth of the claim, "The Eiffel Tower exists in Paris, France."

The testimony of experts in some area, domain, field, or discipline.

   For example, the engineer of the Eiffel Tower, Gustave Eiffel, tells other engineers that the tower can support an elevator system to bring people to the top, and the elevator engineers begin construction on the elevator because they take Gustave's testimony to be the support for the truth of the claim, "The Eiffel Tower can support an elevator system."

Authoritative explanations as one finds in the sciences.

   For example, researchers since Isaac Newton have shown that gravity is at work in the universe, and this is what accounts for why the Eiffel Tower (and any other dense physical object) does not simply float away into Earth's atmosphere.

Logical or mathematical entailment.

   For example, if it's true that the Eiffel Tower is located in Paris, and it's true that Paris is located in France, then by a logical property of the "located in" relationship known as *transitivity*, these two truths *entail* that (or we can conclude with absolute certainty that) it's true that the Eiffel Tower is located in France.

Arguments can act as evidence, too.

For example, the *reductio ad absurdum* (reduction to absurdity) argument has been used for thousands of years to show that someone's claim is false. One form of the argument looks like this:

(1)   If your claim X is true, then this absurdity, contradiction, or craziness Y results.
(2)   <u>But, we cannot accept this absurdity, contradiction, or craziness Y.</u>
(3)   Therefore, your claim X is not true (it's false).

We can put flesh on the argument using this example:

(1)   If it's true that Noah fit two of every species of living thing on the ark, then the ark would need to have been the size of Australia, which is absurd (and not communicated in the Bible anyway; it was about 520 feet long by 86 feet wide by 52 feet high).
(2)   <u>We cannot accept that Noah built an ark the size of Australia.</u>
(3)   Therefore, it's false that Noah fit two of every species of living thing on the ark.

There are other forms of evidence, but this should suffice for now. Referring back to our lettered list of true (A)–(D) and false (E)–(H) claims, we can note that:

(A)   is true because of direct sense evidence – we can see that spiders are orange.
(B)   is true because of expert testimony – the data gathered from doctors and researchers show that most children are born with two hands.
(C)   is true in terms of expert testimony through historical records and accounts.
(D)   is true because of direct sense evidence (we can see the craters with the naked eye) as well as sense evidence that is indirect through a telescope (ever since Galileo did it in the early 1600s).
(E)   is false because of direct sense evidence – we can see that the sun is not cube-shaped. (E) is also false because of the well-established law of gravity, part of which means that celestial bodies such as stars are uniformly "pulled" in toward their center of mass as they rotate, creating a sphere-shaped (and not a cube-shaped) object.
(F)   is false because of sense evidence that is indirect through a microscope – there are only organelles (nucleus, ribosomes, mitochondria, etc.) inside an animal cell.
(G)   is false in terms of expert testimony through historical records and accounts – Leo Tolstoy wrote *War and Peace*.

(H) is false because of many well-established laws of physics as well as laws of math and logic. Through the principle of non-contradiction in logic, it can't be true that "Frank is standing" and "Frank is not standing (assumed when he's sitting)" at the same time and in the same respect.

As critically thinking, rational beings, we want to make sure that any claim we put forward – or anyone puts forward – is in fact true by virtue of the evidence for it. You will often hear questions like, "Where's the proof for what you're saying?" or "Give me an example of what you're talking about?" and these are other ways of saying, "What is the evidence that supports the truth of your claim?"

Certain claims are easier to support with evidence than others. In general, we think that direct sense evidence resulting from sober, sane people provides a decent support for claims made about the spatiotemporal world. If several folks are on a street corner when a car chase zooms by them and they all claim, "The vehicle being chased by police was a red SUV," then the officer interviewing them thinks, "Well, it must be true that it's a red SUV because the witnesses saw it." (Of course, it's possible to misperceive something or project something into existence that's not really there – even groups of folks are known to have done this – so one must be careful when taking another's "word" for something.)

So too, data are gathered from researchers about entities and relationships that are the focus of sciences such as physics, chemistry, and biology, and those researchers make claims about the data which most everyone takes to be true. When a respected astrophysicist says, "The sun is roughly 75% hydrogen and 25% helium," or a world-renowned chemist says, "There are currently 118 different elements that comprise the Periodic Table," or an Oxford University biologist says, "In African nations, malaria is transmitted to humans by the female mosquitoes of the genus *Anopheles*," we have no problem believing what they say is true.

Conversely, certain claims are much harder to support with evidence. "Humans have souls that survive the death of the body," "All events in the universe are determined to occur the way they do, including events caused by humans," "There are several alternate universes," and other like philosophical and theoretical claims require forms of evidence that go well beyond merely pointing at something in the spatiotemporal world. And some claims, like "I truly exist because I am aware of myself existing," "I recall that I had eggs for breakfast this morning," and "This object in my visual field appears green to me," may have evidence that is only acceptable to *that* person – the person who is aware, or recalling, or perceiving – and no one else.

Inferences and Arguments

There are plenty of times when we reason in an attempt to draw a conclusion from another claim or claims that we think or know to be true. For example, let's say that you have a convertible that is parked out front in your driveway, you left the top down, and you hear from the local meteorologist on TV that there's a 100% chance of rain in the next hour. You think to yourself, "If it rains outside, then the interior of my convertible gets wet." This is a little piece of reasoning, actually, where you are assuming that the claim, "The interior of my convertible gets wet" follows logically from the claim, "It rains outside." *Follows logically from* means the same thing as *can be legitimately inferred from* – one can legitimately infer that "The interior of my convertible gets wet" from "It rains outside." So, if we know it's true that "If it rains outside, then the interior of my convertible gets wet" and we know it's true that "It rains," then we can logically infer (or it follows logically that) "The interior of my convertible gets wet."

Here are some other examples:

We know it's true that:	And we know it's true that:	So, we can conclude/infer that:
Catholics are Christians.	Christians are believers in One God.	Catholics are believers in One God.
Most Republicans are conservative.	Jim is a Republican.	It's likely (though, not necessarily) that Jim is conservative.
Cats are a different species altogether from dogs.	Mittens is the name of my friend's cat.	Mittens is not a dog.
Fire requires a certain amount of oxygen to burn.	There's no oxygen in a perfect vacuum chamber.	Fire won't burn in a perfect vacuum chamber.
If all of the conditions are present for rain, then it rains.	All of the conditions are, in fact, present for rain.	It rains.

The car starts only if the battery works.	The battery does not work.	The car does not start.
Team X won the championship game the last two years.	Team X has had the best statistics of all of the teams this season.	Team X probably (not necessarily) will win the championship game today.
The sign says Chicago is 10 miles away from here.	Qualified highway personnel placed the sign where it is located.	Chicago is (most likely) 10 miles away from here.
If you want to go downtown, then you must take your car.	If you must take your car, then you'll need some gas for your car.	If you want to go downtown, then you'll need some gas for your car.

When we try to show what claim follows from or can be inferred from another claim or claims we take to be true, we are putting forward an *argument*. An argument is made up of at least two claims, one of which plays the role of the *conclusion*, while the other plays the role of a *premise*. A *premise* is the claim that is supposed to support, back up, justify, or give a reason for accepting the conclusion, while a *conclusion* is the claim that is supported by, backed up by, justified by, or shown to be what follows from the premise. The following is a simple argument with one premise and a conclusion:

Premise: <u>Given that Frank is a bachelor.</u>
Conclusion: This shows us that Frank is an unmarried male.

We can see that the claim "Frank is an unmarried male" follows from the claim "Frank is a bachelor" because what it means to be a bachelor is to be an unmarried male. That Frank is a bachelor (stated as a premise) supports, backs up, justifies, or gives the reason for accepting that Frank is an unmarried male (stated as the conclusion). Here is another simple argument with one premise and a conclusion that is straightforwardly obvious:

Premise: <u>Jane has two apples and two oranges in her shopping cart.</u>
Conclusion: Thus, Jane has four fruits in her shopping cart.

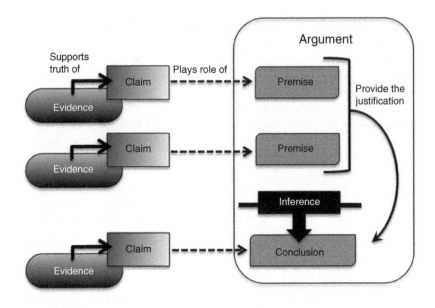

Usually an argument has more than one premise, as in the examples in the table above, a few of which we can put in argument form below. Note that an argument in *argument form* usually has the premises of the argument listed first, then a horizontal line – demarking premise(s) from conclusion – followed by the conclusion of the argument. Also, often (though, not always) there will be a *premise-indicating word* such as *because, since, given that, as, for*, or *for the reason(s) that* (there are others) that indicates a premise in an argument, while often (though, not always) there will be a *conclusion-indicating word* such as *So, Hence, Thus, Therefore, This shows us that*, or *We can then conclude/infer that* (there are others) that indicates a conclusion in an argument. A few of these indicating words are evident in the examples given above and below.

(1)   Since Catholics are Christians.
(2)   And Christians are believers in One God.
(3)   Therefore, Catholics are believers in One God.

(1)   Because most Republicans are conservative.
(2)   And because Jim is a Republican.
(3)   Hence, it's likely (though, not necessarily) that Jim is conservative.

(1)   The car starts only if the battery works.
(2)   The battery does not work.
(3)   This shows us that the car does not start.

(1) Given that Team X won the championship game the last two years.
(2) <u>And given that Team X has had the best statistics of all of the teams this season.</u>
(3) So, Team X probably (not necessarily) will win the championship game today.

Persuasion is the Primary Reason for an Argument

When someone puts forward an argument in written or spoken form, she is trying to convince you or persuade you of the truth of the conclusion of the argument – in fact, this is *the* ultimate goal of, or primary reason for, an argument. This is most clearly the case in the Team X example above: let's say that Peter and a bunch of other folks are sitting in the bleachers just before the championship game is about to begin, and Peter makes the claim, "Team X probably will win the championship game today" – he obviously wants any and all persons (himself included) to believe that this claim is in fact true. However, Paul is sitting next to Peter, he's an intensely inquisitive kind of person, and he wants to know why Peter believes this and why anyone should believe this, so he says to Peter, "Oh yeah, prove it. Demonstrate it. Show me why I should accept that claim as true. I'm not convinced. I'm not persuaded. I want you to convince me, to persuade me, that the claim is true." Basically, Paul is asking for Peter's argument that concludes to the claim, "Team X probably will win the championship game today." So, Peter lays out his reasons for why anyone should accept his conclusion as being true, and those reasons take the form of premises in an argument. "Well," Peter continues, "Team X won the championship game the last two years. And Team X has had the best statistics of all of the teams this season. And those are the reasons that support my conclusion. Another way to say it is this: *that* Team X will win the championship game today follows from, or can be inferred from, the fact that Team X won the championship game the last two years and Team X has had the best statistics of all of the teams this season." Paul then may say, "Well, if it's true that Team X won the championship game the last two years and it's true that Team X has had the best statistics of all the teams this season, then I, too, am convinced that Team X probably will win today."

Oftentimes, a definition, an account, or an explanation looks like an argument. Consider this argument again:

(1) Since Catholics are Christians.
(2) And Christians are believers in One God.
(3) Therefore, Catholics are believers in One God.

It only becomes an argument if someone needs to be *convinced* or *persuaded* that "Catholics are believers in One God." However, when one does some investigation, one sees that, by definition, Catholics are Christians and again, by definition, Christians are believers in One God, so one really need not be convinced that "Catholics are believers in One God." It's not really something about which one need debate or argue.

Also, this argument really has the flavor of an explanation:

(1)   The car starts only if the battery works.
(2)   <u>The battery does not work.</u>
(3)   Thus, the car does not start.

We could easily see someone's asking an auto mechanic, "Hey, why doesn't my car start?" and the auto mechanic's responding, "Well, the battery doesn't work, and the car won't start if the battery isn't working. So, there's the explanation for your problem. If he's a competent, experienced, trusted auto mechanic, then "The battery doesn't work" is what explains the car's not starting, and the claim is not really something about which one need debate or argue.

And this next example from the table above also has the flavor of an explanation or an account – we can imagine someone waking up from a long nap in the car on a road trip and asking, "How much further to Chicago?"

(1)   The sign says Chicago is 10 miles away from here.
(2)   <u>Qualified highway personnel placed the sign where it is located.</u>
(3)   Chicago is (most likely) 10 miles away from here.

Notice that if someone claimed, "Margaret Thatcher was the first female Prime Minister of the United Kingdom," this would be easy to show as true or false by virtue of historical evidence. However, if someone claimed, "Margaret Thatcher was the *best* Prime Minister of the United Kingdom," then we can see that it "cries out" for a justification in terms of an argument. The person making this claim would need to *convince* others that Thatcher was the best PM of the UK by providing an argument complete with evidence for the truth of any premises.

Usually any *prescriptive claim* – a claim communicating that one should, ought to, or must do something – requires an argument. For example, the typical person will kill a spider he sees in his home, usually with a shudder and an "Ewww" right after. If someone said, "Hey, you shouldn't kill the spiders you see in your home," the argument might look like the following:

(1)   Spiders set up webs near cracks and crevices of your home and eat insects that would become nuisances if they got inside your home, like ants and mosquitoes.

(2) *That* spiders do this is a good thing, and they need to be alive to do it.

(3) You *should do and/or promote* what is good and, conversely, you *should not do and/or promote* what is bad.

(4) Thus, you shouldn't kill the spiders you see in your home.

So, too, these claims we saw at the beginning of this introduction, in essence, are conclusions requiring premises and evidence as justification. One needs to be convinced or persuaded that they're true, no doubt. That's why they're the fodder for (usually intense) debate and discussion in classrooms, on TV and radio featuring political programs, around dinner tables, in articles and books, and at conferences and colloquia:

> The love of money is the root of human-perpetuated evils in this world.
> Welfare programs actually create more poverty and should be abolished altogether.
> Abortion is immoral.
> There is an all-powerful, knowledgeable, and good God who cares deeply for humanity.

Reasoning

We have seen so far that, as rational beings, we must support the claims we think are true with evidence. We have also seen that we need to, at times, convince or persuade others of the truth of a claim through an argument whereby we try to show that the claim we think is true – the conclusion – follows from or can be inferred from another claim or claims we take to be true – the premise(s).

> *It is the logical move from premise(s) to conclusion – inference – that primarily concerns us here in this book.*

In fact, *the very essence of reasoning* is concerned with this logical move. There are plenty of times when we reason correctly. You may come to the immediate conclusion that "I have to take Main St. to work today" from the claims, "There are only two ways for me to get to work, either Highway 1 or Main St." and "Highway 1 is closed due to construction." In argument form, this piece of reasoning looks like the following:

(1) There are only two ways for me to get to work – either Highway 1 or Main St.

(2) Highway 1 is closed due to construction.

(3) I have to take Main St. to get to work today.

And if it really is the case there are only two ways for you to get to work – either Highway 1 or Main St. – then we can see that it follows that, or we can infer, deduce, or conclude that, you have to take Main St. to work today. That move, the one from premise (or premises) to a conclusion, is a straightforward example of reasoning – and, in this case, reasoning correctly. Here are a couple more examples of reasoning correctly.

(1)   Politicians in the Crack Down Party are all conservative about spending.

(2)   <u>Congresswoman Smith is in the Crack Down Party.</u>

(3)   Congresswoman Smith is conservative about spending.

If you found out that it is true that Congresswoman Smith is in the Crack Down Party and you know that it is true politicians in the Crack Down Party are conservative about spending, then you would reason (infer, deduce, conclude) correctly that Congresswoman Smith is conservative about spending.

Now, let's say you're watching your favorite courtroom drama on TV and the attorney for the defendant puts forward this argument:

(1)   If my client committed the crime, then he would have been in Chicago.

(2)   <u>But he was not in Chicago; check the gas receipts, GPS, and witness testimony.</u>

(3)   Therefore, my client did not commit the crime.

Again, if the two premises are absolutely, positively true, and there is nothing else to consider in the case (in other words, this was the so-called *linchpin*), then the defense attorney, jury, judge, and any of us familiar with the case would be reasoning correctly that the defendant did not commit the crime.

Sometimes, we are confronted with claims that require us to reason through their connections slowly, in a more conscious fashion. Consider a certain apartment lease agreement. Let's say that you got a new job in Denver, Colorado, six months into a 12-month lease agreement you signed with an apartment in San Francisco, California, so you need to move from your apartment and would like to break your lease. The contract states:

The leasee may be let out of the 12-month lease agreement *if and only if*:

(1)   He can find another leasee to take his place for the remainder of the agreement;

(2)   *or* He is moving out of the state for work purposes only.

However, if (1), then the new leasee (the one replacing the leasee who broke his lease agreement) must sign an additional 12-month lease agreement. If (2), then the leasee must provide a notarized copy of the offer of employment. If neither of these conditions can be met, then the leasee will not be let out of the 12-month lease agreement.

Since you have a notarized copy of your offer of employment for the job in Denver, Colorado, you reason correctly that you, the leasee, will be let out of your 12-month lease agreement.

Deductive Reasoning and Arguments

Broadly speaking, there are two types of reasoning: *deductive* reasoning, which utilizes deductive arguments, and *inductive* reasoning, which utilizes inductive arguments. In a *deductive argument*:

The conclusion is supposed to follow necessarily (absolutely, apodictically) from the premise(s);

If the conclusion does, in fact, follow from the premise(s) *and* if, in fact, all of the premises are true, then it is impossible for the conclusion to be false – the conclusion must/has to be true;

The premise(s) is/are supposed to *entail* the conclusion – in other words, the conclusion can already be found in the premise(s).

These arguments are all deductive arguments utilizing deductive reasoning:

(1) There are only two ways for me to get to work – either Highway 1 or Main St.
(2) <u>Highway 1 is closed due to construction.</u>
(3) So, I have to take Main St. to work today.

(1) Politicians in the Crack Down Party are all conservative about spending.
(2) <u>Congresswoman Smith is in the Crack Down Party.</u>
(3) This shows us that Congresswoman Smith is conservative about spending.

(1) If my client committed the crime, then he would have been in Chicago.
(2) <u>But he wasn't in Chicago (check the gas receipts, GPS, and witness testimony).</u>
(3) Therefore, my client did not commit the crime.

(1)   If it's raining we'll stay inside, and if it snowing we'll go outside to play.

(2)   <u>It's either raining or snowing.</u>

(3)   Hence, we'll either stay inside or go outside to play.

We can see that the conclusions drawn in each argument are the *only* ones that could possibly follow, so the conclusions follow necessarily (absolutely, apodictically) from the premises. Also, given the truth of the premises, it has to be the case that the conclusions are true as well. Finally, if the conclusions were not explicitly stated, they still are there *implicitly* or *implied by* the premises – we can logically "see" (so to speak) that the conclusions are already present in the premises or, understood differently, we can "read" the conclusion from the premises.

In this book, we will be concerned with two standard forms of deductive reasoning: the first considers reasoning with *categories* of things that dates back to Aristotle, called *categorical logic, traditional logic, syllogistic logic,* or simply *Aristotelian logic*; the second considers the reasoning associated with *claims*, which are statements, propositions, or declarative sentences (or parts of declarative sentences), aptly called *propositional logic* or *sentential logic*.

Categorical Logic

In his *Prior Analytics*, Aristotle (384–322 BCE) laid out a system of logic that would dominate Western and much of Middle Eastern thought for some 2,000 years. Aristotle's logic concerns categories of things (kind of like sets, groups, or types/kinds), the characteristics that the members (individuals, instances) of those categories possess or do not possess, and what appropriate inferences can be made from our knowledge of the categories and the characteristics of their members. Aristotle was able to capture these relationships in four categorical claims, which have come to be known as:

A Claim: All A are B.

All	*A*	*are*	*B.*
All of the members of	*Category A*	*are members of*	*Category B.*
Examples:			
"All	cats	are	mammals."
"All	Christians	are	monotheists."
"All	bachelors	are	unmarried males."

E Claim: No A are B.

No	A	are	B.
None of the members of	*Category A*	*are members of*	*Category B.*
Examples:			
"No	cats	are	dogs."
"No	Christians	are	atheists."
"No	bachelors	are	married males."

I Claim: Some A are B.

Some	A	are	B.
At least one member of	*Category A*	*is a member of*	*Category B.*
Examples:			
"Some	cats	are	black."
"Some	Christians	are	Catholics."
"Some	bachelors	are	bald."

O Claim: Some A are not B

Some	A	are not	B.
At least one member of	*Category A*	*is not a member of*	*Category B.*
Examples:			
"Some	cats	are not	black."
"Some	Christians	are not	Catholics."
"Some	bachelors	are not	bald."

The fundamental instrument of reasoning in Aristotle's system of logic is the *syllogism*, which he defines in the *Prior Analytics* as "discourse in which, certain things being stated, something other than what is stated follows of necessity from their being so." In its simplest form, a syllogism is an argument composed of exactly two premises and one conclusion, the claims of which are A, E, I, and/or O claims. The following are examples of properly formed syllogisms that should be intuitively obvious:

(1)   All cats are mammals.
(2)   <u>All mammals are warm-blooded animals.</u>
(3)   All cats are warm-blooded animals.

(1)   No Christians are atheists.
(2)   <u>All Catholics are Christians.</u>
(3)   No atheists are Catholics.

(1)   Some cats are black.
(2)   <u>All black things are harder to see at night.</u>
(3)   Some cats are harder to see at night.

(1)   No Republicans are Democrats.
(2)   <u>Some Republicans are socially liberal people.</u>
(3)   Some socially liberal people are not Democrats.

(1)   All men are mortal.
(2)   <u>Socrates is a man.</u>
(3)   Socrates is mortal.

Propositional Logic

There is a tradition of reasoning with propositions or sentences in the West that goes back to Aristotle as well but received its first serious treatment with the Stoic philosopher Chrysippus (ca. 280–205 BCE). Whereas categorical logic deals with the attributes of categories of things and what can be inferred from the relationships between and among these things, propositional logic concerns the attributes of claims (propositions, sentences) and the reasoning possible when claims are related to one another. Among others, Chrysippus noted these pieces of correct reasoning:

(A)   If the 1st, then the 2nd. But, the 1st. Therefore, the 2nd.
(B)   If the 1st, then the 2nd. But, not the 2nd. Therefore, not the 1st.
(C)   Either the 1st or the 2nd. But not the 1st. Therefore, the 2nd.

Examples of these arguments, which we saw above already, are all in the realm of propositional logic:

(1)   There are only two ways for me to get to work – either Highway 1 or Main St.
(2)   <u>Highway 1 is closed due to construction.</u>
(3)   So, I have to take Main St. to work today.

Notice that this argument is an example of the form of reasoning utilized by Chrysippus in (C).

(1)   If my client committed the crime, then he would have been in Chicago.

(2)   But he wasn't in Chicago (check the gas receipts, GPS, and witness testimony).

(3)   Therefore, my client did not commit the crime.

Notice that this argument is an example of the form of reasoning utilized by Chrysippus in (B).

(1)   If it's raining we'll stay inside, and if it snowing we'll go outside to play.

(2)   It's either raining or snowing.

(3)   Hence, we'll either stay inside or go outside to play.

You can see how the conclusions of these arguments can be deduced (inferred) from the premises.

Inductive Reasoning and Arguments

In an *inductive argument*, on the other hand:

The conclusion is supposed to follow *likely* or *probably* from the premise(s), not necessarily – in other words, the inference to the conclusion is one of degree and on a percentage scale from 0.000...1, which is the *least* likely or probable case where the conclusion may be drawn from the premise(s), through 0.1, 0.2, 0.3, 0.4, 0.5, 0.6, 0.7, 0.8, and 0.9 to 0.9999..., which is the *most* likely or probable case where the conclusion may be drawn from the premise(s).

If all of the premises are true, then it is *still possible* for the conclusion to be false.

The premise(s) does/do not *entail* the conclusion – the conclusion cannot already be found in the premise(s), at least not in the same way the conclusion is entailed by the premise(s) of a deductive argument.

These arguments are all inductive arguments utilizing inductive reasoning:

(1)   My old running shoes were Brand X, genuine leather, and lasted me a year.

(2)   These new shoes I'm thinking of buying are Brand X and genuine leather.

(3)   So, these new shoes will last me a year, too.

Note that it's still possible that the new shoes won't last you a year. Also, it's more appropriate to conclude, "So, *it's likely that* or *probably the case that* these new shoes will last me a year, too." Finally, you'd feel more confident about the conclusion if you had more cases/examples of other running shoes lasting a year – one case offers some support for the conclusion, while 100 similar cases would offer more support for the conclusion, and 1,000 similar cases would offer *even more* support for the conclusion, etc.

(5)   (1)   Team X won the championship game the last two years.

(2)   <u>Team X has had the best statistics of all of the teams this season.</u>

(3)   Thus, Team X will win the championship game against Team Y today.

Again, it's still possible that Team X loses the game for any number of reasons. And again, it's better to state, "Thus, Team X *probably* or *likely* will win the championship game against Team Y today." Finally, you'd feel more confident about the conclusion if we knew this information, too: "Team Y's star player has an injury and won't be playing in the game" and "Team Y is playing in Team X's arena."

(6)   (1)   I know there are 10 beans total in this bag, but I don't know their color.

(2)   <u>The last nine beans I pulled from this bag have been red.</u>

(3)   The next bean I pull out will be red, too.

Could the last bean you pull out be a different color? Of course. So, you might want to conclude that the last one has a *chance of being* red and not that it will absolutely, positively, definitely, without a shadow of a doubt, be red. Notice that you'd feel less confident about the conclusion following from the premises if the second premise was "The last five beans I pulled out of this bag have been red" and *even less confident* if that premise was "The last two beans I pulled out of this bag have been red."

Fallacies

Oftentimes, unfortunately, we do not reason correctly.

We may think that because we had a bad meal at a restaurant, therefore all of the food at the restaurant is lousy, and we never frequent the place again. How can we conclude that all of the food is lousy if we've never had *all of* it?

Or you may think that the reason you caught a cold was that you weren't dressed warmly enough last Friday night, when in fact the rhinovirus that was on the doorknob you touched at work made it into your system when you rubbed your eyes a few moments later, and that's what caused your cold. What makes you continue to believe the myth that "you'll catch a cold" if you don't dress warmly enough, especially since there have been literally hundreds of studies featuring tens of thousands of participants where it has been consistently shown that there is no correlation between lowered body temperature and catching a cold?

Or we conclude that a product or service is the best one on the market because some celebrity who has been compensated uses it. Why do we take one person's word for it? Especially when it's a paid endorsement?!

Or we may "jump to the conclusion" that a politician from a party with which we disagree has nothing of value to say about public policy *just because she's from the opposing party*. How can we think that when we haven't even heard her out?

The examples of incorrect reasoning just mentioned are all types of fallacies.

> A *fallacy* is an error in reasoning whereby someone attempts to put forward an argument whereby a conclusion supposedly has been appropriately inferred from a premise (or premises) when, in fact, the conclusion *does not and should not be inferred* from the premise(s).

In other words, a fallacy is a bad thing, logically, and from a critical thinking standpoint should be avoided at all costs. Further than this, whoever is putting forward the fallacy may innocently be unaware of the fact that the conclusion does not follow from the premise(s). That is probably the case for a majority of the fallacies put forward in human history, and thinkers have had to point out the error in reasoning after the fact upon analysis of the argument. On the other hand, someone may want to dupe people into thinking that the conclusion follows from the premise(s) of an argument, which is how many feel about the kind of rhetoric utilized by politicians who "push their agendas" upon a populace. People who want to *sell you* on almost anything – a product, service, idea, policy – often will utilize a fallacy in their so-called *pitch*. So there is often vagueness and ambiguity in the language of a fallacy, coupled at times with an intention to deceive that the critical thinker must be cognizant of as a possibility.

Formal Fallacies

Broadly speaking, there are two types of fallacies, *formal fallacies* and *informal fallacies*. Formal fallacies are found in the deductive realm of reasoning (we already talked about two logical systems, categorical logic and propositional logic) whereby it is determined that a conclusion does not follow from a premise or premises based upon an examination and under-standing of the argument's structure or *form*, rather than its content. Here, one need only examine whether the argument is set up correctly or not according to the principles of the particular logical system – if not, then the argument is fallacious. Here are examples of formal fallacies from everyday life.

In the realm of propositional logic, you may think that "If it's raining, then the sidewalks are wet," and you see that in fact "the sidewalks are wet" and then conclude "it's raining." This an example of a famous type of formal fallacy called *affirming the consequent*. In argument form, it looks like this:

(1)   If it's raining, then the sidewalks are wet.
(2)   The sidewalks are wet.
(3)   It's raining.

When the claims have been symbolized in argument form, the argument looks like this:

(1) $R \supset S$.
(2) S.
(3) R.

And it reads like this:

(1)   If it's **R**aining, then the **S**idewalks are wet.
(2)   The **S**idewalks are wet.
(3)   Therefore, it's **R**aining.

You cannot logically and rationally draw the conclusion that it's raining from these two premises because it could be that a sprinkler made the side-walks wet, or there was a break in the local water main, or it *had* rained earlier that day, or any number of other reasons for the sidewalks' being wet. That said, if you reasoned like this, you would be *correct* in your thinking:

(1)   If it's raining, then the sidewalks are wet.
(2)   It's raining.
(3)   The sidewalks are wet.

When the claims have been symbolized in argument form, it looks like this:

(1) $R \supset S$.
(2) R.
(3) S.

This is a basic and powerful piece of deductive reasoning known as *modus ponens* (Latin for "method of affirming"). If it's true that "If it's raining, then the sidewalks are wet" and it's true that "It's raining," then we can conclude absolutely, positively, definitely, without a shadow of a doubt that "The sidewalks are wet." (Notice that this argument is an example of the form of reasoning utilized by Chrysippus in (A) above.) Now compare these two:

(1) R ⊃ S.	(1) R ⊃ S.
(2) <u>R.</u>	(2) <u>S.</u>
(3) S.	(3) R.
Modus ponens	Affirming the consequent

Once you observe the *modus ponens* argument symbolized, it becomes clear to the critical thinker that the argument's structure or form is correct, showing that it is an appropriate piece of reasoning. And once you see that the correct structure or form has been *altered* – the R and the S are in the wrong places – this demonstrates the fact that it is a formal fallacy. When *modus ponens*' form is altered exactly in the way shown above, then it is the formal fallacy of affirming the consequent. Here is another example of affirming the consequent:

(1)   If it's icy outside, then the mail is late.
(2)   <u>The mail is late.</u>
(3)   So, it's icy outside.

No! You can't logically draw that conclusion. It could be that the mail truck had a flat tire, or that the mail carrier got caught up at a previous site, or there could be any number of other reasons for the late mail.

Informal Fallacies

Informal fallacies, on the other hand, are found in the inductive realm of reasoning whereby it is determined that a conclusion does not follow from a premise or premises based upon an examination and understanding of the argument's *content*, rather than its structure or form. And the argument's content consists of claims, as we noted above, which are expressed using a language. So, it's really through an investigation of the *language used* in an informal fallacy – and the things to which that language refers – that informal fallacies are identified. An informal fallacy involves such things as the abuse or misuse of words or grammar, misconceptions or faulty understanding due to biases or underlying pre-suppositions, misstatements of fact or opinion, or illogical sequences of thought.

One of the most common informal fallacies people commit is known as a *false cause*, which itself comes in a variety forms, as we'll see in this book. In a false cause, a supposed cause of some event or other phenomenon is put forward as a premise of an argument, and the event or other phenomenon the cause is supposed to explain is put forward as the conclusion of the same argument; however, upon inspection the cause meant to explain the event or phenomenon is not the correct one. Superstitions are straight-forward examples of the fallacy of false cause. Consider these, which are almost laughable:

(1) Every time I watch my favorite team play at Casey's Bar, they win.
(2) <u>Tomorrow night my team is playing.</u>
(3) Thus, I have to be at Casey's Bar to watch the game to ensure they win again.

(1) <u>I hit the side of my TV when the picture was fuzzy, and it no longer was fuzzy.</u>
(2) So, it's obvious that my hitting the side of the TV is what fixed it.

(1) <u>A black cat crosses your path.</u>
(2) Hence, that's why you trip a minute later and fall.

But there are other, less laughable, examples of false cause. Consider all of the people who think that one particular substance in pill form is *the key* to losing weight, or improving memory, or clearing up skin blemishes. The late-night, multi-billion-dollar-a-year infomercial culture *depends upon* people's thinking fallaciously like this. Or, think about how many times we have heard someone say that the President is *solely responsible* for unemployment, or inflation, or any other calamity in a particular nation.

As will be shown in this book, false cause is normally classified as an *informal fallacy of presumption*. A fallacy of presumption occurs when an argument rests on some hidden assumption – it could be an unknown factor, a condition, set of circumstances, state of affairs, or idea – that, if not hidden, would make it clear that the assumption is not sufficient to be able to reason to (draw, infer) the conclusion.

So, in the first example in the list immediately above, we all know that there are myriad causes, events, and states of affairs that go into a team's winning a game and that it is mere coincidence that it wins every time you watch the team play at Casey's bar – your watching them at Casey's has absolutely no effect on whether the team wins or not. You *presume* that there's a causal connection between the two (thus, it's a fallacy of presumption), but if you had knowledge of the myriad causes, events, and states of affairs associated with each game – a kind of *god's eye view* – then you would know the correct causes and processes involved in (the reasons for) your team's winning.

The second example is subtler, because your hitting the TV was not the *direct* cause of the picture's becoming clear; rather, it probably jostled something related to the internal antenna, perhaps knocking the node at the end of the antenna (that had fallen off) back onto the TV's receiver and reestablishing the connection between the antenna and the receiver, and that reestablished connection is the actual, correct cause of the clarity of the picture. It may be that, if you hit the TV once more, the antenna node would detach from the receiver, causing the picture to be fuzzy again.

The final example is as absurd as the first. You tripped and fell a minute later because of something other than the supposed superstitious power associated with a black cat's crossing your path.

In addition to false cause, other typical fallacies of presumption that we will see in this book include *false dilemma, suppressed evidence, complex question, hasty generalization*, and *begging the question*. You beg the question when you assume in your premise(s) what you're trying to prove in your conclusion, so that you really haven't proven anything. You have just restated your premise as your conclusion (or your conclusion as your premise, if you look at it from that angle). Here is a famous example:

(1) It says so in the Bible that God exists.
(2) Therefore, God exists.

You may ask a believer, "Why do you think that God exists?" or "What evidence or proof do you have that God exists?" and the believer may respond, "Well, it says in the Bible that God exists. In fact, the Bible talks about God all throughout." Now, many fallacies are squirrely and difficult to see (as we intimated above), and in fact that is part of the reason their conclusions seem to convince so many people. In the above argument, God's existence is implicit in the premise because God is supposed to be a co-author – if not *the* author, according to some religious groups – of the Bible, so the argument more clearly and explicitly should look like this:

(1) It says so in the Bible (written by a God that exists) that God exists.
(2) Therefore, God exists.

So in this fallacy, what is supposed to ground the fact that God exists? Put another way, what is supposed to be the proof or justification for God's existence? Well, the fact that God exists! The person putting forward this fallacious argument wants you to think that the fact that God exists demonstrates that God exists or from the fact that God exists, we can conclude that God exists. The fallacious reasoning should now be evident. Begging the question is a form of *circular reasoning*, and we can see the circularity present here: God's existence is proved by God's existence, which proves God's existence, which is proved by God's existence, which proves God's existence, which is proved by God's existence, which proves God's existence, and so on. You can see how the argument really just restates the premise in the conclusion, thus demonstrating nothing. It's kind of like saying this:

(1)   When you move your legs quickly across a solid surface in a steady gait, it's beneficial to your body.
(2)   Therefore, running is good for you.

Above we mentioned *hasty generalization* as a type of fallacy of presumption, and people commit this fallacy almost daily when they conclude "they're all like that" from an experience of just a few instances (or even just one instance) of the "they" in question. More specifically, someone may hold a prejudice that goes like this:

(1)   My experience of a person from that ethnicity, creed, or sex has been negative.
(2)   So, they're all like that. (Every experience I have, or anyone will have, of a person from that ethnicity, creed, or sex will be negative.)

Can one rationally or logically draw that conclusion? Of course not. The main reason is that you will never be able to experience *all* people from that ethnic background, creed, or sex. Other examples: Sally will jump to the hastily generalized conclusion that "Cars from Brand X are all lemons" from the fact that she had one bad experience with a car from Brand X. Or think of how a restaurant in a small community can literally go out of business because it has gotten around by word of mouth that "Frank got a case of *E. coli* from that place" even though the restaurant has always been up to code and recently had a thorough, independent inspection performed. People hastily and incorrectly generalize that if *one* patron got a case of *E. coli* from the restaurant, then *all* patrons will get a case of *E. coli* from the restaurant, which may be an unfounded, illogical, fallacious move to make in one's thinking.

Besides fallacies of presumption, informal fallacies can be classified as *fallacies of relevance (or irrelevance)* and *fallacies of ambiguity*. A fallacy of relevance occurs when the premise(s) of an argument is/are found to be logically irrelevant to the conclusion, even though they may appear to be relevant, because of an appeal to psychological or emotional relevance. Typical fallacies of relevance that we will see in this book include *appeal to the person (ad hominem)*, *appeal to force*, *appeal to inappropriate authority*, and *appeal to the people (ad populum)*.

Coast to Coast AM with George Noory is a radio program featuring topics in conspiracy theory and the paranormal that airs on XM satellite radio as well as on terrestrial radio stations in the middle of the night. On January 5, 2016, the topic was cryptozoology, a pseudoscience concerned with the supposed existence of cryptids, creatures like Bigfoot, the Loch Ness monster, and chupacabra. A caller noted something like the following:

> That there is no hard evidence of these cryptids is baffling because they exist. There are too many accounts of these creatures for them *not* to exist. One of these days, someone will find a carcass. They *have* to.

There are a few things to note about this piece of poor reasoning. First, the caller seems to see the value of "hard evidence" and one can only assume that the carcass he mentions later would be an instance of that evidence. Yet, he has not appealed to that hard evidence in order to justify the existence of cryptids. What he has appealed to, however, is known as one of the most unreliable forms of evidence: witness testimony. "There are too many accounts of these creatures for them *not* to exist," he claims. Crack open any law school textbook dealing with courtroom evidence, and you will see references to hundreds of studies that have been performed in the last 50 years showing how people will claim to have witnessed events that did not occur or see objects that do not exist. There's even a phenomenon known as a *mass* or *collective hallucination* whereby several people claim to see something that really does not exist. What the caller has committed is a form of the informal fallacy known as *appeal to the people*, *appeal to the masses*, or in Latin, *argumentum ad populum*, which looks like this:

(1)   <u>Several people claim X is true or is the case.</u>
(2)   Therefore, X *is* true or *is* the case.

The caller fallaciously concludes that cryptids exist because "There are too many accounts of these creatures for them *not* to exist," when what he really should do is suspend judgment until someone finds a carcass.

A fallacy of ambiguity relies on some ambiguity (vagueness, obscurity, non-clarity) in wording or phrasing, the meanings of which shift/change to various degrees of subtlety during the course of the argument. Consider this argument:

(1)   The conflict in the Middle East is no news.
(2)   <u>And no news is good news.</u>
(3)   So, the conflict in the Middle East is good news.

Our intuition is that not only is the conflict in the Middle East *not* good news (in other words, the conclusion is false) but also that the conclusion does not follow from the premises. But why? What has occurred with this argument is known as *equivocation*, which refers to a term's changing its meaning throughout the course of a sentence, discussion, or, in this case, an argument. Equivocation is a bad thing, logically, linguistically, and for many other reasons. Specifically, the meaning of *no news* has changed: in the first premise, it means something like "known by all or most people" while in the second, it means something like "nothing bad is happening, or otherwise, that grabs our attention." When made explicit, we can see that the conclusion does not follow from the premises:

(1)   The conflict in the Middle East is known by all or most people.
(2)   <u>And nothing bad is happening that grabs our attention is good news.</u>
(3)   So, the conflict in the Middle East is good news.

So, if for some crazy reason you wanted to justify the claim that "The conflict in the Middle East is good news," you would need to do it some other way because your argument here is fallacious and should be rejected.

One more thing should be pointed out in relation to this argument that gets at the distinction between formal fallacies and informal fallacies. Read purely from a formal perspective, the argument might appear to be valid. If we symbolize the elements of the argument *formally*, without diagnosing its *content*, it looks like this:

(1)   CME is NN.
(2)   NN is GN.
(3)   So, CME is GN.

The link from CME to GN is clearly, and validly, made through NN. However, it is vital to look at the content of the claims as we have done above, since even formally, then, the argument's conclusion does not follow from the premises, as can be seen:

(1)   CME is KBA.
(2)   NBH is GN.
(3)   So, CME is GN.

There is no longer a link from CME to GN and now, even formally, the argument is invalid.

In addition to equivocation, other typical fallacies of ambiguity that we will see in this book include *amphiboly*, *accent*, *composition*, and *division*. And there are countless other types of informal and formal fallacies – complete with examples from famous writings, speeches, interviews, debates, stories, lore, and colloquialisms – that exist in the world today.

Why Be Concerned about Fallacies?

Fallacies are so rampant in our thinking that they affect public policies, civil laws, and even what are taken to be moral laws all over the world. Unfortunately, fallacious thinking has led to much pain and suffering in human history. Consider again the question-begging argument that fallaciously concludes to God's existence. How many people have used that very argument in the history of Western civilization as a justification for all kinds of unjust, exploitative, and atrocious activities? Or the hasty generalization that concludes, "They're all like that." Think of all the countless slavery laws, or religious laws, or voting laws that have been a part of various cultures throughout human history that have this fallacious conclusion as a basis, *in addition to* the base fact that one group, race, creed, or culture is always dominating and exploiting another.

The Logical Two Step

In addition to describing claims, evidence, support for the truth of claims, arguments, persuasion, and inference, above we mentioned reasoning correctly vs. reasoning incorrectly. Reasoning incorrectly is what leads to fallacious thinking and the creation of fallacies. Reasoning correctly is part and parcel of forming your own good arguments as well as evaluating an argument to see if it is a good one or not. In general, there is a two-step process to the evaluation (analysis, critique) of an argument:

Step 1: Make sure the conclusion follows from the premise(s).
Step 2: Make sure all of the premises in the argument are true.

Recall that a fallacy occurs when one thinks a conclusion follows from a premise (or premises) when in fact it does not. We must be constantly on the lookout for this possibility when evaluating an argument, and the suggestion here is that it is *the very first thing a critical thinker needs to check*. (Note that one of the reasons it is important to place an argument in argument form is so that one can more easily *visually* determine whether a conclusion follows from a premise (or premises) or not.) Consider this argument:

(1)   Computers can calculate things.
(2)   <u>The human mind can calculate things, too.</u>
(3)   Therefore, the mind is a computer.

There is something intriguing about this argument, and our immediate reaction may be to say that it all makes sense, especially given the emergence of work in artificial intelligence in the past 60 years or so. However, the argument is fallacious, as can be demonstrated by this more intuitive argument, which is of the exact same form:

(1)   Birds can fly.
(2)   <u>Airplanes can fly, too.</u>
(3)   Therefore, an airplane is a bird.

We can see that not only does the conclusion not follow from the premises, but also that, in this case, the conclusion is false. Airplanes are not the same things as birds just because they both can fly. Notice that it is absolutely true that computers can calculate things and that human minds can too but that we cannot conclude, therefore, that the mind *is* a computer – at least not from the two premises in that particular argument. The fallacy committed above is the formal fallacy known as the *fallacy of the undistributed middle term*, which you can see described in this book in more detail.

So, once again, it is absolutely imperative that you first check an argument to see if it commits a fallacy or not, namely, whether the conclusion follows from the premise(s) or not. And we will see numerous examples of formal and informal fallacies in this book.

However, that's not enough when evaluating an argument. You have to make sure that all of the premises are, in fact, true. That's the second step of the two-step process involved in the evaluation (analysis, critique) of an argument. Why? Because it's possible that a conclusion follow from a premise (or premises) and that the conclusion be *still false* or unsupported because the *premise(s) is/are false*. Believe it or not, there is no fallacy committed in the following argument:

(1)   Our sun is a star.
(2)   <u>All stars are cube-shaped.</u>
(3)   Therefore, our sun is cube-shaped.

The conclusion absolutely, positively follows from the premises in this argument and, in fact, you can't conclude anything other than "Therefore, our sun is cube-shaped." Yet, something is not right here. We know that our sun is most definitely *not* cube-shaped. Yes, it's true that our sun is a star as is noted in the first premise, but the second premise is false and, in this particular argument, this makes the conclusion false as well. Now consider this argument:

(1)   In over 1 million controlled studies, it was shown consistently that people lost 10% of their body weight in a month on a 5,000-calorie-a-day diet.
(2)   <u>You are starting that same diet at the beginning of next month.</u>
(3)   Therefore, all things being equal, you too will likely lose 10% of your body weight in a month on a 5,000-calorie-a-day diet.

No fallacy is committed here. However, the first premise is absolutely false (it was just concocted). Once again, in this particular argument, given the falsity of the first premise, the conclusion is false, too. If someone were trying to convince you of the truth of the conclusion utilizing this argument, hopefully you would not be convinced.

Good and Bad Arguments

Above we mentioned deductive reasoning and arguments vs. inductive reasoning and arguments. There are good arguments and there are bad arguments in both the deductive and the inductive realm. A good argument, in either realm, is one that meets the conditions of the two-step process mentioned above: (1) the conclusion does in fact follow from the premises and (2) all of the premises are in fact true. If either one of these conditions is absent, then the argument is bad and should be rejected.

In the deductive realm, that a conclusion follows from premises means that the argument is *valid* – it is *invalid* if the conclusion does not follow. *Strictly speaking, in the deductive realm, an invalid argument is one where a formal fallacy has been committed.* When an argument is valid and all the premises are true in the deductive realm, the argument is said to be a good, *sound argument.* If the argument is invalid or any of the premises are false, then the argument is *unsound* – thus, both conditions, validity and truth of all of the premises, must be met. This will make it so that the conclusion absolutely, positively, without a doubt, is true, and this is a good thing!

So, the "Our sun is cube-shaped" argument is valid but still unsound because the second premise is false. It is thus a bad argument and should be rejected.

This is true →	(1)	Our sun is a star.	
This is false →	(2)	<u>All stars are cube-shaped.</u>	← *Valid, but not all premises*
Does follow →	(3)	Therefore, our sun is cube-shaped.	*are true, so unsound*

On the other hand, the "The mind is a computer" argument has true premises but is still unsound because it's invalid. It, too, is a bad argument and should be rejected.

This is true →	(1)	Computers can calculate things.	
This is true →	(2)	<u>The mind can calculate things, too.</u>	← *All premises are true, but*
Doesn't follow →	(3)	Therefore, the mind is a computer.	*invalid, so unsound*

In the inductive realm, that a conclusion likely will follow from premises means that the argument is *strong* – it is *weak* if the conclusion likely does not follow. *A weak argument is one where an informal fallacy has been committed.* When an argument is strong and all the premises are true in the inductive realm, the argument is said to be a good, *cogent argument.* If the argument is weak or any of the premises are false, then the argument is *uncogent* – thus, both conditions, strength and truth of all of the premises, must be met. This will make it so that the conclusion most likely or probably is true, and this is a good thing, too!

So, the 5,000-calorie-a-day weight loss argument is strong but still uncogent because the first premise is false. It is thus a bad argument and should be rejected.

False →	(1)	In over 1 million controlled studies, it was shown consistently that people lost 10% of their body weight in a month on a 5,000-calorie-a-day diet.
True →	(2)	<u>You are starting that same diet at the beginning of next month.</u>
Follows →	(3)	Therefore, all things being equal, you too will likely lose 10% of your bodyweight in a month on a 5,000-calorie-a-day diet. *← Strong, but not all premises are true, so uncogent*

On the other hand, the following argument has true premises but is still uncogent because it's weak – a fallacy has been committed. It's an example of the informal fallacy known as *appeal to inappropriate (or false) authority* or *inappropriate appeal to authority.* It, too, is a bad argument and should be rejected.

This is true →	(1)	He is an accountant by trade.
This is true →	(2)	<u>In his opinion, global warming occurs.</u> *← All premises are true,*
Doesn't follow →	(3)	Therefore, global warming occurs. *but weak, so uncogent*

Below are two diagrams. The first shows that there are two types of good argument, a sound argument in the deductive realm of reasoning and a cogent argument in the inductive realm of reasoning. Again, for an argument to be sound, it must meet two conditions: it must be (1) valid – the conclusion absolutely/positively does, in fact, follow from the premise(s), and (2) all of the premises in the argument must be true. And for an argument to be cogent, it must meet two conditions: it must be (1) strong – the conclusion likely/probably does, in fact, follow from the premise(s), and (2) all of the premises in the argument must be true. If an argument is valid in the deductive realm, then no formal fallacy has been committed. And if an argument is strong in the inductive realm, then no informal fallacy has been committed.

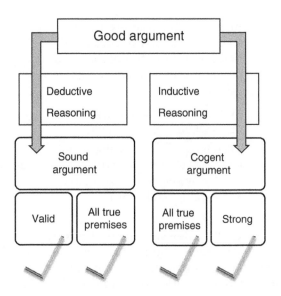

The second diagram shows that there are two types of bad argument, an unsound argument in the deductive realm of reasoning, and an uncogent argument in the inductive realm of reasoning. However, there are three ways that an argument can go bad in each realm. In the deductive realm, if an argument (1) is invalid, (2) has a false premise, or (3) both, then it's unsound. In the inductive realm, if an argument (1) is weak, (2) has a false premise, or (3) both, then it's uncogent. If an argument is invalid in the deductive realm, then a formal fallacy has been committed, and if an argument is weak in the inductive realm, then an informal fallacy has been committed.

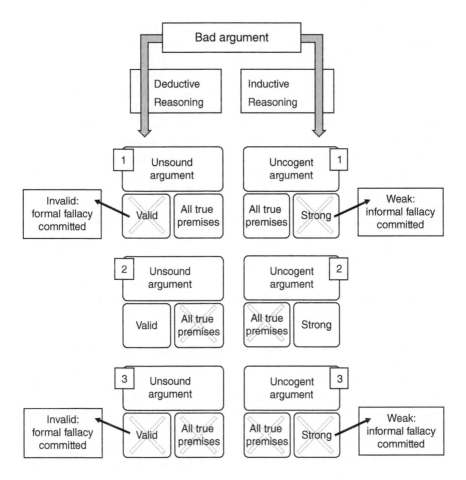

In Summary

What it comes down to is this: we all have beliefs (thoughts, opinions) about ourselves, the world around us, and reality, as we perceive it, and we make those beliefs known to ourselves in our own minds or in spoken or written form through claims. If you want to be a critical thinker, then you need to support the claims you put forward with evidence for the truth of those claims. If you can't do that, then you should reject the claim and not hold onto the corresponding belief (thought, opinion).

There are times, however, when you need or would like to reason to a claim, or from a claim, and when you do this, you are beginning to form an argument (unless you're simply providing an explanation or account). The claim you are reasoning to (or inferring) is the conclusion of the argument, while the claim(s) you are reasoning from is/are the premise(s). The conclusion is the claim you're trying to persuade or convince others (and yourself) is true, while the premise(s) is/are the claims that are supposed to support (justify, demonstrate) the conclusion such that the reasoning involved in the move from premise(s) to conclusion is correct (appropriate, legitimate).

The reasoning involved in the move from premise(s) to conclusion is an essential part of constructing a good argument because a good argument is one where the conclusion you are reasoning to actually does, in fact, follow from the premise(s). *If the conclusion does not follow from the premise(s), then it's a fallacy, either formal (deductive realm) or informal (inductive realm).* The other essential part of a good argument has to do with all of the premises in the argument being shown to be true with evidence. Thus, there is a logical two-step process that you have to go through when constructing your own arguments as well as evaluating the arguments of others: (1) make sure the conclusion follows from the premise(s) and (2) make sure all of the premises are true.

When you evaluate an argument and note that the conclusion actually does not, in fact, follow from the premise(s), *then you have located a fallacy.* If the argument is a deductive argument in the realm of deductive reasoning, then you have located a formal fallacy, several of which you will find described in this book. With formal fallacies, the argument's structure will make the fallacy apparent. If the argument is an inductive argument in the realm of inductive reasoning, then you have located an informal fallacy. With informal fallacies, an investigation of the content of the argument's claims will make the fallacy apparent. You will see that there are a good deal more informal fallacies described in this book precisely because many types of informal fallacies have been identified throughout human history.

We hope that you will benefit from the information in this book. The contributors have done an excellent job of explaining the fallacies. But don't *merely* take our word for it – go ahead and see for yourself, and the evidence for the truth of our claim, "The contributors have done an excellent job of explaining the fallacies," should become clear.

Part I
Formal Fallacies

Propositional Logic

1

Affirming a Disjunct

Jason Iuliano

> You have two choices with Obama. You either believe that he is a man of Christ, or you think he's a liar.
>
> Penn Jillette

Can you spot the logical error in Penn Jillette's statement? If so, you've identified the fallacy known as affirming a disjunct (AAD). If not, don't worry. In short order, you'll see just where Penn's argument went astray. Let's begin by considering a straightforward example:

> Either Madison likes cats or she likes dogs. I know she likes cats. Therefore, she doesn't like dogs.

This argument is flawed because it fails to account for the possibility that Madison likes both cats *and* dogs. Here's the example mapped out in logical form.

	Example	*Logic*
Premise 1	Madison likes cats or she likes dogs.	A or B.
Premise 2	Madison likes cats.	A.
Conclusion	Madison doesn't like dogs.	Not B.

Bad Arguments: 100 of the Most Important Fallacies in Western Philosophy, First Edition. Edited by Robert Arp, Steven Barbone, and Michael Bruce.
© 2019 John Wiley & Sons Ltd. Published 2019 by John Wiley & Sons Ltd.

As you can infer from the table above, this fallacy is caused by an ambiguity in the English word *or*. Because context makes the meaning clear in everyday usage, you might never have thought about this ambiguity before, but you actually use the word *or* in two very distinct ways. One type of *or* is known as "inclusive," and the other type is known as "exclusive." Since this difference is the key to understanding the fallacy of AAD, let's take a moment to explore it.

When you were a child, your mother probably had a hard time convincing you to eat your vegetables. At some point, she likely said, "Either you eat your veggies or you're not getting dessert." Chances are, you diligently ate your vegetables and your mother brought out dessert a short while later. But why did you understand your mom's statement as a bargain? What made it clear that if one event happened (i.e., eating your vegetables), then the other would not (i.e., not getting dessert)? The answer lies in your belief that your mother was using an exclusive *or*.

Now, suppose that you ate your vegetables, but your mom failed to provide dessert. You would've approach her and complained, "Mom you promised dessert if I ate my vegetables!" But what if she responded, "No, I didn't, Sweetie. I said, 'Either you eat your veggies or you're not getting dessert.' You ate your veggies and you didn't get dessert, so my statement is truthful. You really should listen more carefully."

Aside from ensuring that you'll never again eat your vegetables in exchange for dessert, what has your mother taught you? Well, she has given you a valuable lesson in the difference between two types of *or*.

Let's break them down, so you'll never be fooled again. On the one side, there is the inclusive *or*. This is the *or* used in classical logic. Take the basic proposition "Either A or B." If this proposition is using an inclusive *or*, it is true in three circumstances:

(1)   A is True.
(2)   <u>B is True.</u>
(3)   Both A and B are True.

Therefore, if your mother intended to use this inclusive *or*, her statement would have been true in three situations:

(1)   You eat your veggies.
(2)   <u>You don't get dessert.</u>
(3)   You eat your veggies AND you don't get dessert.

Unlucky for you, it was this third possibility that played out. Lest you think your mother played a terrible trick on you, let me point out that this is the type of *or* that online search engines use. Go try it now to see for yourself.

If you type "apple or banana" into Google, it will return results that have the word "apple," results that have the word "banana," and results that have both "apple" and "banana" in them.

Exclusive "or" is quite different. It is true only in two circumstances:

(1)   A is True.
(2)   B is True.

If *both* A and B are true, then an exclusive *or* statement is false. If Google searched using this form of *or*, it would return results that had the word "apple" and results that had the word "banana," but it would exclude results that had both "apple" and "banana."

To sum up, for inclusive *or*, there is an implicit *or both* that follows the statement. However, for exclusive *or*, there is an implicit *but not both* that follows the statement (Crain and Thornton 2013).

AAD occurs when someone mistakenly believes that an inclusive *or* is an exclusive *or*. To return to the original example, this is precisely what Penn Jillette did when he said, "You have two choices with Obama. You either believe that he is a man of Christ, or you think he's a liar." Penn failed to realize that there is a third choice: someone can believe that Obama is both a man of Christ *and* a liar.

Importantly, not every *or* statement can fall prey to AAD. Consider the following argument:

Either George Washington is dead or alive. George Washington is dead. Therefore, he is not alive.

This argument – known as a disjunctive syllogism – is sound because the first premise correctly uses an exclusive *or*. In other words, that premise sets out two possibilities that are mutually exclusive. When someone is dead, s/he is not alive, and when someone is alive, s/he is not dead.

The next time you make an *or* statement, think a little bit harder about which *or* you intend to use, and make sure you don't fall prey to AAD.

Reference
Crain, S., and R. Thornton. 2013. "Unification in Child Language." In *From Grammar to Meaning: The Spontaneous Logicality of Language*, edited by Ivano Caponigro and Carlo Cecchetto. Cambridge, UK: Cambridge University Press, 235–236.

2

Affirming the Consequent

Brett Gaul

> If Sophia is in the Twin Cities, then she is in Minnesota. Sophia is in Minnesota. Therefore, she is in the Twin Cities.
>
> John Doe

Affirming the consequent is a fallacious form of reasoning in formal logic that occurs when the minor premise of a propositional syllogism (an argument consisting of a general statement known as the major premise, a specific statement known as the minor premise, and a conclusion) affirms the consequent of a conditional statement. A conditional statement is an "if-then" sentence that expresses a link between the antecedent (the part after the "if") and the consequent (the part after the "then"). A conditional statement does not assert either the antecedent or the consequent. It simply claims that *if* the antecedent is true, then the consequent is also true. In the example, "Sophia is in the Twin Cities" is the antecedent and "she is in Minnesota" is the consequent. Affirming the consequent makes the mistake of assuming that the converse of an "if-then" statement is true. In other words, if "If p, then q" is true, then the converse, "If q, then p," must also be true. However, the converse of an "if-then" statement isn't necessarily true. Although affirming the consequent is an invalid argument form, it is similar to, and sometimes mistaken for, the valid argument form *modus ponens*

Bad Arguments: 100 of the Most Important Fallacies in Western Philosophy, First Edition.
Edited by Robert Arp, Steven Barbone, and Michael Bruce.
© 2019 John Wiley & Sons Ltd. Published 2019 by John Wiley & Sons Ltd.

(the mode of putting). While the valid argument form *modus ponens* asserts or affirms the antecedent of a conditional statement, the invalid argument form affirming the consequent asserts or affirms the consequent of a conditional statement.

Modus ponens (valid)	Affirming the consequent (invalid)
If p, then q.	If p, then q.
p.	q.
Therefore, q.	Therefore, p.

Modus ponens is a valid argument form because the truth of the premises guarantees the truth of the conclusion; however, affirming the consequent is an invalid argument form because the truth of the premises does not guarantee the truth of the conclusion. Put another way, if an argument is in the form of *modus ponens*, the structure of the argument makes it impossible for the argument's premises to be true and the conclusion to be false. Affirming the consequent is an invalid argument form, though, because the structure of that argument allows the premises to be true and the conclusion to be false.

To see how *modus ponens* is valid, assume that p = "Sophia is in the Twin Cities" and that q = "she is in Minnesota."

(1)   If Sophia is in the Twin Cities, then she is in Minnesota. (If p, then q)
(2)   <u>Sophia is in the Twin Cities. (p)</u>
(3)   Therefore, Sophia is in Minnesota. (q)

Given the form of *modus ponens*, if Sophia really is in the Twin Cities, then it is impossible for her not to be in Minnesota, because if she is in the Twin Cities, then she is in Minnesota. In other words, being in the Twin Cities is a sufficient condition for being in Minnesota. If something is a sufficient condition, it guarantees something else. In this case, being in the Twin Cities is a sufficient condition for being in Minnesota, because being in the Twin Cities guarantees that one is in Minnesota. To deny that Sophia is in Minnesota if she is in the Twin Cities is to make a mistake in reasoning. The truth of the premises guarantees the truth of the conclusion. However, this is not the case in affirming the consequent.

(1)   If Sophia is in the Twin Cities, then she is in Minnesota. (If p, then q)
(2)   <u>Sophia is in Minnesota. (q)</u>
(3)   Therefore, Sophia is in the Twin Cities. (p)

This argument form of affirming the consequent is invalid because if Sophia is in Minnesota, it is possible that she is somewhere other than the Twin Cities. Just being in Minnesota does not guarantee that one is in the Twin Cities. As Elliot D. Cohen puts it in *Critical Thinking Unleashed* (2009), the fallacy of affirming the consequent "confuses a necessary condition with a sufficient one" (40). The conditional statement in the example says that being in the Twin Cities is a sufficient condition for being in Minnesota and that being in Minnesota is a necessary condition, that is, one that is needed or required, for being in the Twin Cities. However, it does not say that being in Minnesota guarantees that one is in the Twin Cities.

The validity of *modus ponens* and the invalidity of affirming the consequent are confirmed by truth tables. In propositional logic, truth tables are used to represent the relation between any statement and its denial. For example, if p is true, then not p must be false. If p is false, not p must be true.

p	Not p
True	False
False	True

Truth tables are also used to represent the relationship between conjunctions (*and* statements), disjunctions (*or* statements), and conditionals (*if-then* statements). The truth table for conditionals looks like this:

p	q	If p, then q
True	True	True
True	False	False
False	True	True
False	False	True

The first line of the truth table indicates that if p is true and q is true, the conditional "If p, then q" is true. If p is true and q is false, then the conditional is false. If p is false and q is true, the conditional is true. Finally, if both p and q are false, the conditional is true.

For an argument to be valid, it must be impossible for the premises to be true and the conclusion to be false. *Modus ponens* is valid because there is no place on the truth table where all of the premises (If p, then q, and p) are true and the conclusion (q) is false. On the one line where both premises are true (the first line), the conclusion is also true.

Modus Ponens

Premise	Premise	Conclusion
p	If p, then q	q
True	True	True
True	False	False
False	True	True
False	True	False

Affirming the consequent is an invalid argument form, however, because the third row of the truth table below shows all true premises (If p, then q, and q) and a false conclusion (p). The truth of the premises does not guarantee the truth of the conclusion.

Affirming the Consequent

Premise	Premise	Conclusion
q	If p, then q	p
True	True	True
False	False	True
True	True	False
False	True	False

To return to the original example, given the conditional "If Sophia is in the Twin Cities, then she is in Minnesota," if she is in Minnesota, it's possible she is somewhere other than the Twin Cities. Simply being in Minnesota does not guarantee being in the Twin Cities. The fallacy of affirming the consequent is committed when one concludes that she is in the Twin Cities if she is in Minnesota. Avoid committing this fallacy by coming up with examples (p's and q's) to test the form of your argument. Is it true that the conclusion is true while the evidence is false? Is there another possible explanation? If Sophia is in Minnesota, could she be somewhere other than the Twin Cities? If you find that the argument does commit the fallacy, try to rework the structure of the argument to use *modus ponens*: If Sophia is in the Twin Cities, then she is in Minnesota.

Reference
Cohen, Elliot D. 2009. *Critical Thinking Unleashed*. Lantham, MD: Rowman & Littlefield.

3

Denying the Antecedent

Brett Gaul

> If Sophia is in the Twin Cities, then she is in Minnesota. Sophia is not in the Twin Cities. Therefore, she is not in Minnesota.
>
> Jane Doe

Like affirming the consequent (see Chapter 2), denying the antecedent is also a fallacious form of reasoning in formal logic. This time the problem occurs when the minor premise of a propositional syllogism denies the antecedent of a conditional statement. Denying the antecedent makes the mistake of assuming that if the antecedent is denied, then the consequent must also be denied. In other words, if the antecedent is not true, then the consequent must not be true either. However, that is not the case. To see this, assume again that p = "Sophia is in the Twin Cities" and that q = "she is in Minnesota."

(1) If Sophia is in the Twin Cities, then she is in Minnesota. (If p, then q)
(2) Sophia is not in the Twin Cities. (not p)
(3) Therefore, Sophia is not in Minnesota. (not q)

If Sophia is not in the Twin Cities, it does not follow that she is not in Minnesota. She could be in many other places in Minnesota.

Bad Arguments: 100 of the Most Important Fallacies in Western Philosophy, First Edition.
Edited by Robert Arp, Steven Barbone, and Michael Bruce.
© 2019 John Wiley & Sons Ltd. Published 2019 by John Wiley & Sons Ltd.

Just as the invalid affirming the consequent is similar to the valid *modus ponens*, the invalid denying the antecedent is similar to the valid *modus tollens* (the mode of taking). While *modus tollens* denies the consequent of a conditional statement, denying the antecedent denies the antecedent of a conditional statement.

Modus tollens *(valid)*	Denying the antecedent *(invalid)*
If p, then q.	If p, then q.
Not q.	Not p.
Therefore, not p.	Therefore, not q.

Like *modus ponens*, *modus tollens* is a valid argument form because the truth of the premises guarantees the truth of the conclusion; however, like affirming the consequent, denying the antecedent is an invalid argument form because the truth of the premises does not guarantee the truth of the conclusion. Given the form of *modus tollens*, if Sophia is not in Minnesota (not q), then she is not in the Twin Cities (not p), because the Twin Cities are in Minnesota. It's impossible for her to be in the Twin Cities if she is not in Minnesota, because being in Minnesota is a necessary condition – one that is needed or required – for being in the Twin Cities. However, being in Minnesota is not a sufficient condition – one that guarantees a result – for being in the Twin Cities, because being in Minnesota does not guarantee that one is in the Twin Cities. Nor is being in the Twin Cities necessary for being in Minnesota.

The invalidity of denying the antecedent is confirmed by a truth table.

Premise	Premise	Conclusion
If p, then q	Not p	Not q
True	False	False
False	False	True
True	True	False
True	True	True

The third row of the truth table indicates that the argument form allows true premises (If p, then q and not p) and a false conclusion (not q). For an argument to be valid, though, it has to be impossible for the premises to be true and the conclusion to be false. Thus, denying the antecedent is an invalid argument form.

Categorical Logic

4

Exclusive Premises

Charlene Elsby

> From two negative premises no conclusion is deducible ... *e.g.*, though I assert
> *Syrius is not a planet, Procyon is not a planet*, these dicta prove nothing.
> Samuel Neil, *The Art of Reasoning* (1853)

The categorical logic fallacies are called "formal" fallacies, because they are all violations of proper syllogistic form. The categorical syllogism is the foundation of Aristotelian logic, and Aristotle's logic is the foundation of modern logic. These fallacies, however, have only been termed "fallacies" for a couple hundred years. When Aristotle wrote his description of the categorical syllogism in the *Prior Analytics*, he pointed out that in only certain combinations of terms, no syllogism is possible, no syllogism is produced, or no syllogism can be made. Alexander of Aphrodisias (1991) referred to these combinations as "non-syllogistic" in his commentary on Aristotle's *Prior Analytics*. These were combinations of propositions that simply didn't lead anywhere.

Proper fallacies, at the time, were rather errors in reasoning based on ambiguities, such as those Aristotle speaks of in *Sophistical Refutations* and on which Galen comments in *De Captionibus* (*On Fallacies*). In the Aristotelian tradition, arguments are describable in terms of their matter and form, but in the case of these modern "formal" fallacies, there is no form and, therefore, no argument. William of Sherwood, a medieval thinker,

Bad Arguments: 100 of the Most Important Fallacies in Western Philosophy, First Edition.
Edited by Robert Arp, Steven Barbone, and Michael Bruce.
© 2019 John Wiley & Sons Ltd. Published 2019 by John Wiley & Sons Ltd.

whose *Introduction to Logic* explains the rules for the proper formation of a syllogism, called them "useless combinations." The tradition of calling them "fallacies" in modern logic really begins with Richard Whately's *Elements of Logic*, the 1826 book that is an expansion of his earlier article in *Encyclopaedia Metropolitana*. The book to which Whately claims he is most indebted, Henry Aldrich's *Artis Logicæ Compendium* of 1691, talks about such problems as illicit processes of terms and undistributed middles, but they are not included in Aldrich's appendix on formal fallacies.

Formal fallacies, according to Aldrich, include any reasoning that violates the law of identity, law of non-contradiction, or law of excluded middle. It is only since Whately's *Elements of Logic* that a standard table of fallacies, that is, reasons for the invalidity of certain combinations of premises, includes an illicit major or minor (see, for instance, Thomas Solly's *A Syllabus of Logic* from 1839 or Samuel Neil's *The Art of Reasoning* from 1853).

Each categorical fallacy is a violation of a rule for the formation of valid syllogisms. Aristotle defines the syllogism in *Prior Analytics* at 24a19–22:

> A syllogism is a discourse in which, certain things being stated, something other than what is stated follows of necessity from their being so. I mean by the last phrase that it follows because of them, and by this, that no further term is required from without in order to make the consequence necessary.

While a syllogism is by no means the only kind of argument, it is the *best* kind of argument, just as Alexander of Aphrodisias (1991) says it is:

> When a part is justified from the whole, such a justification is called a syllogism; and this is the most compelling type of justification. For anything which applies to or holds of a universal and a totality, by necessity also holds of what is within it and is included in it. (104)

The reason a syllogism is so great is because if the syllogism is of the correct form, and as long as the premises are true, then the conclusion is guaranteed to be true – necessarily. Aristotle describes syllogisms that are not formed correctly and hence, fallacious. This chapter deals with the exclusive premises fallacy (EP). Also see the other chapters on the fallacy of four terms (Chapter 5), the illicit major and minor terms fallacies (Chapter 6), and the fallacy of the undistributed middle term (Chapter 7).

EP occurs when a syllogism has two negative premises, which are propositions that deny a connection between the subject and predicate. For example, the proposition, "No monkeys are cats," makes the claim that there is no connection between the set of monkeys and the set of cats. Likewise, the proposition, "Some monkeys are not plants," claims that there is no necessary connection between the set of monkeys and the set of plants. In all, negative premises usually (not always!) contain the word "not" or "no" in them.

The quality or quantity of the premises of a syllogism can make them *exclusive* to one another. By quality, I mean whether the premise is affirmative or negative, and by quantity, I mean whether the premise is particular or universal. While nobody spoke of the EP until relatively recently, everyone has always known that no good syllogism has two negative premises. Aristotle notes the problem in *Prior Analytics* at 26a9–13.

> Nor again can a deduction be formed when neither the first term belongs to any of the middle, nor the middle to any of the last. As an example of a positive relation between the extremes take the terms science, line, medicine: of a negative relation science, line, unit.

We can see this illustrated in one of Aristotle's examples of a non-syllogism at 27a21–23:

> Nor is a syllogism possible when M is predicated neither of any N nor of any O. Terms to illustrate a positive relation are line, animal, man: a negative relation, line, animal, stone.

If we fill in the blanks for a negative relation:

(1)   No animals are lines.
(2)   No stones are lines.
(3)   Therefore, ...?

And there's nothing we can conclude from that. Alexander of Aphrodisias (1991) quotes the former passage in his commentary, explaining the reasoning behind it:

> The reason why nothing is deduced syllogistically in this combination is that the middle bears no relation to either of the extremes (it is as if the middle had not been taken at all – and syllogisms depend on the middle term).

Basically, we have a middle term and it is related to each of our major and minor terms in some way but in such a way that doesn't allow us to make any connection between the major and minor terms in order to form a conclusion. For example, if I say:

(1)   No monkeys are cats.
(2)   No monkeys are plants.

then I still have nothing to conclude from these statements when I take them together. It's as if the premises have nothing to do with each other besides the fact that both of them mention monkeys. They are *exclusive*. These two premises, taken together, tell me nothing of the relation between the sets of cats and plants. This was a well-known rule for the formation of any and all syllogisms, right from Aristotle, through the medievals, and into the modern era. William of Sherwood (1966) includes it in his rules for syllogisms: "Note that nothing follows from two negatives or from two particulars" (68). So does John Buridan (2015): "Second Conclusion: No syllogism can be validly drawn from two negatives" (119). And so does Walter Burley (2000): "Therefore, I say that there are two general rules for every syllogism, in no matter what figure or mood it occurs, namely that it have (a) one universal proposition and (b) one affirmative one. For nothing follows syllogistically from negatives or from particulars" (26).

In summary, you can't have a good syllogism with two negative premises, or else your premises won't be related in the right way, and you won't be able to conclude anything at all.

Neil (1853) uses the "agreement/disagreement" terminology to describe assertions and negations, which helps to elucidate the fact that from two statements about what things *aren't*, we can't form any conclusion.

References

Alexander of Aphrodisias. 1991. *On Aristotle's Prior Analytics 1.1–7*, translated by Jonathan Barnes, Susanne Bobzien, Kevin S.J. Flannery, and Katerina Ierodiakonou. London: Gerald Duckworth.

Aristotle. 1984. *Prior Analytics*. In *The Complete Works of Aristotle: The Revised Oxford Translation*, edited by Jonathan Barnes. Princeton: Princeton University Press.

Buridan, John. 2015. *Treatise on Consequences*, translated by Stephen Read. New York: Fordham University Press.

Burley, Walter. 2000. *On the Purity of the Art of Logic*, translated by P.V. Spade. New Haven, CT: Yale University Press.

Neil, Samuel. 1853. *The Art of Reasoning*. London: Walton and Maberly.

William of Sherwood. 1966. *Introduction to Logic*, translated by Norman Kretzmann. Minneapolis: University of Minnesota.

5
Four Terms

Charlene Elsby

> The war against ISIS is no news. And no news is good news. So, the war against ISIS is good news.
>   Used by Rob Arp in every logic primer he gives to students

Humans are natural classifiers, sorting all kinds of things into categories so as to understand, predict, and control reality better. A category is a class, group, or set containing things (or members or elements) that share some feature or characteristic in common. We can construct a category of things that are dogs, a category of things that are human, a category of things that are red and left shoes, a category of things that taste sweet and fly, and on and on. In fact, it's possible to classify anything that exists or you can think of into one category or another.

Aristotle was one of the first thinkers to lay out rules for describing the relationships between and among categories of things, as well as for reasoning with categories – thus, he's considered the father of *categorical logic*. As he notes in Book I, Part I of the *Prior Analytics*, Aristotle's principal tool for reasoning and for explanation is the syllogism: "discourse in which, certain things being stated, something other than what is stated follows of necessity from their being so." And in Book II, he lays out probably the most well-known syllogism: "If then it is true that A belongs to all that to which B belongs, and that B belongs to all that to which C belongs, it is necessary

Bad Arguments: 100 of the Most Important Fallacies in Western Philosophy, First Edition.
Edited by Robert Arp, Steven Barbone, and Michael Bruce.
© 2019 John Wiley & Sons Ltd. Published 2019 by John Wiley & Sons Ltd.

that A should belong to all that to which C belongs, and this cannot be false."
We recognize this syllogism today as:

(1)   All A are B.
(2)   All B are C.
(3)   All A are C.

Aristotle also describes other syllogisms that are well formed as well as ones
that are not well formed and hence, fallacious. This chapter deals with the
fallacy of four terms (FT). Also see the other chapters on the exclusive premises
fallacy (Chapter 4), the illicit major and minor terms fallacies (Chapter 6),
and the fallacy of the undistributed middle term (Chapter 7).

The fallacy of FT violates the very first rule of constructing a valid syllogism:
any syllogism must contain three and only three terms. These terms have, since
Aristotle, been called the major, the minor, and the middle. The major and
minor are also called the "extremes" of a syllogism, since they lie on either
extreme of the middle term. This rule is already explicit in Aristotle's *Prior
Analytics*, where he deduces at 41b36–8 that it "is clear too that every demon-
stration will proceed through three terms and no more, unless the same conclusion is established by different pairs of propositions." And again at 42a30–35:

> So it is clear that every demonstration and every deduction will proceed
> through three terms only. This being evident, it is clear that a conclusion
> follows from two propositions and not from more than two for the three
> terms make two propositions unless a new proposition is assumed, as was said
> at the beginning, to perfect the deductions.

Aristotle's reasoning for the idea that each syllogism must have three, and
only three, terms is that three is the minimum number of terms required to
make a deduction. In order to form a valid syllogism, we must at least be
able to relate two different terms (the major and minor) to one and the
same term (the middle) such that we can make a valid inference that
relates the major term and the minor. Of course, it is possible to have an
argument with more than three terms, but a syllogism is but one deduction.
If we are constructing a syllogism with more than three terms, then we
either have multiple syllogisms or no syllogism at all.

In this example, there are two syllogisms, each one of which is valid on its
own:

(1)   All cats are cute.
(2)   All cute things are blue.
(3)   All blue things are smelly.
(4)   Therefore, all cats are smelly.

In order to put this argument into proper syllogistic form, we would have to elucidate an implicit conclusion – that all cats are blue. The argument reduces to two syllogisms:

(1)   All cats are cute.
(2)   All cute things are blue.
(3)   Therefore, all cats are blue.

And then

(1)   All cats are blue.
(2)   All blue things are smelly.
(3)   Therefore, all cats are smelly.

In each of the above syllogisms, we have one term that is in both the premises (the middle term) and disappears in the conclusion, and two other terms, one of which is in the first premise, and the other of which is in the second premise, which both appear in the conclusion. The conclusion of each of these syllogisms is a necessary result of two premises, and the syllogism as a whole contains only three terms.

Without the middle term to connect the premises, no deduction is possible. That is why if we have two premises with four completely unrelated terms, then we cannot form any conclusion. That is, one of the terms needs to repeat in the first and second premises in order for any deduction to be made. If it doesn't, then we have no way of making a reasonable connection. If instead we have four terms, then no deduction is possible. For example:

(1)   All cats are blue.
(2)   Your mom smells funny.
(3)   Therefore, ...?

But there is a sneakier way to commit the fallacy of FT, which is to use in place of the middle some ambiguous term that actually has two meanings, when we need it to have one. For example:

(1)   All asses eat hay.
(2)   Aristotle is an ass.
(3)   Therefore, Aristotle eats hay.

Looked at from the perspective of bare language, this looks like a valid syllogism, but the meaning of the word "ass" shifts between the first and second premise. Where in the first, "ass" refers to the animal that is the offspring of a horse and donkey, the second use of "ass" is metaphorical, referring to a human having some of the same qualities as the animal from which we derive this usage. What we have in reality is another supposed syllogism where the two premises aren't related at all, since the middle term is actually two terms.

On the converse side of things, a syllogism can't have any fewer than three terms either. If it did, then we would run into the problem illustrated by William of Sherwood (1966) in his *Introduction to Logic* of the thirteenth century, namely that with only two terms, you would only have one premise and not be able to make any deduction at all. He summarizes the first rule of syllogisms:

> There will be no more and no fewer than three terms, since propositions cannot share two terms, for then they would be one and the same proposition. This is because there are exactly two terms in one proposition – viz., the subject and the predicate – for the proposition is analyzed (*resolvitur*) into the term. So there will be three terms in every syllogism. (60)

To summarize, every good syllogism has three and exactly three terms. There are two premises, one of which relates the major term to the middle, and the other of which relates the minor term to the middle. In a valid syllogism, the major and minor terms are related in the conclusion, and their relation is absolutely necessary and completely justified by the premises alone. When there are four terms, either the terms are unrelated and no deduction is possible, or there are multiple syllogisms.

There's another thing about negative premises, that is, premises that deny a relationship between the subject and predicate. As soon as you have a negative premise, your conclusion must be negative as well. If you try to conclude something affirmative when one (or more) of your premises is negative, you commit the fallacy of illicit negative. This fallacy is the violation of Whately's (1840) sixth rule of syllogisms:

> 6th· *If one premiss be negative, the conclusion must be negative;* for in that premiss the middle term is pronounced to disagree with one of the extremes, and in the other premiss (which of course is affirmative by the preceding rule) to agree with the other extreme; therefore, the extremes disagreeing with each other, the conclusion is negative. In the same manner it may be shown, that *to prove a negative conclusion one of the Premises must be a negative.* (87)

In general, Aristotle claims that to prove any sort of conclusion, there must be a premise of the same kind previously in the argument.

And it is clear also that in every syllogism either both or one of the premises must be like the conclusion. I mean not only in being affirmative or negative, but also in being necessary, pure, or problematic (*Prior Analytics*, 41b27–30).

This fallacy is the converse of that rule: If you want to prove a negative conclusion, one of your premises must be negative, and if you have a negative premise, your conclusion must also be negative. The modern logicians like to speak of this fallacy in the "agreement/disagreement" terminology, as Whately (1840) does above. An affirmation is an agreement, and a negation is a disagreement. Now, if one of the terms agrees with the middle, and the other disagrees, then they necessarily disagree with each other.

Just take a look at this terrible forgery of a syllogism:

(1)   All cats are clowns.
(2)   Some clowns don't do drugs.
(3)   Therefore, some cats do drugs.

But we don't know anything about cat habits from the information given. From those two premises, we can't conclude anything at all.

And then there's this other terrible sham of a syllogism:

(1)   All cats are clowns.
(2)   No cats do drugs.
(3)   Some clowns do drugs.

This doesn't even make sense. In fact, we could conclude something from the premises given, namely that there are some clowns who don't do drugs. That's because if all cats are clowns, then some clowns are cats. And if no cats do drugs, then those ones that are clowns don't do drugs. And therefore there are some clowns who don't do drugs. But there's absolutely no reason to think that you could prove the opposite.

References

Alexander of Aphrodisias. 1991. *On Aristotle Prior Analytics 1.1–7*, translated by Jonathan Barnes. London: Gerald Duckworth.

Aristotle. 1984. *Prior Analytics.* In *The Complete Works of Aristotle: The Revised Oxford Translation*, edited by Jonathan Barnes. Princeton: Princeton University Press.

Whately, Richard. 1840. *Elements of Logic.* London: B. Fellowes.

William of Sherwood. 1966. *Introduction to Logic*, translated by Norman Kretzmann. Minneapolis: University of Minnesota.

6
Illicit Major and Minor Terms

Charlene Elsby

> McNuggets are fast food, but Big Macs aren't McNuggets, so Big Macs aren't fast foo... Wait. That doesn't work.
>
> John Doe, thinking through categorical logic for the first time

The categorical syllogism is the foundation of Aristotelian logic, and he defines it in *Prior Analytics* at 24a19–22:

> A syllogism is a discourse in which, certain things being stated, something other than what is stated follows of necessity from their being so. I mean by the last phrase that it follows because of them, and by this, that no further term is required from without in order to make the consequence necessary.

There are 15 valid syllogisms, of which these three are examples:

(1)	All A are B	All cats are mammals.
(2)	All B are C	All mammals are warm blooded.
(3)	All A are C	All cats are warm blooded.

(1)	All A are B	All Christians are monotheists.
(2)	No B are C	No monotheists are polytheists.
(3)	No A are C	No Christians are polytheists.

Bad Arguments: 100 of the Most Important Fallacies in Western Philosophy, First Edition.
Edited by Robert Arp, Steven Barbone, and Michael Bruce.
© 2019 John Wiley & Sons Ltd. Published 2019 by John Wiley & Sons Ltd.

(1)	All A are B	All wolves are canines.
(2)	Some A are C	Some wolves are black-colored.
(3)	Some C are B.	Some black-colored things are canines.

The categorical logic fallacies are called *formal* fallacies because they are all violations of proper syllogistic form. This chapter deals with the illicit major and minor terms fallacies. Also see the other chapters on the exclusive premises fallacy (Chapter 4), the four terms fallacy (Chapter 5), and the fallacy of the undistributed middle term (Chapter 7).

The fallacies of illicit major term and illicit minor term have to do with distribution in syllogisms. The rule for making a good syllogism is that you can't have a term distributed in the conclusion that's not distributed in the premise. So if you are only talking about some of something, then you can't go on to conclude something about all of that something. For example:

(1)   All cats are blue.
(2)   All cats are furry.
(3)   Therefore, all blue things are furry.

In the premise, we haven't extended the whole class of blue things, so we can't go on to make a claim about all blue things in the conclusion. This argument is an example of the illicit process of the minor term. The illicit process of the major term is much the same, except we would illicitly process the major term as opposed to the minor:

(1)   All cats are blue.
(2)   All cats are furry.
(3)   Therefore, all furry things are blue.

It just doesn't work with either term. We could conclude, on the other hand, that *some* furry things are blue – all the ones that are cats. Then we are not distributing the term "furry things." At least, according to Aristotle we could conclude that. Nowadays, those who follow Boolean logic would claim that's an example of the existential fallacy.

Sometimes, our terms are so undistributed that we can't even make a valid conclusion, and that's when we get the rule for all syllogisms that you can't make a valid one from two particular premises. For example:

(1)   Some cats are blue.
(2)   Some cats are furry.
(3)   ...?

There's no way to know if the same cats are both blue and furry, because none of the terms are distributed in that example. That is, we don't know anything about cats in general, we don't know anything about blue things in general, and we don't know anything about furry things in general. We don't even know if the cats that are blue are the same as the ones that are furry, because the middle term is also undistributed. Aristotle gives a ton of examples of arguments that fail due to mismatched distributions, and the medieval logicians formalized rules based on these observations.

In short, you can't distribute anything in the conclusion that wasn't distributed in the premises. But feel free not to distribute in the conclusion whatever was distributed in the premises. That's just fine.

Reference

Aristotle. 1984. *Prior Analytics*. In *The Complete Works of Aristotle: The Revised Oxford Translation*, edited by Jonathan Barnes. Princeton: Princeton University Press.

7

Undistributed Middle

Charlene Elsby

> Minds are computers, since minds calculate and computers calculate, too...
> The typical freshman in college

This chapter deals with the fallacy of the undistributed middle term. Also see the other chapters on the exclusive premises fallacy (Chapter 4), fallacy of four terms (Chapter 5), and the illicit major and minor terms fallacies (Chapter 6).

In order to understand the fallacy of undistributed middle, we need to know that the middle term is the term that appears in both of the premises but not in the conclusion. In addition, we need the concept of distribution. "Distribution" is meant to describe the extension of the term, that is, how many things it applies to. If it's all of them, then the term is distributed, as is the term "cats" in "All cats are blue." I have said something about all of the cats, and so that term is distributed in my premise. "Blue" is not distributed, since I haven't included all of the blue things in my statement. (There could be other blue things besides cats, like the sky, or it could be that all and only cats are blue, but the statement does not tell us whether that is true.) With regard to its place in the history of logic, William Kneale and Martha Kneale (1985) credit the medieval logicians with applying the term "distribution" to this property of terms: "it came later to indicate the property which a

Bad Arguments: 100 of the Most Important Fallacies in Western Philosophy, First Edition.
Edited by Robert Arp, Steven Barbone, and Michael Bruce.
© 2019 John Wiley & Sons Ltd. Published 2019 by John Wiley & Sons Ltd.

general term is supposed to have when it is used to stand for all the individuals to which it is applicable" (272).

Stated succinctly, the fallacy of undistributed middle occurs when the middle term isn't distributed in either premise. This fallacy was apparent to medieval scholars like John Buridan in his *Treatise on Consequences* in *Summulae de Dialectica* (1350/2001): "Sixth Conclusion: No syllogism is valid in which the middle is distributed in neither premise, unless the middle is used in the minor with a relative of identity" (121).

That's not to say that the problem wasn't already apparent in Aristotle. It is the reason many of the possible combinations of premises result in "no syllogism." Many forms of argument fail due to their middle term's being undistributed, and while Henry Aldrich (1862) uses the undistributed middle term to explain why an argument is invalid, it doesn't seem to have been formalized as a "fallacy" until Richard Whately's *Elements of Logic* (1827). Still, in Aristotle, we get the idea through his examples of situations where no syllogism is possible. One of these situations is where the middle term is undistributed. Another note on terminology – where the middle term is that which is repeated twice in the premises, the "extremes" are the other two terms of the syllogism. If, for instance, we have "substance" as a middle term and "animal" and "human" as extremes, then the start of a non-syllogism with an undistributed middle would look like this:

(1)   All animals are substance.
(2)   All humans are substance.

And from that we can't conclude anything, because neither all of the animals nor all of the humans are enough to extend the reach of all substance.

Aristotle formulated this rule in the *Prior Analytics*: "But if M is predicated of every N and O, there cannot be a syllogism. Terms to illustrate a positive relation between the extremes are substance, animal, man; a negative relation, substance, animal, number—substance being the middle term" (27a19).

We cannot conclude anything from the two statements above, since we have not accounted for the entirety of substances in either of the premises. It is completely possible that the animals that are substances and the humans who are substances aren't the same substances. Alexander of Aphrodisias (1991) fully comprehends the reasoning behind this, although he doesn't use the term "distribution."

> The reason why there is no syllogistic combination from two universal affirmatives in the second figure is that the middle is predicated of both extremes, and the predicate is the major term. Thus, being major in relation to both, it may be predicated of one extreme term in virtue of one of its parts, and of the other in virtue of another. And in this way there is nothing which the extremes

share with each other, if they each share with the middle term in virtue of different parts of it. For the extremes must share in one and the same thing if there is to be a syllogism. (151)

Basically, demanding that the middle term be distributed in at least one of the premises ensures that there's going to be some overlap between the two premises so that it is possible to deduce their relation. If the middle term is undistributed, the argument is invalid.

There exist any number of ways this fallacy could be avoided; that is, the way to avoid the fallacy of undistributed middle is to create any valid syllogism. While not all syllogisms with distributed middles are valid, a syllogism must have a distributed middle in order to be valid. Distribution of the middle term is thus a necessary but not sufficient condition for a valid syllogism. If we imagine a world where no humans are substance, then we could reform the example above to look like this:

(1)   All animals are substance.
(2)   No humans are substance.

And from these premises we could conclude

(3)   No humans are animals.

In order to do so, we have had to distribute the middle term – the fact that the classes of "human" and "substance" are mutually exclusive means that, at some point in our syllogism, we have taken all of substance into account. That is, all of substance is excluded from being human.

References

Aldrich, Henry, and H.L. Mansel. 1862. *Artis Logicae Rudimenta, from the Text of Aldrich*. Oxford: Clarendon Press.

Alexander of Aphrodisias. 1991. *On Aristotle's Prior Analytics 1.1–7*, translated by Jonathan Barnes, Susanne Bobzien, Kevin S.J. Flannery, and Katerina Ierodiakonou. London: Gerald Duckworth.

Aristotle. 1984. *Prior Analytics*. In *The Complete Works of Aristotle: The Revised Oxford Translation*, edited by Jonathan Barnes. Princeton: Princeton University Press.

Buridan, John. 1350/2001. *Summulae de Dialectica* (Compendium of Dialectic), translated by Gyula Klima. New Haven, CT: Yale University Press.

Kneale, William, and Martha Kneale. 1985. *The Development of Logic*. Oxford: Clarendon Press.

Whately, Richard. 1827. *Elements of Logic*. London: J. Mawman.

Part II
Informal Fallacies

Fallacies of Relevance

8

Ad Hominem: Bias

George Wrisley

> My opponent says that we should return the municipal garbage-disposal to private hands. But why does he say this? What are his underlying motives? Could it be that he and his friends want to get in on a profitable little monopoly?
>
> Patrick Hurley, *A Concise Introduction to Logic*

In our dealings with each other, how much weight do we and should we give to considerations of character? After all, we can quite reasonably think of a person's character as the wellspring of her actions. As such, we quite rightly pay attention to a person's character in judging the truth and significance of what she says. If you are considering deepening your friendship with someone, then it might be helpful for you to know how he has treated his past friends. Thus, if someone who is trustworthy impugns the friend's character, you rightly might question whether to spend the time deepening the bond between you. In political contexts, particularly very public and popular ones, character is quite relevant, and thus it is a context in which we often find mention of a person's character.

However, it is because of the importance of character and the power to influence others that comes with commenting on another's character that we must be very cautious how and when we do it. The *ad hominem* argument form is one way of engaging another's character. The *ad hominem*

Bad Arguments: 100 of the Most Important Fallacies in Western Philosophy, First Edition.
Edited by Robert Arp, Steven Barbone, and Michael Bruce.
© 2019 John Wiley & Sons Ltd. Published 2019 by John Wiley & Sons Ltd.

argument is an argument "to," "toward," or "against" the person. That is, it is an argument that calls into question a person's character, her credibility and trustworthiness, by appealing directly to some *negative* aspect of her person, or indirectly by making some negative claim about the person's relationships, actions past or present, commitments, views, or still more. It is the direct or indirect impugning of a person's character that unites the various forms of the *ad hominem* argument.

Many textbook accounts of the *ad hominem* argument are much too cavalier in their approach, often treating the *ad hominem* argument form as usually/always fallacious. However, as Walton, for example, has made clear, things are not so easy. One of the greatest challenges in thinking about the *ad hominem* argument type and the possibility of particular cases being fallacious is finding a way to distinguish between those cases that are fallacious and those that aren't. And as we will see in the chapters for the different *ad hominem* subtypes, the very same case may be considered fallacious or legitimate depending on how it is read, what the conclusion of the respondent is.

This chapter deals with *ad hominem*: bias. Also see the other chapters on *ad hominem*: circumstantial (Chapter 9), *ad hominem*: direct (Chapter 10), and *ad hominem: tu quoque* (Chapter 11).

We are very often rightly disturbed by bias, as it represents a kind of ungrounded prejudice in favor of one thing, person, group, and so on. However, is bias always problematic? What about my bias for Japanese food over Mexican? How about a salesperson's bias for his product? One would expect a salesperson to be biased toward his product. However, bias becomes a problem in contexts in which the goal is fairness and the discovery of impartial truth, as far as that's possible. In such contexts, bias can be particularly pernicious as it can impede the dialogue's goal of impartial inquiry, as it involves the "suppressing of critical doubt (when critical doubt is appropriate)" (Walton 1998, 132). Further, accusing someone of bias can be a powerful way of impugning her character and making suspect what she says since it is purportedly driven by bias. Such is an *ad hominem* bias argument.

As with all the *ad hominem* argument forms, the *ad hominem*: bias has both fallacious and legitimate uses. Thus a central question becomes: How do we differentiate the fallacious from the legitimate instances of *ad hominem* attack? This is particularly important because of how powerful an influence *ad hominem* arguments can have on the proponent's ability to support her position in a meaningful way. Fallacious uses of the *ad hominem* argument type are pernicious, in part, because of how difficult it can be to respond to them in an effective way. Think about how hard it can be for someone to recover from accusations that paint him as a bad person or hypocrite.

What makes an example of an *ad hominem*: bias argument fallacious is that there is not sufficient reason to believe that the proponent's vested interests compromise her ability to engage fairly in argument. There may be cases where it does, but bias alone is not sufficient, and, thus, trying to turn others against the proponent in a case of unproblematic bias is a dirty and fallacious move, one that illicitly shifts the issue from the subject of the argument to the character of the proponent.

The basic form of the fallacy looks like this:

Respondent: Claims the proponent of argument/position *x* is biased.
Respondent: Claims that the proponent's bias interferes with her ability to argue fairly.
Respondent: Therefore, the proponent's character and credibility are not trustworthy.
Respondent: Therefore, argument/position *x* "should not be given as much credibility as it would have without the bias" (see Walton 1998, 255).

(1) What reason is there for thinking the proponent is biased?
(2) If the proponent is biased, is she biased merely in the sense of having a vested interest or has the bias also interfered with her ability to argue fairly?
(3) Are the details about the proponent's purported bias relevant to the argument/position in question or the dialogical context?
(4) Is the respondent's conclusion the weaker claim that the proponent's argument/position is questionable and in need of further support or the stronger claim that her argument/position is refuted?

Let us look at some examples to illustrate the use of these questions:

Example 1

A school teacher argues for increased pay for school teachers and a critic attacks his argument by replying, "Sure! It's easy to see why *you're* in favor of a raise!"
(Walton 1998, 75)

Regarding our first critical question, clearly as a school teacher he stands to benefit if school teachers receive a raise, assuming his argument concerns school teachers in his area. Thus, we can see that he has a vested interest in the matter. However, from the example, we know of no reason for considering the teacher biased in the sense of his letting his vested interest influence his argumentation in a negative way. Thus, whatever bias he has in the sense of having a vested interest, it is not, from what we know, detrimental to his ability to take part credibly in the dialogue in question. Further, consider that teachers are often viewed as underpaid. Thus, it is not surprising that a teacher would advocate for increased pay. Thus, it does not seem that we have good reason for thinking that the proponent, the teacher, has a bias that is problematic. Thus, we have not been given sufficient reason to think that the bias is such that it reflects poorly on his character.

Even if there was some potentially problematic bias, how relevant is it to the quality of the argument/position in question? It is at the very least questionable that the teacher's vested interest is relevant to whether his premises support his position regarding teacher pay. The main reason is that he *has put forward an argument* in support of his position. If we interpret his argument deductively, then whether the premises of his argument actually support his conclusion to increase teacher pay depends on the form of the argument—for example, the deductively valid *modus ponens* is valid because of its form: If p, then q. / p. / Therefore, *q*. Alternatively, if we interpret his argument inductively, then whether the reasons of his argument support the conclusion will depend on their content, that is, what they say. The teacher's bias is completely irrelevant to whether his argument is an instance of a deductively valid form. Similarly, the inductive strength of his argument is completely independent of any bias. This is further true because how well the premises of an argument support the conclusion does not depend upon whether they are actually true. Thus, the respondent's allegations are irrelevant in regard to whether the premises of his argument support his conclusion.

And, thus, since we have not been given reason to believe that the teacher's bias compromises his argument/position, and since the bias is not relevant to whether his premises support his conclusion, we have not been given reason to believe that the proponent's argument/position has been called into question, much less refuted, by the *ad hominem*: bias argument. As such, the respondent has argued fallaciously against the proponent's person.

Example 2

> House speaker Nancy Pelosi has argued strongly against oil and gas exploration in the Arctic National Wildlife Refuge. But what would you expect? She represents the city of San Francisco, which is loaded with environmentalists. If she didn't take this position, she would be run out of office. Thus, her arguments on this issue really have no merit. (Hurley 2008, 144)

As we'll see, this example is less straightforward than the first one. What reason is there for thinking the proponent, Pelosi, is biased? Well, she would certainly have a vested interest in the views of her constituency. Is such a bias problematic? Well, there is certainly a place for politicians to go against their constituents' wishes when they think their constituents are dangerously mistaken, for example. But there also seems to be a widespread presumption that politicians will do whatever they can to remain in office.

We can perhaps get a better idea of whether the bias here is problematic or whether the *ad hominem* is problematic (fallacious) if we consider the conclusion of the respondent. Is the respondent merely trying to cast doubt upon Pelosi's argument/position x in a way that would call for further evidence, or is he claiming that the bias here shows that Pelosi has let her bias influence her such that her character is so bad that her argument/position x is refuted? Regardless of how biased she may be, it is irrelevant to either the strength or the validity of the argument, as both of those depend on the nature of the inferential relationship between the premises and conclusion of her arguments and not at all on her character. Moreover, the bias we have reason to expect her to have certainly does not imply that her premises are false. Perhaps they are cherry-picked, but none of this would imply the refutation of her position/argument.

Concerning the question of calling her argument/position x into doubt, on the one hand, given that she would be expected, generally, to argue in favor of her constituents' desires, it does not seem justified to conclude that her bias in this situation reflects poorly on her character. Thus, it does not seem we have reason to doubt her arguments without further evidence. Nevertheless, on the other hand, given the state of political debate in the United States in the latter part of the twentieth century and now, in the first part of the twenty-first, it seems like good practice not to trust what any politician says or argues without further, third-party evidence. Perhaps we should wish her, and other politicians, to be the "bigger person" and stand above the pressures to pander to voters. However, be that as it may, it seems open to serious doubt that the present state of US politics is sufficient reason for thinking that Pelosi, in arguing for her constituents' position, is demonstrating a bad character, much less one that is sufficiently relevant to seriously question the quality of her argument/position. If this is correct, then the respondent's attempt to undermine Pelosi's argument/position x with the charge of bias is fallacious. We can see in the next example how complex the considerations can be.

Example 3

A Monsanto representative argues that the company's genetically modified seed is perfectly safe because of studies, A, B, and C. Steve responds by saying that what the Monsanto representative says can't be trusted because it has so much invested in the genetically modified seed and would lose too much if the studies indicated the seed was unsafe.

This case is interesting as Monsanto's bias is easy to see. However, is the vested interest Monsanto has enough to indicate a problematic bias, one that indicates less credibility or trustworthiness? It is difficult without further information to say for sure. One thing that would be relevant would be the nature of the studies cited by Monsanto. Who paid for them? What journals were they published in? If, for example, Monsanto paid for them and published them in something like *Monsanto's Agri-Journal*, then that may well be reason to think that they have a problematic sort of bias and that, therefore, the representative's credibility has been impugned. The next question, of course, concerns what exactly the respondent's conclusion is. If it is that the representative's argument/position is refuted, then that would be a fallacious inference. What about if the conclusion is that the representative's position/argument is questionable and in need of further evidence from an unbiased party?

References

Hurley, Patrick. 2008. *A Concise Introduction to Logic*, 10th edition. Belmont, CA: Wadsworth Cengage Learning.

Walton, Douglas. 1998. *Ad Hominem Arguments*. Montgomery, AL: The University of Alabama Press.

9

Ad Hominem: Circumstantial

George Wrisley

> Mr. Lipperty advocates immediate desegregation of the schools, yet he himself sends his son to a private school to avoid the integrated school in his neighborhood.
>
> Douglas Walton, *Ad Hominem Arguments*

This chapter deals with *ad hominem*: circumstantial. You perhaps should start with *ad hominem*: bias (Chapter 8), then read this one, as well as the other chapters on *ad hominem*: direct (Chapter 10) and *ad hominem: tu quoque* (Chapter 11).

The circumstantial variety of the *ad hominem* argument is distinct from the direct form in that instead of directly attacking the character of the arguer, one draws attention to an inconsistency in the personal circumstances of the proponent (her commitments) and the content of her argument/position as a way to question her sincerity or credibility. As with all of the *ad hominem* argument subtypes, the *ad hominem*: circumstantial occurs in the context of some kind of dialogue or exchange, real (face to face) or imagined (in dialogue with a text, for example). That is, an *ad hominem* occurs in response to the stated argument/position of another person (the proponent).

As Walton (2006, 99ff) notes, the scope of "circumstances" is quite broad and includes a variety of possibilities. For example, circumstances might be

Bad Arguments: 100 of the Most Important Fallacies in Western Philosophy, First Edition. Edited by Robert Arp, Steven Barbone, and Michael Bruce.
© 2019 John Wiley & Sons Ltd. Published 2019 by John Wiley & Sons Ltd.

the arguer's current or past actions, promises, jobs, relationships, ownership of material goods, and so on. The two important aspects of the circumstances for this argument type are: (1) that they indicate some kind of commitment to values, beliefs, courses of action, and so on; (2) the mark of what counts as a *relevant* circumstance in an *ad hominem*: circumstantial argument is that there is some sort of practical conflict with the proponent's circumstances/commitments and the proponent's argument/position. The important issue is whether the practical inconsistency indicates the compromising of one's character and, further, whether that is relevant to the issue in question.

As with all the *ad hominem* argument forms, the *ad hominem*: circumstantial has both fallacious and legitimate uses. Thus a main question becomes: How do we differentiate the fallacious from the legitimate instances of *ad hominem* attack? This is particularly important because of how powerful an influence *ad hominem* arguments can have on the proponent's ability to support her position in a meaningful way. Fallacious uses of the *ad hominem* argument type are pernicious, in part, because of how difficult it can be to respond to them in an effective way. Think about how hard it can be for someone to recover from accusations that paint him as a bad person or a hypocrite.

The basic form of the fallacy looks like this:

Proponent: Gives argument/position x.
Respondent: Questions or attempts to refute argument/position x, not by attacking x, but by drawing attention to circumstance y, where y demonstrates one of the proponent's commitments which is in some way inconsistent with argument/position x.
Respondent: Claims the proponent's credibility in regard to argument/position x is called into question.
Respondent: Concludes that the proponent's argument/position x is less credible/refuted.

One of the main issues with *ad hominem* arguments is telling which are fallacious and which are not. To help identify whether an *ad hominem*: circumstantial argument is fallacious, it will be helpful to ask the following four questions:

(1)   Is there good reason to believe that the proponent has identifiable commitments and that the proponent is being practically inconsistent?
(2)   If the proponent's practical inconsistency has been correctly identified, could she give more details concerning the circumstances such that either (a) the appearance of inconsistency is lessened or (b) her credibility is not called into question by the inconsistency?

(3) How relevant are the proponent's circumstances, character, and credibility to the quality of her argument/position?
(4) Is the respondent's conclusion the weaker claim that the proponent's character is open to question, and thus her argument/position is in need of further support, or the stronger claim that the her argument/position is refuted?

Let us look at an example to illustrate the use of these questions:

Example 1

PARENT: There is strong evidence of a link between smoking and chronic obstructive lung disease. Smoking is also associated with many other serious disorders. Smoking is unhealthy. So you should not smoke.

CHILD: But you smoke yourself. So much for your argument against smoking. (Walton 1989, 141–142)

Regarding the first question, what exactly is the parent committed to with his smoking? Is he thereby committed to the claim that smoking is healthy? Presumably not, since we are all familiar with doing things that we know aren't healthy, whether for sheer pleasure or because of addiction. We would thus need more information about whether the parent is committed to the view that smoking is a good idea. Hence, the parent could respond to the child's allegations by saying that he is addicted to smoking, that he doesn't want to smoke, and that he is trying to keep the child from being in his position. This would greatly mitigate the appearance of inconsistency. However, for the sake of analyzing this example, let us say we have reason to believe that the parent's smoking reveals commitments that imply he is being inconsistent in telling his child not to smoke.

With our second question, if there is reason to think the proponent is practically inconsistent, we can still ask whether this reflects on his credibility. In this case, it will depend on the nature of his commitment to smoking and his reasons for arguing to the child that he should not smoke. Our answer above already touched on this issue to an extent. Further, perhaps the proponent believes not that smoking is bad in general but that it is bad for children because they are still developing. If this were the case, then the appearance of inconsistency is lessened and so is the hit taken to his credibility. However, if it turns out that he is, for example, merely attempting to deprive the child of something enjoyable when there is nothing wrong with it, then this would presumably be a mark against his character and credibility. In such a case, he is both willfully depriving the child of something he thinks is harmless and enjoyable, and he is using dishonest means to do so as he apparently does not believe the evidence he has given the child.

With our third question, on the one hand, the parent's actions and character are irrelevant to the question of whether his argument against smoking is any good. If we interpret his argument deductively, then whether the reasons of his argument actually support the conclusion that the child shouldn't smoke depends on the form of the argument – for example, the deductively valid *modus ponens* is valid because of its form: If p, then q. / p. / Therefore, q. That is, it does not depend on the parent's actions and character. Alternatively, if we interpret his argument inductively, then whether the reasons of his argument support the conclusion will depend on their content, that is, what they say. The proponent's practical inconsistency and even his poor character (if the practical inconsistency implies it is poor) have nothing to do with the form of his argument or with whether the premises inductively support his conclusion. However, on the other hand, because the respondent in this context is in a special position of dependence, as a child, on the parent, we should note that the parent's inconsistency may well give the child a reason to question the truth of the reasons given against smoking. That is, the inconsistency gives reason for the child not to take the argument seriously since one of his main authority figures is not endorsing it, practically speaking. From this point of view, the child's *ad hominem* argument is not fallacious. However, whether it really is depends on the fourth critical question.

The fourth question forces us to clarify what exactly the respondent's conclusion is. Does the child claim that the allegations are (a) sufficient to refute the parent's argument/position or (b) sufficient at least to bring the parent's character into question in a way relevant to question the proponent's advocacy of the argument/position in question? How we formulate the respondent's conclusion will have implications for whether she has committed an *ad hominem*: circumstantial fallacy. For even if her allegations do not refute the proponent's argument/position, we may still ask whether the allegations give us reason to question his advocacy of it. Do they do either? Well, as we have seen, since the allegations are irrelevant to both the validity and the strength of the proponent's arguments, they do not refute or give us reason to question whether the conclusion follows from what he says. However, depending on the answers given to the other three critical questions, the child may have given reason for questioning the parent's advocacy of the argument/position, which may, in turn, give us reason to want more evidence from another source. If the proponent has been practically inconsistent in such a way that his credibility and character have been tarnished, and that credibility is important in regard to endorsing the argument, particularly the truth of the premises, then it is legitimate for her, at least until more evidence/information is given, not to endorse the parent's argument/position. Thus, the respondent's *ad hominem* argument is fallacious only if she takes it to refute the proponent's argument/position. But if her conclusion is the weaker claim that the proponent's inconsistency gives us reason to question his character, and thus indirectly call the argument/position into doubt until further evidence is given, then no fallacy has been committed.

Example 2

> It is ridiculous to hear that man from Peru complaining about America's poverty. Peru has twice as much poverty as America has ever had.
> (Hurley 2008, 146)

With this example, it is clear to see that the issue of commitments is important. Is the Peruvian man committed to the superiority of Peru over the United States simply by being Peruvian? Certainly not. But let us say for the sake of analysis that with further questioning, he is committed to the superiority of Peru over the United States in regard to poverty. Might he say something that lessens the blow to his credibility? It will depend in part on whether he is lying or ignorant in regard to Peru's poverty. If he is downplaying it in the hopes that others don't know, then that speaks poorly of his credibility. However, it's possible that he admits that Peru has twice as much poverty as the United States but that the way Peru deals with the impoverished is better than how the United States deals with them. This would also lessen the appearance of inconsistency.

How relevant are the proponent's circumstances, character, and credibility to the quality of his argument/position? From the example, it is unclear whether in "complaining" the proponent has given an argument or merely stated an opinion. If he has given an argument, then the usual considerations apply, as demonstrated above in our first example, regarding the irrelevance of circumstances, character, and credibility to the validity or strength of an argument. If no argument was given, then the proponent's character is central to whether we put any stock in his claims.

The real question, again, is whether the respondent's claim is that the proponent's argument/position should be taken to be refuted or whether the proponent's credibility is in question such that there is reason to question his argument/position. If the proponent's character has not been impugned via commitments that show problematic inconsistency, then it seems the respondent has succeeded in neither refuting nor calling the proponent's argument/position into question. Thus, on either reading, the proponent has given a fallacious *ad hominem*: circumstantial argument.

References
Hurley, Patrick. 2008. *A Concise Introduction to Logic*, 10th edition. Belmont, CA: Wadsworth Cengage Learning.
Walton, Douglas. 1998. *Ad Hominem Arguments*. Birmingham, AL: The University of Alabama Press.
Walton, Douglas. 2006. *Fundamentals of Critical Argumentation*. Cambridge, UK: Cambridge University Press.

10

Ad Hominem: Direct

George Wrisley

> Richard Nixon's statements on foreign affairs policies in relation to China are untrustworthy because he was forced to resign during the Watergate scandal.
>
> Douglas Walton, *Fundamentals of Critical Argumentation*

This chapter deals with *ad hominem*: direct. You perhaps should start with *ad hominem*: bias (Chapter 8), then read this one, as well as the other chapters on *ad hominem*: circumstantial (Chapter 9) and *ad hominem: tu quoque* (Chapter 11).

An *ad hominem* argument is an argument "to," "toward," or "against" the person. The direct variety of the *ad hominem* goes directly against the person, particularly in regard to some aspect of character, as opposed to indirectly by, for example, pointing out some pragmatic inconsistency between a person's actions and various commitments (as in the *ad hominem*: circumstantial). As with all of the *ad hominem* argument subtypes, the *ad hominem*: direct occurs in the context of some kind of dialogue or exchange, real (face to face) or imagined (in dialogue with a text, for example). That is, an *ad hominem* occurs in response (the respondent) to the stated argument/position of another person (the proponent). Instead of addressing the argument/position of the proponent, the respondent addresses the proponent's character in such a way that his credibility is questioned in order to either question or refute his argument/position.

Bad Arguments: 100 of the Most Important Fallacies in Western Philosophy, First Edition.
Edited by Robert Arp, Steven Barbone, and Michael Bruce.
© 2019 John Wiley & Sons Ltd. Published 2019 by John Wiley & Sons Ltd.

The central complication when dealing with the *ad hominem*: direct is that while *ad hominem* arguments are often fallacious, they are also often legitimate. Thus, a main question becomes: How do we differentiate the fallacious from the legitimate instances of *ad hominem*: direct arguments? This is particularly important because of how powerful *ad hominem* arguments can be in regard to the proponent's ability to support her position in a meaningful way. Fallacious uses of the *ad hominem* argument type are pernicious, in part, because of how difficult it can be to respond to them in an effective way. Think about how hard it can be for someone to recover from accusations that paint her as a bad person or a hypocrite.

The basic form of the fallacy looks like this:

> Proponent: Gives argument/position x.
> Respondent: Questions/attempts to refute position x, not by attacking x, but by attacking the Proponent's character.
> Respondent: Concludes that the proponent's argument/position x is less credible/refuted. (Walton 2006, 123)

One of the main issues with *ad hominem* arguments is telling which are fallacious and which are not. To help identify whether an *ad hominem*: direct argument is fallacious, it will be helpful to ask the following three questions.

(1)   How well justified are the allegations made against the proponent's person?
(2)   Are the details about the proponent's person relevant to the argument/ position in question or the dialogical context?
(3)   Is the conclusion of the respondent's *ad hominem* argument that the proponent's argument/position should be rejected outright, or is the conclusion merely that the proponent should be viewed with less credibility as a supporter of the original argument/position x? (Walton 2006, 123)

Let us look at two examples to help illustrate the nature of *ad hominem* arguments and the use of these three critical questions. As we will see, since we are focusing on the *ad hominem* argument, the proponent's side is often not given explicitly or in detail.

Example 1

> Respondent: General Petraeus's argument for aggressively pursuing ISIS can't be trusted because it is likely that he gave classified documents to a reporter with whom he was having an extramarital affair.

Following our critical questions above, we should first inquire as to whether the allegations against Petraeus are well founded. If they are not, then to the extent that they are not, the *ad hominem* argument does not get off the ground as they do not give reason to impugn Petraeus's character. If they are true, then we need to move to ask the other critical questions.

The second critical question concerns the relevance of the respondent's allegations to the proponent's argument/position and the dialogical context more generally. This first issue of relevance concerns whether his character is relevant to how well the premises of his argument support his conclusion. It is at the very least questionable that Petraeus's giving classified documents to his mistress is relevant to whether his premises support his conclusion regarding ISIS. The main reason is that Petraeus *has put forward an argument* in support of his position. If we interpret his argument deductively, then whether the premises of his argument actually support his conclusion to pursue ISIS aggressively depends on the form of the argument – for example, the deductively valid *modus ponens* is valid because of its form: If p, then q, / p. / Therefore, q. Alternatively, if we interpret his argument inductively, then whether the reasons of his argument support the conclusion will depend on their content, that is, what they say. Petraeus's character is completely irrelevant to whether his argument is an instance of a deductively valid form. Similarly, the inductive strength of his argument is completely independent of his character. This is further true because how well the premises of an argument support the conclusion does not depend upon whether they are actually true. Thus, the respondent's allegations are irrelevant in regard to whether the premises of his argument support his conclusion.

So, we've seen that the allegations regarding Petraeus's personal life are not relevant to whether his argument supports his position. So, has the respondent committed a fallacy with her *ad hominem* argument? Before we can answer, we must address the third critical question. The third question requires us to clarify what exactly the respondent's conclusion is. That is, is she claiming that the allegations are (a) sufficient to refute his argument/position or (b) sufficient to at least bring Petraeus's character into question as a supporter of his argument/position in such a way that we might have reason to question the truth of his argument's premises and whether he may be leaving out pertinent information? That is, do the allegations reveal something about Petraeus's character that would justify calling for further evidence from another, untarnished, source? How we formulate the respondent's conclusion will have implications for whether she has committed an *ad hominem* fallacy. For even if her allegations do not refute Petraeus's position, we may still ask whether the allegations give us reason to question it.

Do they do either? Well, as we have seen, since the allegations are irrelevant to his argument's validity and strength, they do not refute or give us reason to question whether the conclusion follows from what he says. But they also don't give us reason to think that he has made an error in formulating the premises, that is, the allegations don't speak to his competence. Since a part of the allegation is that he had an affair and another that he shared classified information with someone unauthorized, then we might have reason to question his integrity. But in what sense is his integrity relevant to the argument? Perhaps his motive is relevant, that is, if he were really a spy, then we might question his motives and thus his reasons for putting forward his argument. But, again, in this case the allegations don't seem to pertain to his motive. Thus, it is difficult to see the allegations as relevant to questioning what Petraeus says, much less refuting it. Thus, the respondent's *ad hominem* argument fails to be relevant for questioning or refuting Petraeus's argument/position, and, thus, she commits the fallacy of *ad hominem*: direct.

In our General Petraeus example, the respondent commits an *ad hominem* fallacy if we read her argument along the lines of either questioning or refuting Petraeus's argument/position. However, as we will see, it is possible for a respondent's *ad hominem* argument to be fallacious read one way but not fallacious read another way. Usually, when there is a difference, it will be a matter of the argument being fallacious if read as refuting the proponent's position but not if read as calling it into question.

Example 2:

An eyewitness is on the stand, testifying to the guilt of the accused. The defense attorney asks the eyewitness: "Isn't it true that you've been convicted of perjury twice before, and, thus, you are a perjurer, a liar?"

Has the attorney committed an *ad hominem* fallacy? Let us consider our three critical questions. First, it would presumably be straightforward to assess whether the attorney's allegations of perjury are true. If they aren't, then his *ad hominem* argument is immediately beside the point (though it may still be damaging if not caught).

Second, note that the eyewitness, the proponent, is committed to two things: (1) to being in a position to know what happened, and (2) to speaking honestly about what happened. As a position to know argument, the support for the eyewitness's claims comes from the claimed position to know. This is in contrast to an argument with explicit premises whose truth and relevance for the conclusion we could examine independently of the proponent's character. Thus, the proponent's character and credibility are highly relevant in regard to whether his testimony supports what he says. For if he is untrustworthy, we do not have good reason to trust what he says.

Third, what is the conclusion of the respondent's argument? Is it that what the eyewitness says is false or that we should question it and not assent to it without further evidence from another source since the witness's character is questionable? Well, being an untrustworthy liar does not mean that everything one says is false. At most, it means that one is not trustworthy and that others are fools if they uncritically accept what one says. Thus, if the respondent claims that the proponent's testimony is false, then the respondent has argued fallaciously. However, if the respondent claims that the proponent's testimony cannot be trusted, then we have been given reason to believe that is true given the truth of his being a perjurer. Thus, on this weaker reading, no fallacy has been committed. And since, in this example, it is a court case, the attorney need not attempt to show that the testimony is false; he merely needs to show that there is reason not to trust it.

Reference

Walton, Douglas. 2006. *Fundamentals of Critical Argumentation*. Cambridge, UK: Cambridge University Press.

11

Ad Hominem: Tu Quoque

George Wrisley

A public school teacher argues for increased pay for public school teachers and a taxpayer attacks his argument by replying, "Sure! It's easy to see why *you're* in favor of a raise!" To which the teacher replies, "Well, I can say the same of you; it's easy to see why you're against it!"

Douglas Walton, Ad Hominem *Arguments*

This chapter deals with *ad hominem: tu quoque*. You perhaps should start with *ad hominem* bias (Chapter 8), then read this one, as well as the other chapters on *ad hominem*: circumstantial (Chapter 9) and *ad hominem*: direct (Chapter 10).

An *ad hominem: tu quoque* argument is often seen in political debate. When one party impugns the character of another, it is often countered with a response, "you, too!" Presumably the goal of such a response is to distract from or deflate the power of the first party's allegations. However, the *tu quoque ad hominem* argument is not merely the claim that the other party is just as guilty as oneself. As Douglas Walton (1998) emphasizes: "The main problem with the textbook treatment of the tu quoque ad hominem fallacy is that according to the way it is most often defined, it becomes essentially the same type of argument as that in the two wrongs make a right fallacy" (233). What makes the *ad hominem: tu quoque* not merely an instance of the latter but a genuine *ad hominem* is that it involves both parties' characters in

Bad Arguments: 100 of the Most Important Fallacies in Western Philosophy, First Edition.
Edited by Robert Arp, Steven Barbone, and Michael Bruce.
© 2019 John Wiley & Sons Ltd. Published 2019 by John Wiley & Sons Ltd.

some way. As Walton (1998) stresses: "The primary case of the tu quoque type of ad hominem retort occurs when an ad hominem reply is used to respond to an ad hominem attack" (16). Thus, the *ad hominem: tu quoque* necessarily involves one of the other *ad hominem* subtypes.

As with all the *ad hominem* argument forms, the *ad hominem: tu quoque* has both fallacious and legitimate uses. Thus a main question becomes: How do we differentiate the fallacious from the legitimate instances of *ad hominem* attack? This is particularly important because of how powerful an influence *ad hominem* arguments can have on the proponents ability to support her position in a meaningful way. Fallacious uses of the *ad hominem* argument type are pernicious, in part, because of how difficult it can be to respond to them in an effective way. Think about how hard it can be for someone to recover from accusations that paint him as a bad person or a hypocrite.

The basic form of the fallacy looks like this:

Proponent: Questions/attempts to refute respondent's position *x*, not by attacking *x*, but by attacking the respondent's character directly or by appeal to circumstances or bias.
Respondent: Questions/attempts to refute proponent's *ad hominem* argument/position by alleging that she is equally guilty in a similar way of having a bad character (Walton 1998, 233).

One of the main issues with *ad hominem* arguments is telling which are fallacious and which are not. To help identify whether an *ad hominem: tu quoque* argument is fallacious, it will be helpful to ask the following three questions (see Walton 1998, 16):

(1)   How good of an argument is the proponent's *ad hominem*? Is it fallacious given the critical questions one should ask about it?
(2)   How good of an argument is the respondent's *ad hominem*? Is it fallacious given the critical questions one should ask about it?
(3)   If the proponent's argument is a good one, how credible is the respondent in regard to her allegations?

Let us look at some examples to illustrate the use of these questions:

Example 1

At a promotional event, after a businessman gives a lecture on the charitable activities of his company, a student accuses him and his company of selling weapons to countries that use them to kill innocent citizens.

The businessman replies, "The university you attend has investments in these very companies that manufacture weapons. Your hands aren't clean either!" (Walton 1989, 147)

In evaluating this *tu quoque* argument, we begin by evaluating the quality of the proponent's *ad hominem*. In this case the proponent is the student, since he is giving the first *ad hominem* argument. Is it any good? Well, what kind of *ad hominem* is it? Presumably the argument concerns some inconsistency between the claims being made about the charitable activities of the company in order to promote its value and the accusation of selling weapons that end up being used to kill innocent citizens. As such, it is best read as an *ad hominem*: circumstantial, which has its own set of critical questions to ask. What exactly is the inconsistency? It is that the businessman claims that both he and the company he represents are good (because of charitable activities) while both are, however, involved in doing things that are reasonably seen as inconsistent with a good character, that is, selling weapons that kill innocents. Is the businessman/company thereby displaying a commitment that is inconsistent with his/its actions? Possibly. Perhaps not if he doesn't know that the weapons are being used to kill innocents – though in such a case we might still ask whether he is culpable for his ignorance. One might argue that selling weapons of any kind is inconsistent with the ideals of charity and generosity in the name of improving people's welfare. These are difficult issues. However, it is not hard to imagine an argument in favor of inconsistency here. Given that the point of the businessman is to promote the image of himself and the company with the claims of charity, such an inconsistency is relevant in this case, as the nature of the inconsistency undermines the force of the businessman's claims, potentially even showing that it is false that the company is a (morally) good one. Thus, the argument is not fallacious.

What about the respondent's *ad hominem*? He is presumably intending an analogous kind of attack in response. That is, since he is claiming the student's hands aren't clean either, he presumably intends to say that the student's character is not one that can sustain such a charge, that is, the student is just as inconsistent as he is. Is he? And is he in a relevant way? The student did not offer up evidence of his own moral superiority. Though perhaps we can justifiably attribute to the student a commitment to the claim that selling weapons that are used to kill innocents is bad. If that's right, then he could be charged with being inconsistent since he pays tuition, thereby supporting the university, which itself invests in the weapons companies. But we should note that even if there is such a connection between the student's money and the weapons companies, it is not nearly as direct as the businessman's due to the differences in the businessman's and the student's roles.

We should ask, too, whether the student has knowledge of such investments, or if not, if he is culpable for not knowing. For now, let's say for the sake of analysis that he does know that a portion of his tuition goes to the university's investments in weapons manufacture. What is the conclusion of the respondent's argument? Does he intend it to imply that the proponent's *ad hominem*/position is refuted or that his advocacy of it is questionable? Either way it doesn't seem that the respondent's *ad hominem* is relevant. The student's original *ad hominem*: circumstantial does not depend upon his own moral high ground, so to speak, at least not in the same way as the businessman's. The businessman was attempting to show the moral high ground of his company, something that is called into question given the weapons allegations. Given his presumably indirect involvement in the university's weapons deals, and given that the student is not himself attempting to make himself look good, the businessman's "you, too!" falls flat regardless of his conclusion.

Lastly, if the proponent's (student's) argument is a good one, how credible is the respondent (businessman) in regard to his allegations? We've seen that the proponent's argument is a good one. We saw above that even if the respondent is telling the truth about the student, his *ad hominem* argument is fallacious. So, it won't matter if the respondent is credible or not, either way, he's arguing fallaciously. The issue of the respondent's credibility would only really come up in the case in which the proponent had given a legitimate *ad hominem* argument against him and the respondent had given a legitimate *ad hominem* argument in response. At that point, if it turned out that the respondent was not credible in regard to the allegations, then that would undermine their force. However, in such a case, no fallacy would be committed.

Example 2

"I know you like Heidegger, Jon, but his philosophy can't be taken seriously, given what we now know about his active involvement in the Nazi party. He was clearly not a good man." "What?! That's ridiculous, especially coming from you. I heard you talking about your dedication to the Tea Party."

Let's consider our three questions. In this *tu quoque ad hominem* both parties use *ad hominem*: direct arguments to impugn someone's character. How good of an argument is the proponent's *ad hominem*? Since it is of the direct subtype, we need to consider the critical questions appropriate to it. How well justified are the allegations made against the Heidegger's person? Well, we've learned more and more about Heidegger's involvement in the Nazi party in recent years. So it seems that there is good reason to accept the basic allegation that he was an active member, even if he wasn't directing a death camp or the like. Are the details about Heidegger's person relevant to the argument/position in question? This is much more difficult to assess. You will find some philosophers arguing that his involvement did and others that it did not have negative consequences for Heidegger's philosophical work. Much more information would be needed to decide this. This is particularly true since much of Heidegger's work concerned not simply abstract metaphysics but what it means to live an authentic human life. Thus, it is conceivable that his involvement in the Nazi party might indeed prove problematic for his philosophical work, as his views about Jews and the Nazis might impact his views about authenticity and the authentic life. But the key question is whether the proponent's conclusion is that Heidegger's involvement with the Nazis is a sufficient reason to take his work as a whole to be refuted or indirectly called into question via Heidegger's allegedly poor character. If the proponent intends the former, then that is clearly a fallacious inference, as Heidegger's involvement with the Nazis is simply not sufficient reason to reject all of his work as false, poorly reasoned, or otherwise compromised. If the proponent intends the allegations merely to call Heidegger's character into question and thus cast some kind of shadow on his work, perhaps in relation to what he included and what he left out, or what he claimed to be true, then given the truth of the allegations, it seems sufficient to do just that. Thus, such a move would not be fallacious.

How good of an argument is the respondent's, Jon's, *ad hominem*: direct? Again, our three questions: How well justified are the allegations made against the proponent's person? We can't say with the information provided, but it is unlikely that such an allegation would be made if it wasn't something that was likely to be true. For if it were false, it would be easy for the proponent to deny it and end that part of the conversation. Though that might be different if there are others around who don't really know the proponent. Nevertheless, for the sake of analysis, let's assume that the allegations are true, that the proponent is a dedicated Tea Party member. Are such details about the proponent's person relevant to the argument/position in question? What is the respondent's argument? Presumably something like: "The Proponent rejects Heidegger's work because he was a Nazi. But we shouldn't listen to that since the Proponent is himself a Tea Party member. Belonging to the Tea Party reflects poorly on the Proponent's character and credibility." Whether one thinks this last claim is true or not, let's assume it is for the sake of our analysis. If it were true, would it give us reason either to question the proponent's argument/position or to reject it as refuted? Perhaps if Heidegger were extremely liberal in his political affiliation, then given the conservative nature of the Tea Party, one might wonder if the proponent has a negative bias that would influence his judgment regarding what he asserts, and so on. However, the Nazi party isn't exactly liberal; so this doesn't seem to be a possible relevant connection. Would the conservative traits that the respondent presumes to belong to Tea Party members make the proponent less reliable in his ability to assess the relationship between Heidegger's being a Nazi and the quality of his philosophy? It is hard to see the connection. Thus, it doesn't seem that the respondent's *ad hominem*: direct is really relevant to the proponent's *ad hominem*: direct.

Thus, regardless of whether the respondent intends us to question the proponent's character, and indirectly his argument, or whether the respondent takes the proponent's position to be refuted, we have not been given sufficient reason to do either. Thus, on either reading the respondent is giving a fallacious version of an *ad hominem*: direct and so the example is a case of a fallacious *ad hominem: tu quoque*.

Reference

Walton, Douglas. 1998. *Ad Hominem Arguments*. Birmingham, AL: The University of Alabama Press.

12

Adverse Consequences

David Vander Laan

> If the six men win, it will mean that the police are guilty of perjury, that they are guilty of violence and threats, that the confessions were invented and improperly admitted in evidence and the convictions were erroneous .... This is such an appalling vista that every sensible person in the land would say that it cannot be right that these actions should go any further.
> Lord Denning in his judgment on the Birmingham Six, quoted in Catherine Elliot and Frances Quinn, *English Legal System*

The argument from adverse consequences has this general form:

(1) If P were true, then something bad would be the case.
(2) Therefore, not P.

Since the bad consequences of P are not generally relevant to P's truth or falsity, arguments of this form typically commit a fallacy of relevance. Here are some examples:

> If we're required to declare rental income to the Internal Revenue Service, then I've been calculating my taxes incorrectly for about six years. I'd have to collect a lot more information, and I'd worry about an audit of the previous years. So I think we don't really have to report rental income.

Bad Arguments: 100 of the Most Important Fallacies in Western Philosophy, First Edition. Edited by Robert Arp, Steven Barbone, and Michael Bruce.
© 2019 John Wiley & Sons Ltd. Published 2019 by John Wiley & Sons Ltd.

Margaret Chemise says to Claude Nads: "I was reading about a sociologist who has found that there are differences in the average intelligence of different racial groups. She found this out by conducting what she claims was a culturally neutral IQ test." Claude responds: "Well she must have got it wrong. There isn't an average difference in IQ between different races of people because if there was, it would allow bigots to justify their racism." (Clark and Clark 2014, 25)

I am a busy man; I have no time for the long course of study which would be necessary to make me in any degree a competent judge of certain questions, or even able to understand the arguments. [So I need not always have evidence for what I believe]. (Clifford 1876)

Of course, the conclusion of such an argument could turn out to be correct. But if the conclusion is a factual statement (i.e., a true or false statement, as opposed to a proposal for action), we cannot show that it is true simply by pointing out that its negation would have unfortunate consequences. After all, unfortunate things often do happen.

A common variant of the fallacy has this form:

(1)   If people believed that P, then something bad would be the case.
(2)   Therefore, not P.

The example about alleged IQ differences between races can be interpreted as an argument of this form. We might take Claude's thought to be that the *belief* in IQ differences would allow bigots to justify their racism. Here's another example:

Are human beings physical objects such as biological organisms, or do they have immaterial souls? New psychological evidence sheds light on this ancient dispute between physicalism and dualism. A recent survey found that people who affirm dualist beliefs are more likely than physicalists to have reckless attitudes toward health and fitness. Dualists were also found to prefer and eat less healthy food than physicalists. These results suggest that adopting dualism may well have a negative impact on health-related behaviors.

Here, as often, the conclusion is not entirely explicit. However, the second sentence suggests that the intended conclusion is that dualism is probably false. Even if it were true that believing dualism had negative effects on one's health, though, those effects would not be closely related to the matter of whether dualism or physicalism is correct. (This example also includes a dubious inference from correlation to causation.)

The argument from adverse consequences can be seen as an argument that is intended to be pragmatic – about what we should *do*, not about what is true – but then comes to the wrong kind of conclusion. The arguer may intend to use a form like this:

(1)   <u>If P were true, then something bad would be the case.</u>
(2)   Therefore, we should hope that not P.

Or this:

(1)   <u>If people believed that P, then something bad would be the case.</u>
(2)   Therefore, we should not believe that P.

But the arguer instead conflates one of the above conclusions with the unsupported claim that P is false.

It is possible that the pragmatic argument lurking behind the fallacy is faulty as well. It may be that P has bad consequences but also very good ones, and so we should hope that P, all things considered. Or it may be that, although some bad things would result from the belief that P, we have a moral obligation to form our beliefs truthfully regardless of the results. But whether the pragmatic argument is faulty or not, the adverse consequences usually have very little to do with whether P is true or false.

In many genuinely pragmatic arguments, however, adverse consequences are relevant to the conclusion and no fallacy is committed. So it is important to notice exactly what the conclusion of the argument is. Consider the thought process described below:

> For the physicians who ran the ASCC, popular interest in meat and other foods as causes of cancer threatened to undermine [an early detection and treatment] approach to cancer control. ... On the one hand, if people believed that their diet was healthy and unlikely to cause cancer, they could easily use this as a reason to avoid their physician if they spotted any of the early warning signs of cancer. On the other hand, if they believed that their diet was unhealthy and might be the cause of cancer they could easily succumb to a paralyzing fear that nothing was to be done. ... Either way, the result was likely to be that people waited too long to see their physician. ... From this perspective, the ASCC believed, it was better to question any role for diet as a cause of cancer than to risk giving people an excuse not to seek early treatment. (Cantor, Bonah, and Dorries 2015, 117)

The ASCC's conclusion was that they should question the idea that diet plays a role in causing cancer; it was a conclusion about what they should do. The claim about consequences – that people will probably delay going to their physician if they believe that diet plays a role in causing cancer – *is* relevant to that conclusion. (It may not be decisive, but it is relevant.) On the other hand, if their conclusion had been that diet plays no role in causing cancer, the claim about consequences would not have been relevant, and it would have done nothing to support the conclusion.

So when you suspect that someone has given an argument from adverse consequences, first identify the conclusion. Sometimes you will find the confusion characteristic of the fallacy, in which a pragmatic conclusion has been conflated with a factual conclusion. Sometimes – rather frequently, in fact – you will find that the arguer has not settled on a conclusion, or at any rate has left the conclusion implicit. In that case the arguer may be in danger of committing the fallacy without yet having done so. Sometimes the arguer may have a pragmatic conclusion in mind without confusing it with a factual conclusion.

And sometimes it will be unclear. Lord Denning's conclusion in the quotation at the beginning of this chapter may appear to be a pragmatic one. On the other hand, it also seems likely that he intends to decide what to do on the basis of the factual statements he believes, for example, that the police have not committed perjury. Since the "appalling" character of the situation (assuming the police did commit perjury and so on) does not do much to support those factual statements, it is likely that he has implicitly made an argument from adverse consequences.

References

Cantor, David, Christian Bonah, and Matthias Dorries, eds. 2015. *Meat, Medicine and Human Health in the Twentieth Century*. New York: Routledge.

Clark, Jeff, and Theo Clark. 2014. *Humbug! The Skeptic's Field Guide to Spotting Fallacies and Deceptive Arguments*. New York: Nifty Books.

Clifford, W.K. 1876. "The Ethics of Belief." *Contemporary Review* (29): 289–309

Elliot, Catherine, and Frances Quinn. 2007. *English Legal System*. London: Longman Publishing Group.

13

Appeal to Emotion: Force or Fear

George Wrisley

> If workers of this company do not agree to a 25% cut in salary, then the company may have to shut its doors. Therefore, the workers of this company must agree to a 25% cut in salary.
>
> Stan Baronett, *Logic*

Emotions have long been seen as suspect because of their power to overwhelm us. Plato, for example, held that reason must dominate the spirited (emotional) part of the soul. And today we view crimes of passion as deserving of less punishment than premeditated acts of violence. In the context of dialogue and argument, emotion also plays an important and powerful role. Fear can be debilitating, but it can also spur someone to do things he ordinarily wouldn't, or couldn't, do. In moments of pity and compassion, we often let our guard down and open to the needs of others. It is because of the wide variety of their effects and because of their centrality to our lives that emotions are so important to consider carefully.

Fear of negative consequences is a great motivator. Because it is such a strong tactic, appeals to force or fear can be quite powerful in persuading others to act. An argument that appeals to force or fear attempts to make the audience feel fear at the threat or possibility of harm in order to get them to accept a conclusion. The threat or evoking of fear can be direct or indirect, physical or psychological.

Bad Arguments: 100 of the Most Important Fallacies in Western Philosophy, First Edition.
Edited by Robert Arp, Steven Barbone, and Michael Bruce.
© 2019 John Wiley & Sons Ltd. Published 2019 by John Wiley & Sons Ltd.

This chapter deals with fallacies that appeal to force or fear; also see the chapter that considers fallacies that appeal to pity (Chapter 14).

Sometimes evoking fear in, or threatening, another can be a legitimate part of arguing, particularly if emotion is part of what is at issue. However, often appeals to fear or force are irrelevant to the point at issue and are fallacious attempts to convince an audience to accept one's argument/position. Thus, a central problem in regard to appeals to force or fear arguments is figuring out when such appeals are legitimate and when they're fallacious. In order to address this, we'll employ several critical questions (see Walton 1992 and 2006).

The basic form of the fallacy looks like this:

Proponent: Gives reasons x, y, and z, one or more of which are intended to instill fear if some action, C, does or does not happen.
Proponent: Concludes C should or should not happen.

The two basic issues relevant to considering whether an appeal to force or fear is fallacious are:

(1) What exactly is the conclusion?
(2) What is the understood point of the dialogue? In regard to that point, is the proponent equivocating in the conclusion she has drawn? That is, is one party of the argument operating with a sense of the conclusion appropriate to one purpose, but the proponent illicitly shifts from one sense to a sense appropriate to a different purpose? (See Walton 1992 and 2006.)

Let's look at several examples to illustrate the meaning and use of these questions.

Example 1

In regard to his support of a particular bill, a lobbyist reminds a representative that he (the lobbyist) can influence so many thousands of voters in the representative's constituency, or so many potential contributors to campaign funds. (Walton 1992, 144)

Copi comments on this example, writing, "Logically [the lobbyist's] considerations have nothing to do with the merit of the legislation that the lobbyist is attempting to influence. But they may be, unfortunately, very persuasive" (see Walton 1992, 144–145). Copi rightly points out the issue of relevance. Whether the bill is any good, whether it ought to be adopted, is surely a matter of the bill's quality. Thus, if we take the conclusion of the argument to be, "You should adopt this bill" in the sense of, "it is worthy legislation," then clearly the influence of the lobbyist is irrelevant and the argument fallacious. One context of considering whether a bill should be adopted focuses on the bill's worth. If this is the context in which the discussion is occurring, then when the lobbyist implies that bad things will happen if the representative does not support the bill, he is illicitly shifting from the sense of "should" that pertains to that context to the context of a "should" that pertains to the representative keeping his position. As Walton writes:

> Whether a fallacy has been committed depends on what the representative and the lobbyist are trying to do. If they are discussing the merits of the legislation, then offers or threats to influence voters or funding are beside the point and make no contribution to the discussion. In that case the lobbyist's "reminder" could be dismissed as a fallacious move on the grounds of its irrelevance to the issue of the discussion. (Walton 1992, 144–145)

However, as Walton further emphasizes, it's possible that the conversation is not in the context of discussing the worth of the bill but rather is in the context of negotiating more generally whether the representative is going to support it. In such a context, the lobbyist's purpose is to persuade the representative that it is in his best interest to support the bill; the issue isn't the quality of the content of the bill. In such a context, we could read the lobbyist's conclusion, "You should support the bill" in the sense of, "if you know what's good for you." On this reading, there is no illicit shift, no equivocation on the meaning of "should." And, thus, the argument is not fallacious.

Example 2

> A graduate school student supervisor demands sexual favors from a graduate student over whom he has control in return for continuation in a PhD program (Damer 2009, 107).

Such a straightforward demand may not seem like an argument. However, we can reconstruct the situation as an implicit argument susceptible to our questions regarding whether it is a legitimate or fallacious use of fear/threat. The "conclusion" of the argument is presumably something like, "You should have sex with me" or "We should have sex." We have to ask, then, what is the point of the dialogue? If the point of the dialogue was something like the playful planning of a sexual encounter between people in a reciprocal relationship of attraction and affection in which there have been previous sexual encounters, then we don't have good reason to think of the "argument" as fallacious. However, given the language used to describe the situation, for example, the supervisor is said to "demand" sexual favors, and given that it is occurring in the context of power inequality, the "should" does *not* mean something like "as we're mutually attracted to each other and amorous"; rather, the supervisor has "shifted" from that meaning to "as you surely want to continue in the program." As such, and given the mores/ethics surrounding appropriate exchanges regarding sex, that is, sex should not be coerced, the reasons given are irrelevant to the context of the discussion of whether to have sex. Thus, the supervisor has argued fallaciously in his appeal to the student's fear of losing her position in the program.

References

Damer, Edward. 2009. *Attacking Faulty Reasoning: A Practical Guide to Fallacy-Free Arguments*, 6th edition. Belmont, CA: Wadsworth Cengage Learning.

Walton, Douglas. 1992. *The Place of Emotion in Argument*. State College, PA: The Pennsylvania State University Press.

Walton, Douglas. 2006. *Fundamentals of Critical Argumentation*. Cambridge, UK: Cambridge University Press.

14
Appeal to Emotion: Pity
George Wrisley

> You are my daughter. An aunt who has always taken a special interest in your well-being – has treated you with kindness, remembered your special occasions, helped with your educational expenses, and so on – has fallen on hard times and is in ill health and lonely and depressed. I remind you of her many kindnesses and present you with a detailed account of her present difficulties. I say to you after all this, "You really ought to pay Aunt Tillie a visit."
> Douglas Walton, *Fundamentals of Critical Argumentation*

Emotions have long been seen as suspect because of their power to overwhelm us. This chapter deals with fallacies that appeal to pity; also see the chapter that considers fallacies that appeal to force or fear (Chapter 13).

Sometimes evoking pity can be a legitimate part of arguing, particularly if emotion is part of what is at issue. However, often appeals to pity are irrelevant to the point at issue and are fallacious attempts to convince an audience to accept one's argument/position. Thus, a central problem in regard to appeal to pity arguments is figuring out when such appeals are legitimate and when they're fallacious. In order to address this, we'll employ several critical questions.

The basic form looks like this:

Proponent: Gives reasons x, y, and z, one or more of which are intended to evoke pity.
Proponent: Concludes C should or should not happen.

Bad Arguments: 100 of the Most Important Fallacies in Western Philosophy, First Edition. Edited by Robert Arp, Steven Barbone, and Michael Bruce.

The two basic issues relevant to considering whether an appeal to pity is fallacious are:

(1) What exactly is the conclusion?
(2) What is the understood point of the dialogue? In regard to that point, is the proponent equivocating in the conclusion she has drawn? That is, is one party of the argument operating with a sense of the conclusion appropriate to one purpose, but the proponent illicitly shifts from one sense to a sense appropriate to a different purpose?

Let's look at two examples to illustrate the meaning and use of these questions.

Example 1

A student who missed practically every class and did nothing outside class to master the material told me that if he failed the course he would probably be drafted into the army. (Walton 1992, 262)

What exactly is the conclusion of the student's argument? It appears to be something like, "You [the professor] should give me a passing grade." What is the reason given? That the student will be drafted if this doesn't happen. But does the latter support the conclusion? Let's begin by noting that the reason the student gives is not what we might call logically relevant to the conclusion. That is, ordinary practice is to assign students grades based on their academic performance in the course. Thus, what a student should get is determined by his performance, not factors outside that performance. Thus, whatever results from the earned grade is not relevant to determining what the grade should be. The conclusion "You should give me a passing grade" is false as it relates to the student's performance.

However, as it relates to the reason given by the student, namely, his being drafted if he fails, it may be true, not as it relates to his performance but as it relates to other considerations. For example, say the student knows that the professor is anti-war and against the draft, thinking it is immoral for anyone to be subjected to it. Given such commitments, the student may indeed give the professor reason to give him a passing grade. In this sense, the student is equivocating on the sense of "You should give me a passing grade." On one reading of it, the "should" relates to what is deserved in relation to performance, and on the other, what needs to happen based on moral commitments. What makes this example fallacious is that the professor is talking about the grade from the standpoint of logic, but the student shifts from that standpoint, since it is a dead end for him in regard to getting a better grade, to the moral standpoint that war is bad and he shouldn't be subjected to it. The latter considerations are not relevant to what grade should be given from the perspective of being the professor of the course in which a student performed so poorly. Thus, while it's possible that the student has given a kind of moral reason to give him a passing grade, that is not the perspective under discussion.

Further, we might ask whether the student really intends the moral argument. He may not think at all of appealing to the professor's anti-war sentiments (after all, he might not have any or the student may not be aware of them); instead, he may just fear death and want the professor to feel bad for him, pity him, and not want to be responsible for sending him to his death. If the latter is what is going on, then we can see even more clearly the problematic nature of such an appeal to pity. For even though assigning degrees of culpability is tricky, it would presumably strike many as perverse to claim that the professor's giving the student the grade he has earned, which results in the student's being drafted and, say, killed, caused the student to die.

Example 2

> Your honor, before you sentence my client for bank robbery, I ask you to consider his situation. He is an orphan and has been in and out of facilities and homes his whole life, never learning how to feel at home or at peace.

What is the conclusion of this argument? Presumably, something like, "You [the judge] should, minimally, commute any sentence given for the bank robbery." This is much different than the conclusion, "You [the judge] should find my client innocent." We'll return to this difference in a moment, but consider the claim that the judge should commute the sentence. What is the reason given? That the defendant was an orphan who experienced great instability and (presumably) a concomitant lack of direction, and so on. Does this support the conclusion that the sentence should be commuted? As with our first example, the reason the lawyer gives is not what we might call logically relevant to the conclusion. That is, ordinary practice is to sentence the guilty based on the nature of the crime committed, along with intent, and so on. Thus, what a convicted criminal should receive is determined by his actions, not factors external to those actions. Thus, whatever happened to the defendant prior to the crime in question is irrelevant to its nature and the sentence deserved. The conclusion "You [the judge] should, minimally, commute any sentence given for the bank robbery" does not follow from the facts about the defendant's childhood, as bad as they might be, and as much as one justifiably would feel pity for the defendant. Thus, in regard to the conclusion, we have reason for thinking that the lawyer has illicitly shifted from the sense of "should" that pertains to judicial practice to a sense of "should" that pertains to outside factors not relevant to judicial practice. Thus, the lawyer has given a fallacious appeal to pity argument.

However, things are more complicated than that. One issue that is important in this case is the purpose of sentencing a criminal. That is, is any punishment supposed to be for the purposes of rehabilitation, retribution, or what? If the judge were to view punishment's main purpose as rehabilitation, then the kind of punishment handed down might well take into account the pitiable conditions of the defendant's childhood. Thus, it's possible that the mentioning of the defendant's past is meant not to distract from the real issue by evoking pity but rather to facilitate the judge's carrying out a sensible sentencing.

Consider a different conclusion, however. Instead of concluding that the judge should commute the sentence, let's say the conclusion is that the judge should find the defendant innocent. If this is the conclusion of the defense lawyer, then we can see even more clearly the problematic nature of the case. That is, it is quite clear that it does not follow from the defendant's history that he should be found innocent of bank robbery, even if the judge was interested in rehabilitation and not retribution. If that were the import of the defense lawyer's argument, then it is clear that he is attempting to make the judge feel bad for the defendant, perhaps, making him think he's been punished enough already.

I leave you with one more appeal to pity, from Damer (2009):

> I think that we ought to give the Teacher of the Year award to Professor Raley. Ever since his wife died last year, he just hasn't been the same. I think that this award would really lift his spirits. He always seems so sad. I think this year has been hard for him. And he's not really that bad a teacher. (116)

References

Damer, Edward. 2009. *Attacking Faulty Reasoning: A Practical Guide to Fallacy-Free Arguments*, 6th edition. Belmont, CA: Wadsworth Cengage Learning.

Walton, Douglas. 1992. *Fundamentals of Critical Argumentation*. Cambridge, UK: Cambridge University Press.

15

Appeal to Ignorance

Benjamin W. McCraw

> I do not have much information on this except the general statement of the agency that there is nothing in the files to disprove his Communist connections.
>
> Senator Joe McCarthy

McCarthy's point is to show that someone is a communist based on the lack of evidence that he is *not* a communist. This maneuver in an argument commits the appeal to ignorance fallacy (or *ad ignorantiam*). For Copi, Cohen, and McMahon (2010), an argument "commits the fallacy *argumentum ad ignorantiam* if [it] argues that something is true because it has not been proved false, or false because it has not been proved true" (126). On this definition, *ad ignorantiam* arguments will exhibit one or the other of the following forms:

(a) ~[proof that ~ p] → p
(b) ~[proof that p] → ~p

Put this way, we can see that any instance of the *ad ignorantiam* fallacy uses lack of evidence as the grounds for accepting some claim. Thus, Woods and Walton (1989) describe the appeal to ignorance as a fallacy "located within confirmation theory as a confusion between the categories of 'lack of

Bad Arguments: 100 of the Most Important Fallacies in Western Philosophy, First Edition.
Edited by Robert Arp, Steven Barbone, and Michael Bruce.
© 2019 John Wiley & Sons Ltd. Published 2019 by John Wiley & Sons Ltd.

confirming evidence' and 'presence of disconfirming evidence'" (161; also see Walton 1999a). Thus, we might reformulate (a) and (b) with "evidence" replacing "proof":

(c_1) ~ [evidence that ~ p] → p
(c_2) ~ [evidence that p] → ~p

As Woods and Walton (1989) note as well, we can give a broad epistemic version of the *argumentum ad ignorantiam* whereby "knows" replaces "proof" (or "justified belief," "warranted belief," or any other epistemological honorific):

(d_1) ~ [knows that ~ p] → p
(d_2) ~ [knows that p] → ~p

One can also "modalize" these formulations, shifting the argument from *actual* proof/evidence/knowledge to *possible* proof/evidence/knowledge or *the ability for one to give* proof/evidence/knowledge. Thus:

(a^*) ~ [◊ proof that ~ p] → p
(b^*) ~ [◊ proof that p] → ~p
(c_1^*) ~ [◊ evidence that ~ p] → p
(c_2^*) ~ [◊ evidence that p] → ~p
(d_1^*) ~ [◊ knows that ~ p] → p
(d_2^*) ~ [◊ knows that p] → ~p

This yields 12 versions of the *argumentum ad ignorantiam* built on the same general framework.

Richard Robison (1971) develops another way of launching an *ad ignorantiam* that works by using a rhetorical question to commit the illicit move: "In many inferences from ignorance there is no explicit mention either of ignorance or of knowledge [...]. Instead, the ignorance is implied by putting the argument in the form of a question" (99). He calls this the "interrogative" form of the *argumentum ad ignorantiam*. It has the following structure:

(e) may it not be that p? → p

The maneuver goes from not answering that it may not be that p to p actually being the case. And when put in those terms, the move common to (a), (b), (c), and (d) reappears.

A slightly different way to frame the fallacy sees it "as an attempt to unfairly shift the burden of proof in a dialectical game" (Woods and

Walton 1989, 161). This "burden of proof" model of an *ad ignorantiam* would look something like this:

(f)   A: p
      B: Why p?
      A: Why~p? (Where A takes this question as grounds to reject B's question)

In (f), A commits the *ad ignorantiam* fallacy by shifting the burden of proof that B prove the negation of A's original assertion, effectively arguing that p by B's non-proving of~p. When we see the "shifting the burden of proof" in that light, it clearly fits the schema above in (a)–(e).

Now, why think arguments exhibiting any of these maneuvers to be fallacious? Consider Copi, Cohen, and McMahon (2010):

> Just because some proposition has not yet been proved false, we are not entitled to conclude that it is true. The same point can be made in reverse: If some proposition has not yet been proved true, we are not entitled to conclude that it is false. Many true propositions have not yet been proved true, of course, just as many false propositions have not yet been proved false. The fact that we cannot now be confident rarely serves as good reason to assert knowledge of falsity, or of truth. Such an inference is defective. (126)

The point here intuitively underlies thinking of an appeal to ignorance as fallacious: not having a proof, evidence, or knowledge that p isn't a decent reason (given obvious human cognitive limits) to think that p is false. If this intuitive point is true, then we can see why logicians think of an *ad ignorantiam* as fallacious or "defective." Consider Goldbach's Conjecture (that every odd integer equal to or larger than seven can be expressed as the sum of three primes). It's either (necessarily) true or false but, as of my writing this, it's unproven. Does our lack of a proof imply that the Conjecture is false? Certainly not. And the lack of a disproof doesn't show that the Conjecture is true either.

Another way to approach the *argumentum ad ignorantiam* as defective comes from Robinson (1971):

> The argument from ignorance neglects the facts that every statement has its contradictory and our job is to choose between the two contradictories. To the argument that "we don't know that not-p, therefore", the answer is that "we don't know that p, therefore not-p"; and the strength or weakness of the two arguments, once they are contrasted, is obviously exactly the same. (102)

Thus, Robinson's assessment of the *ad ignorantiam* fallacy comes to the point that not knowing p doesn't favor grounds to think that p or~p. That is, lacking a proof for p doesn't settle the truth of p or~p and, therefore, such ignorance won't give one reason to deny or to accept p.

A few passages from classical philosophical texts may (arguably) commit an *argumentum ad ignorantiam*. Consider a famous point from Kant's *Groundwork of the Metaphysics of Morals*:

[I]t cannot be assumed here that [a shopkeeper] had, besides, an immediate inclination toward his customers, so as from love, as it were, to give no one preference over another in the matter of price. Thus the action was done neither from duty nor from immediate inclination but merely for the purposes of self-interest. (G 4:397)

Given one plausible reading, Kant is arguing that the shopkeeper acts from self-interest because we cannot assume that he has an immediate inclination (of love) to be impartial with respect to price. That is, we can't know (assume) he has an inclination toward his customers; hence, we know that he has no inclination toward them (but, rather, himself). This moves from ignorance of his motives toward customers to claiming that he has no motives toward them. And, supposing that's the correct reading, the *ad ignorantiam* fallacy as described above is committed.

Also, Descartes makes the following point in his Third Meditation's proof of God's existence: "For how could I understand that I doubted or desired – that is, lacked something – and that I was not wholly perfect, unless there were in me some idea of a more perfect being which enabled me to recognize my own defects by comparison?" This seems to be an instance of the "interrogative" *ad ignorantiam* of (e): how could it not be the case that p? → p.

Could there be non-fallacious instances of the *argumentum ad ignorantiam*? Wreen (1989) has argued that the *ad ignorantiam* maneuver is not fallacious (full stop), whereas other philosophers accept the *general* fallacy of an appeal to ignorance but note some instances where lack of evidence *does* provide good inductive grounds for some statement. More specifically, Wreen (1989) claims, "There are only inductive arguments, inductive arguments which differ in strength, some very strong, some very weak, most somewhere in-between [...]. Far and away the weakest *ad ignorantiam*s I know of occur as examples, made up by authors, in logic texts" (314). The most obvious instance where ignorance does play a positive role would be in courts. The US courts have an "innocent until proven guilty" standard whereby a defendant has a default status of "not guilty" unless proven otherwise. Thus, when the prosecution is unable to prove guilt, this is thereby adequate for a "not guilty" verdict. But this maneuver is allowed as a substantive principle of jurisprudence rather than a general point of logic.

More interesting for a wider *logical* discussion would be cases of what Walton (1996, 15–17) calls "negative proof" (also see Walton 1999a). In some cases, it seems plausible to think that a lack of evidence or proof for something *does* give one reason to accept its denial. *Ex silentio* (from silence) arguments generally occur in history: moving from the claim that we haven't seen evidence of p, so ~ p. What makes this sort of reasoning work is the following principle: if p were the case, then we'd have evidence/proof that p. The presumption is that historical documents would provide evidence of important events, practices, persons, and so on, so lack of evidence in these documents is at least *prima facie* evidence for their falsity. What makes this non-fallacious, I suggest, is the plausibility of the principle above. When it's false, then the *ex silentio* becomes the defective *ad ignorantiam*.

Similarly, scientific research can turn on what looks like an *ad ignorantiam*. Suppose, for instance, that after a significant run of particle collisions, we have detected no sign of the Higgs boson. Intuitively, this would have been some reason to deny its existence. But that's because we're assuming some principle like the following: if there were such a particle, we would have some evidence for it (after running n tests).

What these non-fallacious appeals have in common is the truth of the following: if p were the case, then we'd have proof/evidence/knowledge that p. Walton (1999b, 57) calls this the "depth of search premise" presuming that p's truth would be available on an in-depth search or inquiry. Denying the proof/knowledge of p in question, under this principle, would be a successful argument. Thus "negative evidence has the kind of plausibilistic *modus tollens* form characteristic of typical *ad ignorantiam* arguments: 'if A then one would normally expect B; not B, therefore (plausibly) not A'" (Walton 1999b, 60). Thus, if this principle holds, an *ad ignorantiam* simply converts to a straightforward *modus tollens*.

We can see, then, that the truth or falsity of this sort of principle can settle whether an argument type is an instance of a fallacious *ad ignorantiam* or a valid *modus tollens*. For instance, in considering the argument from evil in philosophy of religion, a heated issue concerns our cognitive situation with respect to any reasons why God would permit evil. Some argue that any reasons God would have to permit evil would be known to us, and others (skeptical theists) deny this – arguing that our ignorance of God-justifying reasons is not evidence that there are no such grounds (because we'd plausibly lack cognitive access to such reasons). Arguments from evil presuppose, using Stephen Wykstra's (1996) language, a "noseeum" principle: if God has evil-justifying reasons, we would know them. If this is true, then ignorance of such reasons cuts against the rationality of belief in God. Whether the evidential argument from evil succeeds then turns on whether this "noseeum" principle is true. But *that* principle is just an instance of the "depth of search premise" above. Thus, how one views the plausibility of *this* instance of the premise (the "noseeum" principle) will determine whether one thinks the argument from evil is categorized as an *argumentum ad ignorantiam* or a *modus tollens*, and that sort of question determines the argument's success or failure.

References

Copi, Irving M., Carl Cohen, and Kenneth McMahon. 2010. *Introduction to Logic.* Upper Saddle River, NJ: Prentice Hall.

Robinson, Richard. 1971. "Arguing from Ignorance." *Philosophical Quarterly* (21): 97–108.

Walton, Douglas. 1999a. "The Appeal to Ignorance, or *Argumentum Ad Populum.*" *Argumentation* (13): 367–377.

Walton, Douglas. 1999b. "Profiles of Dialogue for Evaluating Arguments from Ignorance." *Argumentation* (13): 53–71.

Walton, Douglas. 1996. *Arguments from Ignorance.* University Park, PA: Pennsylvania State University Press.

Woods, John, and Douglas Walton. 1989. *Fallacies: Selected Papers 1972–1982.* Dordrecht: Foris Publications.

Wreen, Michael. 1989. "Light from Darkness, From Ignorance Knowledge." *Dialectica* (43): 299–314.

Wykstra, Stephen. 1996. "Rowe's Noseeum Argument from Evil." In *The Evidential Argument from Evil*, edited by Daniel Howard-Snyder. Bloomington, IN: Indiana University Press, 126–150.

16

Appeal to the People

Benjamin W. McCraw

> Among these diversities of opinion about injustice, it seems to be universally admitted that there may be unjust laws, and that law, consequently, is not the ultimate criterion of justice.
>
> John Stuart Mill

> If the end, which the utilitarian doctrine proposes to itself, were not, in theory and in practice, acknowledged to be an end, nothing could ever convince any person that it was so. No reason can be given why the general happiness is desirable, except that each person, so far as he believes it to be attainable, desires his own happiness.
>
> John Stuart Mill

The appeal to the people fallacy (ATP; also known as *argumentum ad populum*) comes in two distinct variations. First, there's what Woods and Walton (1989) call the "argument from popularity" (212). On this view, an ATP occurs "whenever someone takes a belief to be true merely because large numbers of people accept it" (Kelly 1990, 113). Thus defined, ATP has the following form: (a) Some large group of people believe/accept that if p, therefore p. Let's call this the epistemic version of the ATP since it turns on the beliefs of the people. John Stuart Mill's first quotation above is an instance of (a): everybody believes that there are unjust laws; therefore, there are unjust laws. Or, at least, this is how Mill appears to make the case.

Bad Arguments: 100 of the Most Important Fallacies in Western Philosophy, First Edition.
Edited by Robert Arp, Steven Barbone, and Michael Bruce.
© 2019 John Wiley & Sons Ltd. Published 2019 by John Wiley & Sons Ltd.

Another version is the "emotive" ATP, again in Woods and Walton's language (213). When this variant occurs, one attempts "to win popular assent to a conclusion by arousing the feelings of the multitude" (213; also Copi, Cohen, and McMahon 2010, 108). Here, the appeal is not to the beliefs or acceptances of the majority or populace but to their feelings or emotions. The emotive *ad populum* has this structure: (b) Some large group of people have strong (positive) feelings that if p, therefore p. The appeal to group feelings about p motivates an emotional response grounding the acceptance of p. And this, I suggest, looks like the second quotation from Mill: we desire happiness as the chief human end; therefore, happiness is the chief human end. Or, again, this provides one plausible interpretation of the passage. Following Wreen's (1993, 64) analysis, I propose a disjunctive account of the ATP. So, whenever an argument commits either (a) or (b), it makes the *ad populum* maneuver. We can develop (a) and (b) into subtypes.

Some texts distinguish a "bandwagon" version whereby the following occurs: (c) Everyone does A, feels X, or believes p, you don't want to be left out, therefore, do A, feel X, believe p. However, this just seems like a minor tweak on either (a) or (b) rather than a distinct subtype on its own. So, we'll not define this as a separate variant of the *ad populum*. But one may appeal to a certain type or group of "the people" to whom one appeals. Generally, this is called the appeal to "snobbery" or "vanity" by picking out some exclusive, elite, or desirable group of people, motivating belief on the basis of this group's beliefs or feelings. Thus:

(a*)   Some exclusive group of people believe that p therefore p.
(b*)   Some exclusive group of people have (positive) feelings about p therefore p.

Clearly, though, (a*) and (b*) serve only as limited, specified variations on (a) and (b).

There might be space here for a negative ATP: some exclusive (bad, inappropriate, disliked) group of people believe that p therefore not p. One can reason that if some scorned group has a belief (or has certain feelings about) p, then one infers the falsity of p. Political beliefs seem ideally representative of this point: some political person or political party with whom one typically disagrees advocates p, so one infers that p is false. But this won't change the substance of the maneuver described in either (a*) or (b*) – just an interesting "tweak" of the *ad populum* maneuver.

Why think ATP is fallacious? Is it, in fact, fallacious? Well, the reasoning here for the defectiveness of ATP seems to be the following: simply believing that p or having (positive) feelings about p does not entail p, so appealing to a group or everyone's belief that p will not guarantee the truth of the conclusion in (a) or (b) above. Thus, the ATP cannot be deductively valid.

Yet we might think that, at least, some ATPs may be inductively strong. I'll just briefly mention a few plausible candidates and see if we can draw conclusions about when the ATP may succeed and when it is defective. First, we may deflate objections to (a*) especially but perhaps (b*) as one deflates an appeal to inappropriate authority by showing that the group to which one appeals has qualified authority on the issue. Mill (2001) famously argues that "competent judges" provide standards distinguishing higher (better) pleasures from lower (less good) ones. And Plato's (1997) Gorgias has Callicles's suggesting that we need a "craftsman" to distinguish good from bad pleasures (844). One may take it that "competent judges" *qua* competent and Callicles's craftsman (by exercising the know-how of a craft) are adequate authorities on pleasure. Supposing Mill and Callicles are correct, this seems less an ATP and more of an inductively decent appeal to appropriate authority. Here is my general point: if the group to which one appeals in the ATP is (plausibly taken to be) an authority on the topic at issue, the maneuver seems inductively adequate and, thus, not fallacious. Otherwise, the appeal could be defective.

Another potentially successful *ad populum* could come from what is called *consensus gentium* (common consent) arguments. While more popular in the past and less so for contemporary philosophers, some thinkers find a way for *consensus gentium* arguments to offer some kind of (inductive) evidence that some widely believed proposition is true. Linda Zagzebski (2011) and Thomas Kelly (2011) focus on theistic *consensus gentium* arguments: Belief that God exists is widespread, therefore, probably, God exists. Whether this is a defective ATP fallacy or inductively innocent hangs upon the wider arguments that common consent does provide at least some probabilistic grounds to think the content of the consent is true.

References

Copi, Irving M., Carl Cohen, and Kenneth McMahon. 2010. *Introduction to Logic*. Upper Saddle River, NJ: Prentice Hall.

Kelly, David. 1990. *The Art of Reasoning with Symbolic Logic*. New York, NY: W.W. Norton.

Kelly, Thomas. 2011. "Consensus Gentium: Reflections on the 'Common Consent' Argument for the Existence of God." In *Evidence and Religious Belief*, edited by Kelly James Clark and Raymond J. VanArragon. Oxford: Oxford University Press, 135–156.

Mill, John Stuart. 2001. *Utilitarianism*. Indianapolis, IN: Hackett.

Plato. 1997. *Gorgias*. In *Plato: Complete Works*, edited by John M. Cooper. Indianapolis, IN: Hackett.

Woods, John, and Douglas Walton. 1989. *Fallacies: Selected Papers 1972–1982*. Dordrecht: Foris Publications.

Wreen, Michael. 1993. "Jump with Common Spirits: Is an *Ad Populum* Argument Fallacious?" *Metaphilosophy* (24): 61–75.

Zagzebski, Linda. 2011. "Epistemic Self-Trust and the *Consensus Gentium* Argument." In *Evidence and Religious Belief*, edited by Kelly James Clark and Raymond J. VanArragon. Oxford: Oxford University Press, 22–36.

17

Appeal to Personal Incredulity

Tuomas W. Manninen

I fail to understand how teachers can call themselves Christians, go to church, talk about God, talk about Christ, and then go to school five days a week and talk about Darwin, and teach it as if it's fact, not a theory, but that's how it happened. I don't understand it. To me that's talking out of both sides of your mouth.

Bill Buckingham, in *Judgment Day: Intelligent Design on Trial*

The fallacy of appeal to personal incredulity is committed when the arguer presumes that whatever is true must be easy to understand or to imagine. Hence, if something is easy to understand or to conceive, it must be true; conversely, if it is difficult (or impossible) to understand, then it is false (Baggini 2009; Bebbington 2011). This line of reasoning seems to undercut the fact that we rely on expert opinions in many (if not most) parts of our lives. After all, we visit doctors when we seek an explanation for something that ails us. Likewise, we seek expert opinions in innumerable other facets. The fallacy seems to be most frequent when the contrasting expert opinions differ from our deeply held beliefs. As a result, we try to discount the expert view by appealing to the perceived difficulty in understanding it.

The fallacy is very commonly found in debates over science. In the *Judgment Day* documentary, Bill Buckingham is incredulous of how someone can both claim to be a Christian and teach science – especially Darwin's theory of evolution (NOVA 2007). In *Darwin's Black Box*, its author

Bad Arguments: 100 of the Most Important Fallacies in Western Philosophy, First Edition.
Edited by Robert Arp, Steven Barbone, and Michael Bruce.
© 2019 John Wiley & Sons Ltd. Published 2019 by John Wiley & Sons Ltd.

Dr. Michael Behe cannot see how natural selection could produce biological systems that appear to be irreducibly complex (cited in Bebbington 2011 and in NOVA 2007). But the fallacy becomes clear when we take a step back from these claims. Just because Mr. Buckingham cannot imagine how someone can be a scientist and profess Christian faith does not mean that these two viewpoints cannot be reconciled. Similarly, because the fact that Dr. Behe cannot see how natural selection could produce irreducibly complex biological systems may be more of an indictment of Dr. Behe's understanding of natural selection, and less of the fact that natural selection can produce seemingly irreducible complex systems. To be fair, Dr. Behe does qualify his statement on irreducibly complex systems by adding "… if there is such a thing" (cited in Bebbington 2011, 28).

In a variant of the fallacy, a person may to appeal to her lack of understanding on a subject matter in a seemingly more self-deprecating manner as a backhanded way of undermining expert authority. This has been a recent talking point for many American politicians, as a number of them have responded to questions on whether they accept the scientific consensus on anthropogenic climate change. As if read from a common script, the politician has acknowledged "I am not a scientist," only to proceed to discuss the negative impact of policies based on the scientific consensus (Chait 2014). The general pattern of the fallacy in these cases (roughly) follows these steps:

Step 1: Politician X is asked whether or not s/he accepts the scientific consensus on topic Y.
Step 2: X acknowledges that s/he doesn't understand Y, because s/he is not a scientist; X defers any such question to the experts.
Step 3: X goes on to promote her/his own initiative on Y on the grounds of economy.

Curiously, Step 3 is offered without any qualifications on X's expertize on economics.

The steps to avoid committing the appeal to personal incredulity fallacy are rather straightforward. However, this is not to say that these steps are easily taken. When faced with a claim that one does not understand, the epistemically responsible thing to do would be to seek to expand one's understanding. However, when the claim in question challenges one's ideology – or any other belief one holds near and dear – one can become extremely reluctant to entertain such a challenge with an open mind. The same considerations apply, and the same difficulties are present, whether we deal with our own case or that of our opponent in an argument. Ultimately, it seems to come down to the level of obstinacy, either in ourselves or in our opponent.

References

Baggini, Julian. 2009. *The Duck that Won the Lottery*. London: Penguin Books.

Bebbington, Dene. 2011. *Think* 10(28): 27–28.

Chait, Jonathan. 2014. "Why Do Republicans Always Say 'I'm Not a Scientist'?" *New York Times Magazine*, May 30. http://nymag.com/daily/intelligencer/2014/05/why-republicans-always-say-im-not-a-scientist.html (accessed September 25, 2017).

NOVA. 2007. *Judgment Day: Intelligent Design on Trial*. PBS, November 13. http://www.pbs.org/wgbh/nova/evolution/intelligent-design-trial.html (accessed September 25, 2017).

18

Appeal to Ridicule

Gregory L. Bock

> Criticize Donald Trump? Sure. Question his sanity? That's nuts.
> Title of Howard Kurtz's article in Fox News Politics Online

To ridicule a point of view is to disparage or make fun of it. When someone uses ridicule as part of an argument, she commits an appeal to ridicule, which is a fallacy of relevance. According to Stan Baronett in *Logic* (2013), a fallacy of relevance is one that attempts to support a conclusion using an irrelevant premise. Premises that contain ridicule are irrelevant because making fun of a claim does not make it false, and a point of view may still be true even if it sounds ridiculous.

An appeal to ridicule is closely related to an *ad hominem* argument because both attack the person. An *ad hominem* argument usually attacks the person directly – for example, "You're an idiot!" – while an appeal to ridicule attacks the person indirectly by mocking her point of view – for example, "That is the most asinine thing I've heard all week!" There is little difference between saying someone is a fool and calling her opinions foolish. It is difficult to ridicule a point of view without implying that the same descriptor applies to the person herself.

There is also a similarity between an appeal to ridicule and an appeal to emotion in that both attempt to bypass rational assessment of a point of view and elicit an emotional reaction from the audience. An appeal to

Bad Arguments: 100 of the Most Important Fallacies in Western Philosophy, First Edition.
Edited by Robert Arp, Steven Barbone, and Michael Bruce.
© 2019 John Wiley & Sons Ltd. Published 2019 by John Wiley & Sons Ltd.

ridicule may be an attempt to elicit humor at another's expense, or it may be an attempt to elicit enmity, playing on the fears and prejudices of the group. Insofar as it promotes group prejudices, it may also be related to an appeal to the people.

Perhaps the most common instance of this fallacy occurs when someone says, "That's crazy!" This is not problematic when it is simply intended to communicate surprise or amazement, as in "I can't believe he just won the lottery! That's crazy!" However, it is a fallacy when a speaker uses it to dismiss an argument without taking it seriously. This expression is so common that there are probably few circumstances in which one has not heard it used, and I have heard it many times in the classroom. For example, when I was a graduate student, one of my professors dismissed a moral theory regarding the sanctity of life with "That's crazy!" I remember it well because the theory that was so quickly dismissed was one I held – although my professor did not know this at the time. In addition, I frequently hear my students use the expression in my world religions classes when we encounter very unusual religious practices. For example, we may be talking about snake-handling churches in Appalachia and watching videos of these folks dancing with venomous snakes and drinking strychnine. Inevitably, someone will say, "That's crazy!" and means for the craziness of the belief to constitute a sufficient reason for rejecting it. If we were to reconstruct the argument with its implied premises, it would look something like this:

(1)   Any point of view that seems crazy to me is false.
(2)   <u>This point of view seems crazy to me.</u>
(3)   So, this point of view is false.

The trouble is that just because a belief sounds crazy to us does not mean that it is false. In fact, many crazy-sounding beliefs turn out to be true. For example, the wave–particle duality theory of light sounds crazy, but it is well confirmed by modern physics. Also, certain Christian beliefs sound crazy to non-Christians, but this does not mean these beliefs are false. The Christian example works well with my students in the Bible Belt who hold a Christian worldview. What is important is to recognize that crazy-soundingness is not proof that a claim is false.

One way to avoid this fallacy is to recognize and employ its non-specious counterpart: a *reductio ad absurdum*, or reduction to absurdity. This argument refutes a claim by showing that it is absurd. In *Understanding Arguments: An Introduction to Informal Logic* (2010), Walter Sinnott-Armstrong and Robert Fogelin show how to use a *reductio* to refute the claim that there is a largest integer: "Suppose there is a largest integer. Call it N. Since N is an integer, $N+1$ is also an integer. Moreover, $N+1$ is larger than N. But it is absurd to think that any integer is larger than the largest integer. Therefore, our supposition – that there is a largest integer – must be false." This argument assumes a claim is true for the sake of argument and continues to show that such an assumption leads to a contradiction (or absurdity) and hence is false. The difference between a *reductio ad absurdum* and an appeal to ridicule is that the former uses good evidence while the latter does not.

Perhaps the best way to avoid this fallacy is to cultivate an attitude of respect for other points of view. This kind of respect does not mean agreeing with everyone, which is impossible. It does, however, mean recognizing that people often have good reasons for believing what they do and that very different (even contradictory) beliefs can be rationally justified. A good example of this is William Rowe's "friendly atheism," according to which Rowe thinks that both atheism and theism are equally justified, although theism, on his view, is false. A friendly theist, on the other hand, would acknowledge that an atheist's beliefs may be justified even though they are false.

This attitude of respect is connected to the virtue of intellectual humility. A person is intellectually humble when he has an accurate assessment of his epistemic position, thinking neither too highly nor too lowly of himself. Humility is a virtue because as epistemic agents we are limited and must rely on others in our epistemic communities for knowledge. Humility facilitates the acquisition of truth and requires taking other points of view seriously no matter how silly they sound, recognizing all the while that we (or others) could be mistaken. To ridicule a point of view fails to show respect to others as epistemic agents and is incompatible with the virtuous life of the mind.

References

Baronett, Stan. 2015. *Logic*, 3rd edition. Oxford: Oxford University Press.
Sinnott-Armstrong, Walter, and Robert Fogelin. 2010. *Understanding Arguments: An Introduction to Informal Logic*. Belmont, CA: Wadsworth Cengage Learning.

19

Appeal to Tradition

Nicolas Michaud

> I cannot help but wonder whether, by continuing and expanding the school lunch program, we aren't witnessing, if not encouraging, the slow demise of yet another American tradition, the brown bag.
>
> Charles Mathias, Jr.

To appeal to tradition (ATT) means to ignore the evidence that we should change because we have been doing something for a long time. ATTs are tremendously useful fallacies. Politicians, as in the quotation above, seem to have found them particularly powerful when manipulating their audiences. It is a fallacy that hinges on our sentimental tendencies and our unwillingness to change, and it is particularly dangerous when it prevents change. Simply, ATT can prevent us from moving beyond harmful and dangerous beliefs and institutions only because we are used to them.

From a purely logical standpoint, ATT simply means that one uses the fact that we've done something in the past, usually with regularity, as a reason why we should continue doing it into the future. It is "[a]ttempting to persuade others of a point of view by appealing to their feelings of reverence or respect for a tradition instead of to evidence, especially when a more important principle or issue is at stake" (Damer 2009, 115). ATT seems to suggest that there is something good about tradition that trumps any other concerns.

Bad Arguments: 100 of the Most Important Fallacies in Western Philosophy, First Edition. Edited by Robert Arp, Steven Barbone, and Michael Bruce. © 2019 John Wiley & Sons Ltd. Published 2019 by John Wiley & Sons Ltd.

ATT has been used for a very long time to justify just about every act of oppression humans have indulged in. It is difficult, for example, to justify slavery, preventing women from voting, and segregation. So we often find ourselves looking about for any justification. When an institution such as slavery is old enough, it becomes common to say, "Well, we have always done things this way." The problem is that just because something has always been done, it does not mean it *should* be done. The fact that is has been done in the past does not make it right.

Notice, in performing an ATT there is something of a tendency to romanticize the past. The word "tradition" may not even be used. We might simply be arguing that it is the only way we have ever done things, or that we have always done things that way, or that we've been doing something for so long that, even if there is a good reason to change, we should keep on the same path. The problem is that since tradition has nothing to do with morality, it is really easy for ATT to be used to justify *anything*, from continuing to tell children that Santa exists to preventing an oppressed group of people from voting.

Perhaps at the core of ATT is our belief that our family and cultural traditions are important. And, if we do anything for long enough, even if it is unwise, stupid, or simply evil, we start to view it with a sentimental perspective. It is kind of like a truly terrible TV show that you grew up with when you were a kid. It was dumb, you didn't like it, but it was the only thing on at the time or your parents always watched it. As an adult, though, you might find yourself romanticizing it, missing it, or even making your own kids watch it. After all, how many children have whined to their parents, "Aw, why do we have to do this?" and the parents reply, "Because we did it when I was a kid, and it will make Grandma happy, dammit!" Some part of us recognizes that whatever is being asked of the child is unfair or ridiculous, but we do it anyway, because it is just the way things are.

In some ways, ATT is a popular fallacy of grandmothers all over the world. After all, isn't there something good about our traditions? Shouldn't we preserve them, remember them, and maintain those actions and beliefs that make us a family and a culture? Perhaps there is something to that idea. Remember, though, that recognizing the flaws in appealing to tradition isn't saying that traditions are bad or that cultural identity is unimportant. When we recognize that appealing to tradition is logically flawed we are just recognizing that just because something has been done in the past does not justify continuing to do it in the future, *especially when there are other moral issues at stake as well.*

Sometimes even those harmless grandmother traditions have more at stake than we realize. We might, for example, think that if we ask Grandma, "Why do we *always* have to have turkey for Thanksgiving???" she is well within her rights to say, "Because it's *traditional!*" That does seem like a fair enough argument. The problem is that, even in this seemingly innocent case, there is a genuine moral issue at stake – the treatment of non-human animals. Some believe that turkeys, particularly the ones mass produced to meet our needs for holidays such as Thanksgiving, suffer tremendous torture in factory farms. Does the fact that we have "always" eaten turkey for Thanksgiving truly trump the tremendous suffering that turkeys are said to experience to meet our need to feel connected to our pasts and our childhoods? Consider some of the following examples:

> Look, I'm not saying anything bad about women. Our military academy has never allowed women to enroll. It is part of who we are. From the day our hallowed institution was founded, we have been men only. This has nothing to do with women; it is about staying true to who we are!

Notice, in the argument above, there is no time or attention given to all of the arguments that are relevant to allowing women to enroll in a military academy. No consideration is given to the harms done to women, to the way the institution may be perpetuating sexism, and to the way the institution may be harmed by not changing with the times The only consideration given is to maintaining the traditions of the past.

> Our family has always been Jewish. We marry Jewish; it is just what we do. I understand you are in love, but some things are even more important than love.

Notice, here, no time is given to other arguments and considerations regarding whom one should marry. In defending the argument, the speaker makes no mention of religious reasons for preferring Jewish unions, or of scripture, or of morality. The only concern is that the family has always acted a certain way, and so it is assumed that it should continue to act that way, even if there are good reasons to change.

> We have a great American tradition of lunches made at home. Sure, some of these children may benefit from having lunches more available to them at school, but that connection to home is something that makes America what it is. We have lost enough of who we are to people who don't respect our heritage already!

This example plays with the quotation that we started this chapter with. Notice that the fact that children might benefit from having free or subsidized lunch is mentioned but is glossed over as unimportant when in comparison with the damage that would be done to the seemingly holy institution of American traditions.

Just remember, our sentimentality for the past can be used against us. Worse, it can be used to justify any kind of inequality, inequity, and oppression. Morality likely is not as much something that defines us based on what others have done in the past but, rather, more by what choices we make as we move into the future.

Reference

Damer, Edward. 2009. *Attacking Faulty Reasoning: A Practical Guide to Fallacy-Free Arguments*, 6th edition. Belmont, CA: Wadsworth Cengage Learning.

20

Argument from Fallacy

Christian Cotton

The Sun is made out of gas, and stars are made out of gas, so the Sun is a star.
A fallacious piece of reasoning with all true claims

Also known as *argumentum ad logicam*, argument to logic, fallacy fallacy, and fallacist's fallacy, the argument from fallacy occurs when one reasons that because the argument for some conclusion is *fallacious*, the conclusion of that argument is *false*. Truth and falsity are features of claims. Fallacies are errors in reasoning, not errors about truth or falsity. That is, if someone has committed a fallacy, then he has made an error in reasoning; but it doesn't follow that he has made a factual error. Consider the following example.

(1)   If Atlanta is the capital of Georgia, then it is in the United States.
(2)   Atlanta is in the United States.
(3)   Therefore, Atlanta is the capital of Georgia.

This argument illustrates the fallacy of *affirming the consequent*. As a deductive argument, it is invalid – one cannot draw/infer the conclusion from the premises – and yet the conclusion is true. As such, it should be clear that poor reasoning (committing a fallacy) does not entail a false conclusion. One would not, in the above example, respond reasonably if she were to

Bad Arguments: 100 of the Most Important Fallacies in Western Philosophy, First Edition.
Edited by Robert Arp, Steven Barbone, and Michael Bruce.
© 2019 John Wiley & Sons Ltd. Published 2019 by John Wiley & Sons Ltd.

suggest that, because a fallacy has been committed, it is false that Atlanta is the capital of Georgia. Nevertheless, the conclusion of the fallacious argument may well be false. The reason is that it's one thing to commit an error in reasoning and quite another to get the facts wrong. The one does not follow from the other. Therefore, because the truth or falsity of a claim cannot be inferred solely from the quality of the reasoning, concluding that a claim is false because an error in reasoning (a fallacy) has occurred is itself an error in reasoning. Hence, the name fallacy fallacy.

To take another example, suppose someone commits the slippery slope fallacy (see Chapter 94), and you respond that because he has used a fallacy, the conclusion of his argument is false. This is the argument from fallacy.

> BRAD: Dammit, Janet! We simply cannot allow same-sex marriage. If we allow same-sex couples to marry, then the next thing you know we'll have to allow people to marry their parents, their pets, even monkeys. I mean, where do we draw the line?
>
> JANET: Oh, Brad! That's the slippery slope fallacy, and you can't use fallacious reasoning to support an argument. So, see, you're wrong that we shouldn't allow same-sex marriage.

Does such an error in argumentation really need an explanation? Sadly, it does. This kind of fallacy occurs all the time in casual conversation, especially online. No doubt the thought process is something like this: "If I can show my interlocutor has committed some kind of fallacy, that means I don't have to accept his argument, so I can dismiss his position." Notice that our imagined fallacist has just made an argument to justify dismissing her interlocutor's position. While it's an example of good reasoning to claim that if there is a fallacy, then one need not accept the argument, the further inference that one is justified in dismissing the position, that is, the conclusion of that argument, isn't good reasoning. It is, in fact, bad reasoning because it conflates the quality of an argument (i.e., the logical connection between the premises and the conclusion) with the truth-value of the position (i.e., the conclusion of the argument). In other words, while we needn't accept a fallacious argument, it doesn't follow that we can reject the conclusion of the argument *as false*. So, while Janet is perfectly correct to call out Brad on his fallacious reasoning, Brad's sloppy thinking doesn't justify asserting that his conclusion is false. In other words, while the conclusion may not follow from the premises, it doesn't follow that his conclusion is false.

Suppose someone commits the *post hoc fallacy*, and you respond that because she has used fallacious reasoning, the conclusion of her argument must be false. This is the fallacy fallacy.

JON: Look, man, I'm telling you: I prayed for this gig to open up for us – every night for a week – and when I checked my messages last night, there was one that said we got the gig! It worked, man!

RICHIE: Dude, saying that you prayed for something and it then happened, so it must have happened *because* you prayed for it, is a fallacy called the *post hoc fallacy*. That means prayer doesn't work.

Maybe this is a bit less clear than the previous example because many of us believe in the efficacy of prayer. So, we have to be clear about what is being said here and why it's problematic. Jon believes that his praying for the gig worked. But, whether the prayer actually worked is not clear; it may just be a coincidence that one night he prays for a gig and the next day there's a message to confirm the gig. So, Richie is correct to point out the fallacy (the *post hoc* fallacy, very briefly, is the fallacy that assumes that because one thing occurs after another, it must have been caused by that thing). But, it remains an open question whether the prayer actually worked. Because it is an open question, Richie is not justified in then concluding that prayer doesn't work. To be sure, the question of whether prayer works is closely related to another fallacy of explanation called *untestability*: Is there any way to test whether or not prayer really works? If not, the claim that prayer works is an *untestable* claim and thus fails to be informative about the efficacy of prayer.

This fallacy is truly one of the easiest fallacies to avoid. As long as you understand that no matter how poor the reasoning of an argument, nothing follows from that about the truth or falsity of the conclusion, you won't fall prey to this one. Also, it helps when entering into spirited debate not to think of your interlocutor as an opponent whom you are attempting to defeat in some kind of intellectual battle. Very often this is a cause of fallacious reasoning of all sorts. Instead, think of yourselves as companions in search of the truth or, failing that, something that more closely approximates the truth. In this way, when a fallacy is committed, you can point it out, and then go about the business of clarifying the position in a way that avoids the initial fallacy without thereby committing a second fallacy.

21

Availability Error

David Kyle Johnson

> I'm never getting in a plane again. They're just too dangerous. Seems like there's another plane crash every month. From now on, I'm driving everywhere I go.
>
> Anonymous

One commits the availability error when one pays attention to, or is compelled by, the readily available evidence – the evidence that is obvious, memorable, or psychologically compelling – instead of taking into account all the evidence or the reliable evidence. If you believe that a full moon makes people crazy (the so called "lunar effect"), and take special notice of crimes committed during full moons while ignoring the same kind of crimes on all other nights, you are subject to the availability error.

The availability error contributes to confirmation bias, the tendency to only pay attention to the evidence that confirms what you believe and ignore the evidence that doesn't. But the error can also just appear on its own. In the quotation that begins this chapter, the person (who shall remain anonymous) is only paying attention to the stories about plane crashes she hears on the news and ignoring the statistical evidence that traveling by automobile is far more dangerous than traveling by plane. In reality, you have a 1/98 chance of dying in a vehicle accident in your lifetime, but your chances of dying in a plane crash are 1/7178. Why do people think plane travel is less safe? Because plane accidents are so rare and compelling, they get news

Bad Arguments: 100 of the Most Important Fallacies in Western Philosophy, First Edition.
Edited by Robert Arp, Steven Barbone, and Michael Bruce.
© 2019 John Wiley & Sons Ltd. Published 2019 by John Wiley & Sons Ltd.

coverage and thus are immediately apparent to one's mind. Traffic accidents, on the other hand, are so common we don't even think twice about them. But the fact that they are so common is why, rationally, we should be more wary of driving to work than flying to a distant location.

The availability error also encourages other fallacies, such as hasty generalization – where you generalize about an entire group based on a statistically insignificant portion of that group. If you conclude that all members of some race are violent criminals just because you noticed a few people of that race that are, you are paying attention to the psychologically compelling evidence (the stories about the criminals) and ignoring the better, less compelling evidence (the much larger number of people in the group who are not violent criminals).

Many people try to take advantage of our propensity to commit the availability error in order to fool us. Self-professed psychics, mediums, and astrologers are great examples. Psychics take advantage of this by putting out hundreds of predictions at the beginning of the year and then only mentioning the ones they got right at the end of the year. Or consider this real-life dialogue from an astrological reading given on one of my favorite television shows, *Penn & Teller's Bullshit*:

READER: Are you living near a railroad, or a diamond store, or a government building?
SITTER: There's a train track in front of my complex now.
READER: Yeah, that's the Capricorn Moon.

The reader is actually using two tricks here. One is that he is stating things that are true of almost everyone; railroads, diamond (jewelry) stores, and government buildings are everywhere, so most people live near at least one. (I currently live near all three.) But he is also counting on the reader's focusing on what he gets right (in this case the train track) and ignoring what he doesn't. In another part of the reading, the reader asked this same sitter whether she lived near a jungle, the woods, the country, a zoo, a church, a courthouse, a publishing house, a college, or the outdoors. She answered no to all, yet afterwards she still ranked the accuracy of the astrologer's reading as a 10 out of 10. Why? Because of the availability error. She's remembering the hits and forgetting the misses.

In fact, memory is especially susceptible to the availability error because we are apt to remember only what is memorable, and that is often only what is psychologically compelling. This is why people often think they always get stuck in the slow lane in traffic jams. Think about it. When you are stuck in the slow lane, what's it like? You're frustrated, it's likely to make you late, you're there for a long time, and you'll stew about it for hours. But when you're in the fast lane, you're calm, you're not there for long, and you'll likely forget about it a mile later. Statistically speaking, you're in the fast lane just as often as the slow lane, but you remember being in the slow lane more often because being in the slow lane is more memorable.

Or take another experience that most of us have had: being suddenly reminded of a dream you had because of some event that happened during the day. Such an event causes some people to suspect that they have psychic powers – that they can dream the future before it happens. But in reality, we should expect for such a thing to happen to us every now and again. According to Ted Schick and Lewis Vaughn (2014), authors of *How To Think about Weird Things*, although we only experience four or five periods of REM (rapid eye movement) cycle sleep a night, we normally experience at least 250 dream *themes* each night (117). We of course forget most of them and thus ignore all the counter-examples that show that our dreams don't predict the future. So when an event during the day triggers a memory of something we dreamed, it may seem remarkable – but statistically speaking it's bound to happen every now and again.

Take the story (mentioned in chapter one of *Weird Things*) of someone who dreamed of not being able to save his father from falling off a cliff only to (in real life, three weeks later) fail to save his father from falling out of a second-story window to his death while painting a windowsill. This too may seem remarkable but (a) this person is failing to recall the hundreds of his dreams that didn't come true and (b) we are failing to recognize all the people to whom this hasn't happened.

In other words, given the large number of dreams that are had every night and the large number of accidents that happen to people during the day, "premonitions" such as this are statistically likely. Just about every day someone, somewhere, has a dream at night about an accident and then experiences or is reminded of a similar accident during the day. It may be unlikely to happen to any particular individual, but it is likely to happen to someone – no supernatural powers required.

But this is not the only way that memory can lead us astray. In fact, memory is notoriously unreliable – much less reliable than people assume. We think of memory as being like a video camera, able to record events and play them back just as they happened (see Maynes2011). In reality, the process of storing and recalling memories is highly unreliable and apt to failure. When we store a memory of an event, we don't record all the specifics. We store general themes and leave out the details. When we recall that event, we harken back to the theme but fill in the details according to what might make sense – or even to what would make the memory align with our expectations. When we store the memory away again, some of those confabulated details can be stored away with it. And the next time we recall that event, we are not remembering the first time it happened but the last time we remembered it (see McDermott and Roedifer n.d.). Consequently, those confabulated details can seem just as accurate as things that actually happened.

Worse still, the more often you remember something, the less accurate the memory becomes; every time you remember, you create a new opportunity for something to go wrong in the memory process (see Fernyhough 2014). This is why, when you go back and watch a movie you only saw once but haven't seen in a while, individual scenes (or even major plots points) are often very different than you remembered them being the first time.

In fact, recent research into memory has shown that eyewitness testimony – which was once thought to be one of the most reliable methods for gathering evidence in the courtroom – is notoriously unreliable (see Arkowitz and Lileinfeld 2010). Indeed, it's often the case that the more confident an eyewitness is that their memory accurately reflects what happens, the less likely it is that it actually does (see Crowell 2011). We all think we can justifiably believe that something happened if we saw it with our own eyes, yet the research suggests that far more often than we realize, our memory of what we have seen with our own eyes is not accurate.

Even memories of large events – so called "flashbulb memories," like your memory of where you were when you heard about 9/11 – aren't as reliable as we assume. Now they do *seem* especially clear and vivid, and we do recall them with confidence. But in one study, led by New York University psychologist W. Hirst (2009), researchers asked and recorded the details of where people were, what they were doing, and whom they were with when they first heard of the 9/11 attacks. When they followed up with the same people one year later, their memories were only 63% accurate. After three, they were down to 57%!

This wasn't a fluke. Many such studies have been done and they all show basically the same thing. To be fair, it seems that most of the confabulating and forgetting that will be done has been done after three years. The flash-bulb memories of 9/11 weren't that much less accurate 10 years out (see Law 2011). But still, 57% is much less accurate than most assume our flash-bulb memories to be. In fact, that's probably less reliable than you assumed your normal memories to be.

All in all, we make the availability error simply because we are prone to. Of course we pay attention to what is more psychologically compelling – that's what "psychologically compelling" means. Of course we remember what is most memorable – that's what "most memorable" means. But if we want avoid being led astray—into believing that which is false—we must be aware of the availability error and strive to avoid it.

References

Arkowitz, Hal, and Scott O. Lilienfeld. 2010. "Why Science Tells Us Not to Rely on Eyewitness Accounts." *Scientific American Mind*, January 1. http://www.scientificamerican.com/article/do-the-eyes-have-it (accessed September 25, 2017).
Crowell, Jeremiah, dir. 2011. "Brain Games: Remember This!" *Brain Games*, National Geographic, October 9.

Fernyhough, Charles. 2014. *Pieces of Light: How the New Science of Memory Illuminates the Stories We Tell about Our Pasts*. New York, NY: Harper Perennial.

Hirst, W., E.A. Phelps, R.L. Buckner, A.E. Budson, A. Cuc *et al.* "Long-term Memory for the Terrorist Attack of September 11: Flashbulb Memories, Event Memories, and the Factors That Influence Their Retention." *National Center for Biotechnology Information*. U.S. National Library of Medicine, May 2009. http://www.ncbi.nlm.nih.gov/pubmed/19397377 (accessed September 25, 2017).

Maynes, Andrew. 2011. "Memory Is Not as Reliable as We Think." *Meeting of The British Psychological Society, September 8, 2011*. University of Keele, Newcastle-under-Lyme.

Law, Bridget Murray. 2011. "Seared in Our Memories." *American Psychological Association*, September 15. http://www.apa.org/monitor/2011/09/memories.aspx (accessed September 25, 2017).

McDermott, Kathleen B., and Henry L. Roedifer. n.d. "Memory (Encoding, Storage, Retrieval)." *Noba*. http://nobaproject.com/modules/memory-encoding-storage-retrieval (accessed September 25, 2017).

Schick, Theodore, and Lewis Vaughn. 2014. *How to Think about Weird Things: Critical Thinking for a New Age*. New York, NY: McGraw-Hill.

22

Base Rate

Tuomas W. Manninen

According to the National Crime Victimization Survey by the Bureau of Justice Statistics, between 1999 and 2011, the number of whites who were killed by the police was 2151, which is nearly twice the number of blacks killed by the police during the same period, 1130. This looks more like black privilege.

Collected from the Internet

The base rate fallacy is a fallacy that occurs in probabilistic reasoning when available general information (the base rate, which pertains to a population as a whole) is omitted from the calculations – either accidentally or deliberately – and attention is given to specific information only (e.g., information pertaining to the sample group) (FallacyFiles 2015).

Consider the following scenario in Philip K. Dick's (1987) short story "Minority Report," with some details augmented by the 2002 movie adaptation by Steven Spielberg. The felony crime rates in New York City in the 2050s have dropped by 99.8%, thanks to the "PreCrime" unit: the information made available to this unit by Precogs – individuals who can foresee criminal acts before they happen – allows the potential perpetrators to be apprehended before they commit the criminal act.

Setting aside many other questions about this approach – and the fact that neither Dick nor Spielberg fleshed out all the details – let us focus on the "99.8%" figure both for sensitivity and selectivity. That is, suppose that of

Bad Arguments: 100 of the Most Important Fallacies in Western Philosophy, First Edition.
Edited by Robert Arp, Steven Barbone, and Michael Bruce.
© 2019 John Wiley & Sons Ltd. Published 2019 by John Wiley & Sons Ltd.

the individuals detected as criminals by the PreCrime unit, a full 99.8% of them were going to commit a criminal act (selectivity, or the rate for true positives). Similarly, of the individuals identified as not-criminals, a full 99.8% of them are not-criminals (sensitivity, or the rate for true negatives). Having granted this, we have the 0.2% possibility for false positives (i.e., someone identified as a criminal when he is not) and for false negatives (i.e., someone identified as not-criminal when she actually is one) alike. Given all this, suppose – as the protagonist of the story, John Anderton, must come to realize – if you are identified by the PreCrime system as a future criminal, what are your odds of being innocent?

Looking at the numbers given above (99.8% versus 0.2%), it seems far more likely than not that you are guilty of a precrime if you are identified by the system. However, this appearance is misleading, because we do not know the base rate of criminal activity. Drawing from information in 2014, the New York City's crime rate was 639.3 violent crimes per a population of 100,000, or 0.0065, and the population was 23,462,000 ("Crime in New York City"). Assuming these numbers remain the same for the scenario, we can apply Bayes' Theorem to solve the question: What is the probability that an individual is guilty if she has been identified by PreCrime as a criminal? More formally, what is the value of p(guilty/PreCrime+)?

Using the aforementioned percentage for the PreCrime's sensitivity and selectivity, together with the base rate information (of how many crimes there are), we can represent the results in the following chart:

Result	Means	Probability	# of Cases
True Positive	guilty of precrime, identified as such	.998	152,192
True Negative	not guilty of crime, identified as innocent	.998	23,415,076
False Positive	guilty, but identified as innocent	.002	46,924
False Negative	not guilty, but identified as guilty	.002	305

We could apply Bayes' Theorem to make these determinations (i.e., P (A / B) = P (A) P (B / A) / P (B) for the conditional probability of event A, given that B). But just from looking at the number of cases, we see that for each of the 152,192 *true* positive results, we have 46,924 *false* positives; this shows a ratio of 3 to 1 between *true* positives and *false* positives. So despite the seemingly high rate of PreCrime's accuracy (99.8%), a positive result only means that you were guilty of a precrime in just two cases of three.

Despite using the fictional example here, this problem comes up in various real-life situations. After all, no breathalyzer, drug test, personality test, criminal profile, and so on, can claim to score 100% both in terms of selectivity and in terms of sensitivity. As such, the seemingly high rate of accuracy of – or the seemingly devastating positive result from – these tests is not so much so, after all.

In recent years, many US state legislatures (Arizona, Kansas, Mississippi, Missouri, Oklahoma, Tennessee, and Utah) have enacted laws that require those who apply for Temporary Assistance for Needful Families (TANF) or for other welfare programs to pass a drug test as a condition of their eligibility. The rationalization for such laws is that those who use illicit narcotics should be ineligible to receive government welfare; if an individual has enough income to dispose on narcotics, then the state should not provide him with funds to enable his illicit activities. Other states are also considering similar legislation (e.g., Florida, Michigan, Wisconsin) despite the fact that the initial results have not been exactly encouraging; according to Covert and Israel's (2015) analysis:

> The statistics show that applicants actually test positive at a lower rate than the drug use of the general population. The national drug use rate is 9.4 percent. In these [seven aforementioned] states, however, the rate of positive drug tests to total welfare applicants ranges from 0.002 percent to 8.3 percent, but all except one have a rate below 1 percent.

The legislative approach seems to be based not just on the base rate fallacy but on assuming a base rate that is divorced from reality, that the drug use rate among welfare applicants is significantly higher than the national rate. The justification does not omit the base rate from consideration – it just uses a wildly inaccurate value for the base rate.

How do we avoid the fallacy? Let us return to the example from the epigraph. Stated more formally, we can put the argument as follows:

(1) Between 1999 and 2011, the number of whites killed by the police was 2151.
(2) Between 1999 and 2011, the number of blacks killed by the police was 1130.
(3) Implied: 2151 is greater than 1130.
(4) Therefore, it seems inaccurate to speak of "'white privilege" when it comes to police violence, because more whites than blacks were killed by the police.

Although the argument seems to be valid, it can be shown to be unsound for the reason that it deals with absolute numbers rather than numbers proportioned to the racial breakdown of the US population. If the US population was evenly divided by whites and blacks, then the argument would be sound. However, using the available figures from the US Census Bureau, we can see the argument's unsoundness quite clearly. According to the 2010 Census numbers, the US population was 72.4% white and 12.6% black.

If we apply these percentages to the above argument, we get the following:

(1) Between 1999 and 2011, the number of whites killed by the police, in proportion to the population, was $(2151/0.724) = 2971$.

(2) Between 1999 and 2011, the number of blacks killed by the police, in proportion to the population, was $(1130/0.126) = 8968$.

(3) Implied: 8968 is greater than 2971.

(4) Therefore, it seems *accurate* to speak of "white privilege" when it comes to police violence, because more blacks than whites were killed by the police in proportion to the respective populations.

Thus, once the accurate base rate is applied (be it the proportions between the races in the US population, or the percentage of drug users among the people receiving government welfare, etc.), we can clearly see that the original conclusion does not follow.

References

Covert, Bryce, and Josh Israel. "What Seven States Discovered after Spending More than $1 Million Drug Testing Welfare Recipients." *ThinkProgress*, February 26. http://thinkprogress.org/economy/2015/02/26/3624447/tanf-drug-testing-states/ (accessed September 26, 2017).

"Crime in New York City." *Wikipedia*. https://en.wikipedia.org/wiki/Crime_in_New_York_City (accessed October 22, 2017).

Dick, Philip. 1987. *The Minority Report and Other Classic Stories*. New York, NY: Kensington Publishing.

FallacyFiles. 2015. "The Base Rate Fallacy." http://www.fallacyfiles.org/baserate.html (accessed September 26, 2017).

23

Burden of Proof

Andrew Russo

> You say there's no proof for God's existence. Well, you can't prove that God doesn't exist!
>
> A typical response from a theist

The burden of proof (BOP) fallacy is an informal fallacy involving the failure to recognize or properly assign the BOP in a persuasive reasoned dialogue, that is, an interchange between two or more parties whose aim is to prove or defend a position and, in doing so, persuade the other side of its truth or plausibility. In some such dialogues, the amount or strength of evidence required in order to accomplish this goal reasonably may differ for one of the parties involved. That is to say, sometimes one side incurs the BOP and thus must do more in order to persuade the other side of his or her position (Walton 1988, 234).

The BOP fallacy can occur in two ways. The first is when one side of the dialogue fails to recognize that its opponent incurs the BOP. Walton (1988) presents the following hypothetical exchange between members of a legislature:

BILLY: Why are my constituents the targets of such savage and unacceptable cutbacks?

SUZY: The government is doing the best it can to retrain employees and proceed in a humane manner. (235)

Bad Arguments: 100 of the Most Important Fallacies in Western Philosophy, First Edition.
Edited by Robert Arp, Steven Barbone, and Michael Bruce.
© 2019 John Wiley & Sons Ltd. Published 2019 by John Wiley & Sons Ltd.

Billy's question presupposes that the cutbacks are "savage and unacceptable," and this may be a matter for further debate. Thus if Suzy had challenged this, it is Billy who incurs the burden of showing why the cutbacks are "savage and unacceptable." However, since Suzy failed to recognize where the BOP lies in this instance, she conceded to Billy more than he deserved. As this case illustrates, the failure to recognize where the BOP lies can amount to a failure to recognize one's strongest argument.

The second way the BOP fallacy can occur is when one side of the dialogue assigns the BOP incorrectly. Suppose that Jane is a skeptic and John an apologist of the paranormal:

> JANE: The existence of entities such as ghosts should be given no credence whatsoever since there is no evidence that such things exist.
>
> JOHN: Your skepticism is unwarranted. Science has never disproven the existence of ghosts.

John's reply assumes that it is Jane who incurs the BOP and that belief in ghosts is justified until some evidence against it is presented. But, in fact, the BOP lies with John. Although it is right that one cannot be certain that ghosts do not exist, it is John who has the burden of explaining why no one has ever been able to conduct a repeatable experiment with which to detect the existence of paranormal entities.

It is interesting to note that Jane's argument is an *argumentum ad ignorantiam* as her conclusion that no credence should be given to the existence of ghosts is based on the premise that there is no evidence for their existence (or, more abstractly, that not-P is true because there is a lack of evidence for P). Nevertheless, as Walton (1988) has argued, this form of argument is not necessarily fallacious so long as it is presented in a context where the BOP lies with the opponent to present positive evidence for her position. Thus, whether or not a particular *argumentum ad ignorantiam* is fallacious depends on "the requirements posed by the BOP" (238–239).

As another illustration of this, consider the dictum of American criminal law that the defendant is "innocent until proven guilty." If the prosecution fails to present any evidence of guilt, the inference to a not guilty verdict is entirely legitimate. Additionally, if the prosecution were to claim that no evidence has been presented that disproves the defendant's guilt, he or she would rightly be charged with incorrectly assigning the BOP to the defense. As Walton as well as Pigliucci and Boudry (2013) point out, our moral intuition that it is a greater injustice to convict an innocent person of a crime than allow a guilty person to go free explains why it is the prosecution that incurs the BOP in a criminal trial.

What determines which side of a dialogue incurs the BOP (if there is one)? Without a doubt, there is no simple answer to this question. Sometimes it is our moral intuitions that do the work. However, the example of Jane, the skeptic, and John, the sympathizer of the paranormal, presents a different scenario. What determines the BOP in this case is the present state of our background knowledge in addition to the prior probabilities of the claims under dispute. And, as Pigliucci and Boudry (2013) have argued, these priors are best understood as set by the consensus of a community of experts.

There are still other factors that play a role in determining which side of a dialogue incurs the BOP. Suppose you are wondering whether to replace your home's smoke detector. In a hypothetical debate about whether it is best to replace it or not, the BOP will typically lie on the side of not replacing it since the costs of having a broken smoke detector far outweigh the costs of replacing it (viz., endangering yourself and your family is far worse than the $15 you will spend to purchase a new smoke detector). In this scenario, it is the practical costs associated with each side of the debate that explain where the BOP lies and why there is a presumption in favor of replacing the device.

References

Pigliucci, Massimo, and Maarten Boudry. 2013. "Prove it! The Burden of Proof Game in Science vs. Pseudoscience Disputes." *Philosophia* (42): 487–502.
Walton, Douglas. 1988. "BOP." *Argumentation* (2): 233–254.

24

Countless Counterfeits

David Kyle Johnson

> The existence of [a great deal of] counterfeit money strongly argues for the existence of real money somewhere.
>
> Peter Kreeft

The countless counterfeits fallacy occurs when one argues that the fact that there is an abundance of unreliable evidence for a conclusion is a good reason to think there is reliable evidence for that conclusion. A countless number of counterfeit pieces of evidence are seen as a good reason to think that some such evidence is legitimate. In the quotation above, taken from an article about belief in ghosts (see Townsend 2013), Kreeft is arguing by analogy that, even though most ghost sightings are fakes or hallucinations, the fact that there are so many is good reason to think that some such sightings actually are of ghosts.

Indeed, this fallacy is committed most often in discussions regarding what James Randi (1982) calls "flim-flam" (i.e., pseudoscience and the paranormal). It's utilized to defend belief not only in ghosts, but in UFOs, demons, alternative medicine, and even conspiracy theories. Such discussions usually go something like the following.

As evidence that (for example) UFOs are alien craft, the true believer touts a remarkable story about people seeing a UFO – let's say the Phoenix lights. But you point out that in *Skeptic Magazine*, Tony Ortega in 2008

Bad Arguments: 100 of the Most Important Fallacies in Western Philosophy, First Edition.
Edited by Robert Arp, Steven Barbone, and Michael Bruce.
© 2019 John Wiley & Sons Ltd. Published 2019 by John Wiley & Sons Ltd.

demonstrated that what people saw that night was National Guard Airplanes in formation that dropped flairs. So the true believer points to other evidence, say the 1991 videos of a UFO during a solar eclipse in Mexico City. But you have them watch the 2005 *National Geographic's Is It Real?* episode on UFOs, which exposed the fact that what people were videoing was the planet Venus. (It was made visible by the eclipse but was a blurry out-of-focus dot on cameras; astronomers already knew that Venus would be visible in that exact spot.) "But what about Roswell?" the true believer insists. In 1995, Dave Thomas from *Skeptical Inquirer* (not Wendy's) revealed that what was found that day was a (rather mundane) grounded aerial device from Project Mogul (a then secret military program) – not an alien craft. "Crop circles?!?" Admitted elaborate hoaxes. You might even point out that many UFO pictures that true believers still find convincing today were literally the result of kids taking pictures of pie tins they had thrown in the sky.

"But they can't all be fake," the true believer insists. "I mean, there are just so many examples – so many stories, so many photos. Sure, the ones I mentioned are bogus, but they can't all be bogus, right? And if just one of them is true, that means aliens have visited Earth!"

It's difficult to pin down exactly what's wrong with this line of reasoning, but its fallaciousness becomes obvious once you realize that you could give such an argument for just about anything. Ghosts, Bigfoot, the Loch Ness monster, conspiracy theories, demons, alternative medicine cures, Elvis sightings – there are lots of stories and "evidence" for it all. So you could give the same "they can't all be counterfeit" argument for any of it. Yet, even for the true believer, it's a stretch to believe in *every* bit of flim-flam.

Besides, such conversations usually begin with the most compelling evidence that exists – UFO enthusiasts utter stories about Roswell or the Phoenix lights. Ghost (and demon) hunters go with Ed and Lorraine Warren and *The Amityville Horror*. Bigfoot believers broadcast the Patterson–Gimlin footage. Nessie non-naysayers note the famous "Surgeon's Photograph." Often the cited evidence is even what started all the hubbub in the first place. Yet each is known to be bogus (see Novella and DeAngelis 1997, for example). If the most compelling evidence can't stand up to scrutiny, what chance does some story you found on the net have?

But still, there's more wrong with the argument. As it's stated, the argument actually rests on a false premise. "They can't all be bogus?" Sure they can. That's definitely within the realm of possibility. What the true believer means, however, is that it's *unlikely* that all such evidence is bogus. In the example above, the fact that there is still a large number of (yet to be addressed) UFO stories is taken to be a reason to believe that at least one of them is true. In the Townsend (2013) article, Kreeft suggests that an abundance of counterfeit ghost sightings "strongly argues for" the existence of real ones.

And this is where we find the fallacy. Simply put, the true believer mistakenly thinks that whether or not a piece of evidence is good is a matter of chance, so that the more pieces of evidence there are, the more likely it is that one is reliable. "Throw the dice long enough and eventually you'll get a Yahtzee." But this is not how evidence works. I can't pile up a 1000 pieces of bad evidence that you committed a murder and claim it's likely that one proves you did. Whether a piece of evidence is good is not a matter of chance; it either is or it isn't.

In fact, the more evidence of a particular kind of phenomenon I debunk with a certain kind of explanation, the more likely it is that all such evidence is explained by that kind of explanation. To see why, suppose I wonder whether magicians have real magic powers. After searching, I find perfectly mundane natural explanations for every trick I've seen. Now, there are still thousands of magicians doing hundreds of tricks that I have never seen (and never will). But that doesn't keep "it's just an illusion" from being the better explanation for each and every one of them. By explaining just a few magic tricks, I eliminate the need to explain the rest. Without even looking at them, I know it's more likely that there is a natural explanation for each; I'd likely even find it, if I was able to look.

Of course, this doesn't 100% prove that no magician has magic powers. (After all, it is only inductive evidence, and inductive evidence doesn't 100% prove anything. Finding a million white swans is good evidence that all swans are white, but it's not a guarantee than there are no black swans. But until specific evidence of a black swan is presented to me, the conclusion is justified.) And if a specific trick defies my ability to explain it, that is a different story. (Then I'd have to be careful to avoid the mystery therefore magic fallacy.) But I shouldn't conclude that magic is real simply because there are thousands of magic tricks I haven't examined. By finding the explanation for many magic tricks, I eliminate the need to examine the rest. I'm justified in believing that none involve magic powers.

The same applies for any evidence regarding flim-flam. Cold reading (and sometimes hot reading) explains the "success" of psychic mediums (Hunter n.d.). The placebo effect and the variable nature of illness is the best explanation for anecdotes about the success of alternative medicine, such as homeopathy (Novella). And fakery, misleading perceptions, and/or human credulity/gullibility is the best explanation for all UFO and ghost sightings. I am justified in believing that there is a non-alien/non-paranormal explanation for them all. Once you've debunked a few, you've effectively debunked the rest.

In fact, such explanations reveal how easily fooled we are; it's not surprising that there are so many flim-flam stories out there. Given how gullible we are, we should expect a great number of such stories. So it's actually *quite likely* they're all bogus.

But we should also be careful not to confuse this mistake in reasoning with another that could go by the same name. Instead of suggesting that it's likely that one piece of evidence is good because there are so many bad ones, sometimes people will try to combine a large number of individually weak pieces of evidence into one good one. To avoid confusion, we might call this mistake "the combining counterfeits fallacy."

For example, a juror might make this mistake. As Arkowitz and Lilienfeld make clear, it is now known that eyewitness testimony is notoriously unreliable. Perception and human memory is far more unreliable than we assume and can even be molded by something as simple as leading questions. Knowing this, a juror might not be convinced by the testimony of a single eyewitness who was not carefully questioned. But what if the prosecution produced 50 such testimonies? Would he be convinced then? Probably, but he shouldn't. By asking leading questions, I could produce as many such witnesses as you like, but that doesn't mean the defendant is guilty – it just means I'm good at asking leading questions. "Weak evidence" plus "weak evidence" does not equal "strong evidence."

The same is true for arguments. You can't combine multiple failed arguments to produce a good one. I've heard some argue, for example, that even though there is wide agreement that (individually) the arguments for God's existence fail, together they present a convincing case that God exists. (For a readable rundown of 36 such arguments, and why they fail, see the list at the end of Goldstein 2010. The novel itself is also well worth the read.) But this isn't true. It certainly isn't true of deductive arguments, which fail when they are invalid or have a false premise. But it also isn't true of inductive arguments. Of course, in science, multiple lines of *good* evidence can come together to provide even better evidence for a theory. But if an inductive argument fails, it does so by either having a false premise or by failing to support its conclusion. So you can combine it with as many such arguments as you want, but you still won't have a good reason to accept your conclusion.

So when it comes to weak evidence or arguments, size doesn't matter. Pile up as much bad evidence, as many poor arguments, and as much flim-flam as you want. It doesn't establish anything.

References

Arkowitz, Hal, and Scott O. Lilienfeld. 2010. "Why Science Tells Us Not to Rely on Eyewitness Accounts." *Scientific American*, 1 January. https://www.scientificamerican.com/article/do-the-eyes-have-it/ (accessed September 25, 2017).

Goldstein, Rebecca. 2010. *36 Arguments for the Existence of God: A Work of Fiction*. New York, NY: Pantheon Books.

Hunter, Colin. n.d. "Cold Readings: Confession of a Psychic." *Skeptic Report.* http://www.skepticreport.com/sr/?p=207 (accessed October 24, 2017).

Novella, Steven. 2009 "Closing the Door on Homeopathy." *Science-Based Medicine*, 11 November. http://www.sciencebasedmedicine.org/closing-the-door-on-homeopathy (accessed October 22, 2017).

Novella, Steven, and Perry DeAngelis. 1997. "Hunting the Ghost Hunters." *The New England Skeptical Society*, July 15. http://www.theness.com/index.php/hunting-the-ghost-hunters/ (accessed September 26, 2017).

Ortega, Tony. 2008. "The Phoenix Lights Explained (Again)" May 21. http://www.skeptic.com/eskeptic/08-05-21/#feature (accessed September 26, 2017).

Randi, James. 1982. *Flim-flam!: Psychics, ESP, Unicorns, and Other Delusions.* Amherst, MA: Prometheus.

Thomas, Dave. 1995. "The Roswell Incident and Project Mogul." CSI, August 1. http://www.csicop.org/si/show/roswell_incident_and_project_mogul\ (accessed September 26, 2017).

Townsend, Tim. 2013. "Paranormal Activity: Do Catholics Believe in Ghosts?" *U.S. Catholic*, October 30. http://www.uscatholic.org/articles/201309/paranormal-activity-do-catholics-believe-ghosts-27887 (accessed September 26, 2017).

25

Diminished Responsibility

Tuomas W. Manninen

> There is a need to draw a line between the leaders responsible and the people like me forced to serve as mere instruments in the hands of the leaders.
>
> Adolf Eichmann

The fallacy of diminished responsibility (DR), a variant of the fallacy of accident, is common enough to warrant being treated on its own. In the fallacy of accident, a commonly accepted principle is applied in a case where it should not apply. The fallacy of DR occurs when a principle that could be applicable as a positive defense in common law trials is applied in cases that are typically excluded from the scope of the principle.

The example cited in the epigraph comes from a letter by Adolf Eichmann, written mere days before he was executed (for crimes against humanity – and other sundry charges). After Eichmann was convicted, sentenced to death by hanging, and had his appeals rejected by the Israeli Supreme Court, he appealed to the President of Israel, Yitzhak Ben-Zvi, for clemency on the grounds that he was – put roughly – just following orders. Eichmann's petition was rejected, and he was executed shortly thereafter. In part, the rejection of Eichmann's appeal follows from the Nuremberg Principles (trials which Eichmann was able to avoid by skipping the country) where his

Bad Arguments: 100 of the Most Important Fallacies in Western Philosophy, First Edition.
Edited by Robert Arp, Steven Barbone, and Michael Bruce.
© 2019 John Wiley & Sons Ltd. Published 2019 by John Wiley & Sons Ltd.

co-conspirators were tried and sentenced. In particular, the Nuremberg Principle IV reads:

> The fact that a person acted pursuant to order of his Government or of a superior does not relieve him from responsibility under international law, provided a moral choice was in fact possible to him.

In other words, just because an individual was ordered to do X (whatever the results of Xing would be), as long as the individual who was ordered to do X could have refused to do so – and he didn't – the *moral* consequences of Xing cannot be escaped.

In a more philosophical vein, we can find a corresponding idea expressed already in the writings of Aristotle (384–322 BCE). In the *Nicomachean Ethics*, Aristotle discusses the cases in which it is appropriate to assign blame (or praise) to an individual's actions. One of the preconditions for this is that the individual's actions were voluntary – or that the individual knowingly chose to perform the action. Absent these prerequisites, the assignment of blame (or praise) is misguided (Bk. III, 1109b30–1115a5).

Individuals seeking exemptions to their moral responsibility on ideological grounds abound, there are also those who seek such exemptions on physiological grounds. The following from Miller (2016) will serve to illustrate this:

> In hindsight, it's clear that Brock Turner was desperately trying to fit in at Stanford and fell into the culture of alcohol consumption and partying [...]. This culture was modeled by many of the upperclassmen on the swim team and played a role in the events of Jan 17th and 18th 2015.

This is an excerpt from a letter written by Dan Turner, the father of Brock Turner. The letter was addressed to the judge who ordered the younger Turner to a sentence – deemed by many to be too lenient – for committing sexual assault at Stanford University in 2015. In essence, the letter attempts to diminish Brock Turner's responsibility for the assault on the grounds that he had fallen "into the culture of alcohol consumption and partying." But even if (or, when) Brock Turner had consumed alcohol prior to committing the assault, this does not serve to diminish his responsibility – after all, the actions that led to his diminished capacity were self-inflicted. Moreover, this aligns with the recommendation from the United States Sentencing Commission (2016) (a bipartisan agency of the judicial branch of the US government) when it comes to diminished capacity:

> A downward departure [from the sentencing guidelines] may be warranted if (1) the defendant committed the offense while suffering from a significantly

reduced mental capacity; and (2) the significantly reduced mental capacity contributed substantially to the commission of the offense. Similarly, if a departure is warranted under this policy statement, the extent of the departure should reflect the extent to which the reduced mental capacity contributed to the commission of the offense. However, the court may not depart below the applicable guideline range if (1) the significantly reduced mental capacity was caused by the voluntary use of drugs or other intoxicants ... (§2K.13)

As a further counterpoint to the claim advanced by Brock Turner's father, we take his anonymous victim's impact statement, which was read at the sentencing phase of Turner's trial. Among the most poignant passages of the statement was:

I will now take this opportunity to read portions of the defendant's statement and respond to them: You said, "Being drunk I just couldn't make the best decisions and neither could she." Alcohol is not an excuse. Is it a factor? Yes. But alcohol was not the one who stripped me.

And further:

I fully respected his [Brock Turner's] right to a trial, but even after twelve jurors unanimously convicted him guilty of three felonies, all he has admitted to doing is ingesting alcohol. Someone who cannot take full accountability for his actions does not deserve a mitigating sentence.

(Miller 2016)

In essence, whether the fallacy of DR is committed or not depends on the context in which the claim for diminished responsibility is made. If the factor that is offered as diminishing one's (moral) responsibility is something that results from a voluntary choice, then the claim is fallacious. After all, if individuals make a voluntary choice to do something that can likely impair their judgment, then they cannot claim to be absolved from the consequences of their actions: it was their initial choice that left them (and their judgment) impaired. If, in contrast, the factor is beyond an individual's control, the claim is less likely to be fallacious.

In terms of avoiding the fallacy, as noted above, there are some instances where an individual's moral (or legal) responsibility can be diminished due to factors beyond the individual's control. However, in none of these instances is the causal responsibility diminished. Consider: A person gets in her car and goes driving. All of a sudden, she experiences a debilitating stroke – or some comparable medical emergency – she loses the control of the vehicle and causes a collision that results in fatalities. While the driver is causally responsible for the collision, she may not be morally so due to factors beyond her control. After all, she did not voluntarily choose to have a stroke, and neither did she do anything (at least, not immediately) to bring it about. In such a situation, the person may be absolved from moral responsibility, even if her causal responsibility remains the same. A further question to be explored (elsewhere) would be: How far can this line of reasoning be extended? Revisiting the above hypothetical, consider these variants: What if the debilitated driver had been warned by her doctor to make lifestyle changes to reduce the likelihood of such a medical emergency – and she didn't follow the doctor's orders? What if the driver was a diabetic who didn't take proper care of her blood glucose levels (again, contrary to her doctor's orders) and lost the control of her vehicle due to hypoglycemia? What if the driver was prescribed narcotics that could impair her ability to operate a vehicle, and this was the cause of the accident? And *What if …?*

Reference

Aristotle. *Nicomachean Ethics*, 2e. Translated by Terence Irwin. Indianapolis: Hackett, 1999.

Miller, Michael. 2016. "'A Steep Price to Pay for 20 Minutes of Action' – Dad Defends Stanford Sex Offender." *Washington Post*, June 6. https://www. washingtonpost.com/news/morning-mix/wp/2016/06/06/a-steep-price-to-pay-for-20-minutes-of-action-dad-defends-stanford-sex-offender/ (accessed September 26, 2017).

United States Sentencing Commission. 2016. "Guidelines Manual" https://www. ussc.gov/guidelines/2016-guidelines-manual (accessed September 28, 2017).

26

Essentializing

Jack Bowen

> He definitely cheated on his taxes. I went to high school with him and he cheated on his homework all the time. As the saying goes, "Once a cheat, always a cheat." He's just a cheater by nature.
>
> John or Jane Doe

One commits the fallacy of essentializing when claiming that just because something was one particular way at one point, it will always be that way. It's as though the arguer states something along the lines of "It is what it is" and then makes the illogical jump to "and therefore it will always be that way."

This fallacy is also similar to the genetic fallacy in that it suggests things are a certain way simply "by their nature," such as in the statement, "Men are naturally better drivers than women." The statement is made without any reference to data or sound logic to back it up. This sort of error is often made due to one's reliance on stereotypes and emotionally laden (and often negative) preconceptions that then frame an argument fallaciously.

For example, regarding prison sentences and recidivism, one may argue criminals should serve life sentences based on the premise, "Once a criminal, always a criminal." While this may be enticing on an emotional level, one needs to provide more of a defense than what has been given here, as one has committed essentializing by claiming a criminal is, *essentially*, always a

Bad Arguments: 100 of the Most Important Fallacies in Western Philosophy, First Edition.
Edited by Robert Arp, Steven Barbone, and Michael Bruce.
© 2019 John Wiley & Sons Ltd. Published 2019 by John Wiley & Sons Ltd.

criminal and, based solely on those grounds, should therefore remain incarcerated for life.

Part of this fallacy relies on the metaphysical notion of determinism: that people are determined by their DNA (and brain, etc.) and, additionally, no amount of environmental factors can change specific aspects of a person. In some instances this is true: people with certain brain chemistry or a brain tumor in a specific part of the brain are much more likely to behave in a specific manner. But this would need to be defended and supported with data, not defended merely on essentialist grounds.

In addition, on countless occasions it has been shown that environmental factors can and do affect our actions, regardless of one's particular brain composition and chemistry. That is to say, it is not the case that simply because a person did maintain a particular disposition at some point she will therefore maintain it always.

So often, when we rely on stereotypes and other non-scientific modes of thinking, we formulate a hypothesis and then perform a non-scientific (often emotionally laden) survey seeking to support our hypothesis, all done, for the most part, subconsciously. For example, one may hypothesize, "All drivers of race X are worse than other drivers." Then, while out driving, one may observe a driver of race X committing an error and allow this to confirm one's hypothesis, typically ignoring all non-erroneous driving by members of that same race. We rarely collect data scientifically, for example accounting for all drivers and all errors, but, instead, allow our bias toward confirming our hypothesis to lead us to a fallacious conclusion – in this case, that members of race X are naturally worse drivers than members of all other races. This, then, provides support – wrongly so – for those committing essentializing. In a sense, one could argue that racism results from committing such a fallacy: by (wrongly) asserting that *essential* to being a full-fledged moral entity is that the person must be a human who is a member of this or that race.

We might notice that some form of the fallacy of hasty generalization is committed here as well. For example, one could assume that because one finds a small subset of instances supporting the fallacious claim, "It is what it is and therefore will always be that way," that this claim really is true. But we know that asserting a truth about the world requires more than just a hunch or how things seem to someone on a few occasions – it requires rigorous proof, with sound statistical data to back it up.

At times, deciphering essential properties helps us to make accurate predictions. Knowing something is a poison confers certain qualities about the substance, *essential* to its being called a "poison." Because it is a poison, we know it will likely cause severe damage if consumed. In this case, the essential property of poison is exactly what is of interest: whether there is a harmful chemical in a particular substance. Likewise, the critical thinker will seek to utilize statistics and probabilities in the correct manner, thus leading to conclusions sometimes made not on a basis of certainty but, instead, on the basis of being "highly probable," thus properly framing the conclusion. Lastly, awareness of essentializing motivates the critical thinker to delve into exactly what is "essential" to a certain entity maintaining a particular label. As in the case of avoiding racism, we realize having a certain skin color is not essential to being a human being – having human DNA is. Many animal rights activists claim that something along the lines of this fallacy is being committed when non-human animals are excluded from the category of "moral entity" on the grounds of their not maintaining the essential quality, "has human DNA." They argue, instead, that something else is needed to be considered a moral entity (sentience being the most oft-proposed quality).

When seeking to defend a conclusion, one should avoid the inclination to claim something will always be the way it was. Instead, look at the data. In determining whether someone cheated, his character certainly may be part of the equation – that is, it may be relevant to the conclusion – but poor character at one time does not provide logical *grounds* for concluding poor character at a later time. Likewise, in examining something like recidivism or a particular subgroup's driving skill, look at the data: examine the respective statistics regarding recidivism rates and driving records.

Much of this goes back to an age-old philosophical discussion as to the nature of things. Early philosophers argued on behalf of things and people maintaining essences; later this notion was rejected, primarily by existentialists, as famously summarized by Jean Paul Sartre's, "Existence precedes essence" – through our choices, we determine ourselves instead of coming "pre-packaged" with some essence.

So when you hear someone claim something like, "Boys will be boys," as if to defend the deviant behaviors of a young male, you can recognize this as an instance of essentializing and ask him to provide more defense than just, "the essence of young male humans is that they act violently toward others." As with all good, critical thinking, one must go beyond hunches and gut instincts when seeking to defend a conclusion. While things certainly do *seem* to be one way, that is not enough to demonstrate that things really *are* that way.

27

Galileo Gambit

David Kyle Johnson

> Almost everyone thought Galileo was wrong, but he turned out to be right.
>
> Darin Brown (HIV skeptic)

The Galileo gambit fallacy is committed by those with theories that contradict the mainstream scientific consensus. Such theories are often ridiculed or even laughed at. But to those who commit this fallacy, this is actually a reason to think that their theory is true. "After all," they reason, "the mainstream laughed at Galileo when he said the sun was the center of the solar system; that flew against conventional wisdom too, but that turned out to be right. So my theory is probably right too." The fact that their fringe theory is ridiculed is thought to be a good reason to conclude that it is true.

It's worth nothing, right off the bat, that the fallacy is poorly named because Galileo did not contradict a scientific consensus; he contradicted church dogma. But there are examples of those who did contradict scientific consensus who turned out to be right. Louis Pasteur and his germ theory of disease, Alfred Wegener and his theory of continental drift, and Albert Einstein and his theory of relativity are three prime examples. But since Galileo is the scientist that those who commit this fallacy invoke, that is what it is called.

Regardless, there are many mistakes that underlie this line of reasoning. The one that perhaps most obviously exposes the fact that it is fallacious is related to confirmation bias (see Chapter 73), availability error

Bad Arguments: 100 of the Most Important Fallacies in Western Philosophy, First Edition. Edited by Robert Arp, Steven Barbone, and Michael Bruce.
© 2019 John Wiley & Sons Ltd. Published 2019 by John Wiley & Sons Ltd.

(see Chapter 21), and suppressed evidence (see Chapter 98). The person committing the fallacy is drawing attention to one case where the dissenting view turned out to be right but ignoring the many cases where the dissenting view turned out to be wrong.

It's not surprising that such cases are easily ignored; they are very hard to find because we don't usually learn about the theories that turned out to be mistaken. But, historically speaking, for every Galileo out there that turned the establishment on its head, there are hundreds who challenged the establishment but were proven to be dead wrong – like Urbain Jean Joseph Le Verrier (who proposed a real planet Vulcan), Wilhelm Reich (who essentially proposed that libido was an actual "physical energy" released upon orgasm), René Blondlot (who proposed the existence of N-rays), and Martin Fleischmann and Stanley Pons (who said they had achieved cold fusion; see Schick and Vaughn 2014; Shermer 2002). As Carl Sagan (1984) put it, "The fact that some geniuses were laughed at does not imply that all who are laughed at are geniuses. They laughed at Columbus, they laughed at Fulton, they laughed at the Wright brothers. But they also laughed at Bozo the Clown" (64).

Statistically speaking, if you are challenging scientific consensus, it's more likely that you are a Bozo than a Galileo.

Perhaps the best way to *describe* the fallacy is as an association fallacy or a faulty analogy. The mere fact that two things have one property in common doesn't necessarily mean that those things have a second property in common. Now it does *if* those properties are related to each other. Observing that, like humans, rats are mammals with lungs justifies the conclusion that rats breathe like humans do. That's a relevant similarity. The fact that both humans and rats have lungs doesn't, however, entail they can both do calculus. And that's what the Galileo gambit does: it relies on an irrelevant similarity or association. Yes, Galileo was criticized, but that has nothing to do with why his theory was right. So the fact that your theory is criticized tells us nothing about whether or not it is right.

Actually, that's not quite right; it does tell us something. When a theory challenges the scientific consensus, that's actually a good reason to think it is *wrong*. Whether it be the Wright brothers (and their flying machine), Wegener (and his theory of continental drift), or Einstein (and his theory of relativity), even though they turned out to be right, their contemporaries were right to be initially skeptical. Coherence with established scientific belief is an important criterion by which scientists can and should judge proposed theories. It's called conservatism. It's not the only one, which is good because otherwise we could never learn that we are wrong about something and advance our understanding of the world. But if a theory is not conservative, until it proves itself to be a better explanation than the established one, one is rational in rejecting that theory.

How could such a theory prove itself to be the better explanation? According to Ted Schick and Lewis Vaughn (2014), in addition to conservatism, science uses four criteria to weigh competing theories:

Testability: Does the theory make observable novel predictions?
Fruitfulness: Does the theory get those predictions right?
Scope: Does the theory have explanatory power? Does it unify or expand our knowledge? Or does it just invoke the inexplicable or raise unanswerable questions? The more a theory explains, the wider its scope.
Simplicity/Parsimony: Does it make additional assumptions? Does it require the existence of forces, energies, or things that we don't already know exist? The fewer such assumptions, the simpler a theory is.

When comparing competing explanations or theories, one should accept the theory that best fulfills the most criteria. So even if a theory is not conservative (that is, it conflicts with the consensus view), if it proves over time to be more fruitful, wider scoping, and more parsimonious, then one should accept it.

This is what happened with Einstein's theory of relativity. At first, it was not conservative because it conflicted with Isaac Newton's theory of gravity, which was very well established. But when relativity correctly predicted that the light from a distant star would curve around the Sun but Newton's theory did not, and explained the wonky orbit (the precession of perihelion) of the planet Mercury where Newton's theory never could, people started to take notice. These made relativity more fruitful and wider scoping than Newton's theory. Later we confirmed time dilation and black holes. As recently as 2016, we observed gravity waves – the last thing Einstein predicted but that had not yet been observed. Of course it took time; I'm sure some stubborn old school Newtonian scientists never admitted that Newton was wrong, but eventually the scientific consensus changed. Now if a theory challenges relativity, scientists are rightly skeptical of it.

That of course is not to say that Einstein's theory is perfect. There will likely be an improvement upon it, just as Einstein's was an improvement on that of Newton. But Einstein likely will never be shown to have been completely wrong and misguided. Generally this is how science works. Rarely is an established theory completely overturned; a new theory just comes along that is a little bit better. Modern cosmology was an improvement upon heliocentrism, heliocentrism was an improvement upon geocentrism, and geocentrism was an improvement upon the flat Earth theory. So, if your new fringe theory not only contradicts the established view, but would completely overturn it, that's an even stronger reason to think your fringe view is wrong.

So who is making the Galileo gambit today? It's very common in the alternative medicine community, especially among those who deny the efficacy of vaccines and claim that they cause conditions such as autism. The safety and effectiveness of vaccines is one of the most well-established facts in all of medicine, thus any such claim is suspect (see CDC 2015). If the view that they were dangerous could prove itself worthy – by, say, correctly predicting some novel facts – we'd have to take a closer look. For example, if the rate of autism was higher in vaccinated vs. non-vaccinated kids, we'd want to investigate further. But it's not. Indeed, countless studies have been conducted, all showing no relationship between vaccines and autism (see CDC 2015).

Yet anti-vaxers won't back down. They even gave an award to Andrew Wakefield, the author of the fraudulent study that started the whole "vaccines cause autism" scare. And you'll never guess what they called it. "The Galileo Award."

Others who are making the Galileo gambit today are Rupert Sheldrake (2004) and his morphic resonance/fields, Bigfoot believers, UFO enthusiasts, creationists, conspiracy theorists of all stripes, and (most dangerously) people who deny climate change.

It's worth noting, however, that Darin Brown, the HIV denier whose quotation opens this chapter, actually commits a slightly different version of this fallacy. What follows from the example of Galileo, he thinks, is not that his position (that HIV doesn't cause AIDS) is right, but that "just because almost everyone thinks [you are wrong], doesn't make it so." He claims that those who argue he's wrong by quoting the scientific consensus (The Institute of Medicine, The World Health Organization, the CDC, … every major scientist and relevant expert) are committing an "argument from consensus fallacy." Invoking Galileo is just his way of showing the error of their ways – that the scientific consensus does not "make it so."

But citing relevant scientific experts as evidence for a scientific claim is not fallacious. Neither is invoking the scientific consensus to cast doubt on new theory. Sure, not even scientific consensus could ever prove anything 100%, but hardly anything ever can and no one was claiming it did. Scientific consensus can, however, prove a theory beyond a reasonable doubt and show claims to the contrary to be irrational.

Brown is actually confusing (what he calls) the "consensus fallacy" with the *ad populum* fallacy. The *mere* fact that a large group of people believe something is true is not a good reason to believe it; that's right. Historically, large groups have been wrong about a lot of things. But if that large group of people is a group of experts on the topic at hand with mounds of evidence for their position, *that is* a good reason to accept their claim and to be dubious of claims that contradict it. Yes, the scientific consensus could still be wrong, but that's very unlikely. When you are contradicting the consensus of experts who are better educated and much more versed than you are in the topic at hand, it's much more likely that you are the one that is wrong.

The Galileo gambit is often used to suggest that science is not open to criticism, but nothing could be further from the truth. No one is more open to criticism than the scientist; that's how we make sure we are not wrong and get closer to the truth. But it's also not fair to demand that scientists consider every contrary theory out there; there are just too many. Scientists would never get anything else done. As Michael Shermer (2002) has noted:

> For every Galileo shown the instruments of torture for advocating scientific truth, there are a thousand (or ten thousand) unknowns whose "truths" never pass scientific muster with other scientists. The scientific community cannot be expected to test every fantastic claim that comes along, especially when so many are logically inconsistent. (50)

So if you want your theory to be taken seriously, the burden is on you to do the initial work of proving that it is better than the established view. The mere fact that your theory is contrarian is not enough; indeed, that means it's likely false. If a scientist won't consider your theory before you have shown it worthy, he is not showing an unreasonable bias toward established wisdom. He is correctly asserting the likelihood that your theory is right and allocating his time wisely. As Robert L. Park once put it, apparently as an offhand remark in an academic bulletin for the University of Maryland, "To wear the mantle of Galileo, it is not enough that you be persecuted by an unkind establishment; you must also be right" (see Shermer 2002, 50).

References

CDC. 2015. "History of Vaccine Safety." Centers for Disease Control and Prevention, September 29. http://www.cdc.gov/vaccinesafety/ensuringsafety/history/index.html (accessed September 27, 2017).

Sagan, Carl. 1984. *Broca's Brain: Reflections on the Romance of Science.* New York, NY: Ballantine.

Schick, Jr., Theodore and Lewis Vaughn. 2014. *How to Think About Weird Things: Critical Thinking for a New Age.* New York, NY: McGraw-Hill.

Sheldrake, Rupert. 2004. "Morphic Resonance." The Skeptic's Dictionary, September 12. http://skepdic.com/morphicres.html (accessed September 27, 2017).

Shermer, Michael. 2002. *Why People Believe Weird Things: Pseudoscience, Superstition, and Other Confusions of Our Time.* New York, NY: A.W.H. Freeman/Owl Book.

28

Gambler's Fallacy

Grant Sterling

> On August 18, 1913, at the casino in Monte Carlo, black came up on the roulette wheel a record twenty-six times in succession. There was a near-panicky rush to bet on red, beginning about the time black had come up a phenomenal fifteen times. Players doubled and tripled their stakes, believing that after black came up the twentieth time there was not a chance in a million of another repeat. In the end, the unusual run enriched the casino by some millions of francs.
>
> Darrell Huff and Irving Geis, *How to Take a Chance*

The gambler's fallacy (GF) is committed in the context of random, unconnected events. When (by chance) a certain outcome occurs very often in one period of time, the fallacious reasoner assumes that the opposite outcome will be more likely to occur in the future to "even out" the results.

OBSERVER: That guy just flipped a coin 10 times and it came up "heads" every time.

GAMBLER: Let's go bet on "tails" for the next flip!

As with most fallacies, GF is prevalent because it is similar to a kind of good reasoning. It is true that over a very long period of trials luck tends to "even out." If you flip a coin a billion times, you're likely to end up with

Bad Arguments: 100 of the Most Important Fallacies in Western Philosophy, First Edition.
Edited by Robert Arp, Steven Barbone, and Michael Bruce.
© 2019 John Wiley & Sons Ltd. Published 2019 by John Wiley & Sons Ltd.

approximately the same number of "heads" and "tails." But that's only because a series of a billion random flips randomly produces even results – there's no mechanism by which the coin "keeps track" of how many heads and tails have gone before and adjusts itself to balance things out.

Consider the following case. Suppose I intend to flip a coin 20 times, and I ask you to bet on how many times it will come up "heads." Assuming a fair coin, you should guess 10. Now suppose I start flipping and get six "heads" in a row. I offer to allow you to change your bet. With 14 flips remaining, you should assume that "heads" will come up (approximately) half the time *on the remaining flips*. So you should change your bet to 13 (six already flipped plus seven more). Luck is "evening out" in the sense that the percentages of "heads" will be expected to go down from 100% (the current results) to 65%. But there's no reason to think that the next flip is more than 50% likely to come up "tails" or that a streak of "tails" is likely. If I were flipping 100 times, you should bet on 53 "heads" (six already flipped plus 47 [50% of the remaining 94 flips] more). So now the expected outcome is 53%. After a billion flips, you should expect 6+ 499,999,997 [50% of the remaining 999,999,994 flips] = 500,000,003 total "heads," which rounds to 50%. The more flips you perform, the closer the total percentage can be expected to come to 50%. In that sense, luck evens out. But there is no reason to think that even with a billion flips, there will be any "extra" flips that result in "tails" to even out the original streak of six.

GT is also called, among other things, the Monte Carlo fallacy (from the incident quoted above) or fallacy of the maturity of chances. It's converse is sometimes called the hot hand fallacy, in which the opposite reasoning is used: the arguer assumes that because a string of results have turned up one way, this "streak" will continue – in the coin example above, the reasoner would assume that "heads" would come up again since "heads" are "on a roll." This sort of reasoning is at least slightly less fallacious, since there's a chance (however small) that a streak indicates that the outcomes are not actually random (maybe the coin is actually weighted or the roulette wheel is out of balance).

Notice that GF covers only situations where the results are based on chance. In a game of skill, for example, a streak may indicate the superiority of one player or team (and hence that the streak is likely to continue!) or it may cause the other players to adjust their strategy to stop the currently successful run.

The fallacy also doesn't cover situations where the outcome of one trial affects the outcome of later trials. If I am drawing cards from a deck and not replacing them, if the first two cards I draw are aces, it would be rational to bet against another ace being drawn next, since the previously drawn aces are no longer in the deck.

The easiest way to avoid this fallacy is *not* to think that heads-or-tails kinds of occurrences will more or less likely yield heads or tails based upon a past frequency – two, four, 40, or 400 heads does not mean that tails will come up next, and vice versa. Doing some research on statistics will help too.

29

Genetic Fallacy

Frank Scalambrino

For this situation is nothing new. It has an infantile prototype, of which it is in fact only the continuation. For once before one has found oneself in a similar state of helplessness: as a small child, in relation to one's parents. One had reason to fear them, and especially one's father; and yet one was sure of his protection against the dangers one knew. [...] In the same way, a man makes the forces of nature not simply into persons with whom he can associate [...] but he gives them the character of a father. He turns them into gods.

Sigmund Freud

One commits the genetic fallacy (GnF) when advocating for a conclusion based solely on origin. This is a fallacy of relevance – irrelevance, really – because the origin of a claim may be irrelevant to its truth-value. That is to say, providing an account of the genesis of a claim, its history or origin, may be informative and helpful; however, it need not determine the truth-value of the claim. Therefore, when one draws a conclusion regarding the truth-value of a claim based solely on the origin of the claim, then one may have committed the GnF.

Like other fallacies of (ir)relevance, GnF is sometimes referred to as the "lunatic fallacy." Colorfully, then, the fallacy is characterized by the truism: "Just because a lunatic said it, doesn't mean it isn't true." Neither the origin of a claim nor the process of its genesis determines the truth-value of the

Bad Arguments: 100 of the Most Important Fallacies in Western Philosophy, First Edition. Edited by Robert Arp, Steven Barbone, and Michael Bruce.
© 2019 John Wiley & Sons Ltd. Published 2019 by John Wiley & Sons Ltd.

claim. Just as strong feelings of dislike for the truth of a claim do not make the claim false, strong feelings regarding a claim's origin do not change its truth-value.

As an example, philosopher Paul Ricoeur (1970) has been influential in charging the psychoanalytic reasoning of Sigmund Freud with the GnF, especially in regard to the truth-value of psychoanalytic claims regarding religion. As the above Freud quotation from *The Future of an Illusion* clearly shows, Freud's critique of religion involves tracing the genesis of religious belief for the sake of identifying a "wish" that such belief might be understood as fulfilling. That is to say, given the manner in which, when essentially helpless, children may be said to simultaneously fear parental figures while hoping for care from them, Freud identifies such a relation as the origin of later religious belief.

Though Ricoeur acknowledges that Freud's genetic account may successfully propagate suspicion regarding religious belief and perhaps raise reasonable doubts, it does not necessitate that religious claims are false. Hence, were one to conclude in favor of atheism on the grounds of Freud's argument, then one would be drawing a conclusion from fallacious reasoning.

Similarly, Michel Foucault's (1995) genealogies regarding the claims upon which various societal institutions and conventions stand may also be seen in this light. That is to say, even considering knowledge and belief as social phenomena, illuminating the history upon which a social practice has emerged does not necessitate the falsehood of the principle for which it stands. In other words, though there is value in exposing political corruption, nepotism, financial favoritism, and injustice, it does not negate the truth of the claim that certain individuals whose behaviors endanger the lives of others should be restrained or confined.

Moreover, similar to the ability of Freud's genetic accounts to provoke or incite suspicion, indicating the presence or absence of particular social practices among other historical periods or cultures may be helpful for illuminating different perspectives regarding current social practices; however, even convincingly showing the genesis of current social practices does not determine the truth-value of claims that form the foundation of such practices.

Whereas the fallaciousness of arguing for the truth of a claim regarding its origin should be straightforward in terms of logical reasoning, it is interesting to note the role of such arguments within the context of legal reasoning. For example, claiming that an unlawful action originated from a person deemed certifiably "insane" does not change the truth-value regarding how the action is identified or the fact that the action occurred; however, that a person may be deemed "not guilty by reason of insanity (NGRI)" does indicate the potentially mitigating force of referring to the origin of action.

In the ethical language of "means and ends" reasoning, GnF helps highlight – what many take to be – the problematic nature of the utilitarian-style disconnect between the justice of actions and the goodness of their consequences. In other words, some consequentialists argue that so long as the outcome of a set of actions brings about greater good for a greater number than the pain associated with the set of actions as its means, then the outcome is good. In the same way, though an actual set of events may have conditioned some outcome such as belief in God or the institution of various social practices, there is a clear disconnect between the truth-value of the outcome and the means from which it emerged. Supposing a group of children believe they should not touch a hot stove because there is a wicked spirit in the stove who bites hands, the falsity of the origin of the belief that hot stoves shouldn't be touched does not change the prescriptive value of the claim. In other words, even if there is not a wicked spirit in the hot stove, it does not mean children should therefore place their hands on hot stoves. Ultimately, in order to avoid this fallacy, we should not base the warrant of an argument's conclusion solely on the origin of its concluding claim.

References

Foucault, Michel. 1995. *Discipline and Punish: The Birth of the Prison*, translated by A. Sheridan. New York, NY: Vintage.

Freud, Sigmund. 1989. *The Future of an Illusion*, translated by J. Strachey. New York, NY: W.W. Norton.

Ricoeur, Paul. 1970. *A Philosophical Interpretation of Freud: An Essay on Interpretation*. New Haven, CT: Yale University Press.

30

Historian's Fallacy

Heather Rivera

> All the evidence shows that you should have seen this coming.
>
> Jane Doe

The historian's fallacy (HF) is a logical informal fallacy in which the writing of a historical event has been skewed by way of biased hindsight on the author's part. The historian has written the details of the event down in such a way that the facts of the event, only seen after the event has occurred, cause the initial event to become distorted. At the time of the initial event, the hindsight was not present, obviously, so the evidence or signs could not have pointed to the event's taking place. It is only after the event has occurred and all the historical data can be viewed as hindsight bias that a conclusion of "How was this not seen in advance?" can be made. Only in retrospect do the warning signs seem obvious; signs that pointed in other directions tend to be forgotten. Hindsight is 20/20, so to speak, in the case of HF. Examples include:

How did the United States not see the attack on Pearl Harbor coming? All the signs were there! (Note: only in retrospect were the warnings obvious.)

The German people should have seen what electing to power a man like Adolf Hitler would do. (Note: at the time of his rise to power, Hitler was a well-liked leader who brought stability and hope to the oppressed

Bad Arguments: 100 of the Most Important Fallacies in Western Philosophy, First Edition.
Edited by Robert Arp, Steven Barbone, and Michael Bruce.
© 2019 John Wiley & Sons Ltd. Published 2019 by John Wiley & Sons Ltd.

German people. It is only hindsight that shows us all what a tyrannical monster he would become; at first Hitler was seen as a way to help uplift the German way of life.)

HF should not be confused with a method historians use in the present day when documenting the past. This is called *presentism*, a mode of historical analysis in which present-day ideas (such as moral standards) are projected into the past. For example: "The horrific civilian casualties far outweighed the military victory for the United States over Japan when we dropped the atomic bombs during World War II." In this example, the writer is using a moral judgment of an action that helped bring a long bloody war to its end. The facts remain, the war ended after the second bomb was dropped and Japan surrendered. There is no emotion in that statement, just fact. Presentism is looking back at history and placing moral standards of the present day on the events that took place. This is not an HF.

Another issue to address is that HF should not be confused with *historical fallacy*. The historical fallacy, also called the psychological fallacy, is a logical fallacy originally described by philosopher John Dewey in *The Psychological Review* in 1896. One commits the historical fallacy when one reads into a process the results that occur because of that process. For example, a person not knowing how to make a cake may inspect a baked cake to try to ascertain the method by looking at the known ingredients. When seeing the holes in the cake texture, this person might think that gases of some sort were an actual ingredient rather than baking powder.

John Dewey writes:

> The fallacy that arises when this is done is virtually the psychological or historical fallacy. A set of considerations which hold good only because of a completed process, is read into the content of the process which conditions this completed result. A state of things characterizing an outcome is regarded as a true description of the events which led up to this outcome; when, as a matter of fact, if this outcome had already been in existence, there would have been no necessity for the process. (367)

It is easy to see why these fallacies can become blurred or mistaken for one another in the mind. It is, however, crucial not to make the mistake of using an HF when documenting historical incidents. Remember that the events leading up to a historical episode are only obvious to us in retrospect. These "clues" were not so visible at the time the event took place.

Reference

Dewey, John. 1896. "The Reflex Arc Concept in Psychology." *Psychological Review* (3): 357–370.

31

Homunculus

Kimberly Baltzer-Jaray

KARL PILKINGTON:	Does the brain control you or are you controlling the brain? I don't know if I'm in charge of mine. Do you know what I mean though by that? […] I was making a shopping list, alright. Going, right, I need some rice, kidney beans, and I thought I had everything and I sort of was rolling up the paper and then something went "oh an onion." My brain sort of went, "you forgot something." I didn't think I forgot….
RICKY GERVAIS:	No, no, you are your brain.
KARL:	I was in control of my brain when I was writing down rice and kidney beans […] so what I am saying is who's in charge? […] It just made me think, that was weird, who reminded me of that?
RICKY:	You did! No, you are your brain! […]
KARL:	How does your brain work? You give it information, don't you? […] If I sat in a room with nothing, not feeding it anything, it wouldn't know anything.
RICKY:	No, no, there's this thing that there are two yous. It's this thing where there's […]
STEPHEN MERCHANT:	There's Karl and Karl's brain!
RICKY:	There's not a duality in this! If you go "come on, come on now – think!" that's the brain saying that to itself. […] You are your brain. If you are anything, you are your mind, your brain, your collection of memories, your personality.

Selections from *Ricky Gervais Podcast, Series 2, Episode 6*

Bad Arguments: 100 of the Most Important Fallacies in Western Philosophy, First Edition.
Edited by Robert Arp, Steven Barbone, and Michael Bruce.
© 2019 John Wiley & Sons Ltd. Published 2019 by John Wiley & Sons Ltd.

At its core, the homunculus fallacy (HmF) happens when a person attempts to account for a phenomenon or occurrence in terms of the very phenomenon or occurrence she was supposed to be explaining. This results in an infinite loop that essentially explains nothing. For example:

JANE: How do you think life ultimately began?
SARAH: I think aliens came here from a distant galaxy and planted seeds millions and millions of years ago.
JANE: Okay, so how did those aliens and their galaxy begin? How did life start there?
SARAH: Well, aliens from another farther galaxy came there and planted seeds billions of years ago.

The HmF is not always an easy one to overcome because sometimes we lack specific information or the complete explanation for an occurrence. Looking to the example above, it might be true that aliens are responsible for starting and spreading life, we just don't have the proof for this yet – so it could technically be right – but the way this argument has proceeded will never answer how life ultimately began because it just goes in an infinite loop.

Historically this fallacy is connected to the theory of vision or what is sometimes called the Cartesian theater. Someone might explain human vision by saying that when we look around at objects in the world, the light forms an image on the retinas of our eyes and something or some little person (where the term *homunculus* comes from) in the brain looks at these as if they were images on a movie screen. But if this is true, how does the homunculus see this movie inside my head? Is there a homunculus in his head? If you say yes, then the explanation essentially does nothing and goes nowhere but in an infinite loop.

The HmF was coined by Anthony Kenny in 1971, in his essay by the same name. Following Ludwig Wittgenstein, Kenny describes the fallacy as occurring when we ascribe to the brain attributes that can be ascribed only to the animal as a whole: "This dictum is often rejected in practice by psychologists, physiologists and computer experts, when they take predicates whose normal application is to complete human beings or complete animals and apply them to parts of animals, such as brains, or to electrical systems. This is commonly defended as a harmless pedagogical device; I wish to argue that it is a dangerous practice which may lead to conceptual and methodological confusion." Another example of this variety comes from neuroscience, where the hippocampus is described as playing an important role in memory consolidation and retention. It would, however, be fallacious to say, "My hippocampus remembers everything," since it's you (as a whole person, mind and body) that remembers, not this one part of the brain all by itself. If you were to cut the hippocampus out of your brain, it would be a lump of tissue and not able to remember a thing! Think of it this way, you've never met just a brain but only a whole, living, breathing person. The brain wouldn't be working if there wasn't a body with its organs and vital systems.

In the example above from the *Ricky Gervais Podcast*, the fallacy is actually committed by both Karl and Ricky albeit slightly differently: Karl tends to speak about his brain as separate from himself, like a little homunculus at the controls, whereas Ricky is telling him that he is his brain. Ricky's error is failing to mention the body – Karl is both his brain and body equally – and is more like what Kenny spoke about. Karl's mistake, however, is in the vein of the classic Cartesian theater, since he sees his brain as controlling the rest of himself at times such as when making shopping lists (don't forget that onion!). Similarly, some people will say, "Oh, my stomach was craving chips" or "My legs were just itching to dance." The remedy for this fallacy, for both Karl and Ricky, is easy though: they both need to talk about themselves and other people as whole human beings. Karl might also need some instruction on how his brain and body work together too, as he clearly is confused.

Reference

Kenny, Anthony. 1971. "The Homunculus Fallacy." In *Interpretations of Life and Mind: Essays around the Problem of Reduction*, edited by Marjorie Grene. London: Routledge and Kegan Paul Books, 65–74.

32

Inappropriate Appeal to Authority

Nicolas Michaud

> I was following orders.
> Nazi General Anton Doster's legal defense for atrocities committed
> during World War II

Inappropriate appeal to authority (IAA) has many different facets. At its core, it is a fallacy that assumes that because someone is an authority, we should listen to that person. The problem is that just because someone is an authority doesn't mean that s/he is, in fact, an expert, that s/he is moral, or that s/he is right. As the example above points out, sometimes when an authority tells us to do something that authority can be very wrong indeed.

Logically, IAA is problematic because it means that we are using someone to defend our claims who doesn't really connect with that claim or is not a good justification. Damer (1987) notes that it is an attempt "to support a claim by appealing to the judgment of one who is not an authority in the field, the judgment of an unidentified authority, or the judgment of an authority who is likely to be biased" (109). Notice, then, that there are a few different ways in which IAA can occur. It doesn't necessarily mean following orders. What it rests on is the assumption that authority itself is a justification for action or a validation of truth.

Bad Arguments: 100 of the Most Important Fallacies in Western Philosophy, First Edition.
Edited by Robert Arp, Steven Barbone, and Michael Bruce.
© 2019 John Wiley & Sons Ltd. Published 2019 by John Wiley & Sons Ltd.

IAA seems to be the result of a flaw in human thinking. Social cognitive theory, a theory that helps explain human action, notes that humans tend to act like each other. We mimic the behavior of those around us. We are, however, far more likely to imitate the behavior of those who have the following qualities: perceived competence, perceived similarity to us, perceived status. That psychological tendency likely explains what I like to think of as "the Oprah and Dr. Phil effect." Consider the fact that Dr. Phil became a hugely popular TV psychologist. Despite having questionable credentials, Dr. Phil was believed to be an appropriate authority to give advice to millions of viewers. Likely this is because of the authority of Oprah, who "discovered him." So many people respect and listen to Oprah that when she recommended that people watch Dr. Phil, they did so without really asking, "Is she the right person to validate the competency of a psychologist for millions across the country?"

Similarly, Oprah's book recommendations make guaranteed bestsellers. A university literary professor with four PhDs who has dedicated her life to reading and understanding books could make a book recommendation, and hardly anyone in the country would listen, but because of Oprah's status, if she recommends a book, we buy it. In the same way, when she recommends that we watch Dr. Phil, we do so. The fact that Dr. Phil has "Dr." in front of his name impacts us as well. Interestingly, according to social cognitive theory, perceived competence causes us to listen to others *even when they are not competent in the field they are discussing.* In other words, Dr. Phil could have his doctorate in basket weaving, and something about us would still want to listen to him about psychology and just about anything else he decided to talk about.

The tendency to listen to authorities who are not authorities explains why celebrities are able to sell us stuff. Consider Michael Jordan's fabulously successful career selling underwear. The fact that he was amazing at playing basketball has nothing to do with selling undies. In fact, he is no more an underwear expert than you or I. However, the fact that he was a basketball god causes our brains to think, "Hmmm, I should listen to this guy even though he isn't an underwear scientist or any other kind of underwear expert."

What makes IAA particularly dangerous is the fact that there are, in fact, appropriate authorities. I may be in a discussion about black holes and reference Dr. Stephen Hawking as evidence that my claim is correct, or I might reference former president Bill Clinton when discussing domestic policy in the United States. They are both authorities that may add evidence to my claims regarding facts in their fields of expertise. So, sometimes it can be hard to know when exactly the fallacy is, in fact, a fallacy. One way is simply to be aware that just because someone is an authority in one area does not make that someone an authority on other things. Sure, I might read a book by Bill Clinton on domestic policy on the United States, but I probably should be timid about trusting a book by him on how to keep a spouse happy. True, I don't want to be guilty of using an *ad hominem*; after all, given his marital troubles, the book might be full of advice on "What not to do." But the point is that when we say, "Well, this must be true because so and so wrote it," we are not really thinking clearly.

Simply, the best way to avoid committing this fallacy is to recognize that *no one person is sufficient authority to make something true by herself.* Even when the authority is appropriate and an expert in the field under discussion, this doesn't mean that the argument stops with her. Just because I pull out Dr. Stephen Hawking's book on black holes when arguing with someone about them doesn't mean that he must concede my point. What really matters is *what the book says.* Are his arguments good? Do they make sense? Do they support the evidence? Just because it is Hawking's book isn't enough. It is the content that matters.

So, simply, the problem with IAA is that it ignores content in favor of credentials and power. If we are going to make well-reasoned arguments, we must look deeper than the identity of the people whose arguments we are espousing. Consider the following examples:

(1)   How do I know that birth control is wrong? The Pope says so, that's how I know!

Notice that this argument might work very well if talking with a Catholic. It is important, however, to realize it won't get the same traction with someone who isn't Catholic. While the Pope is a moral authority to Catholics, he is not an authority to many other people. So, sometimes argumentation requires that we recognize that someone is an authority to us but not to others.

(2)   I think I should take that medicine for depression. I saw a doctor talking about it on a commercial.

It isn't uncommon to see doctors selling product on TV commercials. Those commercials appeal to our belief that doctors are trustworthy authorities. The problem is that all of the other reasons to consider taking or not taking a medication are ignored. That TV doctor is not an authority on *you,* which is really the key problem. If the doctor does not know the patient, just because she is a doctor does not mean she can give good medical advice to someone she has never examined.

(3)   Look, I just do what I'm told. I shoot when I'm told to shoot, and I march when I'm told to march. Whether this war is right or wrong isn't up to me to decide.

On one hand, we certainly want soldiers to follow orders. If they don't, they are a danger to themselves and the other soldiers they serve with. The problem is, as in the case with the Nazis, and in numerous other examples, our tendency to defer our moral judgments to others, sometimes even vague and unnamed authorities, means we don't feel the pressure to take responsibility for really important moral decisions. Sometimes, the result is soldiers and citizens who support truly horrific acts only because those in authority tell them to.

The important thing to remember about IAA is that it isn't just a fallacy that comes up in arguments that don't matter. Sure, at the end of the day, it may not matter that much if I appeal to Dr. Hawking a bit too much in my arguments about black holes. The problem is that if we are not careful, we start listening to people who really don't have much expertise at all and as a result buy and believe things that are not in our best interest. It benefits the underwear company when we don't ask ourselves, "What does Michael Jordan really know about underwear?" Worse, though, is the fact that this fallacy makes it so that we don't have to hold ourselves responsible. The beliefs and actions that come from it we can blame on the authority. When that happens, we can justify just about anything, no matter how awful.

Reference
Damer, T. Edward. 1987. *Attacking Faulty Reasoning*. Belmont, CA: Wadsworth Publishing.

33

Irrelevant Conclusion

Steven Barbone

> You cannot convict my client of murder. We have proven that one of the arresting officers made prejudicial remarks, remarks scornful of my client. Look at the videotape, the audiotape, the man's own testimony. He is a full-blown racist; you must not trust anything he says.
>
> Loosely based on the O.J. Simpson case, from PhilosophicalSociety.com

The fallacy of irrelevant conclusion, also known as the *ignoratio elenchi* ("ignorance of the proof") fallacy, is, in effect, the parent of all other fallacies since every fallacy yields a conclusion that even if it be true is not related – that is, is irrelevant – to the premises of the argument (see also Chapter 43 on the red herring fallacy). Arguments that commit the irrelevant conclusion fallacy all end with a conclusion that is not related in any necessary way to the premises. Consider these generalizations (assume for the sake of argument that they're true):

The Japanese eat little fat and have fewer heart attacks than Americans and the English.

The French eat a lot of fat and have fewer heart attacks than Americans and the English.

The Italians drink a lot of wine and have fewer heart attacks than Americans and the English.

The Chinese drink little wine and have fewer heart attacks than Americans and the English.

Bad Arguments: 100 of the Most Important Fallacies in Western Philosophy, First Edition. Edited by Robert Arp, Steven Barbone, and Michael Bruce.
© 2019 John Wiley & Sons Ltd. Published 2019 by John Wiley & Sons Ltd.

What should we conclude? How about, therefore, eat and drink as you like; speaking English leads to heart attacks! We could for the sake of argument even agree that there is some odd causal connection between speaking English and having a heart attack (so the conclusion could be correct), but does this conclusion really follow from the premises? No, it does not. In fact, it's not certain what follows from those premises. Here's another example of an argument with an irrelevant conclusion:

(1) The United States had an active space program in the 1960s.
(2) <u>The USSR had an active space program in the 1960s.</u>
(3) Therefore, the United States was the first to land humans on the moon, in 1969.

In this example, all the premises are true. The conclusion is true too, but it does not necessarily follow from the premises. Except for some who believe that the moon landing is an elaborate hoax, we should believe that humans landed on the moon in 1969, but there being active space programs does not necessarily imply that there was a moon landing.

This parent of all fallacies has no single form except that whatever the conclusion, it does not follow from the premises. We might imagine it like this:

Premise 1 + premise 2 + premise 3 [...] premise infinity.
Conclusion A (where A has nothing to do with any numerical premise).

Avoiding this fallacy is easier said than done, for it requires one to be a critical thinker at all times. Any time someone tries to persuade you of something or you try to convince someone else of something, ask how the conclusion is related to the premises. Is there a necessary, logical connection or is there merely an emotional one? Do the premises really support the conclusion or are the premises ambiguous or possibly misunderstood? Bottom line: Don't just accept a conclusion because it's labeled as such. Make sure it's connected to the propositions that supposedly support it.

34

Kettle Logic

Andy Wible

> The whole plea [...] recalls vividly the defense offered by a man who was accused by his neighbor of having returned a kettle in a damaged condition. In the first place, he had returned the kettle undamaged; in the second place it already had holes in it when he borrowed it; and in the third place, he had never borrowed it at all. A complicated defense, but so much the better; if only one of these three lines of defense is recognized as valid, the man must be acquitted.
>
> Sigmund Freud, *The Interpretation of Dreams*

Kettle logic (KL) is a fallacy in which multiple contradictory premises are presented to support a point. As such, it is logically impossible for all of the premises to be true. Yogi Berra's famous sayings are often contradictory. In the 1960s, while justifying why he didn't go to Ruggeri's restaurant anymore, he gives these two famous contradictory supporting claims committing a KL: "Nobody goes there anymore. It's too crowded."

Formally, KL arguments are valid arguments, for it is impossible for contradictory premises to be true and the conclusion false. The problem is the principle of explosion, which shows that from a contradiction anything follows validly, and consequently all such arguments are trivial. Additionally, the argument cannot be sound for all of the premises cannot be true. It should be noted that paraconsistent logic has been developed to challenge the notion that such inconsistent arguments are trivial.

Bad Arguments: 100 of the Most Important Fallacies in Western Philosophy, First Edition.
Edited by Robert Arp, Steven Barbone, and Michael Bruce.
© 2019 John Wiley & Sons Ltd. Published 2019 by John Wiley & Sons Ltd.

KL gets its name from Sigmund Freud in his book *The Interpretation of Dreams*. Freud relates the story of a man accused of returning a tea kettle with holes in it. The man defends himself saying: (1) he had returned the kettle undamaged, (2) the kettle already had holes in it, and (3) he never borrowed the kettle. Rather than helping his case by offering multiple supporting premises, the man actually undermines his case by making contradictory claims. The more he defends himself, the worse his credibility (Freud 1900, 101).

Freud believes KL is employed in dreams quite often. Contradictory beliefs are commonly offered, which give notice that one is in a dream. For example, in the embarrassment dream of being naked, the person feels shame for being naked and wants to run but for some reason cannot. Also, the people whom she feels embarrassed in front of are strangers whose faces are indefinite and they are indifferent to her nakedness. Such thinking is part of the "logic" of the dream world. She is caring about being laughed at by people who are unknown and don't care. The reasons are not meant by the dreamer to be contradictory, but Freud believes they are.

Unfortunately, KL fallacies also abound in waking life in not so humorous ways. David Swanson, in his article "Cheney's Kettle Logic," points out that Vice President Dick Cheney gave the following defense of the administration's decision to invade Iraq and the subsequent problems there. Cheney said that the intelligence used to justify invasion was sound and accurate, and that the fact it was flawed was the previous administration's fault. When asked about the damage done to Iraq, he said that it was the Iraqis and not the allied forces who did the damage and that any invasion causes unfortunate horrific things to happen. He gives two KL fallacies to explain his administration's decisions and the damage to Iraq.

Not all arguments that seem to have contradictory premises prove, upon closer examination, to be examples of KL. In the Yogi Berra example above, Berra is likely referring to a subset of people when he says "nobody." The reference is likely to his group of friends who longer go there due to the multitudes.

Freud's dream example of KL may also not be fallacious. In the dream, the person may feel embarrassed at being naked in front of anyone, including strangers who don't care. Or there could be a thought that the people appear indifferent but are really laughing on the inside.

Closer examination may also find the person is arguing in the alternative. As in KL, several inconsistent premises are given for the same conclusion, but it is not claimed that all of the premises are true. For example, a defense attorney might claim that his defendant didn't cause the murder because he was at work during the crime, and even if he had been there, he is too short to have stabbed the victim in the head.

Often the problem in evaluating arguments that appear to be KLs is determining whether the arguer is claiming all of the premises are true. Even the man accused of borrowing the kettle might claim in his defense that he didn't borrow the kettle or even if he had done it, he wouldn't have borrowed a kettle with holes in it, and if he had borrowed a good kettle, he would not have returned it with holes. By using these hypotheticals, he is not claiming all of them are true.

Freud's presentation of the tea kettle argument makes it clear that the man presents all of the premises as true. In real life and even in dreams, determining whether the arguer intends for all the considerations to be true, or whether additional information is missing, is much more difficult, but necessary in order to avoid the fallacy.

References

Freud, Sigmund. 1900. *The Interpretation of Dreams*. New York, NY: The McMillan Company.

Swanson, David. 2011. "Cheney's Kettle Logic." *Dissident Voice*, September 2. http://dissidentvoice.org/2011/09/cheneys-kettle-logic/ (accessed September 27, 2017).

35

Line Drawing

Alexander E. Hooke

> Well, the line has to be drawn *somewhere*.
>
> Overheard in moral conversations

Many logic or critical thinking textbooks treat the line-drawing fallacy as a footnote to or subcategory of another fallacy. They view it as a variation of vagueness, false dilemma, slippery slope, or the perfectionist fallacy. A standard definition of this fallacy is "insisting a line must be drawn at some precise point when in fact it is not necessary that such a precise line be drawn" (Moore and Parker 2007, 221). What determines "not necessary" remains unsettled.

Depending on how one interprets a key premise or central term of the argument, detecting a line-drawing fallacy can take several forms. Consider a typical exercise in a textbook:

OFFICER: You are getting a ticket for driving at an unsafe speed.
DRIVER: Oh, then please tell me what is a safe speed? Is it 50 mph, 45 mph, or should I go so slow that I cause a traffic jam?

Clearly the irritated response imputes fallacious reasons to the officer's actions, but it also commits a line-drawing fallacy by implicitly holding that

Bad Arguments: 100 of the Most Important Fallacies in Western Philosophy, First Edition.
Edited by Robert Arp, Steven Barbone, and Michael Bruce.
© 2019 John Wiley & Sons Ltd. Published 2019 by John Wiley & Sons Ltd.

safe and unsafe are indistinguishable since there is no exact number on a car's speedometer indicating an unsafe speed.

This line-drawing fallacy appears as a form of false dilemma since the driver distorts or limits the either/or options. It can also be a problem of vagueness as the key term "safe driving" is not clarified, to the chagrin of the driver. Line-drawing concerns also appear in slippery slope, hyperbole, and straw man fallacies. The driver, somewhat impudently and imprudently, challenges the officer with a critical thinking question that may thwart the possible compassion the officer has for an apologetic driver who might just receive a warning rather than a ticket.

In fact, the driver is implying a challenge to the officer that has perplexed philosophers for centuries. The line-drawing theme poses inherent intellectual problems. If not carefully addressed, there is always the risk of an absurd or paradoxical conclusion. Unable to answer the driver's question, we are in danger of saying that there is no difference between safe and unsafe driving. Or, should the officer also suspect the driver of being under the influence, we claim no one can precisely distinguish which drop of alcohol finally constitutes inebriation.

To correct or to prevent such absurd conclusions, logicians try to identify and/or explain the nature of the line-drawing fallacy. Roy Sorensen, in discussing one of Zeno's paradoxes, regards the line-drawing fallacy as a slippery slope. Once you disagree on the preciseness of point A or line B, then all points and lines are disputed. One way to avoid the paradox is to reassess the actual premises. Others view the line-drawing problem as an extension of the inability to agree on how to measure or evaluate the empirical aspects of an idea or concept. This either/or approach turns the line-drawing fallacy into a variation of the perfectionist or false dilemma fallacy. Those who emphasize vagueness contend that one or more of the central terms are imprecise and to prevent reaching an absurd conclusion, we need to assess or to agree on these terms.

Such cautions clearly can help the critical thinker to spot overt cases of sloppy thinking. When a petulant child whines about having to go to bed at 9 p.m., demands to know why 9:01 p.m. is any different, a line-drawing fallacy lurks on the horizon. Becoming a teenager, he or she will learn these arbitrary or imprecise distinctions when considering the proper age to drink or vote, the SAT score a college uses to accept or reject an applicant, when mom or dad are classified as senior citizens, or the official distinction between a freedom fighter and a terrorist. What makes this fallacy so important is that it intertwines with innumerable ordinary and controversial aspects of human life in which people are agreeing on or disputing where to draw the line.

To draw the line is a perennial source of cooperation and conflict. In sporting events, drawing lines demarcates what is in and out of play.

In international circles, drawing the line distinguishes respected borders and limits of military aggression. Among social contract theorists, drawing the line might determine where privacy ends and the public begins or when the personal domain becomes part of the communal.

This task is also evident in everyday concerns. Establishing the legal ages for voting or drinking, deciding when a stimulant becomes a drug, and distinguishing which student essay is a B+ rather than a B are just a sample of the many instances of when we draw a line, consciously or by habit. A recent animated film, *Ted 2*, drew rebuke for its humorous take on sickle cell disease. A president of a sickle cell organization called for movie makers and parents "to draw the line" on humor that disparages unfortunate victims of a debilitating disease.

Consider one ongoing and relatively recent controversy that illustrates the practical significance and philosophical difficulty in drawing the line. Visualize two photos, one of an anorexic teenage girl and the other an obese middle-aged tycoon. Asked to identify each one, no sensible person would fail. To explain the difference simply in terms of exact numbers, laymen as well as experts have trouble reaching a consensus. Such an inability to "draw the line" has animated social controversies about controlling diets and moral debates about proper eating, and has even been the unexpected cause of tragic accidents. For example, over the last two decades, several small planes have crashed due to excessive and unbalanced loads. The planes were originally built on the assumption that the average passenger weighed 160 pounds. Now, with so many overweight passengers or an imbalanced seating arrangement with too many obese people sitting on one side of the plane, several small planes have crashed at takeoff.

So the practical and philosophical underpinnings of line drawing show how the line-drawing fallacy can readily appear should arguments be developed to support specific answers to some of the following questions. Should airlines begin charging fees based on passenger weight or assign obese people designated seats? Will this draw protests of bias or favoritism? Suppose fatness is not a medical term but a social construct, then isn't this a moot issue? Can we sue the airlines for not safely determining in advance that passengers were gradually getting heavier?

In light of the above, a simple exercise:

PARENT: Please stop eating all that junk food. It will make you fat.
CHILD: What's wrong with a couple of chips and some ice cream? Do you want me to like those skinny models on TV?

Several line-drawing-related fallacies immediately arise, from false dilemma to straw man (distorting the parent's point). Yet this exercise is too obvious to help a student discern the underlying difficulty in recognizing the line-drawing fallacy or avoiding the paradox it raises. As a potential critical thinker, the student or child might acknowledge his or her youthful moment of illogic, but then offer this more earnest rejoinder to the parent: "OK, but where do I draw the line? Exactly how do I decide when an occasional treat becomes too much snacking, or at which pound am I no longer normal but over-weight?" While we don't expect youthful respondents to have Aristotle's "means between the extremes" in the back of their minds, their questions seek some counsel about when or where to draw the line.

Margaret Cuonzo, in a lucid and scholarly discussion of paradoxes, devotes considerable attention to the sorites problem (the more formal category of line drawing) and possible solutions. One she proposes involves the notion of "folk concepts." These refer to ordinary language terms that are not meant to be so precise and that undermine efforts to communicate or to deliberate ideas. Folk concepts such as baldness, space, pollution, fear, time, forgiveness, or beauty are important in everyday deliberations even though users of these concepts are unable to pin down their exact defini-tions, for example, the precise moment when dirty air becomes smog and when smog becomes pollution.

A shortcoming to the folk concepts approach is that folk concepts them-selves are hardly univocal in their meanings or standards. To assert that someone is skinny, normal, or fat is often based on tacit or subjective standards. They might rely on different criteria to make sensible judgments about beauty, health and longevity, functionality, liability for insurance companies, even the risk factor for flying in a small plane.

While the line-drawing fallacy can be subsumed under more standard fallacies, it warrants distinct attention insofar as it raises a perennial problem in everyday thinking and important disputes. Textbook exercises tend to present obvious cases of the fallacy. This has the inadvertent effect of students accepting the charge and moving on.

Instead, students and logic teachers might be encouraged to consider their own examples and experiences that reflect that drawing the line is one of the most enduring issues in critical thinking and philosophical reflection. Rather than offering the quick answer then checking the next exercise, we might first consider whether an apparent line-drawing fallacy can be resolved with a rational or successful decision about when or where the line should be drawn.

Reference

Moore, Brooke, and Richard Parker. 2007. *Critical Thinking*. Boston, MA: McGraw-Hill.

36

Mistaking the Relevance of Proximate Causation

David Kyle Johnson

> Guns don't kill people; people kill people.
>
> NRA slogan

One commits this variety of causal fallacy when one mistakes the relevance of proximate causation. But, of course, knowing this is not helpful unless one understands what proximate causation is and what it would mean to mistake its relevance. So let's deal with each in turn.

When it comes to causation, things are hardly ever as simple as A caused B. Consider this question: "What caused these words to appear on this page?"

We might say that those words were caused to appear by my decision to write those words, but that decision would not have amounted to much without its being followed by an entire series of other causally relevant events. That decision caused my fingers to move, which caused the keys of my keyboard to move, which caused the words to appear in my text document (and on my screen). I then sent that document to the editors, who added it to a larger document, which was eventually printed by a large machine onto these pages. If any of these steps had been missing, those words would not have appeared on this page. Causal stories are usually long and complicated and involve a chain of events.

Bad Arguments: 100 of the Most Important Fallacies in Western Philosophy, First Edition.
Edited by Robert Arp, Steven Barbone, and Michael Bruce.
© 2019 John Wiley & Sons Ltd. Published 2019 by John Wiley & Sons Ltd.

To keep things straight, it will be helpful to clarify some terminology. Let's call the event that starts off the chain the "ultimate cause," the subsequent events the "intermediate causes," and the event that plays the most immediate causal role in bringing about the event the "proximate cause" (because it is closest in proximity to the event in question, which is different than the legal definition of "proximate cause" (see Rottenstein 2015). So, in the example above, the words being printed is the proximate cause.

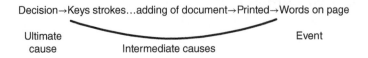

Now, generally speaking, it's true that proximate causes wouldn't exist (or couldn't do much) without their ultimate cause. But that doesn't mean that the proximate cause didn't play an important (or even necessary) role in bringing about the event in question. For example, while it is true that my decision to type the above sentence was the ultimate cause of those words appearing on the previous page, they could never have done so without the printing press that printed them. And this is how one can mistake the relevance of proximate causation. One mistakes the relevance of proximate causation when one thinks the fact that something is a proximate cause makes it irrelevant to the story of how the event in question happened (or whether or not it would have happened).

So take the example from the top of his chapter: the NRA slogan "Guns don't kill people; people kill people." The implied conclusion is that guns are not to blame for the acts of violence (such as a mass shooting) in which they are used because a person is the ultimate cause of the violence (not the gun). Without a person to wield it, a gun can do no harm.

Decision to kill → Firing of gun → Death of person

Ultimate cause   Proximate cause   Event

But, while this is true, it does not follow that guns do not play an important causal role in things like mass shootings – and so it doesn't follow that regulating guns wouldn't do anything to reduce the frequency of mass shootings. Although they are proximate causes, guns do make murdering people *en masse* much easier; so making them harder to attain would reduce the number of mass shootings.

The fallaciousness of this argument becomes obvious when we exaggerate it. Suppose it was legal to own a military-style tank and then someone took the tank, attacked a building, took it down, and killed all those inside.

Suppose that when people then called for owning a tank to be outlawed, someone pointed out that, without an operator, a tank is perfectly harmless. "Tanks don't kill people; people do." Of course this is true, but that doesn't mean that the tank didn't play an important causal role in bringing the building down – and it doesn't mean that outlawing tanks would do nothing to prevent such tragedies. Although they are proximate causes, they do make bringing down entire buildings much easier; making tanks harder to attain would reduce the number of tank-related deaths.

Of course, it's undeniable that tanks are not guns and that there are other arguments and factors to consider regarding whether and how much (and which) guns should be regulated. But it's equally undeniable that pointing out that guns are "merely proximate causes" is irrelevant to that debate. I wouldn't say, as philosopher William Harwood (2015) did, that anyone who makes such an argument is an anti-American bigot (although he makes a good point about the argument itself). I would say, however, that the argument doesn't deserve a place in a rational debate about gun regulations.

Mistaking the relevance of proximate causation can also "go the other way." That is, one can *overinflate* the importance of something being a proximate cause (instead of finding it irrelevant). This is often done by those looking to avoid responsibility for their actions. Suppose you have a rich uncle with cancer in the hospital on life support and that you pull the plug so as to get the inheritance you were promised. Could you rightfully claim that you were not responsible for his death by pointing out, "Hey, I didn't kill him – the cancer did"? Of course not; although the cancer was the most proximate cause, you played an important causal role in this death. Yet this line of reasoning appears quite often in daily life, usually from those wanting to avoid responsibility for their actions. For example, my students often want to blame me for their bad grades – since I am the one who assigned them their grade – instead of blaming themselves, their lack of studying, or their inability to write a well-argued paper.

But, of course, things are not always straightforward. Who's to blame for the execution of a criminal on death row? The criminal himself, those who enacted capital punishment laws, or those who refuse to repeal them? Who is more responsible for the financial crash of 2008 – those who deregulated the financial sector or those in the financial sector who took advantage of its deregulation? Who bears more responsibility for the presence of ISIS in Iraq – the members of ISIS itself, President Obama, whose removal of troops left a power vacuum for them to fill, or George W. Bush, whose invasion of Iraq made a power vacuum in Iraq inevitable? Matters of causation are never simple. And sometimes whether something is a proximate cause is relevant to the issue at hand. But we must be careful to make sure that we don't mistake its relevance.

References

Harwood, William H. 2015. "Those Who Say 'Guns Don't Kill' Are Anti-American Bigots." *The Huffington Post*, October 8. http://www.huffingtonpost.com/william-h-harwood/those-who-say-guns-dont-k_b_8254334.html (accessed October 8, 2015).

Rottenstein Law Group LLP. n.d. "What Is Proximate Cause?" http://www.rotlaw.com/legal-library/what-is-proximate-cause/ (accessed October 22, 2017).

37

Moving the Goalposts

Tuomas W. Manninen

> I am altering the deal. Pray I do not alter it any further!
> Darth Vader to Lando Calrissian in *The Empire Strikes Back*

The fallacy of moving the goalposts (MG) ought to resonate with anyone who has familiarity with – or working knowledge of – 1980s popular culture. Not only have those who have watched *The Empire Strikes Back* seen Darth Vader commit this fallacy quite forcefully, but anyone who has played the classic *Super Mario Bros.* game on a Nintendo console (either around 1985, or thereafter) has come across this particular fallacy. In *Super Mario Bros.*, the game's protagonist – Mario – was set on a quest to rescue Princess Peach. At the end of the final level (World 1–4), and after defeating Bowser, he meets not the Princess, but Toad, who bears him the bad news: "Thank you, Mario. But our princess is in another castle." So, despite fulfilling all the requirements demanded of him (i.e., completing all the levels in World 1), Mario must go on; the expected reward for accomplishing his task was only moved further away, beyond additional goals.

The fallacy that occurs in this example is MG. In brief, this fallacy is typically committed when the following three conditions are met:

Bad Arguments: 100 of the Most Important Fallacies in Western Philosophy, First Edition.
Edited by Robert Arp, Steven Barbone, and Michael Bruce.
© 2019 John Wiley & Sons Ltd. Published 2019 by John Wiley & Sons Ltd.

(1)   Person A requests Person B to meet a certain goal (evidential or otherwise).
(2)   Person B fulfills the goal as stipulated above (step #1).
(3)   Instead of admitting that Person B has met the goals or has discharged the conditions of the contract, Person A stipulates even further goals.

The name of the fallacy derives from football – if the goalposts for one team are moved farther away or closer, this can provide a (dis)advantage to the opposing team. It is quite straightforward to see why MG is incorrect reasoning. If you enter a competition under the assumption that in order to win, you need to satisfy objectives a, b, and c, and if you manage to accomplish this, then you can reasonably expect to be rewarded accordingly. However, if – unbeknownst to you, as this is when the fallacy most commonly occurs – further conditions are stipulated for your meeting the goals, you could call the competition anything but fair.

For a concrete and long-running example of this fallacy, we can turn to Darwin's *The Origin of Species*. In chapter 6, Darwin asks, "as by this theory [of descent by modification] innumerable transitional forms must have existed, why do we not find them embedded in countless numbers in the crust of the earth?" (1902, 134). This has prompted an ongoing inquiry into the fossil record, by both proponents and opponents of Darwin's theory alike. Although the first fossil specimen of *Archaeopteryx* was discovered mere years after Darwin published his book, it has been frequently heralded as a transitional form (by proponents) and decried as a hoax of a genuine "missing link" between dinosaurs and modern-day birds (by opponents). Given the sesquicentennial nature of this argument, it would be practically impossible to include all the instances here. The following version, however, will serve our purposes.

Focusing on the *Archaeopteryx* fossil, the goalposts are shifted when it comes to the interpretations of it. Scientists who conclude that it is a genuine transitional fossil require that it shows features of dinosaurs and of birds, which the *Archaeopteryx* does. In contrast, the critics point out that the *Archaeopteryx* has features that no modern bird has, so it cannot be a direct ancestor of modern birds. Still, the critics' demand goes beyond the scientists' claim: a transitional form only needs to show that an intermediate species existed between dinosaurs and birds, and it does not need to show that all modern birds are related to the *Archaeopteryx*.

Another variant or instance of MG that is common in discussions over transitional forms can be found in a plethora of sources, but it typically takes the following form:

Step 1: Paleontologists present evidence that the fossil A is an intermediate species (or transitional form) between clades X and Y.

Step 2: Critics challenge the significance of the discovery by pointing out the dearth of evidence for an intermediate transitional form between X and A, or A and Y.

Step 3: If evidence for such a transitional form is produced by paleontologists, the process is repeated.

MG is all too commonly found in conspiracy theories, from those focusing on the 9/11 terrorist attacks ("Truthers") to those focusing on Barack Obama's birthplace ("Birthers") and beyond (see Aaronovitch 2009 for more examples). The latter of these insinuates that Obama was ineligible to serve as the President of the United States when he was elected; the US Constitution requires for the president to be "a natural born citizen," and Obama's detractors questioned whether he met this qualification. After several years of rampant speculation, President Obama released a copy of his birth certificate in 2011, and this clearly indicated that he was born in Honolulu, Hawaii, on August 6, 1961. Yet, this hardly served to quell the challenges. "What Obama released," the detractors claimed, "was not a 'Birth certificate,' but merely a 'Certification of Live Birth.'" The document that was released by President Obama to the public to view was not good enough – for the detractors – as it did not meet the criteria they had stipulated. Besides, even if the evidence provided by Obama met the criteria stipulated, it still was not good enough. As many commentators pointed out, there are records of Hawaii's newspapers having run in the "Births Announced" section an announcement that a son was born to Mr. and Mrs. Barack H. Obama, on August 4, 1961. Yet, according to the detractors, these announcements must have fraudulently been placed in the newspapers by conspirators who intended to ensure that Barack Obama could become the President of the United States. Many other conspiracy theories share in MG in a similar way: once a claim advocated by the theorists has been debunked by evidence, the nature of the evidence is questioned or the claim is changed to a more demanding one. And so on.

The most straightforward way in which this fallacy can be avoided only requires a few steps, but these are such that they need to be completed beforehand. First, both (or all) of the parties to the argument should expect the other(s) to be arguing (or entering the contract) in good faith. Second, the parties ought to agree as to what amounts to a successful completion of the task at hand. As long as the terms of the contract or the argument are left ambiguous, one party can (and often will) try to take advantage of that ambiguity. For a recent example from the NFL, both teams should abide by the official standards, for example, that the ball be inflated to a certain gauge pressure, in order to avoid one team's receiving an unfair advantage over the other. Third, one ought to remain wary when making contracts with individuals named Darth Vader (or any other Sith Lord, for that matter), or 'Wimpy' (especially when the contract involves hamburgers, and the payment for those), or arguing with individuals sporting "Where's the birth certificate?" bumper stickers on their car.

References
Aaronovitch, David. 2009. *Voodoo Theories: The Role of the Conspiracy Theory in Shaping Modern History*. London. Jonathan Cape.
Darwin, Charles. 1902. *The Origin of Species*. New York, NY: P.F. Collier and Son.

38

Mystery, Therefore Magic

David Kyle Johnson

Tide goes in, tide goes out. Never a miscommunication. You can't explain that.
Bill O'Reilly, *The O'Reilly Factor* (Fox News, January 4, 2011)

One commits the mystery, therefore magic fallacy (MTM) when one takes the fact that one cannot find a "natural" or "rational" explanation for some event or thing as a reason to favor or to accept a magical, supernatural, or fantastic explanation for that event or thing. "How else do you explain it?" This fallacy gets its name from the fact that we instinctually avoid it every time we watch a good magic show. When a magician does something for which we cannot find a natural explanation, we do not conclude that the magician actually has magic powers. We conclude that there *is* a natural explanation – it's just that we are not smart enough to figure it out or detect it. Even the best magicians don't know how Penn & Teller appear to catch bullets in their teeth, yet none think Penn & Teller actually have the ability to do so. In fact, on their show *Fool Us*, Penn & Teller regularly can't figure out how the guest magicians do their tricks. Yet neither Penn nor Teller ever concludes that their guests have magic powers.

But "It's magic" is not the only kind of magical, supernatural, or fantastical explanation that can be offered up for what one cannot explain. In the outside world (beyond the magic stage), people usually just interject their

Bad Arguments: 100 of the Most Important Fallacies in Western Philosophy, First Edition.
Edited by Robert Arp, Steven Barbone, and Michael Bruce.
© 2019 John Wiley & Sons Ltd. Published 2019 by John Wiley & Sons Ltd.

favorite such explanation. Unexplained noises or temperature variations are often attributed to ghosts. Others conclude that the Egyptian pyramids were built by aliens because they can't understand how the Egyptians could have built them. Thousands have concluded that unidentified flying objects are alien craft, that unknown animals in the forest are Bigfoot, and that unidentifiable objects in Loch Ness are a monster. That no natural explanation is forthcoming is thought to be good reason to interject one's supernatural explanation of choice.

MTM is very common in religious circles since "God did it" is often the religious supernatural explanation of choice. For example, the fact that a disease went into remission is often thought to be evidence of divine intervention, as is the fact that someone endured a terminal disease longer than expected. Religious academics even fall prey to the fallacy, like Lehigh University's Michael Behe (2006). He thinks that irreducibly complex biological systems (e.g., blood clotting) can't be explained by natural selection and are thus evidence of divine intervention. Likewise, apologist William Lane Craig and Christian philosopher Robin Collins think that the inexplicable "fine-tuning" of the universe is good reason to conclude that God fine-tuned it.

Now it's important to note that, quite often, those who make such arguments are mistaken about what is explained and what isn't. For example, as Owen Jarus explains, we actually do know how the Egyptians built the pyramids and most "UFOs" have been identified. Further, there are now tons of pieces of evidence of so-called irreducible complexities that are actually explained quite nicely by natural selection. And, unbeknownst to Bill O'Reilly, the moon's gravitational pull explains the tides.

But even if explanations for such phenomena were not available, these arguments would still be fallacious because they would still commit MTM. For example, what makes Behe's "irreducible complexity" argument fallacious isn't the fact that we actually have explained things like blood clotting via natural selection. (That just makes a premise in his argument false.) What makes the argument fallacious is the fact that Behe thinks that (1) "God designed blood clotting" would logically follow from (2) "We have yet to explain how blood clotting evolved." But even if (2) were true, (1) would not follow.

This fact becomes obvious once you realize that there is no way to delineate one supernatural explanation from another. If Behe's argument were valid, the irreducible complexity would be just as much evidence of *divine* design as it would be of *alien* design or *interdimensional being* design – or even the idea that we live in a computer simulation. This is a weakness to which even Behe himself has admitted.

But we can see *why* such reasoning is fallacious by returning to our "magic show" example. Ask yourself: When you see a magic trick you can't explain, what is the best explanation for why you can't find a natural explanation?

Is it (a) there isn't one because the person on stage has magic powers or (b) you are not as smart as you think (you're not as good as you thought at figuring out magic tricks)? Clearly, it is option (b).

The same holds true when you can't find a natural explanation for something in the regular world. The fact that you can't find such an explanation is much more likely due to your ignorance than it is due to there being no natural explanation. The same even holds when no human has yet explained the phenomenon in question; our collective ignorance is still more likely than an absence of a natural explanation.

In fact, MTM is simply another way of committing the appeal to ignorance fallacy. A person appeals to ignorance, for example, when he takes the fact that *he can't prove some proposition true* to be a good reason to think that proposition is false. When committing MTM, one simply takes one's inability to prove there is a natural explanation (by finding one) to be a good reason to conclude there isn't one.

Now, it's worth noting that appealing to ignorance isn't always fallacious. Sometimes a lack of evidence for something being true is good evidence that it is false. If you look in your fridge and can't find any evidence that there is any milk (i.e., you don't see a milk container), that is good evidence that there is no milk in your fridge. A failed *exhaustive* search for something is evidence it doesn't exist. Likewise, a lack of any evidence for the Earth having a second moon is good evidence that there isn't one. If the evidence of something would be obvious if it existed, a lack of such evidence is good reason to think that thing doesn't exist. In fact, when it comes to existential matters – matters regarding whether or not something exists – an absence of evidence is evidence of absence. The burden of proof is on the believer. If you want to believe in Bigfoot, it's your epistemic duty to show he exists; it's not my duty to show he doesn't. And until you meet that burden, doubt is justified and belief is not.

Could there be such an exception when it comes to MTM? If you experience something weird for yourself, and you have offered multiple natural explanations that have failed, could you be justified in concluding that something "magic" (supernatural or extraordinary) is at work? It wouldn't seem so. After all, such an explanation would have to be the best explanation, and such explanations are (by their very nature) not simple, wide scoping, or conservative. "I just can't figure it out" would always seem to be the better explanation. And even if it's not, which magical explanation should you prefer? God? Ghosts? Aliens? The Illuminati? There would seem to be no way to tell.

So all in all, "How else do you explain it?" isn't a valid argument. The fact that something remains a mystery is not a good reason to invoke magical, supernatural, or fantastical explanations. In order to have evidence of such things, such explanations will have to be the best among the competing alternatives. But it seems that will rarely (if ever) be the case.

References

Behe, Michael. 2006. *Darwin's Black Box: The Biochemical Challenge to Evolution.* New York, NY: Free Press.

Jarus, Owen. 2016. "How Were the Egyptian Pyramids Built?" Live Science, June 14. http://www.livescience.com/32616-how-were-the-egyptian-pyramids-built-. html (accessed September 29, 2017).

39

Naturalistic Fallacy

Benjamin W. McCraw

> If the opinion which I have now stated is psychologically true – if human nature is so constituted as to desire nothing which is not either a part of happiness or a means of happiness – we can have no other proof, and we require no other, that these are the only things desirable. If so, happiness is the sole end of human action, and the promotion of it the test by which to judge all human conduct; from whence it necessarily follows that it must be the criterion of morality.
>
> John Stuart Mill

Unlike many fallacies – formal or informal – it's not likely that one will find the naturalistic fallacy in standard logic textbooks. Typically, one can motivate the fallacy via G.E. Moore – the originator of the term "naturalistic fallacy." For him,

> It may be true that all things which are good are *also* something else … And it is a fact that Ethics aims at discovering what are those other properties belonging to all things which are good. But far too many philosophers have thought that when they named those other properties they were actually defining good; that these properties, in fact, were simply not 'other,' but absolutely and entirely the same with goodness. This view I propose to call the 'naturalistic fallacy' … When a man confuses two natural objects with one another, defining one by the other … then there is no reason to call the fallacy naturalistic.

Bad Arguments: 100 of the Most Important Fallacies in Western Philosophy, First Edition.
Edited by Robert Arp, Steven Barbone, and Michael Bruce.
© 2019 John Wiley & Sons Ltd. Published 2019 by John Wiley & Sons Ltd.

> But if he confuses 'good,' which is not in the same sense a natural object, with
> any natural object whatever, then there is a reason for calling that a naturalistic
> fallacy. (2009, 13–14)

Here the point is that natural properties (e.g., pleasure) are logically and/or metaphysically distinct from normative or moral properties (e.g., goodness) and, thus, any identification of a natural property with a normative property would be defective.

Consider the opening quotation by Mill. In it he moves from certain natural facts about our psychology, namely, that we have exhaustively hedonistic desires, to normative statements about the desirability – the actual goodness – of happiness. This at least appears to fit the model sketched above: purely natural (descriptive) reasons yield a substantive normative or moral claim.

Now, why think this maneuver is fallacious? Moore has wider reasons about metaphilosophical commitments to the non-naturalism of moral values. His metaphysical approach disallows a move from natural to non-natural properties (in Moore's language) because he denies that there are any natural objects possessing normative properties *at all*. Moore's metaphysics of values (metaethics) disallows any movement from natural to non-natural properties. He thinks of normative properties/objects as logically and metaphysically distinct from non-natural properties/objects. Yet if one rejects the wider non-naturalistic moral realism central to Moore's naturalistic fallacy, it seems possible to accept a movement from the natural to normative. The naturalistic fallacy, if this is correct, follows from one's metaphysical (metaethical) commitments rather than simply a *general* defect of reasoning.

For instance, Aristotle (2009) gives the famous "function" argument in *Nichomachean Ethics* for his account of the ultimate human good (*eudaimonia*). "For just as a flute-player, a sculptor, or any artist, and, in general, for all things that have a function or activity, the good and the 'well' is thought to reside in the function" (11). Now, this *appears* to move from the natural/descriptive (what's the function of X) to the normative (what's the good of X). Yet, it's implausible to think of Aristotle's espousing a non-naturalism à la Moore. On Aristotle's view, a thing's function just *is* imbued with the normative properties associated with that object. (Philippa Foot's *Natural Goodness* offers a modern approach entwining natural and normative properties in the ballpark of the interpretation of Aristotle I'm advancing here.) A flute-player's function isn't separate from the value or good of a flute-player. Hence, either it *is* possible to move from the natural to the normative or, more likely in my view, one can claim that at least *certain* natural facts (e.g., about a thing's function) just have an irreducibly normative element, aspect, or basis.

Additionally, consider something like Thomas Aquinas's natural law theory. For him, the very nature of things is normative. Certain facts are true of humans by nature: we preserve our lives, we rear our young, we live in societies, and so on (Aquinas 1997, 775). All of these are natural, descriptive facts true of human beings by nature, and yet Aquinas argues that these features are also *good* for us. Here Aquinas allows – seemingly – a move from natural/descriptive facts to normative ones (about what's good for humans). Why? It's plausibly because Aquinas thinks our nature already contains/implies facts about our good (via our end). He claims that "as *being* is the first thing that falls under the apprehension absolutely, so *good* is the first thing that falls under the apprehension of practical reason" (774). Practical reason follows from apprehension "absolutely" just as the good follows being. Again, the very nature of things contains within themselves normative properties. Like Aristotle, Aquinas doesn't divide the natural and normative as sharply as Moore (or, perhaps, even at all).

In these cases, if I'm right, then the movement from a naturalistic claim or property to a normative one won't be fallacious or defective. That is, given certain meta- physical/ethical/philosophical views that diverge from those of Moore and philosophers like him, there seems to be no inherent or necessary defect in moving from the natural to the normative. Whether the naturalistic fallacy is *fallacious*, then, hangs upon one's more substantive philosophical positions regarding metaphysics and metaethics: some of these commitments yield a naturalistic fallacy, and some allow certain natural-to-normative maneuvers.

References

Aquinas, Saint Thomas. 1997. *Basic Writings of Saint Thomas Aquinas*, edited by Anton C. Pegis. Indianapolis, IN: Hackett.

Aristotle. 2009. *The Nichomachean Ethics*, translated by David Ross. Oxford: Oxford University Press.

Foot, Philippa. 2001. *Natural Goodness*. Oxford: Oxford University Press.

Moore, G.E. 1903. *Principia Ethica*. New York, NY: Macmillan.

40

Poisoning the Well

Roberto Ruiz

> Trump Running Against Crooked Media Supporting Crooked Hillary.
> Headline from the American Thinker blog site (August, 2016)

Poisoning the well (PTW) is a form of *ad hominem* attack – one directed against a person rather than the person's argument. Unlike other forms of *ad hominem* varieties – such as direct (see Chapter 10), circumstantial (see Chapter 9), and *tu quoque* (see Chapter 11) – which are usually a response to an interlocutor's claims, PTW occurs when we illegitimately prime our audience with a pre-emptive strike against, or with adverse information about, an argumentative opponent *before* the latter has had a chance to say anything in her own defense, or in defense of her point of view. This has the insidious effect of creating a conceptual framework according to which the audience – and maybe even the interlocutor herself – will interpret her claims as 'fulfilling' and 'confirming' the presumptions buried inside this conceptual trap. Consider the following exchange between Dilbert and his neighborhood's garbage man:

DILBERT: How much wearable tech can I use before I'm technically a cyborg?

GARBAGE MAN: It doesn't matter because you're a software simulation created by humans who perished after the technological singularity. And you're programmed to scoff at what I just said.

DILBERT: Crazy old coot. (Adams 2014).

Bad Arguments: 100 of the Most Important Fallacies in Western Philosophy, First Edition.
Edited by Robert Arp, Steven Barbone, and Michael Bruce.
© 2019 John Wiley & Sons Ltd. Published 2019 by John Wiley & Sons Ltd.

Notice that what the garbage man says in response to Dilbert's question is quite absurd, but before Dilbert gets a chance to say anything – or to scoff at such a ridiculous statement – the garbage man anticipates Dilbert's likely dismissal of his claim, and frames the issue in such a way that Dilbert's scoff is now made to look like 'confirmation' of the 'truth' of his sci-fi claim. The problem, of course, is that Dilbert's response is actually quite sensible! But the garbage man's clever – if unfair – framing has rigged the rules of the game in his favor.

Or consider that time when, during a hunting trip, former Vice President Dick Cheney accidentally shot his friend Harry Whittington in the face. A famous cartoon by Glenn McCoy depicts Cheney still holding on to his shotgun, smoke coming out of the barrel, and Whittington lying on the ground, legs up. The caption shows Cheney's response to this tragedy: "Just watch," he tells the Secret Service agent standing behind him, "the press is going to try to put some negative spin on this!" (McCoy 2006).

Despite much evidence to the contrary, conservative politicians in the United States often claim that there is a "liberal mainstream media" bias against them. This frame comes in very handy, particularly during embarrassing moments, such as when political candidates are asked such tough 'gotcha' questions as: "What newspapers and magazines do you regularly read?" In the example above, Cheney masterfully utilizes PTW: he has shot his friend in the face, which is clearly a negative thing, but before anyone gets a chance to report on the story, he cleverly invokes the liberal-mainstream-media-bias frame in a way that will ultimately 'confirm' his original self-victimization once the story is reported. The problem, of course, is that it is just not possible to frame this story in a positive light. As a master politician, though, the Cheney in the cartoon knew precisely how to use this inescapable situation to his advantage. Incidentally, and in an epilogue that's probably unrelated to the well-poisoning, Whittington eventually went on national television and apologized to Cheney (and not the other way around!) for the emotional trauma that Cheney must have gone through in the aftermath of having shot Whittington in the face. As it turns out, Cheney may have been the first Sith Lord to preside over the United States of America.

The phrase "poisoning the well" seems to trace back to the egregious medieval European myth that claimed that Jews secretly poisoned wells and drinking fountains used by Christians. If an epidemic or plague hit a town, whether real or imagined, the least tolerant among the locals – and often the most vociferous – would start accusing Jews of having poisoned the water supply upon which the town depended. This lame attempt at a self-fulfilling and *post hoc* 'explanation' was then felt to justify feelings of anti-Semitism and paranoia, as well as any subsequent violence and injustices perpetrated against Jews.

Though PTW is usually understood merely as an *ad hominem* fallacy, this etymological story regarding self-sustaining and irrefutable 'explanations' illustrates an additional and more general concept studied primarily in the philosophy of science which was first articulated and popularized by the philosopher Karl Popper: falsifiability. Popper was interested in the demarcation problem: the question of how to determine the difference between legitimate science and pseudoscience. According to the problem of induction – a problem posed in the eighteenth century by the Scottish philosopher David Hume – nothing short of an infinite amount of evidence can *prove* the truth of a scientific hypothesis. Popper's attempt to solve Hume's problem was to observe that while no scientific theories could be proven *true*, a single observation that contradicts the predictions of a scientific hypothesis can, in principle, *disprove* it. By contrast, Popper thought, pseudoscientific hypotheses are unfalsifiable (or disprovable). They are so flexible that they can be made to be consistent with any and all possible observations.

One of Popper's targets of attack was Freudian psychoanalysis: claims regarding repressed memories, latent oedipal feelings, subconscious denial, wish fulfillment, castration anxiety, penis envy, and others, can be used to 'explain' virtually all possible forms of human behavior and psychology. If you're having a hard time adjusting to the current circumstances surrounding your life, for instance, your therapist might tell you that maybe your mom didn't love you enough as a child, or that maybe she showed you too much affection, or that maybe there was some traumatic and life-altering experience that you have repressed deep into your subconscious mind and that you can't remember, or that maybe you're subconsciously denying your latent homosexual desires, or that you never quite successfully outgrew the anal stage of childhood development, or, if you deny any of this, maybe you're just in denial about the truth of who you really are. The problem, Popper thought, is that this kind of unrestrained flexibility renders such hypotheses completely useless. According to Popper, the problem is not that pseudoscientific claims are false (for all we know, they might even be true!). The problem is that it is impossible to *test* and *know* whether such claims are true or false, right or wrong. And since the purpose of science is to generate knowledge, philosophers of science usually refer to unfalsifiable claims as being so conceptually problematic and methodologically useless that they are "not even wrong."

Other common examples of such epistemically useless claims usually include those with a supernatural component to them, such as:

Teleology or intentionality as applied to inanimate matter: "Everything happens for a reason."
Karma: "What goes around comes around."
Theodicy: "God works in mysterious ways."

Mind–body dualism: "The soul is not limited by the constraints of the physical world."

Reincarnation: "My name is John. In a past life, I was Marie Antoinette, and before that, Cleopatra."

Answered prayers: "Thank you, Jesus, for giving me something indistinguishable from coincidence."

Unanswered prayers: "Your baby is dead. It must be God's will."

The "law of attraction": "Food cannot cause you to put on weight, unless you think it can" (Byrne 2006).

Religious experience: "I have been touched by the Flying Spaghetti Monster's noodly appendage, and I have felt the power of his balls!"

Near-death experiences: "I died temporarily and got a glimpse of heaven and the angels."

Divine judgment: "Can you *prove* that Hurricane Katrina didn't strike a hurricane-prone area during hurricane season as a punishment for homosexuality?"

Popper's criterion of falsifiability has been challenged by philosophers as not producing a fully adequate basis for teasing science and pseudoscience apart. Nevertheless, most of the time it is still quite a useful tool and one that can help us gain a firmer understanding of PTW. One thing you'll notice, if you look back to the Dilbert and Cheney examples above, is that in addition to being instances of *ad hominem* attacks, they are also framed as unfalsifiable statements – purposely designed to be irrefutable – which is ultimately what makes them appear more respectable and legitimate than they actually are.

Unfortunately, this is not merely an abstract and academic philosophical problem. The combination of unfalsifiable accusations and the *ad hominem* pre-emptive strike typical of PTW has been used throughout history to justify some truly horrific practices. Consider the Inquisition or the Salem witch trials: when a person (usually a woman) was accused of witchcraft, a comprehensive and self-fulfilling system of processes of investigation and interpretation of evidence guaranteed the accused, even if innocent, would be found guilty. What kind of evidence might be used to condemn you of witchcraft? So-called Devil's marks: scars, birthmarks, moles, blemishes, boils, pimples, tumors, rashes, and so on. If you happened to have clear skin, 'invisible marks' – often identified by 'prickers' who worked on the equivalent of sales commission, and who consequently had a pecuniary interest in finding blemishes even when they just weren't there – could do the job just as well. 'Confessions' procured through the brutality of torture were also deemed legitimate standard practice. If some pious soul somehow still refused to confess even under torture, the very act of denying involvement in witchcraft was interpreted as presumptive proof of her guilt, since according to this self-fulfilling reasoning whose conceptual well was poisoned from the outset, no real witch would have an interest in admitting to being a witch. At this point a final 'test' would be undertaken: since it was believed that Holy Water would reject the Devil's minions, the accused would be tied up and thrown into a nearby river or lake. If she somehow managed to float, this would be interpreted as proof of her guilt, at which point she would be sentenced to be hanged or burnt at the stake. If she didn't float, this might finally be interpreted as reason to suspect she might not be guilty after all, but it would be too late for her, since she would now have drowned and died. In short, because of the way these procedures and modes of interpretation were framed, once you were accused of witchcraft, any and all evidence, including your own denial of guilt or a watertight alibi, could always be twisted to support the accusations made against you. Such a system was further reinforced by the coercive fact that anyone who dared to question the legitimacy of these practices was automatically accused of being an enemy of the Church, and hence of committing a mortal sin for which the punishment was torture and death (Sagan and Druyan 1997).

Though extending the meaning of PTW (from its traditional role as a mere *ad hominem* attack to the more general problem of dealing with unfalsifiable statements) could result in a loss of specificity, I propose we start using the term *poisoning the well* – regardless of whether such statements also happen to include *ad hominem* attacks – to denote a person's use of sneaky unfalsifiable statements, which cannot be rationally or empirically substantiated, and which therefore do not even merit a refutation.

References

Adams, Scott. 2014. "Dilbert Comic Strip for Friday May 16, 2014." Dilbert Comic Strip, May 16. http://dilbert.com/strip/2014-05-16 (accessed September 28, 2017).

Byrne, Rhonda. 2006. *The Secret*. New York, NY: Atria.

McCoy, Glenn. 2006. "GoComics for Monday February 13, 2006." GoComics, February 13. http://www.gocomics.com/glennmccoy/2006/02/13 (accessed September 28, 2017).

Sagan, Carl, and Ann Druyan. 1997. *The Demon-Haunted World: Science as a Candle in the Dark*. London: Ballantine.

41

Proving Too Much

Kimberly Baltzer-Jaray

> Yes; but you must wager. It is not optional. You are embarked. Which will you choose then? Let us see. Since you must choose, let us see which interests you least. You have two things to lose, the true and the good; and two things to stake, your reason and your will, your knowledge and your happiness; and your nature has two things to shun, error and misery. Your reason is no more shocked in choosing one rather than the other, since you must of necessity choose. This is one point settled. But your happiness? Let us weigh the gain and the loss in wagering that God is. Let us estimate these two chances. If you gain, you gain all; if you lose, you lose nothing. Wager, then, without hesitation that He is.
>
> Blaise Pascal, *Pensées*, #272

Quoted above is what is infamously known as Pascal's wager, an argument that was intended to demonstrate that it is in one's own best interest to behave as if God exists even if it cannot be absolutely proven: if He doesn't exist, no harm done in believing He does; however, if He does exist, then you either have eternal bliss for being good or eternal damnation for being sinful. Pascal's argument is pragmatic in nature as it states that the benefits of believing that God exists (even when there isn't any proof for it) outweigh those of not believing; the possibility of eternal punishment in hell outweighs any advantage had in believing God doesn't exist. However pragmatic it may seem, Pascal's wager contains the fallacy of proving too much,

---

Bad Arguments: 100 of the Most Important Fallacies in Western Philosophy, First Edition.
Edited by Robert Arp, Steven Barbone, and Michael Bruce.
© 2019 John Wiley & Sons Ltd. Published 2019 by John Wiley & Sons Ltd.

and that calls into question its logic. This fallacy has been committed when an argument can be used to also prove something false or leads to contradictory conclusions. An argument that proves too much demonstrates a lack of soundness, since sound arguments can only establish true conclusions, and thus when an argument can be used to prove false conclusions, it becomes evident that there is a flaw in its reasoning. For example, Pascal's wager can be used to prove that it is beneficial to believe in an almighty demon, or a spaghetti monster, or even Bigfoot. It also advocates that you force yourself to believe in something you don't take to be true, and even if it is somehow possible to force yourself to do this, what the wager demands amounts to living a lie (living in sin). Won't that get you into trouble? Is it really better in the eyes of God that you lie to yourself and pretend you believe in Him rather than to live truthfully not believing? The contradictions just pile up.

There are a few forms this fallacy can take on such as when an argument leads to multiple contradictory conclusions. Pascal's wager, once again, fits the bill. If the wager successfully proves we should believe in a benevolent god, then we can also use it to prove the benefit of believing in a sadistic god, or a god that contradicts the existence of all other gods. Another form of this fallacy occurs when an argument leads to a conclusion known to be absolutely false. Great examples are any of Zeno's paradoxes of motion, whereby a person, object, or creature must cross an infinite number of points to get to a destination: if Homer wishes to walk to the end of the pathway, before he can get there he must get halfway, but before he can get halfway he must get a quarter of the way, but before he can get a quarter of the way he must get one-eighth of the way, and so on. These paradoxes end with the conclusion that motion and change – the evidence provided by one's senses – are illusory and thus false, a conclusion that is obviously contradictory. The problem found in the paradoxes of motion is that we have been tricked into thinking about space and time in the wrong way: Hans Reichenbach, for example, proposed that the paradox arises because space and time are considered as separate entities rather than a single space-time continuum (i.e., theory of general relativity). Nick Huggett accuses Zeno of committing the fallacy of begging the question. Regardless of the solution, whether it be that of Reichenbach, Huggett, Aquinas, or Aristotle, the contradictory conclusion reached tells you there's something rotten in the premises – you just need to sniff!

The fallacy of proving too much is not really a single fallacy so much as a great tool for detecting faulty reasoning, since any argument that leads to a contradiction cannot be sound: if the premises are all true, but the conclusion false, then we know something has gone amiss and what is wrong with it is a more specific fallacy. In the case of Pascal's wager, once you notice the contradictions that occur, you can go back through the premises and find the other fallacies at work such as the fallacy of false dilemma (see Chapter 81), and then you notice also the appeal to emotion (see chapters 13 and 14), inappropriate appeal to authority (see Chapter 32), and genetic fallacy (see Chapter 29). As to preventing this fallacy from happening, the best assurance is to make sure your argument has TVS: truth, validity, and soundness. If the premises of the argument are all true, and the conclusion logically follows and is also true, then the argument has TVS. Having TVS means you argue just enough, never too much, and there is a less likely chance other fallacies are at work. Another tip is to understand the far-reaching consequences and implications of what you argue, in other words, consider and critically assess what you are trying to argue: ask yourself, can the argument I'm advocating be used to argue something contradictory, even ridiculous, or can it be turned around to contradict itself? If Bigfoot, demons, or a spaghetti monster start creeping into your argument possibilities, you might need to reconsider some things.

42

Psychologist's Fallacy

Frank Scalambrino

Is my having consciousness a fact of experience? – But doesn't one say that human beings have consciousness, and that trees or stones do not? – What would it be like if it were otherwise? – Would human beings all be unconscious? – No; not in the ordinary sense of the word. But I, for instance, would not have consciousness – as I now in fact have it."

Ludwig Wittgenstein

William James, in his *Principles of Psychology*, coined "the psychologist's fallacy." It is a fallacy of relativism. As the following will indicate, there are three versions of the psychologist's fallacy, which may be listed from least to most extreme. Whereas the first two versions retain the name "psychologist's fallacy," the most extreme version is called "psychologism."

James articulated the psychologist's fallacy as if it were a confusion between first-person and third-person points of view. He noted, "Crude as such a confusion of standpoints seems to be when abstractly stated, it is nevertheless a snare into which no psychologist has kept at all times from falling, and which forms almost the entire stock-in-trade of certain schools [of psychology]" (James 1898, 197). Importantly, an experience and its description are different, and from the first-person point of view, whatever a person experiences is identical with what that experience is. Therefore, the first-person point of view of an experience, because it is the view of actually

Bad Arguments: 100 of the Most Important Fallacies in Western Philosophy, First Edition.
Edited by Robert Arp, Steven Barbone, and Michael Bruce.
© 2019 John Wiley & Sons Ltd. Published 2019 by John Wiley & Sons Ltd.

having the experience itself, is itself the truth of the experience. This is not to say that descriptions of the experience cannot be true. Rather, it is to emphasize that a description of an event should not be confused with the actual event it is supposed to describe.

Now, according to James, "We must be very careful therefore, in discussing a state of mind from the psychologist's point of view"; for, "the poverty of the psychological vocabulary leads us to drop out certain states from our consideration, and to treat others as if they knew themselves and their objects as the psychologist knows both, which is a disastrous fallacy" (James 1890, 197–198). To commit the first version of the psychologist's fallacy, then, is to assume psychological descriptions pertain to the experience itself. The second version is committed when one assumes the psychological descriptions *must* be a part of the experience itself. "Another variety of the psychologist's fallacy is the assumption that the mental state studied must be conscious of itself as the psychologist is conscious of it" (James 1890, 197). The term "psychologism," referring to the most extreme version, according to Edmund Husserl (1969), applies to "any interpretation which converts objectivities into something psychological in the proper sense" (169), that is, descriptions that attempt to "psychologize" experience.

The following is an example of the psychologist's fallacy. Using a psychological vocabulary to describe the first-person experience of an infant facing a mirror, Jacques Lacan popularized the term "mirror stage." The term, though associated with "Lacanian psychoanalysis," of course, comes from a psychological vocabulary; in fact, Lacan's biographer, Elizabeth Roudinesco, "despite her admiration for Lacan, accuses him of plagiarizing [the psychologist Henri] Wallon" (Billig 2006, 17). Lacan (2001), regarding the infant's joy and activity of leaning toward its mirror image, describes the experience's "meaning" in the following way:

> This meaning discloses a libidinal dynamism [...] as well as an ontological structure of the human world that accords with my reflections on paranoiac knowledge. We have only to understand the mirror stage *as an identification*, in the full sense that analysis gives to the term: namely, the transformation that takes place in the subject when he assumes an image [...]. This jubilant assumption of his specular image by the child [...] would seem to exhibit in an exemplary situation the symbolic matrix in which the I is precipitated in a primordial form, before it is objectified in the dialectic of identification with the other, and before language restores to it, in the universal, its function as subject. (2)

Notice, then, to the extent that one understands the infant's first-person encounter with the mirror in terms of Lacan's sophisticated "mirror stage" description, one commits the extreme form of the psychologist's fallacy, that is, psychologism. Commenting in this regard, Michael Billig

(2006) notes, "Lacan is explicit in his acceptance of psychologist' observations and his dismissal of their failures to appreciate what they observe" (11).

Consider the following from Ludwig Wittgenstein's (2009) *Philosophical Investigations*, which may be taken as a criticism of the psychologist's fallacy:

> Do I observe myself, then, and perceive that I am seeing or conscious? And why talk about observations at all? Why not simply say 'I perceive I am conscious'? – But what are the words 'I perceive' for here – why not say 'I am conscious'? But don't the words 'I perceive' here show that I am attending to my consciousness? – which is ordinarily not the case. – If so, then the sentence, 'I perceive I am conscious' does not say that I am conscious, but that my attention is focused in such-and-such a way [...] isn't it a particular experience that occasions my saying 'I am conscious again'? – *What* experience? In what situations do we say it? (§417)

Notice, Wittgenstein highlights the fact that even when the psychologist's vocabulary intuitively resonates with ordinary language, "psychological" features supposed to be aspects of experience require alterations to the first-person perspective to be part of experience; yet, such alteration produces an experience which is, thereby, not the same as the experience from the non-altered-first-person perspective.

To avoid this fallacy, one needs to ground arguments with claims that hold necessarily and universally (Scalambrino 2015). A truism since the time of Aristotle, a science cannot be based on that which is accidental. Thus, on the one hand, psychological development should not be necessarily based on the description of accidental events, which one may or may not experience. On the other hand, whether it is a third-person description of an event which is supposed to include a first-person perspective taking place in the event or a first-person perspective from the experience of an event, in order to avoid the relativity inherent in the psychologist's fallacy, the description must pertain to the event and the experience of the event with necessity and universality. Neither descriptions of experience based on subjective (avowedly "paranoic"-based in Lacan's case) judgments nor the occurrence of specific accidental-psychological events hold necessarily or universally regarding human psychology.

References

Billig, Michael. 2006. "Lacan's Misuse of Psychology." *Theory, Culture & Society* 23(4): 1–26.

Husserl, Edmund. 1969. *Formal and Transcendental Logic*, translated by D. Cairns. The Hague: Matinus Nijhoff.

James, William. 1890. *The Principles of Psychology*. New York, NY: Henry Holt.

Lacan, Jacques. *The Mirror Stage: Écrits, A Selection*, translated by A. Sheridan. London: Routledge.

Scalambrino, Frank. 2015. "Phenomenological Psychology." *Internet Encyclopedia of Philosophy*, June 1. http://www.iep.utm.edu/phen-psy/ (accessed September 28, 2017).

Wittgenstein, Ludwig. 2009. *Philosophical Investigations*, translated by G.E.M. Anscombe. London: Wiley-Blackwell.

43

Red Herring

Heather Rivera

> Ladies and gentlemen of this *supposed* jury, I have one final thing I want you to consider. Ladies and gentlemen, *this* is Chewbacca. Chewbacca is a Wookiee from the planet Kashyyyk. But Chewbacca *lives* on the planet Endor. Now think about it; *that does not make sense!* [...] If Chewbacca lives on Endor, you must acquit! The defense rests.
> Cartoon Johnny Cochran on *South Park*'s "Chef Aid"

A red herring (RH) is a distraction device and refers to an informal logical fallacy that detracts from the actual issue, allowing one to be sidetracked from what is actually happening and to draw a false conclusion. One origin of the term has to do with a police dog exercise in which policemen, while trying to discern the best trail-hunters, use strong-smelling red herring fishes in an attempt to throw dogs off the trail of a scent. So, when someone uses an RH, the claims and argument(s) she puts forward are the "red herrings" she uses to throw you off the "trail" of reasoning that would lead to another, probably more appropriate, conclusion altogether. One form of an RH looks something like this:

Step 1: Argument, issue, or topic A is presented by person 1.
Step 2: Person 2 introduces argument, issue, or topic B.
Step 3: Argument, issue, or topic A is abandoned altogether, like a dog going off trail in search of a red herring.

Bad Arguments: 100 of the Most Important Fallacies in Western Philosophy, First Edition.
Edited by Robert Arp, Steven Barbone, and Michael Bruce.
© 2019 John Wiley & Sons Ltd. Published 2019 by John Wiley & Sons Ltd.

This occurs on a daily basis when a reporter or journalist asks the typical politician a question related to one issue (complete with its associated argument), and the politician responds with a wholly different – but often compelling – issue (complete with its associated argument).

In the 2016 United States presidential election, RHs were flying wild! There was even an article written and published by the *Huffington Post* about how Hillary Clinton's nomination *itself* may be an RH. Anytime one of the two major candidates – Clinton and Donald Trump – were asked a direct question, they diverted and put the attention back on the other person. This even occurred at Clinton's nomination acceptance speech:

> America is once again at a moment of reckoning. Powerful forces are threatening to pull us apart. Bonds of trust and respect are fraying. And just as with our founders, there are no guarantees. It truly is up to us. We have to decide whether we all will work together so we all can rise together. (*Los Angeles Times* 2016a)

This entire speech is an RH, but this particular piece stuck out to me. She is using fear tactics to try to bond others together to rally around her. She uses the Founding Fathers to spark pride in the hearts of Americans and divert from not actually explaining what she plans to do. Then she tries to distract the listener by adding an uplifting message of working together to make things better for everyone, instead of addressing the millions in poverty and how she plans to fix the recession.

Most of Trump's acceptance speech was designed to distract the listener, too:

> What about our economy? Again, I will tell you the plain facts that have been edited out of your nightly news and your morning newspaper: Nearly 4 in 10 African American children are living in poverty, while 58% of African American youth are now not employed. Two million more Latinos are in poverty today than when President Obama took his oath of office less than eight years ago. Another 14 million people have left the workforce entirely.
>
> Household incomes are down more than $4,000 since the year 2000. That's 16 years ago. Our manufacturing trade deficit has reached an all-time high. Think of this, think of this: Our trade deficit is nearly $800 billion last year alone. We're gonna fix that. (*Los Angeles Times* 2016b)

While he seems to offer numbers to drive home "facts," what he is really doing is diverting the listener with what appear to be facts that stir up emotion. People think, "Yes, I am unemployed and in that pool of 14 million people you just mentioned. This candidate wants to help me!" All the while he never lays out a plan to explain how anything will be fixed! Now that the people listening to the speech are emotionally affected and distracted, they no longer expect a planned out explanation of how help is coming for them.

RHs can also be used as a literary device to steer readers off course such as in mystery novels like Perry Mason stories and, of course, Sherlock Holmes. Sir Arthur Conan Doyle's *Sherlock Holmes: The Hound of the Baskervilles* (1902) presents a classic example of an RH. The readers are diverted off the trail of the real murderer and start suspecting the escaped convict and Barrymore. In the end, however, the mystery is resolved by the unexpected confession of Beryl that her husband Stapleton was the real culprit and was behind the whole mystery of the killer hound.

In 1985, an RH was not only used in the film *Clue* but also mentioned by name as well. All the guests in the comedic murder mystery were told a story about how each one of them was tied to some kind of socialist connection; hence, why they were being blackmailed. In the big reveal of "whodunnit," the butler Wadsworth states, "Communism was just a red herring."

Other examples of an RH from common speech include:

DAUGHTER: I'm so hurt that Todd broke up with me.
MOTHER: Just think of all the starving children in Africa, honey. Your problems will seem pretty insignificant then.
MIKE: It is morally wrong to steal, why on earth would you have done that?
KEN: But what is morality exactly?
MIKE: It's a code of conduct shared by cultures.
KEN: But who creates this code?

How do you avoid the fallacy? Actually, the answer is very simple. When asked a question, devise a thought out answer that actually answers the question. Do not try to distract the listener, reader, or interviewer by throwing out information that will lead away from the original topic. When a meteorologist is asked about the rain, answering the questions about rain and not talking about last week's sunshine will avoid an RH. If I were to ask you what 5 plus 5 is and you tell me that Indian people actually invented the number zero, well then, you have distracted me from the question at hand. If a topic is proposed, and you can speak or write about it without departing from the initial trail, then you have successfully avoided an RH fallacy.

References

Clue. 1985. Directed by Jonathan Lynn. Paramount Pictures.
Doyle, Arthur Conan. 1902. *Sherlock Holmes: The Hound of Baskervilles*. London: George Newnes, Ltd.

Los Angeles Times. 2016a. "Hillary Clinton's Complete Convention Speech." July 28. http://www. latimes.com/politics/la-na-pol-hillary-clinton-convention-speech-transcript-20160728-snap-htmlstory.html (accessed September 28, 2017).

Los Angeles Times. 2016b. "Donald Trump's Complete Convention Speech." July 21. http://www. latimes.com/politics/la-na-pol-donald-trump-convention-speech-transcript-20160721-snap-htmlstory.html (accessed September 28, 2017).

44

Reductio ad Hitlerum

Frank Scalambrino

> Green themes like scarcity and purity and invasion and protection all have
> right-wing echoes. Hitler's ideas about environmentalism came out of purity,
> after all.
>
> Betsy Hartmann, "The Greening of Hate"

Reductio ad Hitlerum (RAH) is a species of the *reductio ad hominem* genre
of logically fallacious reasoning. Logically speaking, all of the various species
of *ad hominem* may be refuted by noting that "Just because X or an X said
it, doesn't mean it's false." In other words, we may dislike that Thomas
Jefferson owned slaves, however, his owning slaves does not make all of the
statements he ever made, thereby, false. Similarly, if on a Tuesday Adolf
Hitler noted that it was Tuesday, then we wouldn't say that just because
Hitler said it, it must not be Tuesday.

In this way, it is clear that *ad hominem* arguments, such as RAH, may be
understood as "fallacies of relevance." Yet because in some contexts such
claims may be relevant, the following helps clarify when RAH is logically
fallacious and when it is not. On the one hand, it is clear that the truth-value
of a claim may be understood in most cases as independent from the person
making the claim, that is, excluding various types of claims such as those
with reference to the person making the claim. On the other hand, in certain
social and political contexts, the character of the person making claims

Bad Arguments: 100 of the Most Important Fallacies in Western Philosophy, First Edition.
Edited by Robert Arp, Steven Barbone, and Michael Bruce.
© 2019 John Wiley & Sons Ltd. Published 2019 by John Wiley & Sons Ltd.

plays an intimate role in how one should reasonably relate to the possible truth-value of the claim. For example, when a politician or a potential mate makes promises regarding the future, if we associate the claim-maker with the perpetration of evil acts, a lack of integrity, and infidelity, then it would not be unreasonable to be suspicious of the truth-value of his statements, that is, promises, regarding the future. Yet, it is still true that being a wretched person does not determine the truth-value of the claims such a person may make.

The most notorious example of the RAH in philosophy is the association of Martin Heidegger with Hitler and the Nazi Party. Heidegger was, in fact, a member of the Nazi Party. Yet, logically speaking, the fact of his member-ship in the Nazi Party does not necessitate the falsehood of his philosophical claims. For example, Heidegger (1962) begins "Division Two" of *Being and Time* noting, "our existential analysis of Dasein up till now cannot lay claim to primordiality" (276). The truth-value of this statement does not depend on its author's relation to Hitler. Though, of course, we may find fault and think his membership in the Nazi Party to be blameworthy, the logical truth of his utterances is a separate question. Further, notice that Hitler rose to power in 1933; Heidegger's *magnum opus, Sein und Zeit (Being and Time)* was first published in 1927 and was famously dedicated to Heidegger's Jewish colleague and friend Edmund Husserl.

Tom Rockmore not only associates Heidegger's philosophy with Nazism, he also associates the study of philosophy itself with Nazism in a kind of chain argument from the Heidegger-Nazi identification to the Heidegger-philosopher identification, and ultimately to the "philosophical discipline" itself (1991, 1995). In the general and abstract, of course, the chain argument looks straightforward; however, if we add particular content to the argu-ment, then the fallaciousness of its *reductio* emerges. For example, on the one hand, Heidegger famously criticized the worldview associated with French philosopher René Descartes. On the other hand, there are many different historical instances, subjects considered, and approaches taken in regard to the "philosophical discipline" other than those in which Heidegger participated. Yet, the RAH makes it seem as though philosophically criti-quing the Cartesian worldview or providing proofs of valid inference in a formal logic course would be tantamount to being desirous of perpetrating the Holocaust. Thus, the logical question regarding the truth-value of Heidegger's philosophical claims is separate from the moral question of whether actions perpetrated by "Nazis," or in the name of "Nazism," were evil. Insofar as any murdering of innocent people is evil, then by most accounts those actions were obviously evil.

Originating in regard to the ignorant and routine nature of many online "postings" and "chat room" conversations involving such specific *ad hominem* arguments as RAH, some have suggested a rule that whenever someone first resorts to making a comparison to Hitler or the Nazis in an argument, the argument should be considered over, and the Nazi reference maker considered to have forfeited the argument. Ultimately, in order to avoid this fallacy, we should keep our feelings regarding a person separate from our understanding of the truth-value of the claims she makes.

References

Heidegger, Martin. 1962. *Being and Time*, translated by J. Macquarrie and E. Robinson. New York, NY: Harper & Row.

Rockmore, Tom. 1991. *On Heidegger's Nazism and Philosophy*. Berkeley, CA: University of California Press.

Rockmore, Tom. 1995. *Heidegger and French Philosophy: Humanism, Antihumanism and Being*. London: Routledge.

45

Argument by Repetition

Leigh Kolb

There's a woman in Chicago. She has 80 names, 30 addresses, 12 Social Security cards [...]. She's got Medicaid, getting food stamps, and she is collecting welfare under each of her names. Her tax-free cash income alone is over $150,000.

> Ronald Reagan's 1976 campaign, the birth of the "Welfare Queen"

An argument by repetition (ABR; also known as *ad nauseam* or *ad infinitum*) is a fallacy by which the speaker uses the same word, phrase, story, or imagery repeatedly with the hopes that the repetition will lead to persuasion. According to *Nonsense: A Handbook of Logical Fallacies*, this fallacy is a form of propaganda: "The propagandist says something over and over again. He may use different words each time, but it's the same point. The theory is that if you say something often enough, people will eventually believe you" (Gula 2002, 23).

Often seen in politics, the ABR about the "Welfare Queen" who assumes different identities, has numerous children, and abuses the welfare system while raking in the cash, is an argument that has permeated the last few decades of political and social discourse about government welfare programs. The narrative of the Welfare Queen, which Ronald Reagan began telling in his 1976 campaign, is a story that weaves together three criminals' stories into one symbol of a woman (assumed to be African American)

Bad Arguments: 100 of the Most Important Fallacies in Western Philosophy, First Edition.
Edited by Robert Arp, Steven Barbone, and Michael Bruce.
© 2019 John Wiley & Sons Ltd. Published 2019 by John Wiley & Sons Ltd.

who cheats the system. Kaaryn Gustafson, author of *Cheating Welfare: Public Assistance and the Criminalization of Poverty*, says, "It's one of those persistent symbols that come up every election cycle" (quoted in Blake 2012).

In a *Nieman Reports* study of audience reactions to images in the media – specifically African American mothers on welfare – Franklin D. Gilliam (1999) stated:

> My assumption going into this study was that the notion of the welfare queen had taken on the status of common knowledge, or what is known as a 'narrative script.' The welfare queen script has two key components – welfare recipients are disproportionately women, and women on welfare are disproportionately African-American.

He found that this story had direct effects on audiences' perceptions about who receives welfare and their hostility about government social programs.

Pulitzer Prize-winning reporter David Zucchino wrote *The Myth of the Welfare Queen*, a portrait of welfare mothers in Philadelphia. He found that the "image of the big-spending, lavish-living, Cadillac-driving welfare queen was by then thoroughly embedded in American folklore," and it had a direct effect on people's perceptions of welfare and, in turn, on the recipients themselves (quoted in Gilliam 1999).

While the repetition of this story centers around the "welfare queen," its repetition in politics has taken other forms: "entitlement society," "handouts," "food stamp president" are all loaded terms that are the natural bedfellows of the folklore of the "welfare queen." Gustafson says, "This image of the lazy African-American woman who refuses to get a job and keeps having kids is pretty enduring. It's always been a good way to distract the public from any meaningful conversations about poverty and inequality" (quoted in Blake 2012). ABR controls the script by repeating the script, and it often distracts audiences in the process.

In *The New York Times*, Paul Krugman (2013) examines how voters have completely skewed views of the deficit because politicians typically mislead the public about the real numbers. He says, "Am I saying that voters are stupid? Not at all. People have lives, jobs, children to raise. They're not going to sit down with Congressional Budget Office reports. Instead, they rely on what they hear from authority figures. The problem is that much of what they hear is misleading if not outright false." If they keep hearing repetitive "falsehoods," they will believe them. He says that "In Stephen Colbert's famous formulation, claims about runaway deficits may not be true, but they have truthiness, and that's all that matters." *Truthiness* (which was voted the 2005 Word of the Year by the American Dialect Society) is Colbert's term that means "the quality of preferring concepts or facts one wishes to be true, rather than concepts or facts known to be true." This concept is key to how ABR is a pervasive propaganda technique.

ABR takes many forms: jingles for advertising shampoo, phrases politicians use to evoke fear or gain favor, and narratives to malign – or even kill – certain groups of people. Adolf Hitler's Big Lie technique in *Mein Kampf* extols the usefulness of this technique in swaying masses of people. Hitler and his Propaganda Minister, Joseph Goebbels, utilized this Big Lie technique to repeat the narrative of an "International Jewry," which launched World War I to kill all Germans; this repeated lie helped turn cultural anti-Semitism into the Holocaust, as many would argue (Herf 2006, 3). On a meta note, the phrase "If you repeat a lie often enough, people will believe it, and you will even come to believe it yourself" was attributed to Goebbels in the *Publications Relating to Various Aspects of Communism (1946)*, by United States Congress, House Committee on Un-American Activities; however, no source has ever been located. The phrase is consistently seen attributed to him, and so, by repetition, it's believed to be his.

In "The Truth Behind The Lies Of The Original 'Welfare Queen'" on *NPR*, Gene Demby (2013) examines the real woman whose life inspired the "Welfare Queen" myth. Her name was Linda Taylor, and her crimes were intricate and complicated, as was her race (she identified as white, African American, and Asian throughout her tumultuous life). Demby refers to Josh Levin's investigative story at *Slate* that delves into her crimes and her distracting and disingenuous legacy. She was associated with stealing babies and murdering a woman, but the single story about her that has permeated public opinion about public assistance is that her abuse of the welfare system represented the majority of recipients of welfare. Levin writes, "Linda Taylor's story shows that there are real costs associated with this kind of panic, a moral climate in which stealing welfare money takes precedence over kidnapping and homicide" (quoted in Demby 2013). She was a complicated criminal, yet the repetitive fictionalized story turned into a political beacon that drastically shaped public opinion.

Speakers and writers often fall back on arguments that are familiar and resonate with audiences on an emotional level. The familiarity of these stories or phrases (no matter how mythological or intentionally misleading) makes for an ultimately lazy and dangerous form of rhetoric that relies on a lack of critical thought on the audience's part. Arguments can only be solid and meaningful if they do not rely on repetitive narratives to sway a passive audience. It's worth pointing out that repetition can be artfully used in spoken rhetoric (think of Martin Luther King, Jr.'s "I Have a Dream" speech). The rhythm of repeated phrases serves to add a literary, persuasive quality to the speech; however, it's not used to mislead or distract. To avoid the logical fallacy of ABR, writers and speakers must ensure that their rhetoric is truthful and logical and use varied and complex illustrations that take into account multiple perspectives. Considering and acknowledging the complexity of an argument is always preferable to relying on the same one-dimensional narratives and stereotypes.

ABR seeks to convince an audience not by facts or logic but by the psychological and emotional power of repetition. Argument *ad nauseam* refers to this repetition to the point of exhaustion, or literally, nausea. Repeating words, phrases, narratives, and images are a powerful – but fallacious – propaganda technique to sway an audience.

References

Blake, John. 2012. "Return of the 'Welfare Queen.'" *CNN*, January 23. http://www. cnn.com/2012/01/23/politics/weflare-queen/ (accessed September 28, 2017).

Colbert, Stephen. 2005. "The Word – Truthiness." *The Colbert Report*, Comedy Central. October 17. http://www.cc.com/video-clips/63ite2/the-colbert-report-the-word---truthiness (accessed September 28, 2017).

Demby, Gene. 2013. "The Truth Behind The Lies Of The Original 'Welfare Queen.'" *NPR*, December 20. http://www.npr.org/sections/codeswitch/2013/12/20/255819681/ the-truthbehind-the-lies-of-the-original-welfare-queen (accessed September 28, 2017).

Gilliam, Franklin. 1999. "The 'Welfare Queen' Experiment." *Nieman Reports*, June 15. http://niemanreports.org/articles/the-welfare-queen-experiment/ (accessed September 28, 2017).

Gula, Robert. 2002. *Nonsense: A Handbook of Logical Fallacies*. Mount Jackson, VA: Axios Press.

Herf, Jeffrey. 2006. *The Jewish Enemy: Nazi Propaganda during World War II and the Holocaust*. Cambridge, MA: Harvard University Press.

King, Martin Luther, Jr. 1963. "I Have a Dream …" https://www.archives.gov/press/ exhibits/dream-speech.pdf (accessed September 28, 2017).

Krugman, Paul. 2013. "Moment of Truthiness." *The New York Times*, August 15. http://www.nytimes.com/2013/08/16/opinion/krugman-moment-of-truthiness. html?_r=0 (accessed September 28, 2017).

46

Special Pleading

Dan Yim

> I think it is disgusting, shameful, and damaging to all things American. But if
> I were twenty-two with a great body, it would be artistic, tasteful, patriotic,
> and a progressive, religious experience.
>
> Shelley Winters, on the topic of posing nude

One way to grasp the meaning of the special pleading fallacy is to focus on
a general principle of fairness: We ought to treat individuals alike unless
there is some relevant difference between them that merits the differential
treatment. If there is no relevant difference between individuals, it would be
unfair to treat them in dissimilar ways, especially if the differential treatment conferred a benefit on one, punished the other, or both.

Notice that the principle is consistent with justified differential treatment
of two individuals. Different treatment can be merited if there is a relevant
difference between the two that makes the differential treatment sensible.
For example, suppose that a university is downsizing and is going to make
redundant one of two untenured professors, and that these two professors
are alike in all respects except that one has a good publication record and
the other does not. The difference in publication record is justifiably a relevant difference that would merit differential treatment by the university's
retaining the one and terminating the other. Because the different treatment
is explained by a relevant difference between the two candidates, rewarding

Bad Arguments: 100 of the Most Important Fallacies in Western Philosophy, First Edition.
Edited by Robert Arp, Steven Barbone, and Michael Bruce.
© 2019 John Wiley & Sons Ltd. Published 2019 by John Wiley & Sons Ltd.

one professor with continued employment but not the other is consistent with the principle of fairness.

In argumentation and logical reasoning, there is also a corollary fairness principle:

> Principle of fairness*: We ought to subject competing arguments or perspectives to the same rules of assessment unless there is some relevant difference between them that merits the differential treatment.

The principle states that when we evaluate the rational credentials of two competing claims and their arguments, we should apply the same standards of assessment to both sets of arguments. If the arguments are deductive, then we should evaluate them for validity and soundness using the same standards. If the arguments are inductive, then we should evaluate them for cogency and strength using the same standards. This is rational fair play.

Now take the following example of irrational and unfair play. Suppose two sides are arguing about global climate change and presenting competing arguments about whether human action is a major contributing factor. Side A and Side B agree that it is a general virtue of premises and arguments that they should be self-consistent (i.e., they should neither contain nor imply contradictions). When Side A is made aware of internal inconsistencies in its data and evidence sets, Side A replies that these particular inconsistencies are excusable because the scientists who produced the results are upstanding persons of high moral character. Side A therefore claims an exemption from the general rule about argumentative and evidential self-consistency. The claimed exemption in this case is based on the moral fiber of the scientists on Side A. Notice that even if we grant the high moral caliber of scientists on both sides, this feature of Side A is irrelevant. It is not a rationally relevant consideration or difference that merits the exemption of Side A from the general rule. In fact, it is highly unlikely that Side A would grant the same exception to Side B if the tables were turned. Yet Side A claims the exemption anyway.

This is logically suspicious behavior, and we have a name for it: special pleading (SP). As Morris Engel (1976) explains in *With Good Reason*, "To engage in special pleading is to be partial and inconsistent. It is to regard one's own situation as privileged while failing to apply to others the standard we set for ourselves (or, conversely, failing to apply to ourselves those standards we apply to others)" (192). SP involves breaking rules of fair play, usually in a way that benefits the rule-breaker, and hence can be thought of as a form of argumentative cheating by applying a double standard. Notice that Side A affirms the standards of consistency and believes them to be a virtue of argumentation. It is just that Side A applies those standards only to Side B and then either refuses to abide by those same rules or claims a special exemption that is in fact unjustified.

While SP is most clearly illustrated in the context of two competing, discrete arguments and an explicit, unjustified application of an evidential double standard, this informal fallacy also occurs in simpler, colloquial contexts that apply double standards in the choice of words. Consider these:

> I like to think of myself as firm and steadfast in my beliefs. Others, however, are inflexible and pigheaded.
> Horses sweat; men perspire; women glow.
> We are freedom fighters – the enemy, terrorists.
> We are planners; they are schemers.

In these cases, the double standard is clear in that the very same behavior or feature is either excusable or even admirable in one case but not so in the other, with no evidence presented that there is a relevant difference that would justify the different treatment. In fact, there might even be some relevant differences, but the point of the fallacy is that such evidence is either missing or simply not presented.

SP occurs also in contexts other than pure arguments or colloquial wordplay. Consider that in the past decade in the field of sports media, it has become common for women to appear as professional reporters and commentators on sidelines and as co-anchors in televised commentary studios for the NFL and NBA – career arenas that have traditionally been the domain of men only. One of the criticisms that women in these positions have faced is that many of them lack firsthand athletic experience in those sports – the implication being that such a lack disqualifies them from these kinds of jobs. It often goes uncommented that many of the men who are both successful and popular sports anchors also lack that very experience. In their cases, however, they receive the benefit of an unjustified, "special" indulgence while the other group receives disproportional scrutiny. The fact that SP can be, and so often is, used simultaneously to hide and to underwrite hypocrisy and prejudice makes it an important informal fallacy of reasoning that affects everyday life.

Avoiding SP can be very difficult for two reasons. First, the fallacy takes so many forms. It can appear in the form of an explicit double standard in the assessment of competing arguments. It can appear in the usage of biased language that is designed to convey that bias to the reader or listener. It can also appear in professional practices such as employment and promotion. Second, SP can be difficult to avoid because it is often invisible to the one who commits the fallacy, and in this respect it is like a bad, invisible cognitive habit.

The most explicit form of SP is in the application of double standards to arguments. It takes great effort to change a bad habit, even an explicit one. In fact, it may take a few different strategies. First, one might commit to acquiring knowledge about logical fallacies, such as what one does when consulting a book such as this. Buy and read more books on logic (and recommend this one to friends)! Second, one might begin to introduce new cognitive behaviors into one's argumentative repertoire.

When one is raising a criticism about another view or argument, one should practice a procedure of rational fair play. Explicitly ask, "Is my competing claim or position susceptible to the same or similar critique? Do I pass the very test that I am subjecting my rival to?" This is not a natural behavior for most people. This is why it will likely be the sort of thing that one does through an artificial-feeling rule of behavior, such as when very small children are taught by rote to utter the words "Thank you" as a way of creating a habit of politeness. But this artificial rule of behavior, if repeated over time, can become two things. First, it can become an avenue for a person self-consciously to begin to think about rational fairness. Second, it can initiate the process through which a person actually becomes more fair-minded in her character and cognitive habits. In that respect, the rule is like practicing musical scales for a musician or practicing free throws for a basketball player. Eventually, the behavior can become a fluid habit that feels natural to the musician or athlete. Similarly, practicing fair-mindedness can over time become a sustainable virtue of cognitive character to replace the vice of SP.

Reference
Engel, S.M. 1976. *With Good Reason*. New York, NY: St. Martin's Press.

47

Straw Man

Scott Aikin and John Casey

> The argument for Hillary Clinton was never quite made at the convention, at least other than the fallback that their Trump is purportedly a worse crook and a bigger liar than our Hillary.
>
> Victor Davis Hanson

How one can straw man someone's view or argument happens in a variety of ways. We will focus here on three. The first is the *representational* straw man fallacy. What one does here is represent the opponent's views in worse or less defensible form than that given by the opponent. Consider the way *Salon.com*'s Sophia Tesfaye (2015) represents Ben Carson's claims about guns in schools. Carson, on ABC's *The View*, makes the following statement:

> If I had a little kid in kindergarten somewhere I would feel much more comfortable if I knew on that campus there was a police officer or somebody who was trained with a weapon. [...] If the teacher was trained in the use of that weapon and had access to it, I would be much more comfortable if they had one than if they didn't.

Tesfaye's headline to report what Carson said was, "Carson wants kindergarten teachers to be armed." The force of the headline is that Carson is making a policy proposal and positively *wants*, as opposed to *prefers*, armed

---

Bad Arguments: 100 of the Most Important Fallacies in Western Philosophy, First Edition.
Edited by Robert Arp, Steven Barbone, and Michael Bruce.
© 2019 John Wiley & Sons Ltd. Published 2019 by John Wiley & Sons Ltd.

kindergarten teachers. One may still reasonably disagree with Carson on the matter, but the disagreement needn't now be with someone so extreme.

The second form of the straw man fallacy is that of the *selectional* straw man, or better *the weak man*. In this case, instead of distorting an opponent's view for the worse, one simply finds the worst representative of the opposition and takes that to represent the entire group. One cherry-picks opponents, and the results are, ultimately, men of straw. Consider the way many reacted when a man at a Donald Trump (who was also at the time a candidate for the 2016 Republican nomination for president) rally said: "We have a problem in this country. It's called Muslims. You know our President is one. You know he's not even an American." Trump's reply was that, "We are going to be looking at that and many other things." The criticism of the exchange led Debbie Wasserman Schultz (the Chair of the Democratic National Committee) to say: "Racism knows no bounds. This is certainly horrendous but unfortunately unsurprising, given what we have seen already. The vile rhetoric coming from the GOP candidates is appalling" (De Graaf 2015).

But it is too quick to say that the Republican base is Islamophobic and racist on the basis of this. In fact, many Trump supporters at the rally recoiled in disgust when the man asked Trump the question and again when Trump failed to set him straight. One particularly bad and indefensible version of Republican support and ardor needn't be representative of the entire party's support.

The third and final type of straw man fallacy is what we'll call the *hollow man*. One does not take any particular opponent's view and distort it but rather one just invents a ridiculous view for one's opponents whole cloth. Consider how *National Review* columnist Dennis Praeger (2015) portrays the position of 'The Left' on gun control. It comes down to three things that he maintains are behind their commitment:

> The Left believes in relying on the state as much as possible. [...] The Left is uncomfortable with blaming bad people for bad actions. [...] The Left is more likely to ask "Does it feel good?"

For Praeger, the gun control debate really comes down to having to answer people who want government-dependent, irresponsible, hedonists for citizens. Of course the debate won't look very good when your opponents are so depraved.

Notice that straw manning requires a form of misrepresentation of the overall intellectual situation in an area of dispute. The speaker, the one who straw mans, must portray the opposition in an untoward light. This requires, then, an audience that must not know better. That is, if the audience for a straw man argument knows that there are better versions of the view available, then the argument will not work on it. And so straw man arguments depend on their audience's being generally unfamiliar with the issue or at least with the opposing view on the issue.

This fact, that straw manning depends on audience ignorance, is significant. This is because with straw manning, not only is a conclusion established fallaciously, but a picture of the opposition is painted in a way that yields intellectual contempt. A result of this picture of the opposition as incompetent or mendacious is that one is less likely to want to engage honestly with them in further discussion. And as a consequence, we see the polarization of discourse on matters of significance. Straw man arguments not only produce bad argumentative results at the times they are given, but they have lasting repercussions on the communities they convince.

What makes straw manning fallacious is that one is not responding to the better reasons of one's opponents. And when one does not reply to the better versions, the argument does not cover the intellectual ground it should. Issues are left unanswered, we gain no better understanding of the matter, and the sides are made more polarized by the exchange.

How does one avoid and correct straw man fallacies? Given that the fallacy depends primarily on the fact that the audience is unfamiliar with the views and arguments of the opposition, the best prevention is simply being informed about the variety of views on an issue. This means that one should, when being presented with a criticism of a view, be familiar with the case for the view made by those who hold it. And so when criticism of the American Civil Liberties Union's defense of privacy rights is brought forth, one should be familiar with its reasons, not just the ones that the critics attribute to them. Or when the National Rifle Association is a target for critique on protecting Second Amendment rights, one should go to them for their reasons, not to their critics. This means that one should read widely, watch the news shows from the opposing viewpoint, and have conversations with those who disagree. Straw manning depends on us being unaware of a misrepresentation of opponents, and the only way to detect that is to know what the correct representation is.

References

De Graaf, Mia. 2015. "Outrage as Donald Trump Fails to Correct Ignorant Supporter." *The Daily Mail*, September 17. http://www.dailymail.co.uk/news/article-3239373/ Outrage-Donald-Trump-fails-correct-ignorant-supporter-stood-said-President-Obama-Muslim-not-American-live-Q-A.html#ixzz4IDsBJcpt (accessed September 29, 2017).

Praeger, Dennis. 2015. "Differences Between Left and Right: It's All about Big Government." *National Review*, July 7. http://www.nationalreview.com/article/ 420820/differences-between-left-and-right-its-all-about-big-government-dennis-prager (accessed September 29, 2017).

Tesfaye, Sophia. 2015. "Carson Wants Kindergarten Teachers to Be Armed." *Salon. com*, October 7. http://www.salon.com/2015/10/07/ben_carson_is_just_this_ vile_5_repugnant_ statement_hes_made_since_the_oregon_mass_shooting/ (accessed September 29, 2017).

48

Sunk Cost

Robert Arp

I don't think it would benefit either one of us to give up on this relationship yet because we've both invested so much of ourselves into it already...
Form letter, "Please Forgive Me. (This Relationship Is Worth Saving!)"

In economics, a *sunk cost* is an investment that can never be recovered. Prime examples include money spent on research and development or advertising for a product. However, there's a way to think of *cost* in terms of time, energy, and even emotion, as is hinted at in the quotation above.

In the first few pages of his insightful article titled "The Sunk Cost 'Fallacy' Is Not a Fallacy," Ryan Doody (2013) gives a rough description of the sunk cost fallacy as allowing the reality of unrecoverable costs to influence your current (or future) decision-making about an investment in such a way that the sunk costs legitimize the investment, no matter if the investment is a good or a bad one. The general form of this fallacy looks something like this:

(1) <u>Costs have been sunk into X.</u>
(2) X is worth further investment.

Not only is there no *logical* connection between *past* unrecoverable costs and decisions about *current* (or *future*) investment, but there is also a clear

Bad Arguments: 100 of the Most Important Fallacies in Western Philosophy, First Edition. Edited by Robert Arp, Steven Barbone, and Michael Bruce.
© 2019 John Wiley & Sons Ltd. Published 2019 by John Wiley & Sons Ltd.

"you're fooling yourself" or "you're rationalizing" element to the fallacy because the sunk cost itself emotionally taints rational, objective thought concerning the worth of the investment. Thus, in a certain sense, this fallacy epitomizes poor reasoning – you continue to make bad investments because you fear losing what was already invested. Doody lays out three common examples:

(1)   You buy a non-refundable ticket to the opera, but you really don't want to go on the night of the performance; yet, you go anyway reasoning that you spent money on the ticket and "it'll be a waste of money" if you don't go.
(2)   You devote many years of your life to a certain job – climbing the corporate ladder, so to speak – but now you're unhappy with the career path; yet, you stay in that job and are miserable, figuring that you invested so much time and energy in the career and "it'll be a waste of career investment" if you leave that career.
(3)   A nation allots a ton of money for its military to fight a war, loses many of its soldiers in the fight, and there's even a general belief in the nation that the war is unwinnable; yet, the legislative body in the nation continues to allow the war to be funded.

Many would argue that this last example resonates with the United States' commitment to the Vietnam conflict in the 1960s and 1970s and to the war in Iraq in the 2000s, where sunk costs in terms of dollars spent and lives lost were used to justify continued involvement.

The fallacy is also known as the Concorde fallacy, referring to the production of the first supersonic airplane, the design of which had heating, pressurization, and structural problems, among others. The project was predicted to fail in reports of prototypes early on in the 1950s and 1960s, but after having sunk an incredible amount of money, time, and "blood, sweat, and tears" into the project, key folks involved kept pushing forward and they didn't want to just give up. In David McRaney's (2013) words, "their shared investment built a hefty psychological burden that outweighed their better judgments" (233). Concorde was retired in 2003.

The way to avoid this fallacy is to not allow the fear of losing what was already invested in something to influence your rational, objective decision about a present or future investment. In Eric Nielsen's (2005) words, when making any decision, economic or otherwise, it "makes no sense to factor in sunk costs precisely because they are sunk; no present action can change them. No matter what happens, the sunk costs are always there."

References

Doody, Ryan. 2013. "The Sunk Cost 'Fallacy' Is Not a Fallacy," MIT Department of Philosophy, November 1. www.mit.edu/~rdoody/TheSunkCostFallacy.pdf (accessed September 29, 2017).

McRaney, David. 2013. *You Can Beat Your Brain*. New York, NY: OneWorld.

Nielsen, Eric. 2005. "Jargon Alert: Sunk Costs." Federal Reserve Bank of Richmond, January 15. https://www.richmondfed.org/~/media/richmondfedorg/publications/research/region_focus/2005/winter/pdf/jargon_alert.pdf (accessed September 29, 2017).

49

Two Wrongs Make a Right

David LaRocca

> Two wrongs don't make a right, but they make a good excuse.
> Thomas Szasz, *The Second Sin*

If the notion that "two wrongs make a right" is false – perhaps because it is a fallacy – then it would seem that a hallmark trait of thinking in Western civilization, and a guiding *ethos* from Hebraic antiquity, is predicated on a mistake in reasoning. We must, needless to say, take a closer look.

Let's begin with the calculus of the claim by rendering it this way: 2 wrongs = 1 right. Or put another way: 1 wrong + 1 wrong = 1 right. At first blush, the math seems to suggest a double negative in which 2 negatives equal 1 positive (as in "I'm not not hungry"). Part of the confusion about how to write the claim stems from the fact that its obverse is also prevalent and regularly invoked, namely, "Two wrongs *don't* make a right." This bromide is frequently told to the young, for instance, as a hedge against striking back at a playground bully. In short, the child is assured that committing a wrongful action is not an ethically suitable approach for responding to a *prior* wrongful action; the slugger's strike doesn't create the conditions for the child to become a (justified) slugger himself. Two wrongs *making* a right, however, is a different claim altogether and our focus here.

If the notion that "two wrongs make a right" seems familiar, but also peculiarly stated, it may be owing to the fact that we more often hear it in

Bad Arguments: 100 of the Most Important Fallacies in Western Philosophy, First Edition.
Edited by Robert Arp, Steven Barbone, and Michael Bruce.
© 2019 John Wiley & Sons Ltd. Published 2019 by John Wiley & Sons Ltd.

other, more commonly rendered forms. For example, the most famous ancient instances of the sentiment appear in the Code of Hammurabi and later in Exodus, Deuteronomy, and Leviticus (24:19–21), where it is written:

> And if a man cause a blemish in his neighbour; as he hath done, so shall it be done to him. Breach for breach, eye for eye, tooth for tooth: as he hath caused a blemish in a man, so shall it be done to him again. And he that killeth a beast, he shall restore it: and he that killeth a man, he shall be put to death.

Originally a method to align compensation accurately with the amount of one's loss (hence the emphasis on equivalency $1 = 1$; eye = eye – and coverage of everything from bodily injury to loss of property), Roman law later evolved the notion into *lex talionis*. Today we have inherited this kind of vengeful retaliation – the sort that aims to "even things up" – with theories and practices of retributive justice.

Retributive justice, despite its largely sanitized form in contemporary society (since one does not personally undertake retribution but lets the state do it), retains the core idea that justice can be achieved by the extraction of some quantity of something, such as time. A murderer kills an innocent person; instead of being killed himself, say, by the victim's heirs (where, as Leviticus would want it, the equivalency would be even), he is incarcerated by the state, perhaps for life. In this way, "taking his life" (by taking away his freedom) is translated, or becomes a metaphor for, killing him. Debates about the death penalty are fundamentally debates about the *literalness* of retribution: is justice done *only if* the one who kills is also himself killed? Can the victim's heirs achieve justice if the death is repaid "merely" with the murderer's incarceration time?

But let's say the murderer (of an innocent person) is himself put to death. Then we have a scenario that depicts the math rehearsed earlier: 1 person killed (the innocent) + 1 person killed (the murderer). (Though again, it is likely to be the state that kills the murderer, not the victim's heirs.) Yet what do these deaths (1 for 1) *equal*? If they equal justice and right, then the claim "two wrongs make a right" is sound and not fallacious. But insofar as it is difficult to determine that these two deaths amount to justice or confirm right, then there is a significant danger that a fallacy has been committed.

From Babylon to the Bible and beyond to the present day, it's clear that much of Western civilization has sanctioned, codified, and reified the idea that the way to right a wrong is to commit another wrong (of *at least* equivalent scope). If this is the case, and all signs suggest it is, then much of Western religion *and* moral philosophy (ethics) is predicated on a fallacy, if this be one. And if it is indeed a fallacy, then the discovery becomes a referendum on and indictment of millennia of Western moral, legal, and religious values. To say "two wrongs *do not* make a right" – namely, that its antithesis is a fallacy – necessarily implies a wholesale condemnation of retributive justice.

In recent centuries, petitioners have developed the countermanding theory of *restorative* justice to expose the fallacious thinking (and "logic") at the heart of retributive justice by focusing not on the extraction of compensation in terms of money, time, or life (from the offender) but in terms of mutual understanding (between offender and victim and within the community they share). With restorative justice the aim is, insofar as it is possible, that both parties – the murderer and the victim's heirs – are meant to achieve some kind of healing and consolation. Selective emphasis has made it seem that Babylonian, Hebraic, and Roman law exclusively focused on retribution, but this is not so. The Code of Hammurabi, the Pentateuch, and the Twelve Tables all reflect models and measures of restorative justice.

In the realm of fallacies, the present one is described as "informal" mainly because – despite what seems a nearly mathematic equation – the error in thinking is not a matter of logic per se but of reasoning. Pushing the claim into other territories shows how we are dealing with matters of relative persuasiveness. For instance, "two wrongs make a right" is commonly invoked in economic matters, such as cheating or thievery: stealing money from the bank is a wrong, but, the robber claims, so is the bank's policy of charging high interest rates (viz., analogized here to be another form of stealing); hence, the literal stealing is treated as equivalent to usury (believed to be a sort of metaphorical stealing), and so the two acts cancel one another out. Hegel, of course, noted long ago that if you believe in private property, it's illogical to steal. The bank robber's equivalency introduces a red herring (see Chapter 43) that distracts from his faulty equivalency and evident equivocation.

Likewise in the realm of lying. If a politician lies under oath (and is caught), then her appeal to *other* politicians who have lied (and perhaps not been punished) will draw on the history of the *tu quoque* fallacy (or "you, also"). Her implied defense is that because other politicians have lied, it is hypocritical of her *accusers* to hold her accountable when the other politicians have not been. To be sure, *tu quoque* (see Chapter 11) is a red herring (see Chapter 43) and also an *ad hominem* (since the lying politician must malign the character of others in a similar situation; see Chapter 10).

Victor Lasky has pointed out in *It Didn't Start with Watergate* (1977) that if immoral acts are not prosecuted, then legal precedent may be set and future transgressors should expect to escape punishment as well. Lasky focused on the uneven prosecution of wiretapping (e.g., Kennedy's use without punishment, and Nixon's, which led to his impeachment). Such presumed analogical defenses – if Kennedy got away with it, so should Nixon – can be tallied from many directions: as the citizens of Israel were, historically, the victims of Nazi mistreatment, is present-day Israel justified in its alleged mistreatment of Palestinians? Since innocent noncombatants were attacked and killed on 9/11, does this violation provide justification for the United States to carry out global military operations that achieve the same result (and through a range of methods from "enhanced interrogation" to drones to the instantiation and renewal of the Authorization for Use of Military Force)?

These and related questions *presume* that retaliation – as a form of score-settling or as defense against future harm – is justified (morally, legally, and logically). But the essentially rhetorical nature of the claim, "Two wrongs make a right," assures us that no such logic is in place, and worse, that the so-called justifications for committing wrongful acts are not derived from a rigorous calculus (as the claim wishes to convey) but rather through blunt insistence.

Reference

Lasky, Victor. 1977. *It Didn't Start with Watergate*. New York: Dial Press.

50

Weak Analogy

Bertha Alvarez Manninen

> The eye appears to have been designed; no designer of telescopes could have done better. How could this marvelous instrument have evolved by chance, through a succession of random events? Many people in Darwin's day agreed with theologian William Paley, who commented, "There cannot be a design without a designer."
>
> Robert Jastrow (in *Life—How Did It Get Here?*)

Appeal to analogies can be a successful tool when constructing strong arguments. Typically, arguments from analogy look something like this:

(1) Example X is relevantly similar to example Y.
(2) <u>P follows from X.</u>
(3) Therefore, P follows from Y.

Whether or not an argument from analogy is strong depends on whether premise 1 is true – that is, are X and Y sufficiently and relevantly similar so that you can infer that P follows from Y just because P follows from X. The focus, therefore, should be on the *reasons* P follows from X and whether those reasons also apply to Y. As Patrick Hurley writes, the weak analogy fallacy "occurs when the conditions of an argument depend on an analogy

Bad Arguments: 100 of the Most Important Fallacies in Western Philosophy, First Edition.
Edited by Robert Arp, Steven Barbone, and Michael Bruce.
© 2019 John Wiley & Sons Ltd. Published 2019 by John Wiley & Sons Ltd.

(or similarity) that is not strong enough to support the conclusion" (Hurley 2008, 716). In the citation above, Paley argues that the creation of human artifacts is sufficiently similar to the creation of human organisms (and to the universe in general, as he argues in his 1802 work, *Natural Theology*) to infer the existence of a creator. As we shall see below, philosopher David Hume has given reasons to think arguments of this sort commit the weak analogy fallacy.

Often, vegetarians and vegans will hear the following argument from analogy in defense of carnivorism: "Animals eat each other in nature, so it's permissible for us to eat them as well." The logical structure of this retort to vegetarianism is:

(1)   Animals eat each other in nature (example X).
(2)   Carnivores eat animals (example Y).
(3)   <u>It is permissible for animals to eat each other in nature (P follows from X).</u>
(4)   Therefore, it is permissible for us to eat animals (P follows from Y).

In order for this argument to be successful, there must be relevant similarities between animals' eating each other in nature and humans' eating animals in our industrialized world. What we find, however, is that there are very few similarities and many more dissimilarities. While both humans and animals do indeed eat other animals for nutrition, *unlike* animals in nature, humans have plenty of other options for adequate nutrition that do not involve eating sentient creatures. Moreover, factory farming entails much more suffering for the animal than a quick death at the jaws of a predator and has detrimental health and environmental implications not present when animals hunt each other. Finally, we do not typically look to animals for moral guidance – male lions, when taking over a pride, will kill the cubs of the previous male lion in order to breed with the lionesses, but we wouldn't use this example to justify a step-father killing his step-children. Clearly, then, this is an example of the weak analogy fallacy.

In the quotation above, Robert Jastrow is appealing to an argument that many theists often bring up as evidence of God's existence. We know that complex objects, such as a telescope, have creators and cannot come together on their own. The universe, the argument goes, is similarly complex and, therefore, must also have a creator. This argument – called the design or teleological argument – has been put forth by philosophers for millennia. Many have argued, however, that for various reasons it is not possible to compare the creation of artifacts (like a telescope or a watch) to the creation of a whole universe. For example, Hume notes that while we have empirical exposure to artifacts' being created, we have no similar exposure to universes' being created and so we cannot conclude anything about the creation of the latter based upon the former. Moreover, Hume argues, we cannot conclude that all of the universe is orderly, and therefore created, based solely on our limited exposure to our world and our part of the universe. For all we know, the rest of the universe could be a chaotic mess.

As mentioned above, analogies can indeed be successfully used for making strong arguments. They key is to ensure that the things you are comparing are *relevantly similar* so that you can draw viable inferences from those similarities. This does not mean that they will be similar in *every* way – when making comparisons between objects or states of affairs, it is inevitable that there will be some differences. The important thing is to make sure that the cases or things you are comparing are similar in the right way.

Take, for a further example, Judith Jarvis Thomson's well-discussed example of the famous violinist. Doctors have, without your permission, attached a famous violinist to your body for nine months in order to sustain and save his life. Thomson compares this to having an unwanted pregnancy. There are both similarities and differences between the violinist example and the typical case of an unplanned pregnancy. Individuals who are not convinced by Thomson's argument will likely maintain that the dissimilarities between the two are sufficient to render her argument flawed; those who agree with Thomson will likely maintain that the similarities are indeed sufficient to conclude that a woman is no more obligated to sustain fetal life than you are to sustain the violinist.

In the past, some philosophers have argued that animals do not feel any pain. This has typically been defended by appealing to their (alleged) non-rational nature. However, we can feel rather confident in maintaining that animals (especially mammals) do indeed feel pain because their pain behavior and central nervous systems are *relevantly similar* to those of humans. While it may be true that animals lack robust rational properties, that is not relevant for concluding that they lack the capacity to feel pain, lest we also maintain that human infants or humans with severe mental disabilities also lack the capacity to feel pain given their lack of robust rational properties. Notable animal rights activist and moral philosopher Peter Singer puts forth a strong argument from analogy to illustrate that animals do indeed feel pain. He writes:

> Nearly all the external signs that lead us to infer pain in other humans can be seen in other species, especially the species most closely related to us – the species of mammals and birds. The behavioral signs include writhing, facial contortions, moaning, yelping or other forms of calling, attempts to avoid the source of the pain, appearance of fear at the prospect of its repetition, and so on. In addition, we know that these animals have nervous systems very like ours, which respond physiologically like ours do when the animal is in circumstances in which we would feel pain: an initial rise of blood pressure, dilated pupils, perspiration, an increased pulse rate, and, if the stimulus continues, a

fall in blood pressure [...]. We also know that the nervous systems of other animals were not artificially constructed – as a robot might be artificially constructed – to mimic the pain behavior of humans. The nervous systems of animals evolved as our own did, and in fact the evolutionary history of human beings and other animals, especially mammals, did not diverge until the central features of our nervous systems were already in existence (Singer 1990, 11–12).

By focusing on these similarities between animals and humans, and by arguing that these similarities are indeed relevant to the issue at hand, Singer presents a strong argument from analogy in favor of the conclusion that animals are indeed sentient beings.

References

Hurley, Patrick. 2008. *A Concise Introduction to Logic*. Belmont, CA: Wadsworth Cengage Learning.

Jastrow, Robert. 1985. *Life—How Did It Get Here? By Evolution or by Creation?*. New York: Watch Tower.

Singer, Peter. 1990. *Animal Liberation*. New York, NY: Avon Books.

Thomson, Judith Jarvis. 1971. "A Defense of Abortion." *Philosophy and Public Affairs* 1(1): 47–66.

Fallacies of Ambiguity

51

Accent

Roberto Ruiz

> Peter Ustinov retraces a journey made by Mark Twain a century ago. The highlights of his global tour include encounters with Nelson Mandela, an 800-year-old demigod and a dildo collector.
>
> Quoted in Joseph Piercy, *The 25 Rules of Grammar*

I bet you didn't know that Nelson Mandela was an 800-year-old demigod and dildo collector, right? Let's do a little experiment: read the quoted passage again, but this time add a mental comma after *demigod*, and see what happens. I'll wait … Interesting, right? Now it becomes clear that the tour included encounters with *three* separate people: (a) Nelson Mandela, (b) an 800-year-old demigod, and (c) a dildo collector.

Accent is a fallacy of pragmatics. In linguistics and semiotics, pragmatics refers to the study of how speech is used and the ways that context contributes to meaning. Contrary to popular belief, words alone are often insufficient to precisely and unambiguously determine the meaning of a sentence or utterance. To make such precise determinations, we usually rely on additional non-linguistic cues, such as knowledge of local history and customs, inferences about other people's mental states, tone of voice, facial expressions, body language, gestures, analogical and symbolic reasoning, relationships between signified and signifier, fluctuations in lexical stress (the vocal stress placed on syllables within words), variations in prosodic stress (the vocal stress placed

Bad Arguments: 100 of the Most Important Fallacies in Western Philosophy, First Edition.
Edited by Robert Arp, Steven Barbone, and Michael Bruce.
© 2019 John Wiley & Sons Ltd. Published 2019 by John Wiley & Sons Ltd.

on words within sentences), and various other inferences and forms of background knowledge. Consider the text from a common street sign:

SLOW
CHILDREN
AT PLAY

At first glance, this sign appears simply to warn drivers to slow down their vehicles in order to reduce the risk of accidentally running over children who are playing in the vicinity. Notice, however, that this is partly the result of the way in which we read the sign, namely with an implicit pause between *slow* and *children at play*. If we take away the pause, however, we get something closer to the sentence, "Slow children at play," with the implication – which we did not have before—that *the children* are slow. Perhaps this difference can be made even clearer if we write the sentence and include a comma:

SLOW,
CHILDREN
AT PLAY

If you look back at the street sign, you'll notice that there is no comma anywhere on it; it is simply assumed that those reading the sign will have at least a basic understanding of the local, cultural, and legal background under which it is to be interpreted as a warning to motorists to drive slowly, and not as a description of the mental or physical ability of the children in question.

The fallacy of accent takes place, therefore, when a premise in an argument seems to rely for its meaning on one possible vocal emphasis, but a conclusion is drawn that relies on an extrapolation from a different vocal emphasis of the same phrase. Such ambiguities are often the result of unacknowledged differences in background beliefs, attitudes, and expectations that people may implicitly bring to the reading of a passage. These differences in context would lead the person drawing the erroneous inference to place the pause, vocal stress, or emphasis on a different part of the sentence from that originally intended, thereby producing a different line of reasoning.

Although it will not cover all cases of accent, the use of proper and careful punctuation can go a long way towards reducing unnecessary confusion and ambiguity. Consider this sentence: "A woman without her man is nothing." Given your own beliefs, values, life experience, and cultural background, you are probably interpreting it to mean something very specific and unambiguous. However, depending on how you punctuate it, you could actually end up with at least two diametrically opposed meanings: (a) A woman, without her man, is nothing; (b) A woman: without her, man is nothing.

The fallacy, then, was committed in the original sentence because, as it stands – with no punctuation marks other than the period at the end – it gives us no context to understand its intended meaning, and it is therefore open to different prosodic stresses when read out loud, and hence to different interpretations. If it looked like either its second or its third iteration, its punctuation would probably be enough to give us the context to understand it unambiguously, and no fallacy would occur.

Below, on the left-hand column, we have a few more examples that illustrate some of the ways in which the absence of proper punctuation can produce instances of the fallacy of accent, and, on the right, how the misleading ambiguity of said passages can be minimized or eliminated with some context-sensitive punctuation.

For my parents, Ayn Rand and God.	For my parents, Ayn Rand, and God.
Let's eat grandma.	Let's eat, grandma.
Most of the time travelers worry about their luggage.	Most of the time, travelers worry about their luggage.
All fields are closed. No trespassing violators will be prosecuted.	All fields are closed. No trespassing. Violators will be prosecuted.
Don't wear green people.	Don't wear green, people.

To make matters worse, and especially in our digital age of texting, people often forego the use of any punctuation at all. Consider the following excerpt from a letter sent by a reader to the BBC News (2006), with most of its punctuation omitted:

> Dear Mother-in-Law it was a shame you had to stay here for such a short time I thought I might have coped but it was unbearable seeing you leave the relief was immense when I heard we might see you again soon I wanted to end it all by saying goodbye now I hope I will not have to say it to you again for a long time if you have the opportunity to spend Christmas elsewhere next year please do not much love Matthew

Depending on how the letter is punctuated, we could read it either as a very warm and affectionate expression of appreciation and concern or as a not so welcoming note:

Dear Mother-in-Law,

It was a shame you had to stay here for such a short time. I thought I might have coped, but it was unbearable seeing you leave. The relief was immense when I heard we might see you again soon. I wanted to end it all by saying goodbye now. I hope I will not have to say it to you again for a long time. If you have the opportunity to spend Christmas elsewhere next year, please do not.

Much love,
Matthew

Dear Mother-in-Law,

It was a shame you had to stay here. For such a short time, I thought I might have coped, but it was unbearable. Seeing you leave, the relief was immense. When I heard we might see you again soon, I wanted to end it all. By saying goodbye now, I hope I will not have to say it to you again for a long time. If you have the opportunity to spend Christmas elsewhere next year, please do.

Not much love,
Matthew

In addition to questions of vocal emphasis and proper punctuation, a given passage or utterance can sometimes only be understood when set in its proper context, which helps to establish the sense in which it was originally intended. The fallacy of accent can also be committed, therefore, when a passage is quoted without its original context, and erroneous inferences are drawn based on this (often deliberate) distortion.

A classic example of this kind of deliberate form of quote mining is often used by creationists in their attempt to discredit Darwin's theory of evolution by natural selection. To make the case that no sensible person in full possession of her faculties could believe in such a theory, creationists sometimes quote Darwin himself in *On the Origin of Species* (1859/2006):

> To suppose that the eye, with all its inimitable contrivances for adjusting the focus to different distances, for admitting different amounts of light, and for the correction of spherical and chromatic aberration, could have been formed by natural selection, seems, I freely confess, absurd in the highest possible degree. (569)

What the quoted passage does not include, however, is *the rest* of the paragraph in question, which goes on to explain the precise conditions under which such an apparently absurd sequence is not only possible but, in Darwin's view, perhaps quite inevitable:

> Yet reason tells me, that if numerous gradations from a perfect and complex eye to one very imperfect and simple, each grade being useful to its possessor, can be shown to exist; if further, the eye does vary ever so slightly, and the variations be inherited, which is certainly the case; and if any variation or modification in the organ be ever useful to an animal under changing conditions

of life, then the difficulty of believing that a perfect and complex eye could be formed by natural selection, though insuperable by our imagination, can hardly be considered real. (569)

Context is crucial to the proper interpretation and understanding of linguistic utterances, and a careful thinker ought to keep in mind the possibility of drawing potentially misleading interpretations from a passage if no attention is given to possible differences in context, intention, vocal emphasis, and punctuation. In fact, we should keep in mind that even the literal truth can sometimes be used to deceive or mislead. In explaining some of the differences between British and American conceptions of justice, for instance, Tom Cowan (1996, 74) tells the story of a sea captain confronted with the question of what to do about a mate whose love for the bottle was getting out of control. At last, after one too many mishaps, the captain had no choice but to state on the ship's log: "The mate was drunk today." The mate wasn't too pleased with this turn of events, and so on a day when it was his turn to write on the ship's log, he took his revenge and recorded on the log: "The captain was sober today!"

References

BBC News. 2006. "Saying Thank You in Style." BBC News, January 5. http://news.bbc.co.uk/1/hi/magazine/4583594.stm (accessed September 29, 2017).

Cowan, Tom K. 1996. "Are Truth and Fairness Generally Acceptable?" In *Readings in True and Fair*, edited by R.H. Parker, P.W. Wolnizer, and C.W. Nobes. 1996. New York, NY: Garland Publishing, 74–80.

Darwin, Charles. 1859/2006. *On the Origin of Species. From So Simple a Beginning – The Four Great Books of Charles Darwin*, edited by Edward O. Wilson. New York, NY: W.W. Norton.

Piercy, Joseph. 2014. *The 25 Rules of Grammar: The Essential Guide to Good English*. London: Michael O'Mara.

52

Amphiboly

Roberto Ruiz

> Too many good docs are getting out of business. Too many OB/GYNs aren't
> able to practice their [...] their *love* with women all across the country.
>
> George W. Bush

Amphiboly – which has the distinction of being one of the funniest logical
fallacies out there – is a fallacy of syntax. In linguistics, syntax refers to the
study of the principles, general rules, and structure of a given language.
While a typical sentence will be made up of various kinds of words and
other parts (nouns, verbs, modifiers, connectives, punctuation marks, etc.),
these cannot be put together in just any haphazard way because different
arrangements and forms of organization and structure could lead to different sorts of meanings. Such ambiguities can justifiably lead people to
come up with radically different interpretations of the same sentence or
passage, and, furthermore, to draw questionable inferences, often with
hilarious results.

Consider the following newspaper headline: "Condom truck tips, spills
load." The reason you're laughing – or at least snickering – is that this headline can be interpreted in at least two different ways, depending on what the
phrase "spills load" refers to: if it refers to the contents of the *truck*, then it
just means that there are condoms all over the place, but if it refers to the
contents of the *condoms*, then, well .... The ambiguity is produced by bad

Bad Arguments: 100 of the Most Important Fallacies in Western Philosophy, First Edition.
Edited by Robert Arp, Steven Barbone, and Michael Bruce.
© 2019 John Wiley & Sons Ltd. Published 2019 by John Wiley & Sons Ltd.

syntax: by the fact that the location of the phrase "spills load" makes it unclear what it's modifying.

More formally speaking, the fallacy of amphiboly occurs when the meaning of a phrase or sentence is indeterminate or ambiguous, particularly as a result of poor syntax, and especially when further inferences are drawn based on the acceptance of an unintended meaning of such passages.

The ambiguities found in cases of amphiboly usually arise from mistakes in grammar (a dangling modifier, an ambiguous antecedent preceding a pronoun, awkward combinations of adverbs and adjectives, inconsistencies in subject-verb agreement, ambiguous referents, etc.) but also from various forms of linguistic booby traps: from loose or awkward phrasing, from compound phrases that have different meanings depending on whether their parts are being used individually or collectively, from the use of careless arrangements of words, from the ambiguity between the narrow and broad scope of certain phrases, and from inferences drawn based on the difference between what one party means by some utterance and how another party interprets it.

Comedians have been known to exploit these double entendres to great effect. Groucho Marx, who once insightfully quipped that "humor is reason gone mad," basically made a career of his use of amphibolies (and other logical fallacies):

- Outside of a dog, a book is man's best friend. *Inside* of a dog it's too dark to read.
- Those are my principles, and if you don't like them ... well, I have others.
- I've had a perfectly wonderful evening. But this wasn't it.
- I intend to live forever, or die trying.
- One morning I shot an elephant in my pajamas. How he got in my pajamas I'll never know.

It is important to note, however, that not all instances of amphiboly are trivial. The interpretation of carelessly constructed legal contracts and wills, for instance, has been known to produce unnecessary and painful conflicts. Consider the following example: Since Mr. Moneypants stated in his will: "I leave my fortune of half a billion dollars and my pet poodle to Rich and Doug," the court concludes that Rich gets the fortune and Doug gets the poodle. Because Mr. Moneypants did not specify whether the conjunction should be interpreted as including the word *respectively* or *collectively*, it is quite possible that his actual intentions will not be honored and that a regrettable feud will develop between his heirs.

It is particularly important to be careful not to commit this fallacy when addressing small children lest we inadvertently teach them a wrong lesson not only about the subject matter at hand but also about proper communication and the ways in which language can be used to produce unintended meanings. The Wikiquote entry on the popular children's book *Charlotte's Web*, for instance, claims that the book is "about a pig named Wilbur who is saved from being slaughtered by an intelligent spider named Charlotte." Because of the dangling modifier, the phrasing in this description makes it sound as though Charlotte – contrary to fact – is Wilbur's would-be slaughterer.

Amphibolies can also have the potential to either threaten political careers or make them indefinitely memorable. In a speech about the "War on Terror," for instance, former President George W. Bush once said: "Our enemies are innovative and resourceful, and so are we. They never stop thinking about new ways to harm our country and our people, and neither do we" (White House Archives 2004). Of course, when he then went on to make other amphibolous remarks, such as: "There's an enemy that would like to attack America [...] again. There just is. That's the reality of the world. And I wish him all the very best [...]" or "See, in my line of work you got to keep repeating things over and over and over again for the truth to sink in, to kind of catapult the propaganda" (Weisberg 2000, 2009), it's a bit hard not to sympathize to some extent with his more conspiracy-theory-inclined critics.

But perhaps it's somewhat premature to jump to cynical and conspiratorial conclusions when we consider other amphibolies and head-scratchers made by President Bush over the course of his political career: "I remember meeting a mother of a child who was abducted by the North Koreans right here in the Oval Office," "I know the human being and fish can coexist peacefully," "I just want you to know that, when we talk about war, we're really talking about peace," or "They misunderestimated me" (Weisberg 2000, 2009). This ability to be beaten into submission and dizzying confusion by his own words might help to confirm to the rest of his critics that the time the President almost choked to death on a pretzel was probably no accident.

Various real-life stories, ranging from the mundane and comedic to the tragic, have been immortalized by newspaper headlines that, intentionally and unintentionally, have capitalized on the ambiguities created by amphibolies:

Headless Body in Topless Bar
Kids Make Nutritious Snacks
Blind Bishop Appointed to See
Homicide Victims Rarely Talk to Police
Deaf Mute Gets New Hearing in Killing
Enraged Cow Injures Farmer with Ax
Man Shoots Neighbor with Machete
Bullying Session to Be Rescheduled

March Planned for Next August
Lack of Brains Hinders Research
Federal Agents Raid Gun Shop, Find Weapons
Drunk Gets Nine Months in Violin Case
Miners Refuse to Work After Death
Killer Sentenced to Die for 2nd Time in 10 Years

Finally, there are probably no more satisfying cases of amphiboly than those in which there is a dose of poetic justice: when the double meaning of an utterance ends up unwittingly reinforcing an institution's mission statement, as in the following example found outside of a health clinic:

> Family Planning Advice
> Use Rear Entrance

True to its ideological vision, and in a climate of rising healthcare costs, this clinic just couldn't help itself and inadvertently provided its patients with some technically sound – and quite fun! – family planning advice, free of charge.

References

"Charlotte's Web (book)." 2015. *Wikiquote*. October 15. https://en.wikiquote.org/wiki/Charlotte%27s_Web_%28book%29 (accessed September 29, 2017)

Weisberg, Jacob. 2000. "The Complete Bushisms." *Slate Magazine*, March 7. http://www.slate.com/articles/news_and_politics/bushisms/2000/03/the_complete_bushisms.html (accessed September 29, 2017).

Weisberg, Jacob. 2009. "W's Greatest Hits: The Top 25 Bushisms of All Time." *Slate Magazine*, January 12. http://www.slate.com/articles/news_and_politics/bushisms/2009/01/ws_greatest_hits.html (accessed September 29, 2017).

White House Archives. 2004. *President Signs Defense Bill*. October 15. https://georgewbush-whitehouse.archives.gov/news/releases/2004/08/20040805-3.html (accessed September 29, 2017).

53

Composition

Jason Waller

You like to eat onions, carrots, and beef, right? So, I know you'll love this casserole made of onions, carrots, and beef that I cooked for you.

The typical mom

The fallacy of composition occurs when one incorrectly infers that the characteristics, attributes, or features of individuals comprising some group will also be found in the group as a whole.

Consider the following:

(1) Each brick in this building is square.
(2) Therefore, this building is square.

The conclusion here clearly does not follow from the premise, thereby making the argument invalid. It is, of course, possible to make a non-square building from square bricks. So from the fact that the bricks are square, we cannot infer that the building must also be. Similarly:

(1) Each brick in this building weighs one pound.
(2) Therefore, this building weighs one pound.

Bad Arguments: 100 of the Most Important Fallacies in Western Philosophy, First Edition.
Edited by Robert Arp, Steven Barbone, and Michael Bruce.
© 2019 John Wiley & Sons Ltd. Published 2019 by John Wiley & Sons Ltd.

This argument is also clearly fallacious because the weight of a brick will not be the same as the weight of the whole building. From the fact that a part of the building has a certain property (in this example, weighing one pound), it does not follow that the whole building has that property (it weighs much more than one pound.)

The two above arguments are obviously invalid, but there are other arguments that are fallacious for the same reason but which are much less obviously invalid. Consider the following:

(1)   Congressmen Jones, Mark, and Smith are all radicals.
(2)   Therefore, Congress is radical.

It may be tempting to infer that Congress is radical from the claim that Jones, Mark, and Smith are radical. But we cannot infer the radical nature of Congress from this claim alone. Perhaps there are hundreds of other members of Congress who may counteract the radical tendencies of these three. Similarly, consider the following:

(1)   John cannot lift the box.
(2)   Therefore, John and his brothers cannot lift the box.

This argument is also fallacious for the same reason. We cannot infer anything about whether John plus his brothers can lift a given box from the claim that John alone cannot do it.

Inferences from a part to a whole can be made if additional assumptions are added to guarantee that the whole will have the property if the parts do. For example, if the chapter of a book is made of paper and the book is made of only one kind of material, then we can infer that the whole book must be made of paper. This inference is valid because we added the assumption that the book is made of only one kind of material. Without this assumption, the inference would not have been valid.

The easiest way to avoid this fallacy is never to assume that the characteristics, attributes, or features of individuals comprising some group will also be found in the group as a whole. One must inspect and evaluate the characteristics, attributes, or features of the whole separately from the parts of which the whole is comprised.

54

Confusing an Explanation for an Excuse

Kimberly Baltzer-Jaray

> When I suggested that Mother's death had no connection with the charge against me, he merely replied that this remark showed I'd never had any dealings with the law [...].
> "Gentleman of the jury, I would have you note that on the next day after his mother's funeral that man was visiting a swimming pool, starting a liaison with a girl, and going to see a comic film." [...]
> "Is my client on trial for having buried his mother, or for killing a man?" he asked.
> There were some titters in the court. But then the Prosecutor sprang to his feet and, draping his gown round him, said he was amazed at his friend's ingenuousness in failing to see that between these two elements of the case there was a vital link. They hung together psychologically, if he might put it so. "In short," he concluded, speaking with great vehemence, "I accuse the prisoner of behaving at his mother's funeral in a way that showed he was already a criminal at heart."
> Albert Camus, *The Stranger*

Albert Camus summarized his infamous book, *The Stranger*, in 1955 by saying paradoxically: "In our society any man who does not weep at his mother's funeral runs the risk of being sentenced to death" (in Carroll 2008, 47). The plot of this novel demonstrates many fallacies, none so clearly though as the confusing of an explanation for an excuse. This fallacy occurs when there is an uncritical assumption that an explanation given for an

Bad Arguments: 100 of the Most Important Fallacies in Western Philosophy, First Edition.
Edited by Robert Arp, Steven Barbone, and Michael Bruce.
© 2019 John Wiley & Sons Ltd. Published 2019 by John Wiley & Sons Ltd.

action or event is an attempt to justify it. The prosecutor in Camus's story is doing just this, he is taking the fact that Meursault didn't cry at his mother's funeral, along with other events that occurred in the 24 hours after her death (i.e., his fun with Marie), and using this as justification for the claim that Meursault was guilty of the murder of the Arab on the beach that occurs later.

Sometimes this fallacy comes about when there is general confusion about the difference between an explanation and an excuse: explanations are attempts to provide factual accounts of why something happened or is the case, whereas excuses are instances where we provide reasons, evidence, or arguments to justify the action or occurrence. In murder trials, especially where there is discussion of the mental state of the suspects, we often want to know if they are of sound mind or not: if they could understand right from wrong and also form malicious intent. Sometimes mental illness can be both an explanation and an excuse (i.e., it is a fact this person had schizophrenia and was in a state where he didn't know what he was doing), and sometimes it can be one or the other (i.e., someone can have a mental illness that doesn't justify what she did; someone had a sudden mental state come on that caused her to do X).

Other times, we see this fallacy committed intentionally when someone is attempting to use an explanation of facts as some kind of justification or proof for an action. This intentional use of the fallacy is really what the prosecutor is doing in Camus's story; he is taking a fact and using it as justification for convicting him (i.e., a man who does not weep for his dead mother is a monster who is cold enough to murder), a trick not uncommon to the courtroom. He uses the lack of tears to paint Meursault as a cold-hearted, callous monster.

When Meursault is questioned by the magistrate why he paused between the first and second shots fired (he fired five altogether, one and then four together), he has no excuse, and this infuriates the official severely: facts are not enough, he wants to know why Meursault did this, what justified this pause. He is further frustrated that Meursault feels no remorse for the murder. The book, in fact, is filled with more explanation than excuses, and this is part of its unsettling and provocative nature, since we as humans seem to desire both the facts and the justifications for events – we want to know why someone felt the need to shoot another person, not just that he did it.

One of the best ways to avoid this fallacy is simply to ask someone if she is stating facts or justifying some event or action. Sometimes it can be unclear what someone is saying or how she is using certain statements, so it is best to ask. Don't just assume. If a co-worker tells you that "George won't be at work today because he was in a car accident," we can take this as an explanation of events. However, this explanation can form the foundation of an excuse if it is meant to serve as justification for his absence – George should be allowed to miss work today as he has valid reason. In this case, it is best to ask, for example, "Will he be missing work due to the accident and for how long?" just to have things clear.

Another way to avoid committing this fallacy is to listen carefully to what someone is saying, especially when the argument is rather emotionally charged. For example, two friends are discussing the issue of terrorism in the United States, and one friend says, "Politicians like saying that terrorists attacked us because they hate our freedoms and way of life, but really it seems to be more about American foreign policy," and the other responds, "I can't believe you are defending the terrorists! How dare you! You're saying the 9/11 attacks are justified?! So we made them attack us?!?" Now, the first friend was stating something factual, explaining how politicians are misinterpreting the situation to the public, and the second friend took that to be a justification instead and got very upset. This could have been avoided if the second friend had asked the first if it was an explanation, even if it was in fact more of an opinion, or an excuse.

References

Camus, Albert. 1988. *The Stranger*, translated by Matthew Ward. New York, NY: Vintage.

Carroll, David. 2008. *Albert Camus the Algerian: Colonialism, Terrorism, Justice.* New York, NY: Columbia University Press.

55
Definist Fallacy

Christian Cotton

> In war, people are killed. And killing is murder, plain and simple. How anyone can support a war is beyond me.
>
> Anonymous blogger during the George W. Bush administration

We often make use of terms and their concepts in ways that are vague. As a consequence, we regularly define one term or concept by means of another term or concept. In other words, we use synonyms. Ordinarily, this isn't problematic. To say "near" instead of "close" or "big" instead of "large" preserves meaning across terms. It's when we get into more complex concepts that we begin to see that overlap in meaning decrease. It is in such cases that we may seek to define a concept in terms of some other concept with which it is not, properly speaking, synonymous. This is the first way we can commit the definist fallacy.

The name "definist fallacy" was originally given by philosopher William Frankena (1939) to G.E. Moore's "naturalistic fallacy," which Moore characterized as the attempt to define general ethical terms, like "good," in terms of supposedly identical natural terms, like "pleasant." The definist fallacy consists of (1) defining one concept in terms of another concept with which it is not clearly synonymous, (2) as the persuasive definition fallacy, defining a concept in terms of another concept in an infelicitous way that is favorable

Bad Arguments: 100 of the Most Important Fallacies in Western Philosophy, First Edition.
Edited by Robert Arp, Steven Barbone, and Michael Bruce.
© 2019 John Wiley & Sons Ltd. Published 2019 by John Wiley & Sons Ltd.

to one's position, or (3) the insistence that a term be defined before it can be used in discussion.

More generally, the definist fallacy is known as "persuasive definition," a tactic in argumentation that defines a term in an infelicitous a way that is favorable to one's position, and then insists that the discussion should continue on that basis. Moreover, such definitions are often laden and/or vague, both of which serve to make the position they are used to defend seem more persuasive. Consider, for example, the following exchange on the morality of abortion.

> JUDITH: We've come here today to discuss the morality of abortion and the right of a woman to choose what happens in and to her own body. It hardly needs to be said that bodily integrity divorced from personal autonomy makes little sense. For in the absence of bodily integrity, of the right of each person to choose what happens in and to her body, there can be no overt exercise of personal autonomy. Therefore, in securing bodily integrity, it follows that abortion must be understood as a right possessed by women the world over, that it therefore must be a morally permissible practice.
>
> DON: While I agree with Judith that personal autonomy and bodily integrity and the rights that flow from these ought to be respected, I cannot but stand amazed that she would reason that such matters mean that abortion, the practice whereby the fetus, an unborn child – a person – is killed, could be considered not only morally permissible, but a right. For it follows from the fact that a fetus is a person that it, too, possesses the very rights she ascribes to women the world over, viz., personal autonomy and bodily integrity, if not from the womb, then in anticipation of its arrival into the human community. There being no security in those rights where there is not also a right to life – the most basic and fundamental right of all persons – one cannot but conclude that abortion must be morally impermissible.

This interaction may look like the well-reasoned arguments of two seasoned philosophers, presenting the core disagreement on the morality of abortion. It certainly encapsulates the fundamental principles of the right to choose of the woman and the right to life of the fetus, but Don's argument falls prey to persuasive definition. Did you catch it? Notice how, in his exposition, he introduces the salient term "fetus" but then goes on to define it, not only as an "unborn child" – a term laden with emotion and connotations of "innocence" and "vulnerability" – but further as a "person" – a distinctly moral concept in which things like innocence and vulnerability are to be defended – who is "killed," thereby failing to defend those qualities.

Sometimes the definist fallacy refers to a conviction that a term be defined before it can be employed. That is, before any useful discussion can begin about a topic, the term(s) must be clearly defined. The demand for clear definition prior to discussing a topic is not an obvious logical fallacy, but it can become so if it's arrived at by a chain of reasoning: discussions are only productive when terms are clearly defined; we want discussions to be productive; thus, we must have clearly defined terms before we begin discussing. Thus, the person who insists *in this manner* on definition prior to discussion is arguably committing a version of the definist fallacy.

NEAL: Welcome back, everybody. I'm sitting here in the studio talking to Uncle Ron about the poor state of the economy and some of the things the folks in Washington can do to get this train wreck back on the tracks. What do you think about taxes?

RON: Well, Neal, that depends on what you mean by taxation. After all, if we're going to have anything productive to say about tax policy and how it might help our economy get "back on the tracks," we should be clear about what we mean.

NEAL: Hold on, Uncle Ron. I think you and I, and the members of the listening audience, and I'd dare say even those jokers up in Washington, know what taxation is.

RON: I'm not so sure, Neal. I bet half of them think taxation is the means by which our Commonwealth is preserved and sustained, while the other half think taxation is the means by which bureaucrats rip off the people who elected them. So, which is it? [Definitions courtesy of Hurley 2008, 94]

NEAL: Why don't you define taxation for us, then, Ron.

RON: Legalized theft.

In this exchange, Ron commits a version of the definist fallacy by insisting that discussion wait on a clearly defined notion of taxation. But Neal points out that they and the listeners have an adequate understanding of taxation sufficient to have a discussion on tax policy. It's surely not a perfect understanding, but to demand such is to commit this version of the definist fallacy. To add to the fallacious demand for a clear definition prior to discussion, Ron then tosses out not one, not two, but *three* persuasive definitions of taxation. A double definist fallacy!

The simplest way to not commit any version of this fallacy is to define your terms credibly! Avoid using definitions that are laden with emotion or those that are idiosyncratic. That is, use more neutral and accepted definitions. If those definitions seem inadequate for your purposes, then argue for your definition. In other words, give reasons for thinking that a term or concept ought to be defined a certain way. There are even rules for how to test a definition's strength that can tell you whether your definition is too broad or too narrow, for instance, or even if it's both too broad and too narrow. And don't be hesitant to jump right in without having a clear definition established first (which usually turns out badly anyway). Discussing a topic is one of the best ways to get clearer about what a term means because you have the benefit of other people's use of the term to provide grist for the mental mill.

Reference
Frankena, William. 1939. "The Naturalistic Fallacy." *Mind* 48(192): 464–477.
Hurley, Patrick. 2008. *A Concise Introduction to Logic*, 10th edition. Belmont, CA: Wadsworth Cengage Learning.

56

Division

Jason Waller

> You hated this casserole made of onions, carrots, and beef that I cooked for you, so I'll make sure to never buy onions, carrots, or beef for you to eat again.
>
> The typical mom

The fallacy of division occurs when one incorrectly infers that the characteristics, attributes, or features of the group as a whole will also be found in the individuals comprising the group.

Consider the following:

(1)   The Cleveland Orchestra can play the full-orchestrated version of Beethoven's Symphony No. 7.

(2)   Therefore, Mary Kay Fink (the piccolo player) can play the full-orchestrated version of Beethoven's Symphony No. 7.

From the fact that the entire orchestra can do something, it does not follow that each part can do that same thing. Mary Kay Fink can certainly play her part of the symphony, but she cannot play the whole thing. She could never play all of the different instruments at the same time. So even if the whole orchestra can play a certain piece of music, we cannot infer that Mary Kay Fink can play the same piece of music. Similarly, the following argument makes the same mistake:

Bad Arguments: 100 of the Most Important Fallacies in Western Philosophy, First Edition.
Edited by Robert Arp, Steven Barbone, and Michael Bruce.
© 2019 John Wiley & Sons Ltd. Published 2019 by John Wiley & Sons Ltd.

(1) <u>Beethoven's Symphony No. 7 takes around 35 minutes to perform.</u>
(2) Therefore, the second movement of Beethoven's Symphony No. 7 takes around 35 minutes to perform.

Clearly, because the whole symphony performance has some particular property (namely, that of taking 35 minutes to perform), it does not follow that the parts of the symphony have the same property. In fact, the time it takes to perform each movement must be much shorter than the time it takes to perform the whole. To consider another set of examples, consider the case of Congress:

(1) The laws passed by the Congress were radical.
(2) <u>Jones is a member of Congress.</u>
(3) Therefore, Jones is radical.

If the laws that Congress passed were radical and Jones were a member of that Congress, it may be tempting to infer that Jones himself must be a radical. But a moment's reflection reveals that this inference is invalid. Perhaps Jones was outvoted by many other radicals in the Congress. Perhaps the laws were compromises, which no one in the Congress particularly wanted. Perhaps the Congress members did not understand the laws they were passing. There are many possible ways for both Premise 1 and Premise 2 to be true but Premise 3 false. Thus, this argument is clearly invalid. We cannot infer that the parts of something have a property just because the whole of something has that property.

The easiest way to avoid this fallacy is never to assume that the characteristics, attributes, or features of the group as a whole will also be found in the individuals comprising the group. One must inspect and evaluate the characteristics, attributes, or features of the whole separately from the parts of which the whole is comprised. Inferences from a whole to a part can be made, however, if additional assumptions are added to the argument that link together the property had by the whole with the property had by the part. For example, if may be inferred from the claim that a book is made of paper that each chapter of the book is made of paper. But this inference can only be made if the additional assumption is added that the entire book is made of only one kind of material (i.e., paper). Similar arguments can be made about a wall made only from bricks. If the wall is made only of bricks, then we can infer that half of the wall is made entirely of bricks also. This inference is possible only because we added information about the composition of the wall to the premises so that we avoid the fallacy of division.

57

Equivocation

Bertha Alvarez Manninen

> And so my fellow Americans, ask not what your country can do for you, ask
> what you can do for your country.
>
> John F. Kennedy

Patrick Hurley (2015) writes that the fallacy of equivocation "occurs when
the conclusion of an argument depends on the fact that the word or phrase
is used, either explicitly or implicitly, in two different senses in the argument"
(168). President Kennedy commits this fallacy in the famous quotation
above by equivocating on the word "country." When Americans ask, "What
can my country do for me?" they typically mean, "What can my government, or my elected officials, do for me?" But when Kennedy implores us to
ask what we can do for our country, he clearly isn't talking about what we
can do for our elected officials; rather, here the term "country" means something different – our homeland, or our nation, or providing services to our
fellow countrypersons.

Several air conditioning companies deliberately rely on equivocation in
billboard advertisement campaigns. In big letters, a sign reads: "Your wife
is HOT!" while right below this it reads, "Better get your A/C fixed." The
equivocation here is on the word "hot" being used to convey both physical
attractiveness and a response to warm weather. As a child, I remember

Bad Arguments: 100 of the Most Important Fallacies in Western Philosophy, First Edition.
Edited by Robert Arp, Steven Barbone, and Michael Bruce.
© 2019 John Wiley & Sons Ltd. Published 2019 by John Wiley & Sons Ltd.

going to a lecture on the perils of drinking and driving and then refusing
to get into the car with my older sister because she was drinking and driving, even though what she was drinking was a Diet Coke. In my young
mind, I equivocated on the term "drinking" – whereas the danger clearly
refers to drinking alcoholic beverages and driving, I had interpreted it as
meaning the act of drinking anything at all while driving. Consider, also,
this example:

> The sugar industry, for instance, once advertised its product with the claim
> that "Sugar is an essential component of the body [...] a key material in all
> sorts of metabolic processes," neglecting the fact that it is glucose (blood
> sugar) not ordinary table sugar (sucrose) that is the vital nourishment. (Kahane
> and Cavender 2006, 81)

The ad in this example equivocates on the term "sugar" and relies on the
general public's ignorance of the differences (both chemical and health-
related) between glucose and sucrose.

Philosopher Mary Anne Warren (1973) argues that pro-life activists commonly commit the equivocation fallacy when arguing against abortion
rights. Typically, a common pro-life argument runs as follows:

(1)   All human beings have a right to life.
(2)   <u>A fetus is a human being.</u>
(3)   Therefore, the fetus has a right to life.

Warren (1973) argues that an equivocation is made here with the term
"human being." In the first premise, the term "human being" is a *moral*
term, denoting the kinds of beings who are "a full-fledged member of the
moral community" (53). In the second premise, the term "human being" is
a *biological* term, denoting a member of the species *Homo sapiens*. Warren
calls this a "slide of meaning, which serves to conceal the fallaciousness of
the traditional argument" (53). A useful tool for determining whether an
argument commits the fallacy of equivocation can be applied here: replace
the premises of the argument explicitly with the term having the same meaning and then gauge whether the argument is successful.

(1)   All human beings (in the moral sense) have a right to life.
(2)   <u>A fetus is a human being (in the moral sense).</u>
(3)   Therefore, the fetus has a right to life.

Seen this way, Warren argues that the pro-life argument commits the begging
the question fallacy in Premise 2 by assuming the very thing that needs to be
argued; one of the main issues when debating abortion ethics is precisely

whether the fetus is a human being in the moral sense of the term, whether it is the kind of being that should be the bearer of moral rights. That is not to say that the fetus *isn't* such a being but rather that this is the very thing that needs to be argued rather than assumed. The same problem occurs if the term "human being" is used in the genetic sense in both premises.

(1)   All human beings (in the genetic sense) have a right to life.
(2)   The fetus is a human being (in the genetic sense).
(3)   Therefore, the fetus has a right to life.

Here Premise 1 begs the question: Why assume that being biologically human is sufficient for moral rights? Again, it is not that the premise is false but rather than the premise is assumed rather than defended.

Therefore, the traditional pro-life argument, according to Warren, commits the equivocation fallacy, and when we rectify it so that the equivocation fallacy does not occur, the argument begs the question. Pro-life activists have typically responded by refuting that the argument commits the equivocation fallacy by denying that there is a valid distinction between "human being" in the moral sense and in the genetic sense. All genetic human beings, all members of the species *Homo sapiens*, are human beings in the moral sense, that is, being genetically human is sufficient for having full and equal moral rights. Pope John Paul II (1995), in accordance with the accepted view of the Catholic Church, argues that "from the time that the ovum is fertilized, a life is begun which is neither the father nor the mother; it is, rather, the life of a human being with his own growth [... this new human being] is a person with his characteristic aspects well determined" (107). Pro-life philosopher Christopher Kaczor (2011) also argues that all genetic human beings are moral human beings (that is, that all human beings are persons) but emphasizes that this leaves wide open the possibility that other animals may also have moral rights (92). Kaczor doesn't just assume this key premise, however; he presents arguments that are supposed to illustrate that this is the case. Pro-life philosopher Francis Beckwith (2007) also argues extensively that genetic humanity is sufficient for moral humanity. He argues that "the human being, as an organism, begins its existence at conception, that it is a unified organism with its own intrinsic purpose and basic capacities, whose parts work in concert for the perfection and perpetuation of its existence as a whole" (130).

If these arguments are successful, then the pro-life position can get out of committing the equivocation fallacy by asserting that the argument means to use "human being" in the genetic sense in both premises and that a right to life follows from being genetically human.

264   *Bertha Alvarez Manninen*

Ali Almossawi's *An Illustrated Book of Bad Arguments* (2013) contains several humorous examples of informal fallacies, including ones for equivocation, and is an entertaining source for further reading. As Almossawi notes, this fallacy happens often within discussions and debates concerning the alleged tension between science and religion. For example, one argument against the authenticity of Darwinian evolution is that it is "just a theory" – the use of the term "theory" here is meant to deride evolution as an unfounded idea or a mere speculation. While evolution is indeed a theory, this term has a very different meaning within a scientific context; in science, a "theory" is an explanation concerning phenomena in the world that has been subjected to multiple and rigorous instances of experiments and testing. By the same definition, gravity is also a theory. The website notjustatheory.com clearly explains why this argument against evolution is flawed and how it is guilty of the equivocation fallacy.

The best way to avoid the equivocation fallacy is to take care to ensure that key terms, especially ones with multiple meanings, in your arguments are being used consistently; that is, that the words retain the *same meaning* throughout the argument. It is also important, for the sake of lucidity, to ensure that it is clear which meaning you intend to be using throughout your argument. Here is an amusing example of the equivocation fallacy:

(1)   Knowledge is Power.
(2)   <u>Power Corrupts.</u>
(3)   Study Hard – Be Evil.

The equivocation here is on the word "power." In the first sentence, "power" means something akin to an expansion of your mental capacities and knowledge of the world. In the second sentence, "power" refers to something like political or authoritative power. For this reason, the conclusion (that studying hard increases your capacity for corruption and evil) does not follow, and the "argument" is therefore flawed. The way to have avoided such a fallacy here would be to have ensured that the term "power" was being used in the same way throughout the argument (either to denote intellectual power in both instances or political/authoritative power in both instances).

References

Almossawi, Ali. 2013. *An Illustrated Book of Bad Arguments*. New York, NY: The Experiment Publishing.

Beckwith, Francis. 2007. *Defending Life: A Moral and Legal Case Against Abortion*. New York, NY: Cambridge University Press.

Hurley, Patrick. 2015. *A Concise Introduction to Logic*. Stamford, CT: Cengage Learning.

John Paul II. 1995. *Evangelium Vitae*. New York, NY: Random House.

Kaczor, Christopher. 2011. *The Ethics of Abortion: Women's Rights, Human Life, and the Question of Justice*. New York, NY: Random House.

Kahane, Howard, and Nancy Cavender. 2006. *Logic and Contemporary Rhetoric: The Use of Reason in Everyday Life*. Belmont, CA: Thomson Wadsworth.

Notjustatheory.com. http://www.notjustatheory.com/index.html (accessed September 29, 2017).

Warren, Mary Anne. 1973. "On the Moral and Legal Status of Abortion." *The Monist* 57(4): 43–61.

58

Etymological Fallacy

Leigh Kolb

> Ives Goddard – the senior linguist and curator at the Smithsonian Institution – concluded that the word "redskins" was created by Native Americans, and that it was first used as an inclusive expression of solidarity by multi-tribal delegations who traveled to Washington, D.C. to negotiate national policy towards Native Americans. "The actual origin of the word (redskin) is entirely benign," Goddard is quoted as saying.
>
> Redskin Facts website

To understand the etymological fallacy (EF) fully, it's important to break down the word *etymology*, which is a practice that in itself informs the conversation surrounding the fallacy. According to Merriam-Webster, *etymology* is "the history of a linguistic form (as a word) shown by tracing its development since its earliest recorded occurrence in the language where it is found [...] by analyzing it into its component parts," and by tracing and identifying it through translated languages and cognates. The origin of *etymon* is Latin, from Greek: the "literal meaning of a word according to its origin, from *etymos*, true; akin to Greek *eteos*, true." The *logy* suffix refers to a scientific area of study, but its origin is from the Greek *logos*, which means, "word." An etymon, then, is "an earlier form of a word in the same language or an ancestral language."

Bad Arguments: 100 of the Most Important Fallacies in Western Philosophy, First Edition.
Edited by Robert Arp, Steven Barbone, and Michael Bruce.
© 2019 John Wiley & Sons Ltd. Published 2019 by John Wiley & Sons Ltd.

While the linguistic study of tracing words to their origins can be a fascinating exercise, when the natural evolution of language that occurs over time is left out of the study, there is the danger of committing the EF (also known as the appeal to definition or abuse of etymology), which assumes that the way a word is used now should be the way it was used historically (an etymon), usually due to the fact that the etymon is more conducive to the argument. EF is a willful use of a former definition of a word that has changed meaning and/or developed new connotations because the change does not benefit the one committing the fallacy.

As Jesse Sheidlower (2001) points out in "What Is, And Isn't, In a Word," in *The New York Times*: "Some words also fall prey to what linguists refer to as the 'etymological fallacy,' the belief that a word's history has a strong bearing on how it is, or should be, used." He goes on to explain that many words change meaning without raising any question, but that the words that most often fall prey to the EF are the ones that are, or are perceived as, offensive.

The NFL team from Washington, DC, the Washington Redskins, has a name that has been the source of controversy and lawsuits in recent years (Gandhi 2013). Many Native American groups (and their allies) have fought against the use of the name *redskins*, which carries with it the terms "derogatory," "offensive," "outdated," and "disparaging slang" in modern dictionary definitions. Sports journalist Baxter Holmes (2014) writes in *Esquire* that the true meaning of the term "redskin" was the scalps of Native Americans who were killed and mutilated for a bounty. After receiving challenges and pushback from readers, he writes another article and includes an excerpt from an 1863 newspaper in Minnesota that explicitly offers money from the state for each "red-skin" produced.

However, the Redskins team owners have stood firm, and in doing so, produced a website and supporting multimedia that relies heavily on the EF. RedskinFacts.com claims that the origin of the word redskins was "benign" and self-referential. The site relies on the etymon (or at least one linguist's version of the etymon) to support the decision not to change the name. In court, "The team's attorneys and linguistics experts argued that this demonstrated that the term had never really been disparaging – just a 'robust informal synonym' for 'American Indian,' which dictionaries only started to label as offensive in response to political pressure from a few Indian activists" (Nunberg 2014). The EF ignores change, connotations, and context. In his article, Sheidlower (2001) says,

> Guidelines for words' usage are determined not by their history (real or imagined), but by someone who cares one way or the other having the power to convince an audience. Groups that have – or gain – political power can have an influence on what they are called [...] the concerns of Native Americans

have not been taken as seriously (which is also why "Redskins" and "Braves" are still used as the names of professional sports teams).

The EF, when used to attempt to uphold the status quo of offensive language, is typically committed in favor of the dominant political/social group.

Of course, not every fallacious use of etymons involves offensive language. In *Nonsense: A Handbook of Logical Fallacies*, Robert J. Gula (2002) uses the example of an atheist trying to convince a religious person that religion is not about love: it "ties man down; it tries to control him; it shackles and enslaves. Nowhere is love even suggested." The atheist attempts to support his argument this way: "Look at the very words we use. The word reverence comes from the Latin word vereor, a word that means 'fear.' [...] And even the word religion itself comes from the Latin religo, a verb that means 'to bind' or 'to fetter'" (48). Gula points out that this argument is fallacious since it ignores that words change, thus making an argument against something based on the Latin roots of a word is not a good argument at all.

Language is constantly changing, and the evolution of words and their meanings is a largely democratic process. When individuals cling to etymons to make an argument about a word that has long since developed new connotations, that argument is uninformed at best and fallacious at worst. To avoid committing the EF, individuals should approach language as they would a scientific process: they may hypothesize the word means X, but after further research and consideration, realize that indeed a word now means Y. The definition may have formally changed in the dictionary, or the meaning may be currently undergoing a cultural shift. Either way, to be a responsible and respectful rhetorician, the changing nature of language must be considered and individuals should be learned enough and flexible enough to communicate within the time and culture they inhabit.

To date, the Washington Redskins have remained firm in their etymological defense and have not changed their team name. However, many journalists and media outlets have stepped over the fallacy and are refusing to use the team name in their reporting. In 2013, Pew Research reported that many journalists and media outlets – 76 at that point – had spoken up about the word "Redskins" and in many cases restricted (or even banned) its use in their publications.

Gula (2002) says, "The etymology of a word does not necessarily constitute any evidence about how the word is being used. A word is important, not for what it once meant, but what it means now" (48). Sheidlower's conclusion is similar: "A word's 'real meaning' according to its etymology may not match the 'real meaning' of its context and usage. And in matters of taste, it is the usage – the way that we and the words we speak every day exist in the world – that is always the deciding factor." Clinging to etymons while ignoring the evolution and everyday use of language is neither logical nor truthful.

References

Gandhi, Lakshmi. 2013. "Are You Ready for Some Controversy? The History of 'Redskin.'" NPR 9 September 9. http://www.npr.org/sections/codeswitch/2013 /09/09/220654611/are-you-ready-for-some-controversy-the-history-of-redskin (accessed September 29, 2107).

Gula, Robert J. 2002. *Nonsense: A Handbook of Logical Fallacies.* Mount Jackson, VA: Axios Press.

Holmes, Baxter. 2014. "Update: Yes, A 'Redskin' Does, in Fact, Mean the Scalped Head of a Native American, Sold, like a Pelt, for Cash." *Esquire*, June 18.

Nunberg, Geoffrey. 2014. "When Slang Becomes a Slur." *The Atlantic*, June 23. https://www.theatlantic.com/entertainment/archive/2014/06/a-linguist-on-why-redskin-is-racist-patent-overturned/373198/ (accessed September 29, 2107).

Pew Research Center. 2013. "Media Takes Sides on 'Redskins' Name." Pew Research Center, October 30. http://www.pewresearch.org/fact-tank/2013/10/30/media-take-sides-on-redskins-name/ (accessed September 29, 2107).

RedskinFacts.com. 2015. "Redskins Alumni." RedskinFacts.com, November 1. www.redskinsfacts.com (accessed September 29, 2107).

Sheidlower, Jesse. 2001. "What Is, and Isn't, In a Word." *The New York Times*, March 4. http://www.nytimes.com/2001/03/04/weekinreview/what-is-and-isn-t-in-a-word.html (accessed September 29, 2107).

59

Euphemism

Kimberly Baltzer-Jaray

> There is no ethnic cleansing in Bahrain.
> Hamad bin Isa Al Khalifa, King of Bahrain, on whether there's genocide
> being committed in his country

A euphemism is a delicate, indirect, inoffensive, or vague word or phrase that takes the place of one that is unpleasant, blunt, offensive, or graphic. Euphemisms create emotional distance and thus provide a level of comfort and ease when discussing a topic that is sensitive, difficult, or disturbing. In some situations, they are used to prevent inappropriately stirring people's emotions – also known as being politically correct – by expressing an idea or description in neutral terms, such as referring to illegal aliens as "undocumented workers" or persons with disabilities as "handicapable" or "differently abled." In other instances, euphemisms are intentionally used to sway people's opinions or emotions to a particular side, as in the example of politicians' referring to the anti-abortion position as "pro-life," torture techniques as "enhanced interrogation," or the non-combatants civilians who die during armed conflict as "collateral damage." At times they are also used to conceal a person's role in or responsibility for a bad deed, as George Carlin (1990) pointed out later in his standup routine: "The CIA doesn't kill anybody anymore; they neutralize people or they depopulate the area.

Bad Arguments: 100 of the Most Important Fallacies in Western Philosophy, First Edition.
Edited by Robert Arp, Steven Barbone, and Michael Bruce.
© 2019 John Wiley & Sons Ltd. Published 2019 by John Wiley & Sons Ltd.

The government doesn't lie; it engages in disinformation. The Pentagon actually measures nuclear radiation in something they call sunshine units."

Euphemisms are fallacious because they are intentionally used to conceal the truth and obscure any real meaning; they are soft language used to mask or downplay warranted emotional force. They work in a similar way to how Novocain numbs the mouth before dental procedures. In this way, euphemisms take the lifeblood out of life. When you refer to the poor as those with "a negative cash-flow position" or your friend who got fired as someone "whose workplace management wanted to curtail redundancies in its human resources," you feel less sad or stressed about the situation. Worse yet, you think less critically about why the poor are poor or get poorer and why your friend was fired from her job: euphemisms numb us from asking the necessary deeper questions or critically assessing situations or actions to form a reaction, and they prevent us from assigning responsibility for actions or results. In fact, with constant use of euphemisms, you feel nothing at all. They make something bad seem pretty good, the awful are rendered lovely, the unnatural becomes almost natural, and the negatives feel rather positive. In this way, the greatest harm that euphemisms do is enable people to avoid reality.

Being ambiguous or vague in meaning brands euphemisms as a type of weasel word. We see these used frequently in politics, corporate business, and advertising media, but they are quite common in everyday language. Weasel words appear to say something truthful or meaningful, but really they conceal truth and meaning, and thus protect the speaker or advocate from counter-attacks or legal redress. If a product says that it "combats wrinkles" and that "Dermatology experts agree skin appears more smooth," then said product commits the fallacy of weasel wording because (1) "combat" seems to indicate that it fights, but it's not clear how much so, and that choice of word means the product doesn't conquer the wrinkles (so what exactly does it do and what degree should I expect?) and, (2) how many and which dermatology experts agreed, what does agreement really mean, and what is meant by skin "appears" more smooth? It's very hard to argue with or sue a company that makes persuasive claims that are at the same time not very specific.

The key signs that weasel words and phrases are being employed include numerically vague statements (e.g., some experts say, many doctors agree); use of the passive voice instead of directly referencing an authority (e.g., it is said that this cream is a miracle); and heavy use of adverbs (e.g., maybe, probably, often). Weasel words attract people and their money or attention rather than invite them to think deeply or critically about something. In the beauty industry, they play on the insecurities women have about their weight, aging, and sexual attractiveness: claims about "defying age," "erasing wrinkles," and "perfecting the skin" mixed with images of women who are heavily photoshopped convey the idea that this product works beauty miracles, but it does not encourage women to read the fine print, question the science behind the claims, or talk to the test subjects and experts who were part of the research.

Sometimes we use soft language to sound professional, civilized, or to tread lightly around the emotions of others, and while that can be appropriate, we must be sure that we are not fudging the truth. Sometimes you have to "say it like it is" and be unpopular. Using honest, direct language and making sure the neutrality deployed is accurate is the best way to avoid euphemisms and weasel wording. It's correct to keep the racist language in *Huckleberry Finn* since removing it would alter its authenticity and historical context; we need to be confronted sometimes with an ugly past to grow. However, it's not right to say to a parent "your son got a D on his exam because he is minimally exceptional at math." Just say it: he sucks at math (he needs to hear it at some point from someone).

Reference
Carlin, George. 1990. https://www.youtube.com/watch?v=Q1TWZ6u0YLk (accessed October 22, 2017).

60

Hedging

Christian Cotton

> FRANK: The spaghetti at this place is really bad.
> JUNE: You think?
> FRANK: Well, it's bad.
> JUNE: I love it.
> FRANK: I guess it's not *completely* bad.
>
> An exchange at a local Italian restaurant

Often in intellectual conversation, we want to express ourselves clearly and forcefully. That is, we want to present the convictions of our thinking straightforwardly. This is surely an admirable desire. There are times, however, when that desire leads us make claims that simply can't be defended. In such instances, there is the temptation to preserve our position in the face of counter-evidence by weakening the initial claim. By weakening the claim, we make it harder to refute by creating indeterminacy. Hedging is that error in reasoning involving the systematic weakening of a claim – or the putting forward of an unreasonably restricted initial claim – so as to avoid refutation. Hedging occurs when a claim is systematically weakened as the dialogue proceeds in order to avoid the thrust of counter-evidence.

The defining characteristic of the hedge is the use of understatement. To understate a claim is to use words – often, though not always, *weasel words* – which diminish the force or content of the claim. There is nothing

Bad Arguments: 100 of the Most Important Fallacies in Western Philosophy, First Edition.
Edited by Robert Arp, Steven Barbone, and Michael Bruce.
© 2019 John Wiley & Sons Ltd. Published 2019 by John Wiley & Sons Ltd.

inherently problematic about understatement. To be sure, it's often the most appropriate form for a claim to take, especially on subjects about which our understanding is limited. Sometimes, our claims ought to be modest. That is not the case with hedging. Hedging uses understatement the way *slippery slope* (see Chapter 94) uses vagueness, *begging the question* (see Chapter 70) uses latency, and the *straw man* (see Chapter 47) uses overstatement. Jason (1988) identifies several ways to deploy understatement, viz., through detensification, qualification, and/or substitution.

Detensification involves using adverbs of degree to weaken a claim. As with understatement, the use of detensifiers isn't problematic in itself as there may be good reason to weaken a claim. With the hedge, however, detensifiers are used to weaken the claim *in order to avoid refutation* without admitting the weakened claim is different from the original. Consider the following example.

THOMAS: Humans are selfish by nature. Just look at how they treat each other: poverty, crime, war, commercialism, dog-eat-dog competition. I swear, it seems the only thing that keeps them from wiping each other out is the heavy hand of the law that threatens them with severe punishment. And that's just more evidence for my point: it's their own selfish nature that keeps them aligned with the law.

JOHN: All these things may be true, Thomas, but people still act in other-regarding ways: charities and good Samaritans, doctors who heal, lawyers who defend the accused. So, I don't think we can say that humans are selfish by nature.

THOMAS: I can see those kinds of exceptional cases. But, that's what they are: exceptions to the rule. So, I still say humans are basically selfish by nature.

In this example, the claim [humans are selfish by nature], when challenged, is detensified to [humans are *basically* selfish by nature]. Immediately, the sense of the claim is altered, although the proponent may protest that this new claim is nevertheless what he originally intended.

Qualification, the second form of understatement, involves limiting the application of a claim, making it not only weaker as a claim (because it covers fewer instances) but also more resistant to refutation. As even the novice student of logic understands, it only takes one counter-example to refute a universal or absolute statement since they admit of no exceptions. [Humans are selfish by nature] is refuted by the existence of a single unselfish action. Consider the following exchange.

THOMAS: I'm telling you John, David is a totally selfish person.

JOHN: Wait a minute. David? He's a dedicated member of his local church, and that means he gives a lot of his time in service.

THOMAS: Well, he's totally selfish when it comes to money. He won't spend a dime on anyone.

JOHN: But, he helped endow the new chair in Philosophy at the university.

THOMAS: Well, except for that he's totally selfish about whom he gives his money to.

Here, when Thomas is challenged with counter-evidence about David's seemingly unselfish giving of his time, he qualifies his initial claim by restricting David's selfishness to the giving of money. And again, when presented with a refuting claim about David's philanthropy, Thomas hedges by further restricting his assertion. It should be clear that while Thomas continues to insist on the total selfishness of David, his claims have weakened in an attempt to avoid refutation by John.

The third form of understatement, substitution, can take two forms: substituting contradictories for contraries and substituting weaker modalities for stronger ones. In the former, using a contradictory in place of a contrary weakens the claim by leaving open the possibility of a "grey area." Continuing the conversation on selfishness, watch how substitution works to understate the original case.

JOHN: Listen, Thomas, you can't keep hedging about selfishness. First, David is totally selfish; then he's totally selfish when it comes to money; then he's totally selfish about money except for this one case!

THOMAS: You're right, John. But, you have to admit, he's not a selfless person. I think the record is pretty clear on that.

JOHN: There you go again, Thomas! Is there no end to your hedging about this?!

THOMAS: Fine, John. You win. Let's just say that David *can* be selfish about some things.

JOHN: By the heavens, Thomas! How pedestrian of you.

In this last exchange, we see the final way in which the hedge might be deployed, through the substitution of weaker modalities for stronger ones. When they first began discussing David's selfish nature, Thomas made a very strong claim about David, and yet by the end he has exchanged all of his progressively understated claims with a rather uninformative modal (and further qualified) claim that David *can* be selfish about *some* things. But there isn't a person (not even the most selfless saint) to whom that claim doesn't apply!

One either refines the claim in light of counter-evidence by weakening the claim and then treating the revision as though it were what one originally intended or begins with a claim whose meaning is ambiguous and can therefore be more easily altered in light of counter-evidence without being refuted.

Alternately, hedging involves using words whose meanings are ambiguous, then changing the meaning of them later. You are hedging if you refine your claim simply to avoid counter-evidence and then act as if your revised claim is the same as the original.

As with most informal fallacies, hedging can easily be avoided by accepting the counter-evidence against the initial claim and revising the claim in light of that evidence. Thomas could have turned to John, at any of the points where John showed that a claim was arguably false, and said, "Well, maybe I'm wrong. Let me think about what you've said and see if I can come up with a better response." You're not committing the fallacy if you explicitly accept the counter-evidence, admit that your original claim is incorrect, and then revise it so that it avoids that counter-evidence. This is true even if you wind up with a weakened or more restricted claim as a result. Often the truth is weaker than we'd like. Just remember that it doesn't do to hold on to a strong claim that is false. In fact, there are no weaker claims than *false* claims. Temporarily retracting one's claim until better evidence can be found is a reasonable way to save face. Plus, it provides you with more opportunity to engage in philosophical analysis.

Reference

Jason, Gary. 1988. "Hedging as a Fallacy of Language." *Informal Logic* X(3): 169–175.

61

If by Whiskey

Christian Cotton

> If by God you mean the great dictator in the sky, the almighty smiter, the God who created us with imperfections then holds us responsible for the imperfections, the God who took away paradise and eternal life from us because the first man and woman committed a "wrong" against God before they were capable of knowing right from wrong [...] then He is certainly not deserving of our love and worship. But, if when you say God you mean the defender, the protector, creator of heaven and earth, the father of us all, the being of pure love, kindness, and everything good in the world [...] then certainly He is deserving of our love and worship.
>
> Bo Bennett, "If by Whiskey," at Logicallyfallacious.com

A common tactic in political discourse is to appear to take a moderate position, or "middle of the road" approach, on controversial issues, so as not to offend those upon whose vote the candidate or officeholder depends. Often, such a position takes the form of a response to a question that is contingent on the questioner's own stance on the issue and makes use of words with strong emotional connotations, all without actually answering the question. Instead, it avoids the question by *appearing* to answer it. The if by whiskey fallacy is a kind of deception by double talk in which one supports both sides of an issue by using terms that are selectively emotionally sensitive. The name derives from a 1952 speech made by Noah S. "Soggy" Sweat, Jr.,

Bad Arguments: 100 of the Most Important Fallacies in Western Philosophy, First Edition.
Edited by Robert Arp, Steven Barbone, and Michael Bruce.
© 2019 John Wiley & Sons Ltd. Published 2019 by John Wiley & Sons Ltd.

a legislator from the state of Mississippi, on the issue of whether Mississippi should continue its prohibition on alcohol:

> You have asked me how I feel about whiskey. All right, here is how I feel about whiskey: If when you say *whiskey* you mean the devil's brew, the poison scourge, the bloody monster, that defiles innocence, dethrones reason, destroys the home, creates misery and poverty, yea, literally takes the bread from the mouths of little children [...] then certainly I am against it. But, if when you say whiskey you mean the oil of conversation, the philosophic wine, the ale that is consumed when good fellows get together, that puts a song in their hearts and laughter on their lips, and the warm glow of contentment in their eyes [...] then certainly I am for it. (Oglesby)

It's clear that Sweat has taken no real stand, despite all his words. There is nothing from which he could retreat and nothing on which to compromise because he hasn't actually answered the question of whether the prohibition on alcohol should be lifted. He has merely disguised the issue in a host of emotional euphemisms, while leading the audience to see his "stand" as sympathetic to their own *whichever way they swing*. And yet, for all the rhetoric, we still don't know whether the sale of alcohol should be legal. To say, in effect, "It depends on what you mean by whiskey," is to reduce a substantive practical issue to a matter of semantics. This tactic can be deployed for many controversial issues for which there is, ostensibly, a "yes or no" answer. On the question of the legalization of cannabis, Pat Ogelsby (2013) writes:

> You have asked me how I feel about cannabis. All right, here is how I feel about cannabis: if by *cannabis* you mean the Devil's weed, the gateway to the nightmare of hard-drug addiction, the tempter of teenagers that terrifies parents, the cause of Willie Nelson's feeling that the flesh was falling off his bones, the impairer of judgment, the cause of fatal automobile crashes [...] then certainly I am against it. But, if when you say cannabis you mean the symbol of hostility against every form of tyranny over the mind, the miracle drug that treats dozens of diseases, the balm to humanity for millennia, the natural healer that tames the nausea of the cancer-stricken chemotherapy patient and restores appetite to the withering invalid, the safer-than-physically-addictive-opiates reliever of intractable pain [...] then certainly I am for it.

It's clear from these examples that the speaker is relying on a number of descriptors, many of them euphemisms, selectively chosen to appeal to the emotions of listeners. In this way, one could argue that this fallacy is a special case of the appeal to emotion fallacy (see chapters 13 and 14). And yet, we are no closer to an answer to the substantive question of legislation. There is, in fact, no argument at all here. As with the alcohol example, "It depends on what you mean by cannabis" is neither an argument nor an answer. It's semantics. Thus, because it is based on definitions that serve one's purpose rather than generally accepted definitions, one could argue this is a special case of the persuasive definition fallacy (see Chapter 55). However, because of its particular use, to avoid answering a question on a controversial matter in a clear and decisive manner, it certainly warrants its own label. It's important to see that these are *not* cases in which someone is simply conflicted on the issue and therefore isn't arguing for any particular position, but rather the cases in which someone is attempting to understand "both" sides of the issue. What makes examples such as these fallacious is avoiding the question while appearing to answer the question by using emotionally charged language.

The trick to avoiding this fallacy is, simply put, to *take a stand*! Don't play the language games. Don't try to curry favor with all sides in a debate. If you aren't comfortable taking a stand, for example, because you haven't thought deeply enough about the topic, then say so. In a case like that, it isn't a fallacy to weigh in on both sides. It is actually a sign that your critical thinking is engaged, that you are considering alternatives. In other words, it shows genuine conflict in your attitudes. As you grow more knowledgeable in the topic, you can begin to make arguments assessing the relative merits of both sides and choose the one that seems to you the best supported. There is no logical fault in playing it safe and considering multiple angles before making a commitment. The fault is in taking a stand that doesn't stand for anything.

Reference

Ogelsby, Pat. 2013. "Pros and Cons of Cannabis, 'If by Whiskey' Style." September 3. https://newrevenue.org/2013/09/03/marijuana-tax-in-context-if-by-cannabis/ (accessed October 2, 2017).

62

Inflation of Conflict

Andy Wible

> The number of skeptical qualified scientists has been growing steadily; I would guess it is about 40% now. I would like to see the public look upon global warming as just another scientific controversy and oppose any public policies until the major issues are settled.
> S. Fred Singer, founder of the Science and Environmental Policy Project

The inflation of conflict fallacy (IC) is the error of exaggerating the amount of disagreement in a field in order to invalidate claims in that field. In making the above claim, Singer wildly exaggerates the amount of disagreement among experts over global warming and goes on to suggest that it is a common scientific squabble that may safely be ignored for the time being. But multiple peer-reviewed studies have set the proportion of experts that agree on global warming at approximately 97%.

Another form of IC is a type of hasty generalization (see Chapter 84). Two authorities disagree on some topic, so we can say nothing meaningful about that field. For example, someone might say to himself, "Ken Ham and Bill Nye disagree on whether the Earth is 6,000 years old or 4.6 billion years old. So, given all of this disagreement, we have no clear idea how old the Earth really is." The problem with this example is that young Earth creationists like Ham are a fringe group. There is little to no actual disagreement among scientists on the approximate age of the Earth – 6,000 years is way off.

Bad Arguments: 100 of the Most Important Fallacies in Western Philosophy, First Edition. Edited by Robert Arp, Steven Barbone, and Michael Bruce.
© 2019 John Wiley & Sons Ltd. Published 2019 by John Wiley & Sons Ltd.

A juror or judge listening to two expert witnesses disagree on a topic might conclude there is enough reasonable doubt in the field to give a "not guilty" decision. The problem in this case is that payments made to such witnesses render their claims to unbiased expertise suspicious. A wider view of how things stand outside the courtroom may reveal little real disagreement among experts. Conventions in the popular press that promote "both sides of the story" or constant debate formats seem to encourage this type of IC.

Even when the conflict promoted is among genuine experts, concluding that the disagreement is common across the field is a faulty inference. For example, pointing out two credible scientists who disagree on global warming and that with such equal disagreement it is a toss-up on whether global warming is true is a mistake in reasoning.

A final form of IC correctly points to disagreement in a field but incorrectly implies that, as a result, little can be known. One scientist might claim that the Earth is 4.5 billion years old and another that its age is 4.6 billion years. The arguer then concludes that therefore we really have no idea of the age of the Earth. These scientists, though, are in fundamental agreement on the age of the Earth. More work may reveal whose estimate is more accurate, but the disagreement is minor. A similar example is when creationists criticize biologists for widely disagreeing about evolution when in truth the disagreement is on particular details of the theory and not on the core thesis of descent with modification.

IC is not always used to conclude that we can know nothing about a particular field. Often the disagreement is used to support an opposing position. A young Earth supporter may suggest that the disagreement among the "old" Earth supporters implies that her young 6,000-year-old hypothesis is right or just as good. The disagreement is alleged to render the issue subjective or supportive of contrarian views. The biblical evidence for a young Earth, it is claimed, is just as good as the scientific evidence for an old one, or even better due to the agreement among young Earth scientists.

Noting disagreement among authorities can be the basis of a good argument. When there is widespread disagreement on the core aspects of a topic and the participants are *bona fide* authorities, then there is a good reason for a non-expert to suspend judgment on the issue. Currently, physicians disagree on whether patients should take a multivitamin. Pointing out this controversy should lead the novice to suspend judgment and look into the issue more carefully.

Conflict among experts is good reason to question the topic as long as the conflict is not inflated.

63

Legalistic Mistake

Marco Antonio Azevedo

On the occasion of Elizabeth Anscombe's presentation of her paper "The Two Kinds of Error in Action" (1963) at the American Philosophical Association meeting in Columbus, Ohio, 1963, Joel Feinberg objected that *murder* was a "legal concept" so he might not have understood what Anscombe meant by the expression "morally speaking a murderer." Anscombe reacted by saying that no one concerns oneself with questions of legality in calling, for example, the killings practiced by the Hitler regime *murder*. She further claimed that any view such that all unjust killings of people are purely a matter of legality consists of a piece of wicked positivism, comparing it to Thrasymachus's claim in Plato's *Republic* that justice is merely the advantage of the stronger (338c). This was a harsh criticism, and Feinberg's response came one year later in a paper entitled "On Being 'Morally Speaking a Murderer'" (1964). It was in this paper that Feinberg introduced the idea that, sometimes, using legal notions outside legal contexts may lead to a peculiar kind of fallacy he called the legalistic mistake.

In her original paper, Anscombe's intended argument stood for the maxim that sometimes "error destroys action," which is to say that, at times, our lack of knowledge of some circumstances prevents our doing such and such from being a case of voluntarily performing an action of a particular sort. Some of Anscombe's examples were exemplifications of the well-known, albeit controversial, legal theory of *mens rea*. In fact, her approach was mainly the same one presented in her classic book *Intention* (1958a). One problem she had in mind is that "when we consider error about whether doing S in circumstances C *is doing A*, it is very difficult to show the rationale

Bad Arguments: 100 of the Most Important Fallacies in Western Philosophy, First Edition.
Edited by Robert Arp, Steven Barbone, and Michael Bruce.
© 2019 John Wiley & Sons Ltd. Published 2019 by John Wiley & Sons Ltd.

of *A*'s not being imputable to the agent. For he did voluntarily, even intentionally, do *S* in circumstances *C*" (Anscombe 1963, 397–398). One example was the following:

> A famous example is that of the public executioner who has private knowledge of a condemned man's innocence. In some way he knows he cannot make use of it to get the man off; and he is to execute him. The man had a fair trial. The question is whether it is, morally speaking, an act of murder for the executioner, at the command of his superiors, to perform his office in these circumstances. (Anscombe 1963, 398)

It was Anscombe's mentioning of the possibility of one's being called *morally speaking* a *murderer* that drew Feinberg's keen attention. Even though it is possible that Feinberg had in fact misunderstood her point, his remark on the possibility of a fallacious use (or rather, a misuse) of the word 'murder' was spot on. In his response, he explained that:

> In classifying 'murder' as a legal concept, [he] meant only that it finds its original, primary, and clearest application in legal contexts, and that therefore its use in those contexts is a convenient, even necessary, model for our understanding of its extended uses outside of the law. (Feinberg 1964, 158)

Feinberg chose to call these concepts "legal-like" instead of just "legal," hoping that this remark could obviate Anscombe's accusation of a wicked sort of positivism. On widening the use of such legal-like terms, we must be cautious, for we might find ourselves guilty of making inferential mistakes or even proffering pure nonsense. The error, according to Feinberg, is committed by "one who, in stating a moral question using a legal-like term, uncritically imports the precision of that term in its strict legal sense, while excluding appeal to the kinds of criteria which alone can decide its use" (Feinberg 1964, 161).

Feinberg's examples of words that are subject to this kind of abuse are, in addition to *murder*, terms such as *right, duty, responsibility, obligation, criminal, bankrupt, indebtedness, partnership*, all of them legal-like, that is, expressions whose original, primary, and clearest applications are legal or juridical. These terms can be distinguished from others that are widely employed in our normative vocabulary, such as *ought, good, bad, better*, which are not distinctively legal-like. And if the word *law* itself is legal-like, the same applies to *moral law* and the related concepts of *morally obliged* and *morally responsible*.

As Feinberg points out, Herbert Hart and Tony Honoré have suggested a similar kind of error committed by moral philosophers when uncritically using the term 'responsibility' in moral contexts, for, say they:

> Where there is no precise system of punishment, compensation, or reward to administer, ordinary men will not often have faced such questions as whether

the injuries suffered by a motorist who collides with another in swerving to avoid a child are consequences attributable to the neglect of the child's parents in allowing it to wander on to the road. (In Feinberg 1964, 161)

To this, Feinberg (1964) adds that his point is even stronger than that: "[i]n ordinary life, *in abstraction from all practical questions about punishment, compensation, and the like, there is no rational way of answering such questions*" (161). Anyone may use a legal-like term, but suppose one reacts to something you did, saying that you are "morally responsible for the harm." If this was done as an attempt at keeping you from doing the same in the future (maybe making you feel bad about yourself), the statement, so says Feinberg, was well made and meaningful. This is different if "we consider the question as one calling for cool and exact judgment, a 'verdict' issued on past events." In this case, he stresses, the question is ill formed, "for it asks us to sit on a kind of moral jury in a court in which normal juridical rules and reasons can have no relevance, but which has no alternative rules and reasons of a remotely legal-like kind" (Feinberg 1964, 161).

Surprisingly, this remark is rather similar to Anscombe's notorious observation in "Modern Moral Philosophy" (Anscombe 1958b). According to her, concepts such as moral obligation and moral duty and what is "morally right" or "wrong" are "survivals or derivatives from survivals from an earlier conception of ethics which no longer generally survives" (1). In this earlier and renowned paper, Anscombe (1958b) claims that the ordinary (and originally non-legal-like) terms as 'should,' 'need,' 'ought,' and 'must' had the special sense of 'being obliged,' 'being bound,' or 'required to,' in the sense of being obliged or bound "by law" (or as something required by law), as a result of the domination for centuries of the Christian law conception of ethics. In consequence of this cultural dominance, the concepts of being bound, permitted, or excused became "deeply embedded in our language and thought" (5). She claims that in the times of Christian dominance, this usage was perfectly in order; in fact, if you believe in God as a law-giver, as do Jews, Stoics, and Christians, the legal-like effects of those terms are natural and meaningful. So her critical assessment was rather of the usage made by the modern philosophers. At any rate, it is very likely, so she claims, that a legal-like notion could exert its effect even after losing its social and cultural roots; but in this case, it is only a psychological, almost delusionary effect. "It is as if the notion 'criminal' were to remain when criminal law and criminal courts had been abolished and forgotten" (6). Obviously, we are not obliged to agree with Anscombe, nor to support her harsh criticism of her contemporary colleagues; anyway, her criticism is very similar to Feinberg's, that is, when using legal-like terms, we should pay special attention to the criteria that make these terms meaningful in their legal or legislative original contexts. Now, the disagreement between Anscombe and Feinberg is explainable.

Anscombe would agree that 'murder' is a legal-like term with an original or primary legislative origin; in her rebuke of the executioner's case, what she probably had in mind was natural or divine law. For Feinberg (1964), instead, the case seems puzzling because there is a difficult problem of moral appraisal "that has nothing to do with the law or anything legal-like":

> In acting on his mistaken moral judgment, the executioner was at fault, and the fault accurately reveals a defect of character – poor moral judgment in some respects – which counts against a man in a final appraisal. Conscientiousness, on the other hand, is clearly a virtue. [...] Given that the executioner was at fault in killing his victim, and perhaps even therefore to blame for the death, it still does not follow that he is, in some strange moral sense, guilty of murder, or indeed that he is guilty of anything at all. (170)

If Feinberg is right, then philosophers should rethink their use of legalistic concepts in moral deontology. Of course, as a cautionary remark, the legalistic mistake does not preclude the use of legal-like terms in moral discourse; as with other informal fallacies, it is a recommendation for the use of persuasiveness, rigor, and clarity.

The use of "legal-like" terms abounds outside the legal domain. But sometimes the users of these terms commit the fallacy Feinberg called the legalistic mistake. Here is an example. In the abortion controversy, some pro-life advocates say, in a quite energetic tone, that "abortion is murder"; but "murder" is a legal-like concept. It is sometimes said that this statement can be inferred from the assumptions that "abortion" is the act of killing an embryo or a fetus, that human embryos and fetuses are *innocent* human beings, and that the act of intentionally killing an innocent human being is an act of *murder*. But the legal concept of "murder" does not apply to acts of killing human embryos or fetuses. Maybe what these pro-life advocates are trying to say is that abortion is an act of "murder" in a special "moral" sense, but that would be the same mistake Joel Feinberg had warned us against. Anyway, if the advocates are attempting to make an analogy, what they are saying is rather that the wrongness of abortion is roughly similar to (or as wrong as) the wrongness of murder. Nevertheless, abortion can be wrong independently of being morally or legally analogous to murder. Hence, the accusation of "murder" does not seem to contribute to the strength of the argument against abortion.

References

Anscombe, G.E.M. 1958a. *Intention*. Cambridge, MA: Harvard University Press.

Anscombe, G.E.M. 1958b. "Modern Moral Philosophy." *Philosophy* 33(124): 1–19.

Anscombe, G.E.M. 1963. "The Two Kinds of Error in Action." *The Journal of Philosophy* 60(14): 393–401.

Feinberg, J. 1964. "On Being 'Morally Speaking a Murderer'." *The Journal of Philosophy* 61(5): 158–171.

64

Oversimplification

Dan Burkett

> Lazy hands make for poverty, but diligent hands bring wealth.
>
> Proverbs 10:4

The fallacy of oversimplification occurs when we attempt to make something appear simpler by ignoring certain relevant complexities. We are bombarded with oversimplifications on a daily basis: poverty is the result of laziness; wealth comes from hard work; meat is murder; the global financial crisis was caused solely by corporate greed. Perhaps at some point, you've found yourself in a heated political debate and heard a friend blurt out something like the following: "That party is anti-immigration – so if you vote for them, you're a racist!" In saying this, your friend commits a very blatant act of oversimplification. Specifically, she assumes that immigration policy is the most influential factor in deciding which party you'll vote for. Suppose that you do vote for the party. Perhaps you *are* racist, but it's also possible that you strongly disagree with the party's views on immigration while nevertheless endorsing its progressive positions on many other issues.

This is an oversimplification of human motivations, but we can also oversimplify the way in which certain systems function. In 2014, Oklahoma Senator James Inhofe carried a snowball onto the Senate floor, effectively arguing that since it was snowing in Washington, climate change must be a myth. In doing so, he ignored a number of relevant complexities – including

Bad Arguments: 100 of the Most Important Fallacies in Western Philosophy, First Edition.
Edited by Robert Arp, Steven Barbone, and Michael Bruce.
© 2019 John Wiley & Sons Ltd. Published 2019 by John Wiley & Sons Ltd.

the important difference between local "weather" and global "climate." We can make oversimplifications about human-made systems too. The philosopher John Stuart Mill (1843) notes that there are many doctrines that "ascribe absolute goodness to particular forms of government, particular social arrangements, and even to particular modes of education, without reference to the state of civilization and the various distinguishing characters of the society for which they are intended" (553). The claim that the single best form of government is provided by communism, fascism, democratic socialism – or any other 'ism' for that matter – will undoubtedly involve a number of gross oversimplifications.

Sometimes oversimplification makes sense. The world can be a convoluted place, and we may need to ignore certain factors in order to get our heads around certain thorny ideas. But in other cases, oversimplification can be used deliberately to deceive or divide people. Politicians are particularly good at this, such as when – only nine days after the September 11 attacks – President George W. Bush claimed that "either you are with us, or you're with the terrorists." This oversimplification (which is also an example of a false dilemma; see Chapter 81) deliberately ignored a number of nuanced positions that individuals might hold toward the "War on Terror." Clearly, it was possible to object to some elements of the United States' foreign policy without necessarily being "with the terrorists."

Mill (1843) notes that a specific kind of oversimplification – "the fallacy of the single cause" – occurs when we attempt to "explain complicated phenomena by a simpler theory than their nature admits of" (552). Put another way, this version of the oversimplification fallacy involves assuming that a particular outcome has only one simple cause when in reality a number of complex causes may have been involved. These are sometimes referred to as "jointly sufficient causes."

Suppose, for example, that a severe thunderstorm washes away my cliff-side home and leaves me destitute. I might find myself saying something like the following to my friends: "I'm homeless and broke because of that storm." But while the storm was a *necessary* factor in the destruction of my home, it wasn't *sufficient*. There were several other causal factors that led to my current situation including (1) choosing to build my home in such a precarious location in the first place, (2) ignoring the advice of engineers and local officials, and (3) opting to forego comprehensive home insurance in favor of spending this money on more frivolous purchases. The storm wasn't the sole cause of my current circumstance. Instead, all of these factors taken together were *jointly sufficient*, and ignoring any one of them would be a bad case of oversimplification.

Why does this matter? Well, suppose I wanted to prevent the same thing happening again. If I identify the storm as the single cause of my destitution, then it seems there's not a lot I can do. "Storms are acts of God," I might say, "and there's nothing I can do to stop those." But if I recognize the wider set of sufficient causes, it becomes apparent that there are many ways in which I could avoid the same tragedy occurring a second time: I could insure my home, seek expert advice on its construction, or just build it somewhere safer.

This is where the real risk of oversimplification lies. Our understanding of relationships of cause and effect allows us to reason about – and interact with – the world around us. In fact, it's vital to our survival. I know that eating causes me not to starve, and that exposure to extreme heat or cold causes me to suffer harm. Understanding causal relationships is just as important on a more global scale. We cannot prevent another world war or avert the next Cuban Missile Crisis unless we fully understand the complex web of causal factors that brought about such events. If we oversimplify these causes, we may get things horribly wrong. Similar problems occur when we ignore the intricacies of natural systems or of human motivations. We cannot adequately address climate change until we recognize the many moving parts that make up the global environment, nor can we solve a refugee crisis unless we fully understand the myriad reasons *why* people decide to migrate.

In order to avoid the fallacy, we need to become comfortable with accepting complicated answers to certain questions. In cases of cause-and-effect, this means ignoring simplistic single-cause answers in favor of explanations that involve sets of jointly sufficient causes. Suppose, for example, that we were faced with the question: "What caused World War I?" In answering this question, it would be fallacious to reply simply with "the assassination of Archduke Franz Ferdinand." This event was not, on its own, sufficient for the outbreak of World War I. Nor was this event even necessary. Instead, a better answer would be that the assassination was one of a number of factors that – when taken in concert – were *jointly sufficient* for the outbreak of global conflict. Among these would be various domestic political factors, a climate of growing nationalism and militarism, and a precarious system of alliances between nations. This answer may be more complex, and less elegant, but it has the advantage of being a more accurate description of the way in which the world actually operates.

When we obscure, ignore, or simply fail to identify certain factors, we run a high risk of misunderstanding reality. If we try to address an issue on the basis of this mistaken understanding, there's a good chance our actions will – at best – be ineffective, or – at worst – exacerbate the very problem we are trying to solve.

Reference

Mill, John Stuart. 1843. *A System of Logic, Ratiocinative and Inductive*. Cambridge, UK: Cambridge University Press.

65

Proof by Verbosity

Phil Smolenski

> When the Sun shines upon Earth, 2 major Time points are created on opposite sides of Earth, known as Midday and Midnight. Where the 2 major Time forces join, synergy creates 2 new minor Time points we recognize as Sunup and Sundown. The 4-equidistant Time points can be considered as Time Square imprinted upon the circle of Earth. In a single rotation of the Earth sphere, each Time corner point rotates through the other 3-corner Time points, thus creating 16 corners, 96 hours and 4-simultaneous 24-hour Days within a single rotation of Earth – equated to a Higher Order of Life Time Cube.
>
> Gene Ray, see https://en.wikipedia.org/wiki/Time_Cube

A proof by verbosity (PVB) – also known as *argumentum verbosium* and proof by intimidation – is a rhetorical device that seeks to persuade by overwhelming the audience with vast amounts of material, or by making the argument so complex and laden with technical jargon that it makes the argument sound plausible. The resulting argument is so complicated and convoluted that no one is able to refute it, obliging the listeners to accept it as sound lest they have to admit their ignorance.

The fallacy is nicely epitomized by W.C. Fields, "If you can't dazzle them with your brilliance, then baffle them with your bullshit." By using deliberately complex reasoning, the speaker is trying to ensure that the audience won't be able to follow and/or understand the argument. D.S. Maier (2012)

Bad Arguments: 100 of the Most Important Fallacies in Western Philosophy, First Edition.
Edited by Robert Arp, Steven Barbone, and Michael Bruce.
© 2019 John Wiley & Sons Ltd. Published 2019 by John Wiley & Sons Ltd.

describes PVB as a meandering maze of reasoning, which can be made difficult to follow by incorporating a plethora of irrelevant details used to disorient the audience. He concludes that, if, against all odds, an audience member manages to find her way to the conclusion of the argument, the relief of reaching the conclusion may leave her reluctant to reconstruct the torturous route of reasoning needed to question the soundness of the argument adequately. Potentially unsubstantiated claims and invalid inferences and deductions gain an allure of plausibility because it is often too laborious to wade through all the minute details of the argument in order to untangle and verify each of the supporting propositions.

Gene Ray's (2015) Time Cube is a perfect example of a meandering maze of reasoning. Despite his $10,000 reward for anyone who manages successfully to refute his argument, no one in Ray's lifetime had ever ventured publicly to take Ray up on his offer. Ray rambles on for page after page, filling his writing with unintelligible terminology and creating such a complex web of reasoning that it obscures everything, including logical defects.

Even though the argument may be entirely obscure, and totally incorrect, the speaker attempts to prey on an audience's vanity by exploiting its fear of looking ignorant or stupid in the eyes of fellow audience members. The underlying strategy is to shift the burden from the speaker of the complex and verbose argument to the audience members. A PVB succeeds by insinuating that the flaw is not with the argument under consideration but with some potentially dim-witted members of the audience. Far from being an honest attempt to prove the soundness of an argument, it is an effort by the speaker to persuade the audience through bewilderment since any attempt to clearly articulate the argument may only serve to expose its underlying logical flaws and substantive inaccuracies.

Academics are especially susceptible to PVB when the author(s) cites countless obscure sources and includes an extensive notes section. According to John Grant (2015) in *Debunk It!*, the author is relying on the fact that most people won't bother undertaking the gargantuan task of checking the sources, knowing full well that most people will accept the dubious scholarships at face value. If someone is looking to commit the fallacy, Michael Wilkinson (2014) recommends citing something with a very impressive name, offering up the *Craske-Trump Theorem* as a promising candidate. The key is to cite the theorem in a tone implying that anyone in the field should know what it is.

PVB is a favorite device among conspiracy theorists who utilize it to obfuscate the weakness of their case. By supporting their theories with so much random information (and misinformation), it gives the impression that their position is superficially well researched and supported by an avalanche of evidence. 9/11 "Truthers" will often roll out a barrage of alternative (and wildly inconceivable) explanations or will present some fanciful account that questions the veracity of the official story. Faced with an overabundance of claims, it becomes hopeless even to begin to respond intelligibly to each individual claim. Being unable (or more accurately, unwilling) to counter the "Truthers'" position, may give the impression that their argument is irrefutable.

Sometimes PVB takes the form of a proof by intimidation, especially when an argument is made using sophisticated insider jargon, or when a complex and long-winded argument is made by an eminent scholar in the field. The appeal to authority (see Chapter 32), coupled with the verbose nature of the argument, is meant to shock and awe the audience into sub-mission. Audience members may be too intimidated by the speaker's stature, or the complexity of the argument to question its conclusions, opting instead to accept it as correct. Consider Rush Limbaugh's comments from his October 14, 2015 show:

> The reason you don't see huge lines of people waiting in soup lines in this depression is why? Let me just ask you. And let me give you a number [...]. Now, granted, population of the country was less than it is today. There were 12.8 million Americans unemployed during the Great Depression. These were the men pictured in those soup lines. Today, there are 46 million Americans unemployed. And 94 million not working. I don't care what – now these 46 million people, these are the counted unemployed, this is the U-3 number. The counted unemployed represent 14 percent of the population. There are 23 million households on food stamps. There are 123 million households in America and 23 million of them are on food stamps. Therefore 19 percent of all house-holds in America require food stamp assistance to survive.

In the spirit of overwhelming the opposition, a PVB can be committed by employing a litany of numbers and statistics. Figuring out precisely how the number of people that are currently unemployed explains why we don't see people waiting in soup lines is anything but clear. Even if we're able to cobble together the connection, we're still faced with the daunting task of verifying the accuracy of Limbaugh's numbers and the credibility of his sources. Our unwillingness to perform the tiresome task of refuting his claims leads us to accept the reasoning as sound. Now consider Donald Rumsfeld's words from a February 12, 2002 interview:

> Reports that say that something hasn't happened are always interesting to me, because as we know, there are known knowns; there are things we know we know. We also know there are known unknowns; that is to say we know there are some things we do not know. But there are also unknown unknowns – the ones we don't know we don't know. [...] The absence of evidence is not evi-dence of absence.

Responding to whether or not there were weapons of mass destruction in Iraq, Rumsfeld makes every effort to obfuscate the issue. Despite the long-winded explanation, we're still left puzzled about the status of weapons of mass destruction in Iraq, but with all this uncertainty floating around, we may be tempted to question how much the media actually knows.

Articulating your arguments in a clear and concise fashion and substantiating your position with well-founded and mutually intelligible premises is the key to avoiding a proof by verbosity. Clarity is a virtue in writing, and good writing and reasoning does not need to be laden with technical jargon and complex or convoluted reasoning to demonstrate the brilliance of your position. The emphasis should be on distilling any argument into one that is accessible to your audience by placing the onus on the speaker to demonstrate the veracity of her claims and to persuade the audience with the soundness of her position, instead of dazzling it with flash and bullshit. The fallacy may be committed as a result of malice or carelessness, in which case the speaker should employ a greater degree of integrity and care while presenting what she takes to be the strongest case for her position.

References

Grant, John. 2015. *Debunk It! How to Stay Sane in a World of Misinformation.* San Francisco, CA: Zest Books.

Limbaugh, Rush. 2015. *Rush Limbaugh Show.* October 14.

Maier, D.S. 2012. *What's so Good about Biodiversity?: A Call for Better Reasoning about Nature's Value.* New York, NY: Springer.

Ray, Gene. 2017. "Time Cube." Wikipedia, October 20. https://en.wikipedia.org/wiki/Time_Cube (accessed October 24, 2017).

Rumsfeld, Donald. 2012. "DoD News Briefing: Secretary Rumsfeld and Gen. Myers." *News Transcript*, US Department of Defense, February 12. http://archive.defense.gov/ Transcripts/Transcript.aspx?TranscriptID = 2636 (accessed October 2, 2017).

Wilkinson, Michael. 2014. "Cogno-Intellecualism, Rhetorical Logic, and the Craske-Trump Theorem." *Annals of Improbable Research* 6(52): 15–16.

66

Sorites Fallacy

Jack Bowen

> The FDA can't claim one product as *natural* while another is not, because one small change along the continuum of not-natural to natural doesn't matter: you can't draw a line between something that's "natural" and something that's not. So therefore, nothing is natural.
>
> Jane Doe

One commits the sorites fallacy (SF) when claiming that because a continuum exists between two distinct categories or states of affairs, then those categories cannot truly be asserted as distinct. The term *sorites* derives from the Greek word *soros*, meaning "heap." While it can apply to more real-world issues than heaps of sand, the fallacy is best understood in its original conception. Imagine seeing a collection of sand grains upon which you claim it to not constitute a *heap* of sand. (Maybe you refer to it as a mere *pile*?) A friend then adds a grain of sand to the pile and asks whether it is now a heap. You respond with a universally acceptable claim:

> If something isn't a heap, then adding a single grain of sand doesn't make it a heap.

And yet, if one does this enough – trillions of times, let's say – then, clearly, the pile *does become*, at some point, a heap.

Bad Arguments: 100 of the Most Important Fallacies in Western Philosophy, First Edition. Edited by Robert Arp, Steven Barbone, and Michael Bruce.
© 2019 John Wiley & Sons Ltd. Published 2019 by John Wiley & Sons Ltd.

The term *heap* has a fully functioning usage in our language. While we may not need to agree, in this particular case, as to how many grains designate a heap – or a pile, mound, and so on – this should not render the term useless, concluding that heaps do not actually exist.

The paradox works the other way as well. Upon seeing an exceptionally large collection of sand grains, you deem it a *heap* of sand. Your friend meticulously removes one grain and asks if it is still a heap. You vehemently defend that it is. After your friend repeats the action a number of times, each time removing one grain and asking if it remains a heap, you retort:

> If something is a heap, then subtracting a single grain of sand doesn't cause it to cease being a heap.

And yet, we know that doing this enough times will render the collection of sand grains miniscule and, with just three grains remaining, clearly not a heap.

And thus arises the SF: heaps of sand exist. Such fallacious argumentation can apply to any situation involving minor incremental changes, such as a single penny in determining whether someone is rich or poor, or a single day, minute, or second in determining the moral status of a human being such as is the case in asserting when a fetus becomes a moral entity.

Imagine someone's applying this to the abortion argument. Upon encountering an argument that a fetus at the time of the first trimester then becomes a full-fledged moral person and, thus, cannot be terminated, the counter-argument is given:

> But one day (or minute, or second) *after* the first trimester doesn't matter. Since one day doesn't matter, then the second day shouldn't matter either. And then, the day after that, and so on. So, since you can keep adding seconds, minutes, and days to your original position, then the fetus never becomes a moral entity.

In the case of a developing fetus, a continuum exists from conception (which itself is more of a process than an exact moment) to the time of birth. And so the fallacy can be applied both ways. On the one hand, as per above, if you think it's permissible to kill a fertilized egg, then you must think it permissible to kill a human baby. And on the other, if you think it's wrong to kill a new-born baby, then you must also agree it is wrong to kill a fertilized egg.

It's important to recognize a key difference between developing heaps and developing humans. Adding grains of sand to heaps doesn't affect any essential quality of a heap of sand. And yet, the growth of a human being *does* involve its developing what we might consider essential qualities. Throughout the stages in its development – that is, as days upon days transpire – the human fetus *does* change in important ways, developing organs – heart, brain, etc. – and other qualities such as sentience and viability, which we may find more relevant to an entity maintaining moral standing.

The flipside of this fallacy is that a word cannot maintain its meaning void of any criteria for proper usage. For example, if one were to use the word *natural* to include something like Yellow #5 based on the fact that Yellow #5 is made entirely from things "of nature" – that is, carbon, hydrogen, etc. – then it would render the term *natural* as meaningless. The term *natural* must have criteria for using the word correctly in order to maintain meaning. Imagine every item in a grocery store having the stamp, "All-Natural"; it would fail to convey any meaning at all. Thus, with a vague term like *natural*, qualifications must be made. And, simply because incremental additions (or subtractions) in the definition of *natural* can be made between two items on opposite ends of the spectrum doesn't mean that those two items are both "natural," as per the SF.

In addition, the SF helps us to distinguish between vagueness and relativity. For example, the term *rich* is a relative term: a person in one part of the world may be considered rich there – that is, this person has considerably more money than most people living in that region – and yet, were this person to move to a more affluent part of the world, the person may be considered as not-rich or even poor. That is to say, being rich has something to do with one's place in society. But, within that, we can apply the SF to highlight the vagueness of the term. If a person in a specific culture is considered rich, then upon discovering he lost a penny, we would not then deem him as not-rich. Yet, were he to lose a penny repeatedly, it's certainly feasible that he would become not-rich. Were one to claim that no difference exists between rich and poor based on the "losing a penny" defense, one would be committing the SF.

Recognizing the SF is helpful, on the one hand, in highlighting the vagueness of our linguistic constructs and categorical thinking. In a sense, it serves as a reminder of the inherent problem of our natural inclination to think categorically: in our habit of mind that the world fits into and abides by our human-made categories, when it fails to do so, we should not be alarmed but should, instead, recognize this problem of language to begin with. But it also serves to remind us that simply because of the vagueness of categories, we shouldn't render these categories as non-existent or vacuous.

Fallacies of Presumption

67

Accident

Steven Barbone

> This is something in English up with which I will not put!
> Attributed to Winston Churchill on ending sentences with a preposition

The fallacy of accident often occurs when we let our attention become distracted by factors, which may be true, other than those relevant in an argument. Accidents do not have to be unintentional, and, in fact, many times the fallacy of accident occurs when something is done quite intentionally. In essence, the fallacy of accident occurs when we apply a generalization that is usually true or good to a particular case to which it does not apply.

For example, we all know the Golden Rule: do unto others as you would have them to undo you. Generally speaking, it would be a violation of the Golden Rule to wound someone intentionally with a knife. Yet, if you needed an operation, you would welcome the surgeon who slices you open. In this case, it is accidental that the surgeon wounds you since while the surgeon certainly is intentionally cutting you with a knife (if that's not a wound, then it's not certain what is), this is not the surgeon's main goal. The so-called wounding here is just a step (and a necessary one at that) to achieve a larger goal. Those who claim that the surgeon violates the Golden Rule are guilty of using the accident fallacy since they are applying a generalization – and a good one at that – to a case where it does not apply.

Bad Arguments: 100 of the Most Important Fallacies in Western Philosophy, First Edition.
Edited by Robert Arp, Steven Barbone, and Michael Bruce.
© 2019 John Wiley & Sons Ltd. Published 2019 by John Wiley & Sons Ltd.

Another example concerns a student, let's say, Sam. Sam is a notorious cheater, and he is quite well known and appreciated by some for his clever cheat sheets. The instructor, however, knows about Sam's reputation and takes measures to assure that Sam isn't able to cheat on the final exam by scrupulously monitoring him. The exam day comes, and Sam does not cheat. Should the instructor think that Sam's efforts to cheat have been checked? In this case, it is merely an accident that Sam did not cheat because, on this occasion, he misplaced his cheat sheet the day of the exam. Had he had it with him, he would have been able to use it successfully. Again, a generalization – students don't cheat if you monitor them – is applied to a case where it does not fit.

While the fallacy of accident is an informal fallacy, we can imagine that it has something like this as a form:

(1) General principle or rule X applies across the board.
(2) <u>Particular case x is an example of X.</u>
(3) Thus X applies to x (except it doesn't since x is a very particular case).

One way to detect or to avoid this fallacy is to ask yourself what generalization is being applied. Once you have that figured out, you can ask yourself whether it really does apply in all cases across the board or whether there is a reason to make an exception in some particular case. If you can think of or imagine some other possibility to the general rule or principle, then you should consider whether the particular case really is a violation of that rule. If such a case exists, beware for a fallacy of accident may be lurking about! And remember, never ever end a sentence with a preposition like up, with, or about.

68
All or Nothing
David Kyle Johnson

> Laws cannot stop the madness.
> Bill O'Reilly, *The O'Reilly Factor* (Fox News, October 5, 2015)

The all or nothing fallacy (AON) is a variety of the false dilemma fallacy that is committed anytime someone presents only two options when in fact there are more. AON presents a false dilemma (see Chapter 81) by suggesting that there are only two options – either all or nothing – when in fact there are many more options in the middle ground between those two extremes. As an easy example, if someone says you can either eat the whole pie or none of it, he is clearly committing the AON fallacy; part of the whole (a piece) is clearly a third option.

It probably goes without saying that if "all" and "nothing" *really are* the only two options, then the fallacy is not committed. If you are playing roulette and bet on black, either it will land on black or it won't, so you'll either double your money or you will lose it. That is a good bit of reasoning. It really is all or nothing. But reality usually is not so black and red. Of course, in standard logic, every proposition is either true or false; but for any given circumstance, there is usually a number of different propositions that could be true or false. So usually there are more than just two options.

Bad Arguments: 100 of the Most Important Fallacies in Western Philosophy, First Edition.
Edited by Robert Arp, Steven Barbone, and Michael Bruce.
© 2019 John Wiley & Sons Ltd. Published 2019 by John Wiley & Sons Ltd.

As evidence that the all or nothing is especially important to be careful to avoid, consider the fact that it played a fairly major role in enabling Hitler to take control of Germany and start World War II. In *Mein Kampf*, Hitler suggests that taking advantage of people's inclination to see things in such black and white terms – making them think it's either all or nothing – is how propaganda works (Surve 2008). It's either us or them; you're either with us or against us. Perhaps if people had been more careful to identify and to avoid the all or nothing fallacy when responding to his propaganda, the world would be a very different place today.

Sometimes AON involves actual wholes and parts. Biblical literalists, for example, will insist that you have to believe that every word of the Bible is literally true or believe none of it – that doubting just one part is equivalent to doubting it all. But, of course, even if one believes the Bible is God inspired, it's possible to take parts of it literally (e.g., the gospels) and other parts of it metaphorically (e.g., the Genesis creation story). Inspiration aside, it's also possible to embrace parts of it as true (like Jesus's moral teachings), and reject others parts of it as fiction (like Jesus's miracles). Interestingly, Thomas Jefferson actually published a version of the gospels that left out their miraculous supernatural elements; he called it *The Life and Morals of Jesus of Nazareth*. Given that this kind of all or nothing biblical literalism is what motivates creationism, and that the pressure to teach creationism (and avoid teaching evolution) in public classrooms has greatly hindered scientific education in America, we can once again see the importance of avoiding the all or nothing fallacy.

Not surprisingly, AON also happens in the political arena anytime a politician insists that being against one of her policies is equivalent to being against all of them. Often people adopt a kind of all or nothing attitude when it comes to supporting a candidate or political party.

But AON also appears in politics when people are proposing or drafting laws and policy. Take, for example, gun regulations. When people call for gun regulations after a mass shooting, opponents of such regulations often say that gun regulations are useless (and should be avoided) because they cannot stop all gun-related crime. No matter how strict gun laws are, criminals will still be able to get guns and commit crimes. After all, criminals (by definition) don't obey the law – so how could a gun law prevent a criminal from committing a crime with a gun? Gun laws will only stop "good guys" from getting guns, not bad guys.

But this argument employs the all or nothing fallacy in many ways. For one, when it comes to laws and regulations, it's seldom an all or nothing affair. Lawmakers don't expect laws to eliminate all the behavior they are trying to restrict, but that doesn't mean laws shouldn't exist. Speeding laws aren't going to keep everyone from speeding, but that doesn't mean there should be no speed limit. Laws are often merely aimed and lowering the frequency of certain kinds of behavior. So the fact that a gun regulation would not eliminate all gun crime is irrelevant to whether it should be passed – Dowden (2015) calls this the "perfectionist fallacy."

Of course, the argument also suggests that gun laws would be completely ineffectual – criminals would still find ways to buy guns. After all, criminals don't obey laws. But, once again, this invokes the all or nothing fallacy. Sure, *some* criminals would find a way around the new regulation – but not all of them. The harder it is for criminals to acquire guns, the fewer criminals will have them. The argument seems to be suggesting that you can either stop all criminals from acquiring guns or none of them, when obviously there is a middle ground. Notice that it's also true that no amount of illicit drug regulation will keep illicit drugs out of the hands of all users, but that doesn't entail that drugs should be legal or unregulated.

The argument also invokes the all or nothing fallacy when it talks about the difference between criminals and "good guys" – as if a criminal is someone who disobeys all laws and a good guy is someone who disobeys none. But, of course, reality is far more nuanced; even the best of us have disobeyed some laws, and even the worst of us have obeyed others. What's more, many of even the worst of us would not even know where to go to find an assault rifle on the black market – much less be willing to take the risk of buying illegal assault rifles on it. So, gun regulations could still prevent many criminals from buying guns despite the fact that it wouldn't stop them all.

Sadly, however, many perpetrators of mass shootings don't buy the guns they use; they acquire them from others who bought them legally. They don't even steal them, per se; they "borrow" them (with or without permission) from a person they know (and often that person has been stockpiling). But that doesn't mean that regulating gun purchases couldn't lower the number of mass shootings. They could still lower the number of guns in the country, thus making it harder for potential mass shooters to "borrow" guns. Other possibilities include restricting certain kinds of extra-lethal ammunition, extended ammunition clips, certain kinds of extra-lethal weapons, or even the number of guns someone can own. We might even pass laws that would make a gun owner legally responsible if she (intentionally or accidentally) allowed her gun to be used in a crime.

Of course, the reduction of gun crimes is not the only thing to consider in such matters, and such regulations wouldn't eliminate gun violence altogether. Laws cannot stop *all* the madness. But thinking that we shouldn't pass a law unless it will be 100% effective commits the all or nothing fallacy. And since gun violence and gun regulation are two of the most pressing issues of our time, we have one last example of why we should take careful pains to avoid AON.

References

Dowden, Bradley. 2015. "Fallacies." *Internet Encyclopedia of Philosophy*, October 19. http://www.iep.utm.edu/fallacy/#Perfectionist (accessed October 2, 2017).

Surve, Sajid. 2008. "Hitler's Guide to Propaganda – The Psychology of Coercion." BrainBlogger, November 4. http://brainblogger.com/2008/11/04/hitlers-guide-to-propaganda-the-psychology-of-coercion/ (accessed October 2, 2017).

69

Anthropomorphic Bias

David Kyle Johnson

> They have hearts, as much as we do. And they have desires, and they want to give as much as we do. And they do, if not more.
>
> Pet psychic customer on *Penn & Teller: Bullshit*

One displays an anthropomorphic bias when one displays a tendency to ascribe humanlike characteristics, usually mental properties or agency, to things that do not have it. The most obvious (but harmless) example occurs when your computer malfunctions and you yell at it, as if verbal reprimand might convince it to do what you want. If it malfunctions at an inopportune time, you may even conclude that your computer is out to get you. If so, you are ascribing humanlike agency to your computer that it does not have; you're displaying an anthropomorphic bias.

People are apt to do this with animals as well, especially their pets. Now, of course, I am not suggesting that animals do not share some characteristics with humans – even some mentality. My dog, Alex, for example, feels pain, gets hungry, and likely feels some level of wants and desires. He might even feel affection for me. What our pets do not have is a psychology that is as complicated as a human's. Their brains simply are not complicated enough. The lady quoted at the beginning of this chapter, who took her dog to a pet psychic, has not only mistakenly concluded that psychics can read minds; she has also mistakenly concluded that her pet has a mind and psychological

Bad Arguments: 100 of the Most Important Fallacies in Western Philosophy, First Edition.
Edited by Robert Arp, Steven Barbone, and Michael Bruce.
© 2019 John Wiley & Sons Ltd. Published 2019 by John Wiley & Sons Ltd.

life as complicated as a human's. She has anthropomorphized her dog. I'm not saying that there is anything wrong with treating your pets as if they are your children; I'm guilty of that myself. But concluding that they actually have a mental life equivalent to a child's would be fallacious.

An example that is a bit more obvious and egregious is when people conclude that ghosts are the cause of unexplained noises or motions. Although this invokes the mystery therefore magic fallacy (see Chapter 38), it also includes ascribing humanlike agency to something that does not have it: the cause of the noise or motion. One student of mine had a boyfriend who committed this fallacy: "Every time it gets cold in my room I hear a rattling sound. Therefore a ghost must be causing the cold and the sound." Anthropomorphizing the cause of the noise and cold into a ghost kept him from realizing that it was steam moving through the pipes because the heat was kicking on. The results of one study, by Willard and Norenzayan (2013), even shows that the anthropomorphic bias leads to belief in the paranormal.

A similar example is found when we ascribe agency to weather. Even today when lightning strikes, tornados hit, or a hurricane destroys property, we are apt to think that there is some kind of reasoning or purpose behind it. Indeed, it seems likely that this is where belief in gods like Zeus originated. In the absence of an explanation for lightning, the ancients concluded that it was caused by a powerful person. A similar kind of logic could lead you to believe that things like the sun and moon are gods. As I have often thought upon seeing a full moon rise on a clear night: "If I hadn't been taught by science what that was, I'd probably worship it as a god too." Indeed Stewart Guthrie (1995) has argued that all our belief in the supernatural – including our belief in God – originates from the anthropomorphic bias.

Why are we apt to anthropomorphize non-human objects? It's likely hardwired by evolution. The explanation often goes something like this: In our hunter-gatherer days, if we heard a rustle in the nearby bushes, we were better off concluding that it was something with a mind (like a tiger) out to get us. We'd run away, and that made us more likely to survive. Withholding judgment on the matter until more evidence was gathered would have been the more rational conclusion to draw – after all, it's likely just the wind – but given that it occasionally would be a hungry tiger, drawing the rational conclusion would make one less likely to survive. Although a tiger is not a human – so this is not exactly an example of full-blown anthropomorphizing even though humanlike agency is ascribed to it – it is likely from this kind of selective pressure that our tendency comes to ascribe agency where it doesn't belong.

But we are also apt to anthropomorphize because the tendency to do so does involve a bit of sound reasoning. When something behaves in a humanlike fashion, it is somewhat rational to conclude that it has some humanlike properties. The fact that my dog yelps when I accidentally step on his toe is a solid indication that he feels pain like I do.

Indeed, one of the most famous arguments in philosophy follows this line of reasoning: the Turing Test. It suggests that if an artificial intelligence displays an understanding of language that mimics that of a human, one should conclude that the artificial intelligence actually does understand language like a human does. Some have claimed the argument as fallacious because of the anthropomorphic bias, but I have our argued elsewhere (Johnson 2011) that the argument is sound.

Indeed, the solution to another philosophical argument suggests that such reasoning is sound – the problem of other minds. The problem of other minds points out that each person is only aware of his own mentality; I am only aware of my mind, you are only aware of yours. Consequently, every person has no direct evidence for the conclusion that anyone has a mind but herself. For all you know, the argument suggests, you are the only one that has a mind. The solution is found, however, in realizing two things: (1) because everyone else behaves essentially like you do, they behave as if they are minded; (2) the hypothesis that they are minded is the best explanation for such behavior. Thus I am justified in believing others have minds (even though I cannot prove it by observing their minds directly).

So this rule – if something behaves pretty much like I do, it is likely minded pretty much like I am – seems reasonable. This is why, if we one day invent androids that behave essentially like humans, I think we should conclude that they have minds. One is guilty of the anthropomorphic bias, however, when one stretches this kind of reasoning too far – when one sees a single or limited number of things that remind him of humanlike behavior and then jumps to the conclusion that the entity in question possesses a humanlike mind. For more on the anthropomorphic bias see Strongman (2007).

References

Guthrie, Stewart. 1995. *Faces in the Clouds: A New Theory of Religion*. New York, NY: Oxford University Press.

Johnson, David Kyle. 2011. "Watson in Philosophical Jeopardy?" *Psychology Today*, February 15. https://www.psychologytoday.com/blog/plato-pop/201102/watson-in-philosophical-jeopardy (accessed October 2, 2017).

Strongman, L. 2007. "The Anthropomorphic Bias: How Human Thinking Is Prone to Be Self-referential." *Working Papers No. 4–07*. Lower Hutt, NZ: The Open Polytechnic of New Zealand.

Willard, A.K., and A. Norenzayan. 2013. "Cognitive Biases Explain Religious Belief, Paranormal Belief, and Belief in Life's Purpose." *National Center for Biotechnology Information*. US National Library of Medicine. Web. http://www.ncbi.nlm.nih.gov/pubmed/23974049 (accessed October 2, 2017).

70

Begging the Question

Heather Rivera

> The death penalty is wrong, because killing people is immoral.
>
> Jane Doe

Begging the question (*petitio principii*, Latin for "seeking the beginning") is a logical fallacy in which the premise of an argument presupposes the truth of its conclusion; in other words, the argument takes for granted what it is supposed to prove. This is often presented when the conclusion is so ingrained in the mind of the speaker that it becomes the absolute truth and so the initial point is the answer. There is no evidence other than the conclusion itself. When used in this sense, the word *beg* means "to avoid," not "to ask" or "to lead to." This is circular reasoning in which the conclusion is included in the initial point, and the premises include the claim that the conclusion is true with no support for the argument other than its own initial statements, which are its conclusion; this can become a vicious cycle because of the never-ending argument that always reverts to the initial point (Garner 1995, 101). A good way to understand this is to consider the chicken and egg argument – an argument that will go in circles forever. This type of reasoning typically has the following form:

(1) Claim X assumes X is true.
(2) Therefore, claim X is true.

Bad Arguments: 100 of the Most Important Fallacies in Western Philosophy, First Edition.
Edited by Robert Arp, Steven Barbone, and Michael Bruce.
© 2019 John Wiley & Sons Ltd. Published 2019 by John Wiley & Sons Ltd.

Examples of this form in use would be arguments or reasoning such as:

> If such actions were not illegal, then they would not be prohibited
> by law.
> Circular reasoning is bad because it is not very good.
> The Bible is true because God exists, and God exists because the
> Bible says so.
> The rights of the minority are every bit as sacred as the rights of the
> majority, for the majority's rights have no greater value than those of
> the minority.
> Free speech is important because everyone should speak freely.

As one can easily see, begging the question is really just a way to say the
exact same thing by rephrasing it. It therefore becomes circular reasoning
that does not prove the stated conclusion. Begging the question is merely
repeating a point already made by any of the premises.

In works such as *Prior Analytics* and *Topics*, Aristotle was the first to
introduce begging the question by stating what translates to "asking the
initial thing" or "asking the original point":

> Begging or assuming the point at issue consists (to take the expression in its
> widest sense) of failing to demonstrate the required proposition. But there are
> several other ways in which this may happen; for example, if the argument has
> not taken syllogistic form at all, he may argue from premises which are less
> known or equally unknown, or he may establish the antecedent by means of
> its consequents; for demonstration proceeds from what is more certain and is
> prior. Now begging the question is none of these. [...] If, however, the relation
> of B to C is such that they are identical, or that they are clearly convertible, or
> that one applies to the other, then he is begging the point at issue [... B]egging
> the question is proving what is not self-evident by means of itself [...] either
> because predicates which are identical belong to the same subject, or because
> the same predicate belongs to subjects which are identical. (*Prior Analytics*
> II xvi 64b28–65a26)

This particular logical fallacy is very often committed in our modern speech.
We hear fallacies in our daily lives, and most of us don't know that what we
are hearing is fallacious. Labeling an argument as "begging the question" is
often itself using the fallacy's name incorrectly, and yet we accept this incorrect usage. Moreover, this misuse has become commonplace in advertising,
the media, and literature as well. It is worth noting that the media are the
biggest culprits of this misuse; anytime that you turn on any 24-hour news
outlet, you will almost certainly hear a news personality say to whomever is
being interviewed, "Well, this certainly begs the question," and then insert
the question brought up by the answer previously given. What the journalist

really means to say is "This prompts the question of whatever" or "This raises the question of the actions of General So-and-so."

This misuse also happens often in our daily lives. Think of a conversation with a friend, family member, or neighbor about the latest news on some celebrity.

SPEAKER 1:   *Miss Popular Actress* is in court again; I can't understand why they give her so much coverage.
SPEAKER 2:   Yeah, that really begs the question, why does anybody want to hear or read about her?

Another example in common speech would be:

> Timmy told me he is going to attend Big State University this fall. This begs the question, how will he do so far away from home?

The previous examples show the utter misuse of the term *begging the question*. These examples are of nothing more than further questions being raised, issues prompted by the original information being supplied or presented. They are not showing a circular type of reasoning or presenting the initial statement as the conclusion or as a fact to prove the statement.

Politics is a common place for begging the question. Politicians in a debate often beg the question by giving answers that give the conclusion of the person they are citing as a truth or fact and never show any real proof of the matter. "Abortion is ending a life and murder is ending a life, so abortion is murder": that is the usual circle of that particular politically charged argument. Another example from politics might be: "Marriage is between a man and a woman, so same-sex marriage is not marriage." The presupposition that marriage is between a man and woman in this statement "proves" that anything else cannot be marriage; this indirectly states the conclusion in the initial point. Watch any political debate, and you'll likely see that begging the question is a common practice to avoid actually giving a concrete answer to the actual questions presented.

References

Aristotle. 1938. *On Interpretation. Categories. Prior Analytics*, translated by Harold Percy Cooke and Hugh Tredennick. Cambridge, MA: Harvard University Press.

Garner, B.A. 1995. *Dictionary of Modern Legal Usage*. Oxford: Oxford University Press.

71

Chronological Snobbery

A.G. Holdier

Religion comes from the period of human prehistory where nobody – not even the mighty Democritus who concluded that all matter was made from atoms – had the smallest idea what was going on. It comes from the bawling and fearful infancy of our species, and is a babyish attempt to meet our inescapable demand for knowledge (as well as for comfort, reassurance, and other infantile needs). Today the least educated of my children knows much more about the natural order than any of the founders of religion.

Christopher Hitchens, *god is not Great: How Religion Poisons Everything*

First described by the Christian academic Owen Barfield (1967) in the 1920s and later popularized by his friend and colleague C.S. Lewis (1955), the fallacy of chronological snobbery (CS) presupposes that cultural, philosophical, or scientific ideas from later time periods are necessarily superior to those from earlier ages. Grounded on the Enlightenment's concept of "progress," this informal fallacy stems from the assumption that the ever-increasing amount of knowledge in society (often due to scientific and technological advances) naturally and perpetually replaces all outdated, disproven ideas with updated, better-justified beliefs, therefore making old ideas incorrect or irrelevant simply because they are old. Similar to biological evolution and the phenomenon of vestigial organs, CS labels once-normal beliefs to be now obsolete in light of cultural evolution and the

Bad Arguments: 100 of the Most Important Fallacies in Western Philosophy, First Edition.
Edited by Robert Arp, Steven Barbone, and Michael Bruce.
© 2019 John Wiley & Sons Ltd. Published 2019 by John Wiley & Sons Ltd.

contemporary situation, but the lack of reference to either evidence or argument for a specific proposition's inaccuracy is the hallmark of this informal fallacy.

Certainly it is the case that many ideas once popularly held to be true – such as cosmological geocentrism or legal theories that denied rights to individuals based on race or gender – are now indeed known to be false, but such affirmations have always come on the basis of evidence or reason beyond the mere fact of the original idea's age or the time period in which it became popular. As Lewis (1955) points out in his autobiography (where he analyzes his own bygone susceptibility to this fallacy), the mere fact of an idea's age is no guarantee of its inaccuracy; CS is:

> the uncritical acceptance of the intellectual climate common to our own age and the assumption that whatever has gone out of date is on that account discredited. You must find why it went out of date. Was it ever refuted (and if so by whom, where, and how conclusively) or did it merely die away as fashions do? If the latter, this tells us nothing about its truth or falsehood. (207–208)

It is not the case, for example, that geocentrism is false simply because it is archaic but rather because it does not accurately describe reality (nor has it ever), a fact now known to be true given the preponderance of contradictory evidence collected in the years since geocentrism's conception.

In Barfield's (1967) mind, the problem with CS is twofold: first, it promotes an arrogant, *snobbish* attitude that labels the modern *homo sapiens* as the pinnacle of human development in every possible mode as if "intellectually, humanity languished for countless generations in the most childish errors on all sorts of crucial subjects, until it was redeemed by some simple scientific dictum of the last century" (169). While technological advances have certainly answered many questions and made contemporary life more comfortable for human beings than ever before, it is a mistake to assume that this simple fact necessarily makes twenty-first-century humanity philosophically, morally, culturally, artistically, or otherwise *better* than that of any other age. Second, the uncritical acceptance of the contemporary perspective means that CS blinds a thinker to problematic assumptions and perspectives in the modern worldview that a critical eye would otherwise uncover.

Rather than relying on logical reasoning to rebut a premise, the person subscribing to CS assumes that no rebuttal is necessary simply because the concept or the person presenting the concept came from a bygone era when all manner of silly things were believed. As Lewis (1955) points out, a classic example is the equation of the word "medieval" with the word "backwards" (206). Today, when a philosopher ridicules religious philosophy as an "Iron Age conception of God" instead of responding to theistic arguments, when early adopters attack critics of new media and technology – like Neil Postman (2006) – for being "stuck in the Stone Age," or when political commentators lambast proposed policies as being "like something out of *Leave It to Beaver*" without explaining why the Iron Age, the Stone Age, or the Beaver Age are not to be preferred in the case in question, then CS rears its ugly head.

Essentially the opposite of the appeal to ancient authority, CS also relates to guilt by association (see Chapter 83), hasty generalization (see Chapter 84), and poisoning the well (see Chapter 40) fallacies whenever it references unrelated false beliefs held by individuals from the originating time period. Because of its attempt to invalidate a proposition based on the temporal location of its origin or popularity, this fallacy can be considered a hybrid of the genetic fallacy (that focuses on origins; see Chapter 29) and the *argumentum ad hominem* (because it focuses on cultures and peoples, not on propositions or logic; see chapters 8–11). And because it fails to distinguish between the general level of knowledge in a culture and a specific proposition affirmed during a cultural period, CS is an applied example of the fallacy of division (see Chapter 56).

In short, it is a mistake to conclude that an old belief is incorrect simply because a newer belief is available without demonstrating why the newer idea is to be preferred. As Barfield and Lewis's intellectual forebear G.K. Chesterton (2008) wrote:

> An imbecile habit has arisen in modern controversy of saying that such and such a creed can be held in one age but cannot be held in another. Some dogma, we are told, was credible in the twelfth century, but is not credible in the twentieth. You might as well say that a certain philosophy can be believed on Mondays, but cannot be believed on Tuesdays. You might as well say of a view of the cosmos that it was suitable to half-past-three, but not suitable to half-past-four. What a man can believe depends on his philosophy, not upon the clock or the century. (70)

References

Barfield, Owen. 1967. *History in English Words*, revised edition. Grand Rapids, IA: Eerdmans.

Chesterton, G.K. 2008. *Orthodoxy: Centennial Edition*. Nashville, TN: Sam Torode Book Arts.

Lewis, C.S. 1955. *Surprised by Joy: The Shape of My Early Life*. New York, NY: Harcourt, Brace & World.

Postman, Neil. 2006. *Amusing Ourselves to Death: Public Discourse in the Age of Show Business*, twentieth anniversary edition. New York, NY: Penguin Books.

72

Complex Question

A.G. Holdier

> George Walker Bush: *great* president or the *greatest* president? I'll just put you down for *great*.
>
> Stephen Colbert

Commonly referred to as a "loaded" question, the fallacy of the complex question (CQ) appears in two varieties: the implicit form distracts an interlocutor by assuming the truth of an unproven premise and shifting the focus of the argument in an unfounded direction, while the explicit form collapses two distinct questions into a single question such that a single answer would appear to satisfy both inquiries. Although it is possible for a philosopher to commit this fallacy accidentally, its common use as an intentional tactic by debaters and investigators has also earned this example of faulty reasoning the title of the "interrogator's fallacy," with the classic example being that of a journalist asking a senator, "Have you stopped beating your wife?" – a question that implicitly presupposes without justification that the senator has actually beaten his wife at some point in the past. If the senator fails to recognize the fallacious thinking when he answers the CQ, he may unintentionally appear to admit that he is guilty of a crime of which he may be innocent.

The explicit variety of CQ is far easier to identify and is typically not wielded as an argumentative tool but is often played for laughs; when a talk

Bad Arguments: 100 of the Most Important Fallacies in Western Philosophy, First Edition.
Edited by Robert Arp, Steven Barbone, and Michael Bruce.
© 2019 John Wiley & Sons Ltd. Published 2019 by John Wiley & Sons Ltd.

show host asks her celebrity guest a question like "What is your favorite novel and why is it *The Lord of the Rings?*" the interviewer clearly presents two questions concurrently, brazenly forcing the conversation in a desired direction. Nevertheless, because her inquiry operates with two parallel questions instead of a more open single query (such as "What is your favorite novel?" or "What is your opinion of *The Lord of the Rings?*"), the host's question is complex. Essentially, her goal is not to uncover new information but to guide the focus of the discussion in a predetermined direction. Consequently, the CQ is similar to, though not identical with, the courtroom infidelity of a lawyer "leading the witness" where open-ended questions that allow a witness to provide personal testimony (such as "What did you see that night?") are replaced with targeted questions (like "Isn't it true that you saw the defendant murder the victim on the night in question?") that only leave room for a "yes" or "no" answer. Leading questions (such as the example at the beginning of this chapter) are not technically fallacious, however, for they merely suggest their own answer and do not attempt to trick a witness into a confession (see Hurley 2010, 148–149 for more on the difference between leading and loaded questions).

Concerning trickiness, the more problematic form of the CQ is the implicit rephrasing of an enthymeme (an incomplete syllogism) into a question-like structure that can lead a respondent to affirm unintentionally an unstated but distasteful or untrue secondary conclusion. Consider the case of Bart Simpson in the 2004 episode of *The Simpsons* "Bart-Mangled Banner," where a series of unfortunate events land Bart and his family on a talk show because of their perceived lack of American patriotism: when the host, Nash Castor, asks the Simpson family (in a fiery manner similar to many media personalities), "What do you hate most about this country?" he first assumes that they *do* hate the United States of America and instead asks a clarifying question about this preconception. It would be impossible for Bart simply to answer the posed question without simultaneously giving credibility to Castor's unproven assumption (that he does, in fact, "hate [...] this country"), ironically providing the very proof that had to that point been lacking. The possibility that an undetected CQ might lead a speaker to affirm additional, unspoken premises unintentionally makes this a popular tactic in police interrogations and debate cross-examinations; avoiding this rhetorical trap is only possible either by rejecting the question as posed and extemporaneously clarifying the situation on one's own terms or by remaining silent.

It is important to note that the fallacious nature of a CQ may be context-dependent. In the flow of normal conversation, it is often natural to pose questions based on any number of assumptions that one might reasonably expect a conversation partner to accept either on the basis of common knowledge or because they had previously been established; a question like "What color is the President's dog's hair?" assumes, at the very least, (a) that there is a President, (b) that he or she owns a dog, and (c) that said dog has hair, but one need not spell out each of those assumptions to avoid speaking erroneously – indeed, conversations would be both tedious and lengthy without such linguistic shortcuts. Instead, CQ relates specifically to instances where the questioner attempts to force a preconceived conclusion into the subtext of a conversation, especially if that conclusion is an embarrassing or incriminating answer.

Because of its attempt to control the flow of an argument regardless of validity or soundness, CQ can often appear similar to the fallacy of begging the question (see Chapter 70), where the conclusion of an argument simply restates one of its premises. The key difference is that while CQs do suggest a particular conclusion, they do not explicitly state it. Instead, like a false dichotomy (if two oversimplified options are suggested; see Chapter 81) or a red herring (where an unrelated premise intrudes on an argument; see Chapter 43), CQ seeks to distract from the logical flow of the argument and force the fallacy-presenter's desired conclusion – and like poisoning the well (see Chapter 40) and *ad hominem* fallacies (see chapters 8–11), it does so at the expense of the other party with the added twist that it is that very party who ends up expressing his or her own condemnation.

Rhetorically speaking, the CQ is a useful tool, simultaneously making a speaker appear clever while casting doubt on the ability or intelligence of his or her opponent. However, unlike a Socratic question (which is designed to reveal methodically a contradiction or error in the thinking of one's opponent), a CQ aims to trick one's interlocutor into affirming a damaging position, therefore operating essentially as the opposite of the Socratic method (because it aims at obscuring and not revealing the truth). Even if some valid use could be found for such a move, it would unavoidably operate at the expense of an opponent's pride, leaving any logical reason for its employment sorely absent. Instead, CQ is best left to media representatives with their so-called "gotcha" questions; philosophers should instead take care to explain each step in their reasoning processes and be plain about their evidence. Otherwise, it may be best simply to remain silent.

Reference
Hurley, Patrick. 2010. *A Concise Introduction to Logic*. Belmont, CA: Wadsworth.

73

Confirmation Bias

David Kyle Johnson

> After I learned about confirmation bias, I started seeing it everywhere.
>
> Jon Ronson

Confirmation bias is the human tendency only to look for evidence that confirms what one wants to believe or what one already thinks is true. Usually people are not too keen to look for evidence against what they want to believe is true, so they don't. In fact, not only will people merely try to prove themselves right and never try to prove themselves wrong, but when confronted with evidence to the contrary of what they want to believe, they will actively ignore or deny it. The human propensity for self-delusion is strong.

Confirmation bias greatly hinders one's ability to find the truth. Why? Because, in all honestly, you can confirm (that is, you can find evidence for) any belief you want. Want to defend the idea that Santa is real? Millions of people believe that he is. Presents appear under millions of Christmas trees every year for which the recipients have no other explanation. Both of these facts are some evidence for Santa. That's not to say that considering evidence for something you believe is a bad thing, but it can't be all that you do. It shouldn't even be most of what you do. Unless you consider the contrary evidence, you can easily fool yourself into believing something is true when it is not.

Bad Arguments: 100 of the Most Important Fallacies in Western Philosophy, First Edition.
Edited by Robert Arp, Steven Barbone, and Michael Bruce.
© 2019 John Wiley & Sons Ltd. Published 2019 by John Wiley & Sons Ltd.

It may seem obvious that only trying to confirm your beliefs is the perfect way to delude oneself, but it's one of the most common reasoning mistakes that people make. It's comforting to have what we already believed confirmed, so we seek it out. Confirmation bias is why conservatives watch Fox News and liberals watch MSNBC; those channels (mostly) present only evidence that confirms their worldview of choice. When reading about religion, Christians primarily read Christian authors; atheists primarily read atheist authors. In my experience, people are much more likely to skip right to reading the criticisms of a book they disagree with rather than actually read the book themselves.

When we surround ourselves with people and views that already agree with our own, we can draw erroneous conclusions. "Everyone I know voted for Hillary. Trump must have stolen the election with voter fraud," or "Everyone I know supports Trump. His low approval ratings must be fake news." The fallacy is in thinking that the evidence you are aware of, the evidence you sought out because it agrees with your views, constitutes all the evidence that exists.

Unfortunately, confirmation bias may be hardwired into us. Suppose I said I was thinking of a pattern, a way to arrange three numbers, and challenged you to figure out what pattern I was thinking of. You give me three numbers and I'll tell you whether they fit the pattern. So you say "1, 3, 5." I say, "Yes, that fits the pattern I'm thinking of."

So what do think the pattern is? Ascending odd numbers, right? So, instinctively, what kind of sequence would you give me next to test that hypothesis? Three more ascending odd numbers, right? Something like "3, 5, 7"? But that is exactly what you should *not* do. In fact, you should probably already suspect that any three ascending odd numbers will likely fit the pattern, given my first answer. Instead, you should try to disprove your theory to make sure that it's not some other pattern that could fit "1, 3, 5." Maybe it's just numbers ascending by 2. Maybe it's just any odd numbers in any order. Maybe it is ascending odd prime numbers. What you should be doing is trying to prove your "ascending odd numbers" hypothesis false, by trying to prove one of these other theories true. Give me sequences like "2, 4, 6," "5, 3, 1," and "11, 13, 17." If any of these also fit, you'll know your first hypothesis was false, and you'll be one step closer to the truth.

The actual pattern I had in mind was "any three ascending numbers." Notice that if all you tried to do was confirm your "ascending odd number" theory, you would give me sequences that fit the pattern all day – "21, 23, 25" or "37, 39, 41" – and yet never make any progress in figuring out the pattern. The only way to actually figure it out is to generate theories and then try to prove them wrong. But, instinctively, we will just try to prove ourselves right – and that's my point. Confirmation bias is ingrained; we have to learn to fight against it. If our aim is having true beliefs, we should actually try to prove what we believe is wrong.

Something that goes hand in hand with confirmation bias is evidence denial. When one is confronted with sufficient evidence against some belief that one holds, what one should do is reject that belief – at least if one is concerned with truth. But that is generally not what humans do (which is evidence itself that, in general, humans are not concerned with having true beliefs). Studies have actually shown that when people are confronted with evidence that refutes positions they hold, they don't change their mind – they dig in their heels. They believe what they previously believed even more fervently. In one study, "When Corrections Fail: The Persistence of Political Misperceptions" by Brendan Nyhan and Jason Reifler (2010), conservatives more adamantly believed that Saddam had weapons of mass destruction after being presented with direct evidence that he did not.

Ted Schick and Lewis Vaugh (2014), in their book, *How to Think about Weird Things*, explain evidence denial with the most obvious example I can think of – people who think that the end of the world is near and think that they can predict its occurrence. My favorite example came in 2011, when Harold Camping predicted that the rapture (the day when Christian believers are supposed to be physically taken up into heaven) would occur on May 21, 2011. When the May 21 date came and went and no one flew away to heaven, Camping didn't admit that he was wrong. Instead, he said that it was "an invisible judgment day" where "Christ came and put the world under [spiritual] judgment."

Conspiracy theorists are perhaps the most adept at denying evidence, for they will not only deny evidence against their theory but turn it into evidence *for* their theory. Consider 9/11 "Truthers," who argue that the Bush administration actually planned and carried out the 9/11 attacks. What about all the overwhelming evidence that it was actually planned and carried out by al Qaeda under the direction of Osama bin Laden? "All that evidence," the conspiracy theorists will say, "was planted by the Bush administration because that's what they want you to think."

"Yeah, that's what they want you to think" is the perfect way to excuse away evidence against any conspiracy theory, and this actually demonstrates why conspiracy theories are fundamentally irrational. They are unfalsifiable; you can't prove them wrong. To see why this makes them irrational, consider (what I call) "The Ultimate Conspiracy Theory":

> There is a clandestine group, I know not whom, working toward nefarious purposes, I know not what. All I do know is that every conspiracy theory that exists was planted by this clandestine group to throw you off the track. So, you think the moon landing was fake, the CIA killed JFK, that 9/11 was an inside job, and the illuminati control the world? Yeah, that's what THEY want you to think.

Notice that it is tailored specifically to avoid counter-evidence; you could never prove this theory wrong. But this is the very fact that makes this theory completely irrational. It's not that sometimes individuals or small groups don't conspire to do bad things; of course they do. (A group successfully conspired to kill Abraham Lincoln.) But conspiracy theories have evidence denial built right into them; consequently, they are fundamentally irrational. In fact, no conspiracy theory has ever turned out to be true.

And this brings us to why the quotation that started this chapter is so cleverly ironic. Confirmation bias and evidence denial is why you start "seeing something everywhere" once you learn about it. Learn a new word, and you'll likely hear it multiple times that day. Start thinking the number 23 has significance, and you'll see it everywhere. That's because you will be looking for confirmation and ignoring the evidence to the contrary. It's called "remembering the hits and forgetting the misses," which feeds another common error in our thinking, called the availability error (see Chapter 21). And that's why you will now start seeing evidence of confirmation bias and evidence denial everywhere you look.

But all in all, if you really are seeking the truth – if you really want to make sure that a belief you hold is true – you should try to prove it false. After all, if all you have done is tried to prove yourself right (that is, if you have only sought out evidence for your belief), is it really any surprise that you succeeded? Anyone can find some evidence for anything. But if you have tried, genuinely, to prove yourself wrong but couldn't – that's a really good indication that your belief is true. Better yet, invite others to prove you wrong. The more scrutiny a belief can withstand, the more likely it is that it's true. But if sufficient evidence is provided against your belief, don't deny that evidence. Change your belief. As David Hume once said, "A wise man, therefore, proportions his belief to the evidence" (1993, 73).

References

Hume, David. 1993. *An Enquiry concerning Human Understanding*, 2nd edition, edited by Eric Stein. Indianapolis, IN: Hackett.

Nyhan, Brendan, and Jason Reifler. 2010. "When Corrections Fail: The Persistence of Political Misperceptions." *Political Behavior* 32(2): 303–330.

Schick, Theodore, and Lewis Vaughn. 2014. *How to Think about Weird Things: Critical Thinking for a New Age*. New York, NY: McGraw-Hill.

74

Conjunction

Jason Iuliano

The Linda Problem: Linda is 31 years old, single, outspoken, and very bright. She majored in philosophy. As a student, she was deeply concerned with issues of discrimination and social justice and also participated in anti-nuclear demonstrations. Which is more probable?

(A)   Linda is a bank teller; or
(B)   Linda is a bank teller and is active in the feminist movement.

Did you pick (B)? If so, you just fell prey to the conjunction fallacy. You shouldn't feel too bad, though. In fact, you're in very good company. In a classic experiment, psychologists Tversky and Kahneman (1983) found that eighty-five percent of people choose (B).

Nonetheless, (B) is incorrect because it misapplies a basic rule of probability: The occurrence of two events (A and B) cannot be more likely than the occurrence of either A or B alone. As Tversky and Kahneman (1983) explain in their seminal work: "The probability of a conjunction, $P(A\&B)$, cannot exceed the probabilities of its constituents, $P(A)$ and $P(B)$, because the extension (or the possibility set) of the conjunction is included in the extension of its constituents" (293).

In other words, in every possible world in which both A and B occur, A has occurred and B has occurred. However, there may be possible worlds in which A occurs without B's occurring and vice versa. Accordingly, the probability of A's occurring is at least as great as – but may be greater than – the probability of both A's and B's occurring. Likewise, the probability of B's

Bad Arguments: 100 of the Most Important Fallacies in Western Philosophy, First Edition.
Edited by Robert Arp, Steven Barbone, and Michael Bruce.
© 2019 John Wiley & Sons Ltd. Published 2019 by John Wiley & Sons Ltd.

occurring is at least as great as – but may be greater than – the probability of both A's and B's occurring.

Let's apply this concept to the Linda Problem by using a Venn diagram. In the left circle, we have the set of people who are bank tellers. Answer choice (A) places Linda somewhere in this circle. Next, in the right circle, we have the set of people who are feminists. Finally, in the area in which the two circles overlap is the set of people who are bank tellers and feminists. Answer choice (B) places Linda somewhere in this overlapping section.

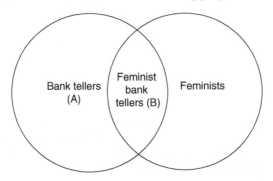

As you can see from the diagram, answer choice (A) is larger than answer choice (B). In fact, there is no part of (B) which is also not also part of (A). However, there is a large portion of (A) that does not overlap with (B). Accordingly, the probability of Linda's falling somewhere in set (A) is greater than the probability that she is in set (B). In plain English, Linda is more likely to be a bank teller than she is to be both a bank teller and a feminist.

When you need to determine the relative probability of different scenarios, one way to prevent yourself from making the conjunction fallacy is to determine whether any of the options is a subset of any other. If so, you can conclude that the subset option is not more probable. This rule works because a specific event can never be more likely than a general event that encompasses the specific event. Consider the following example. Boston hosted the largest football parade in history to celebrate the New England Patriots. Which is more probable?

(A)   The New England Patriots won the Super Bowl the day before the celebration; or

(B)   The New England Patriots played a football game the day before the celebration.

(A) is the more enticing response, but (B) is the correct one. A close look at the options reveals that (A) is actually a subset of (B). Specifically, every Super Bowl is a football game, but only a small percentage of football games are Super Bowls.

When you step back and view the problem in this light, the logical flaw likely seems obvious. Given this, why are people so frequently drawn in by the conjunction fallacy?

There are two primary reasons. First, a detailed description of an event makes the event seem more probable. Let's see how this plays out through another example from Tversky and Kahneman (1983):

(A) A massive flood will occur soon in North America, in which more than 1,000 people drown.

(B) An earthquake will occur soon in California sometime, causing a flood in which more than 1,000 people drown.

One group of participants was asked to rate the probability of (A)'s happening in the near future, and a second group of participants was asked to rate the probability of (B)'s happening in the near future. Interestingly, the (B) group provided substantially higher estimates than the (A) group. Tversky and Kahneman (1983) theorized that this error occurred because people overestimate the likelihood of "specific, coherent" events that are "representative of our mental model of the relevant worlds" (315). Think about how this idea relates to your own experience both detecting and telling lies. Chances are you more readily believe specific lies than vague ones and you are also more convincing when you tell specific lies rather than vague ones.

The second reason the conjunction fallacy tricks people is because humans are wired to seek causal explanations of events. The Super Bowl example illustrates this. Whereas the first causal explanation is consistent with our experience in the world (cities tend to have large celebrations when their team wins the Super Bowl), the second option's causal explanation seems absurd (cities don't have celebrations merely because their team played a football game). Nonetheless, despite its real-world absurdity, this second option is logically more probable.

Now that you know the mechanisms behind the conjunction fallacy, make sure that you don't succumb to this probabilistic error in the future.

Reference

Tversky, Amos, and Daniel Kahneman. 1983. "Probability, Representativeness, and the Conjunction Fallacy." *Psychological Review* (90): 293–315.

75

Constructive Nature of Perception

David Kyle Johnson

> I would like all people to know that I do believe that this is the Virgin Mary, Mother of God.
>
> > Diana Duyser, about a "face" in her grilled cheese sandwich

Many of the things that we believe are generated by our senses interacting with the outside world. If this interaction always generated an accurate representation of the way the world is, that wouldn't be a problem. What we have discovered, however, is that our senses can lead us astray – and do so far more often than we realize or would even suspect. Why? Because our perception is constructive. Consequently, to have the best chance of having true beliefs about the way the world is, we have to guard against the many ways our perception can lead us astray. Otherwise we can fallaciously draw erroneous conclusions about everything from ghosts in houses and UFOs in the sky to Virgin Marys in grilled cheese sandwiches and satanic messages in popular music.

What does it mean for perception to be constructive? Take vision, for example. Our eyes do not just take a picture and then present the world to us as it is. They receive information about the world, send that information to our brain, and then our brain interprets that information in certain ways based on certain criteria. It decides what is relevant, disregards what is not, and then determines how that information should be presented to us.

Bad Arguments: 100 of the Most Important Fallacies in Western Philosophy, First Edition.
Edited by Robert Arp, Steven Barbone, and Michael Bruce.
© 2019 John Wiley & Sons Ltd. Published 2019 by John Wiley & Sons Ltd.

In many cases, that presentation is inaccurate. As Yale neuroscientist Steven Novella (2016) once put it:

> [Our] brains construct [our] image of reality […] we are not passive recorders of reality. What you experience as your stream of consciousness is an incredibly highly filtered, and selected and altered and reconstructed narrative of what's going on. [.… It's] very useful, but largely a fiction [because] in general your brain errs massively on the side of continuity and internal consistency […] not accuracy. It utterly sacrifices accuracy in order for that narrative to be seamless and consistent. […] It will fill in the gaps – we call that confabulation […] it makes assumptions, it alters how you perceive things in order to […] make it all fit.

The easiest example is simple: we perceive all objects in the world as solid despite the fact that they are mostly empty space. That's simply how our brain interprets our sense data (see Matthews 2009). More interesting still, we perceive objects as having color when in fact they have no color at all. They merely reflect wavelengths of light that cause us to see certain colors (see Marder 2015).

This is why "dressgate" was so distressing to people. People fallaciously concluded that the dress must be the color they saw it as (and thus others who disagreed where crazy) because they didn't realize that perception is constructive; they thought there is an objective fact about whether the dress is blue and black, or white and gold, when in fact the dress has no color at all – color is only in the mind (see Johnson 2015). The way you see the world is not necessarily the same as other people see it.

Our brains make decisions about what information to interpret and how to do so mostly based on our assumptions, preconceptions, and desires – our "worldview" if you will. We can see extreme (and interesting) cases of how this can lead us astray in brain-damaged patients. In "The Sound of One Hand Clapping" – one of my favorite chapters in V.S. Ramachandran's book *Phantoms in the Brain* (1999) – Ramachandran tells the story of patients who have had strokes in their right hemisphere but consistently deny the fact that their stroke paralyzed the entire left side of their body. The denial is so strong that when asked to do tasks that require both hands, like tying their shoes, they will try to do them – they'll fiddle at their shoelaces with their right hand (left hand dangling at their side) – and then (incorrectly) insist they completed the task successfully "with both hands." When asked to clap, they will raise only their right hand to the middle of their body, but insist that their left hand is raised too. Indeed, they will even see it moving!

Ramachandran suggests this is because the stroke has inhibited their ability to deal with information that conflicts with their worldview and correspondingly update it. Since their worldview before the stroke included the assumption that their left side was functioning, that's the worldview they are stuck with after the stroke. And since our beliefs largely determine how we perceive the world, these patients literally perceive their arm moving when it is not.

We "normal" (non-brain-damaged) people can be subject to such things as well. Oliver Sacks, in his book Hallucinations (2012), goes into detail about how and why even normal people can suffer from hallucinations. You can probably even think of a few examples from your own personal life. I've seen my dog running in the kitchen when he's not (he's actually asleep upstairs). While I have been in the shower, I've heard the phone ring when it's not. I have felt my phone vibrating in my pocket when it's not; it's not even in my pocket! This is because of the role of expectation in perceptual construction. According to Schick and Vaughn (2014, 101), by simply altering what people expect, studies have shown that you can make people see lights flash, feel electric shocks or warmth, or even smell certain odors all without any of those things actually being present.

This is why, if you really want to know whether a house is haunted, you shouldn't have someone tell you what the ghost is supposedly like or supposedly does. If you are expecting a certain thing to happen in a certain location in the house, you will probably experience it – especially if you go in already believing the ghost is real. This is also why ghost hunters always fail to find ghosts when they haven't been told beforehand what to look for (see Grant 2005).

Another assumption that informs how we interpret the information that our brain receives is that the size, color, and shape of objects is constant. This allows us to perceive an object the same way even if how we are seeing it is changing – for example, even if the surrounding lighting or our distance and angle to the object changes. We see snow as white regardless of whether it is lit by the moon or the sun. We perceive a bus as large even if it is far away.

Obviously this kind of perceptual constancy (as it's called) can help us understand the world accurately – because usually objects aren't changing size, color, or shape. But it can also lead us astray. There are of course countless visual illusions that demonstrate this fact; one of my favorites is the checkerboard shadow illusion in which you will see two squares as completely different colors, when in fact they are the same (due to the way light and shadow affects our interpretation of visual information). But you can also demonstrate this experimentally. In one study, donkeys and trees were each cut out of the same green paper and illuminated with the same red light, yet the subjects still saw the donkey as grey and the tree as green.

Interestingly, however, much (if not all) of our perceptual constancy is learned. Being able to tell how large an object is even though it is far away (and thus appears small) is an acquired skill – one that you would not have if you had spent your entire life living in a thick forest or jungle where you never saw large objects from far away. Indeed, this skill of yours is only good for, at most, around a mile or two because you seldom have the chance to verify the size of objects further away than that. At a certain point, you have no idea whether you are looking at a distant larger object or a close smaller object, especially if that object is against a blank background like the sky.

This is why my friend, Tony, and I were once nearly convinced that a plane was going to slam right into a 7-foot delta kite we were flying in North Dakota one day. The kite was 1,000 feet up, and until the plane passed right over the kite (the plane was much higher), we had no frame of reference to judge the size or altitude of the plane. It's for similar reasons that we all see the moon as large on the horizon but small in the sky. It's not because the lower atmosphere acts as a magnifying lens; that's a myth. It's because of our unconscious assumptions about the shape of the sky and the Ponzo illusion (see Plait 2010). Similar kinds of perceptual mistakes explain why two airline pilots and one national guard pilot were all convinced that they saw a whole squadron of UFOs – so near that the national guard pilot radioed a near collision with the UFOs – even though it was later confirmed that what they were actually seeing was a meteor and its fragments, a full 125 miles away (see Schick and Vaughn 2014, 110).

Another reason people think they see UFOs (and another way our perception leads us astray) is the autokinetic effect. If you stare at a stationary bright object against a solid background for a while, it will start to appear as if it is moving. It doesn't actually take that long, and we don't yet know for sure what causes this effect. (There are a couple of theories; see Rucci and Poletti 2009). But what we do know is that countless people have mistaken the planet Venus for a UFO because of it.

This brings me to the last way our perception leads us astray that I'll mention: pareidolia. One thing that our brain likes to do with the information it receives is impose patters on it. So when we, for example, see a vague amorphous stimulus, we will often impose a pattern onto it and see something that is not actually there: a human face on mars, Jesus on a tortilla, the Virgin Mary on a grilled cheese, and so on. It's often a face because of how much of our brain's visual centers are dedicated to facial recognition, but it doesn't have to be. I've also seen Godzilla in the clouds, a dog on a stained wall, and even the full body of an ascending Jesus in a dog's butt (see Campbell 2013).

But vision is not the only sense susceptible to this effect. Our hearing is too. This is why you can sometimes hear "secret messages" in speech or music when you play it backwards. "Another one's bites the dust" sounds like "It's fun to smoke marijuana" if you play it backwards, and there are supposedly secret messages about the Beatles replacing Paul McCartney with a lookalike in Beatles songs. It's called "back masking," and when I was growing up, many a youth pastor argued that I shouldn't listen to secular music, supporting their arguments by playing popular songs backwards, fallaciously finding nefarious hidden messages in what they heard, and then claiming they were put there by Satan.

Interestingly, however, you will almost never hear these secret messages unless you are told what words to listen for. When I play videos that have Beatles songs played backwards for my students and hide the subtitles, they can't hear anything. But when I play the same thing with subtitles, they can't hear anything else. This is why the TV series *Ghost Hunters* always put up subtitles when they play back the "voices" they mysteriously catch on tape; they are intentionally encouraging audio pareidolia. If they didn't, you would just hear a garbled mess – because that is all there actually is.

All in all, our senses are not nearly as reliable as we think they are. As a result, we must guard against the many ways that they can lead us astray if we want to have any chance at understanding the way the world actually is. This is why science has proved to be such a powerful tool in understanding the world; it is designed specifically to guard against the way our senses (and also all the fallacies in this book) can lead us astray.

References

Campbell, Andy. 2013. "Dog Butt Looks Like Jesus Christ in a Robe." *TheHuffingtonPost.com*, June 13. http://www.huffingtonpost.com/2013/06/13/dog-butt-looks-like-jesus-photo_n_3436086.html (accessed October 3, 2017).

Grant, Eleanor. 2005. "Is It Real? Ghosts." *Is It Real?* National Geographic, April 25. http://www.imdb.com/title/tt0861148/combined (accessed October 3, 2017).

Johnson, David Kyle. 2015. "The Blue/Black White/Gold Dress Controversy: No One Is Right." *Psychology Today*, February 27. https://www.psychologytoday.com/blog/logical-take/201502/the-blueblack-whitegold-dress-controversy-no-one-is-right (accessed October 3, 2017).

Marder, Jenny. 2015. "That Dress Isn't Blue or Gold Because Color Doesn't Exist." *PBS Newshour*, February 27. http://www.pbs.org/newshour/updates/that-dress-isnt-blue-or-gold-because-color-doesnt-exist/ (accessed October 3, 2017).

Matthews, Robert. 2009. "If Atoms Are mostly Empty Space, Why Is Matter not Transparent?" *Science Focus*, October 22. http://www.sciencefocus.com/qa/if-atoms-are-mostly-empty-space-why-matter-not-transparent (accessed October 3, 2017).

Novella, Steven. 2016. "Podcast #570." *The Skeptics Guide to the Universe*, June 11. http://www.theskepticsguide.org/podcast/sgu/570 (accessed October 3, 2017).

Plait, Phil. 2010. "Why Does the Moon Look so Large on the Horizon?" *Slate*, May 13. http://www.slate.com/blogs/bad_astronomy/2010/05/13/why_does_the_moon_look_so_huge_on_the_horizon.html (accessed 14 October 2017).

Ramachandran, V.S. 1999. *Phantoms in the Brain: Probing the Mysteries of the Human Mind*. New York, NY: Harper Collins.

Rucci, Michele, and Martina Poletti. 2009. "Fixational Eye Movements and the Autokinetic Illusion." *Journal of Vision* 9(8): 431.

Sacks, Oliver. 2012. *Hallucinations*. New York, NY: Vintage Books.

Schick, Theodore, and Lewis Vaughn. 2014. *How to Think About Weird Things: Critical Thinking for a New Age*. New York, NY: McGraw-Hill.

76

Converse Accident

Steven Barbone

> We applaud Gov. Fallin in her efforts to stop the influx of Syrian refugees into the United States and into the state of Oklahoma.
>
> State representative Casey Murdock

The fallacy of converse accident (CA) occurs in much the same way as the fallacy of hasty generalization (see Chapter 84). Not unlike its other related fallacy, accident (see Chapter 67), which applies a general principle to a particular case to which it does not apply, CA instead generalizes over some cases, or even over one particular case, to make a more sweeping conclusion. This fallacious way of thinking is especially noxious since it often grounds racist, sexist, or other prejudiced beliefs. For example, soon after the terrorist attacks in Paris in 2016, it was revealed that one of the attackers had a Syrian passport. Based on this one particular case, many governors in the United States announced that they would try to block any Syrian refugees from settling in their states. These governors are guilty of CA. Note: it may be true that some Syrian refugees are dangerous terrorists, but it is unlikely that all or even most are dangerous terrorists. These governors have generalized fallaciously from one particular case to many cases.

Bad Arguments: 100 of the Most Important Fallacies in Western Philosophy, First Edition.
Edited by Robert Arp, Steven Barbone, and Michael Bruce.
© 2019 John Wiley & Sons Ltd. Published 2019 by John Wiley & Sons Ltd.

CA is an informal fallacy, but we can still present it in a general form:

(1)   <u>There is one p that is an example of Q.</u>
(2)   Therefore all p's are Q's.

It should be obvious to most readers how to detect or to avoid this fallacy. Thinking of any counter-example will usually suffice to reveal this fallacy's error. Can you imagine or discover one p that is not a Q? If so, the fallacy is revealed. A good critical thinker, then, examines sweeping claims and tests them with counter-examples.

Here's a test to show how disproving a CA works. Let's agree that this fallacy is boring and not very exciting to read about. From this alone, we might conclude that all other fallacies covered in this book are boring and not very exciting to read about. It's up to the reader to discover whether this is an example of the fallacious reasoning that is converse accident.

77

Existential Fallacy

Frank Scalambrino

> [W]hen I think a thing, through whichever and however many predicates I like (even in its thoroughgoing determination), not the least bit gets added to the thing when I posit in addition that this thing *is*.
>
> Immanuel Kant, *Critique of Pure Reason*

The existential fallacy occurs when we erroneously suppose some class or group has members. In other words, statements may be true about classes or groups even if no members of the class or group exist. Consider the class of things that are unicorns; we can say that it's true that unicorns have one horn, but we need not (and should not) think that individual unicorns (members of the class of unicorns) exist.

In terms of syllogistic argumentation, this is a formal fallacy in that it results when the premises are universal in quantification and the conclusion is particular. That is to say, the premises of an argument may be stated in terms of "All" and "None," and the premises may be true; however, the truth of the premises does not necessitate the truth in regard to "Some" of the contents of the premises since the contents may not exist. For example, the claim "All humans are mortal" is true; therefore, it logically follows that "Some humans are mortal." However, notice that although it is true to claim, "All unicorns are one-horned creatures," it would be false to say,

Bad Arguments: 100 of the Most Important Fallacies in Western Philosophy, First Edition.
Edited by Robert Arp, Steven Barbone, and Michael Bruce.
© 2019 John Wiley & Sons Ltd. Published 2019 by John Wiley & Sons Ltd.

"Some unicorns are one-horned creatures," insofar as "Some" is understood to mean "there are some" unicorns in existence which are one-horned creatures.

Put differently, some universal properties may be true without being instantiated, that is, without existing. For example, it may be true that "All violators will be prosecuted" even if there are no violators. It may be true that "No quitters will win" even if there are no quitters. When we suppose some members of a class or group exist, we might be guilty of erroneously importing existence. Put more concisely, universal claims do not have valid "existential import." Hence, when the truth-value of a claim depends on the existence of members of the class or group under consideration, the question of valid existential import is involved. In this way, the following is not illogical: "All Kings of France must reside in France. Therefore, the King of France lives in France." However, because the conclusion requires that the "King of France" exists, the argument commits the "existential fallacy."

In the history of logic, the existential fallacy may be traced to *dictum de omni*, which refers to the principle in Aristotelian logic that whatever is said universally of a subject is said of everything that is contained under such a subject. Yet, in light of this principle, existence claims may become ambiguous. Therefore, following logician George Boole, "first-order predicate calculus" avoids possible ambiguity by making existential import explicit. In this way, universally quantified statements are treated as if they are conditional. That is to say, "All Ps are Qs" is translated into: "For any/every x, if x is a P, then x is a Q." By replacing the "All" or "None" with "For every," first-order predicate calculus removes the ambiguity.

Controversy regarding the relation between the logic of claims and existence may be found throughout the history of philosophy. One of the more famous examples is associated with the above Kant quotation, namely, that "existence is not a predicate." In his section of the *Critique of Pure Reason* titled, "Of the Impossibility of an Ontological Proof of the Existence of God," Kant (1996) claimed existence is not a property to be predicated regarding an object (A600/B628). The basic idea is that we cannot ensure "existence" by means of the use of language alone. In other words, the truths of semantic logic do not necessitate the *existence* of the entities to which the truths refer. This is the case insofar as by "semantic logic" we mean the logic of the meaning of language. Though not itself a proof against the existence of God, Kant pointed out that the "ontological" strategy (associated with Anselm and Descartes) to argue for the existence of God takes the meaning of terms such as "perfection" and "greatness" to derive a term as a maximum. Yet, though the meaning of the term "perfect" maximally entails not lacking in any way, it does not follow that that to which the maximal term refers must "exist."

In order to avoid this fallacy, one should look for empirical verification of the existence of whatever entity may be in question. Of course, there are cases in which empirical verification may be more or less simple. To verify that your motor vehicle has not been stolen, you may go look. Notice, when you look, you have a clear and distinct concept regulating your investigation. In other words, there are a number of ideas regulating where you look and for what you are looking. In this way, the question of what counts as evidence is, to some extent, tied to our understanding of that for which we are seeking evidence. Thus, in less simple cases when we seek empirical verification of some entity's existence, we should ensure that we properly understand the concept employed in the verification process.

Reference

Kant, Immanuel. 1996. *Critique of Pure Reason*, translated by Werner S. Pluhar. Indianapolis, IN: Hackett Publishing.

78

False Cause: *Cum Hoc Ergo Propter Hoc*

Bertha Alvarez Manninen

> People who eat Shredded Wheat tend to have healthy hearts.
> Advertising campaign for Shredded Wheat breakfast cereal

In general, the false cause fallacy occurs when the "link between premises and conclusion depends on some imagined causal connection that probably does not exist" (Hurley 2015, 149). There are three different ways an argument can commit the false cause fallacy: *post hoc ergo propter hoc*; *cum hoc ergo propter hoc*; and ignoring common cause. We'll deal with *cum hoc ergo propter hoc* here. Also see the chapters for *post hoc ergo propter hoc* (Chapter 80) and ignoring common cause (Chapter 79).

This Latin phrase literally translates to "with this, therefore because of this." This fallacy occurs when one assumes a causal relationship between two events because they occurred simultaneously. Like the *post hoc ergo propter hoc* fallacy, this fallacy is guilty of trying to establish a causal connection between two events on dubious grounds. It is clear that two events can happen at the same time and yet there is no causal connection between them. Perhaps you purchased a car at the exact time when someone else crashed her car – clearly this does not mean that it was your purchase that caused the car accident to occur. In the above-cited advertising campaign, "it does not explicitly state that there is any causal connection between eating

Bad Arguments: 100 of the Most Important Fallacies in Western Philosophy, First Edition.
Edited by Robert Arp, Steven Barbone, and Michael Bruce.
© 2019 John Wiley & Sons Ltd. Published 2019 by John Wiley & Sons Ltd.

Shredded Wheat and having a healthy heart, but it invites viewers of the advertisements to make the connection; the implication is there. Whether or not there is any such connection, the mere fact that the two things are correlated does not prove that there is such a connection" (Logical Fallacies 2009).

This fallacy most typically occurs when there appears to be a constant correlation between two events. For example, say that you trip and fall every time that Bill is around and therefore you conclude that Bill is bad luck. Or you seem to fail an exam every time you use a specific writing utensil and assume that the pen is somehow cursed. Here you have equated the constant correlation of two events with a causal connection without any additional evidence in support of causation.

The phrase "correlation does not imply causation" is often used in scientific and statistical circles to caution against concluding that a causal connection exists between two variables solely based on a correlation (even a constant one) between them. For example, some observational studies illustrated a correlation between women undergoing hormone replacement therapy (HRT) and having a low incidence of coronary heart disease. The conclusion drawn from this was that HRT led to a decreased risk of coronary heart disease. However, subsequent randomized trails illustrated the opposite – that there was an increased risk of coronary heart disease following HRT. What the observational studies failed to note, which the randomized trails did not, was that women undergoing HRT were likely to be more affluent and therefore take part in more rigorous diet and exercise programs – and that these were more likely explanations of the lower incidences of coronary heart disease. When the correlation between two variables can be explained by appealing to a common third variable, this is called a "confounder." As such "the protective effect of HRT found in previous observational studies was likely to be influenced by residual confounding. Inadequate adjustment for socioeconomic position from across the life course would be one source of this residual confounding" (Lawlor, Smith, and Ebrahim 2004, 465).

This is not to say, however, that consistent correlation between two events can never be indicative of causation. For the first half of the twentieth century, the tobacco industry denied that smoking directly increased one's chances of lung cancer, dismissing the correlation between the two as non-indicative of any causal relationship. However, in the 1950s, several randomized clinical studies did indeed illustrate that, in this case, correlation was indicative of causation. The way to avoid committing the *cum hoc ergo propter hoc* fallacy, therefore, is to study correlative relationships more carefully in order to decipher if an actual causal relationship exists rather than assuming the latter follows from the former.

References

Hurley, Patrick. 2015. *A Concise Introduction to Logic.* Stamford, CT: Cengage Learning.

Lawlor, Debbie, George Davey Smith, and Shah Ebrahim. 2004. "Commentary: The Hormone Replacement–Coronary Heart Disease Conundrum: Is this the Death of Observational Epidemiology?" *International Journal of Epidemiology* (33): 464–467.

Logical Fallacies. 2009. "Cum Hoc Fallacy." Logical Fallacies, August 15. http://www.logicalfallacies.info/presumption/cum-hoc/(accessed October 3, 2017).

79

False Cause: Ignoring Common Cause

Bertha Alvarez Manninen

> There is increasing evidence that the easy availability of welfare has greatly increased the incidence of child poverty. For example, the highest increases in the rate of child poverty in recent years have occurred in those states that pay the highest welfare benefit.
>
> White House Task Force Report, 2013

In general, the false cause fallacy occurs when the "link between premises and conclusion depends on some imagined causal connection that probably does not exist" (Hurley 2015, 149). There are three different ways an argument can commit the false cause fallacy: *post hoc ergo propter hoc*; *cum hoc ergo propter hoc*; and ignoring common cause. We'll deal with ignoring common cause here. Also see the chapters for *post hoc ergo propter hoc* (Chapter 80) and *cum hoc ergo propter hoc* (Chapter 78).

The fallacy of ignoring common cause occurs when one notices a constant correlation between A and B and assumes A caused B (or vice versa) while ignoring that there is a third variable, C, that causes both and therefore accounts for the correlation. As Sheila Morton (2014) notes, the quotation above from the White House Task Force report commits this version of the false cause fallacy because "the report ignored many other, more probable, causes of the rising rates of childhood poverty: inflation, job loss, the mass-movement of manufacturing to overseas plants that took place during the

Bad Arguments: 100 of the Most Important Fallacies in Western Philosophy, First Edition.
Edited by Robert Arp, Steven Barbone, and Michael Bruce.
© 2019 John Wiley & Sons Ltd. Published 2019 by John Wiley & Sons Ltd.

Reagan era. All these are more likely causes of childhood poverty than the availability of welfare" (98). Indeed, these reasons can explain both the rise of childhood poverty and the rise of the availability of welfare without making the latter causally responsible for the former.

Harkening back to the smoking example given in Chapter 78, consider the following: "coffee drinking and lung cancer are associated, but coffee drinking doesn't cause lung cancer, nor vice versa. They are associated because both are associated with cigarette smoking. Smokers happen to drink more coffee on average than non-smokers" (McKay Illari *et al.*, 2011, 16). In this case, the tendency to smoke is the common cause that accounts for the correlation between excessive coffee drinking and lung cancer. Ignoring this common cause in an observational study (as was done in the example in Chapter 78 concerning HRT and coronary disease) could lead to the conclusion that it is the coffee drinking itself that increases the risk of lung cancer (thus instilling an unfounded fear among coffee drinkers who are non-smokers).

In general, it is widely agreed that "breast is best" – that is, that a woman's breastmilk is a superior source of nutrition for human infants than formula. Countless studies illustrate a causal relationship between breastfeeding and various health benefits for the mother and the infant. One benefit that has been the subject of debate, however, relates to the finding that breastfeeding is positively correlated to higher IQs in children and whether this implies a causal relationship between breastmilk and childhood intelligence. One concern is that asserting this causal relationship ignores an important confounder (the correlation between two variables that can be explained by appealing to a common third variable) – that women who breastfeed "also often provide a more enriched and cognitively stimulating environment for the child" and that "breastfeeding is associated with higher socio-economic factors that may be the true cause of enhanced intellectual ability" (Jacobson and Jacobson 2002, 258). In other words, it may not be the breastmilk itself that contributes to a child's higher IQ scores; rather, the tendency toward breastfeeding and providing a mentally stimulating environment for a child has a common cause: membership in a higher socio-economic group.

The belief that marijuana use has a causal relationship with the use of harder drugs may also suffer from this fallacy. Again, while it may be true that users of drugs such as heroin or cocaine started experimenting with drugs using marijuana, it may be that the use of both has its roots in a common cause (poor judgment, a reaction to certain socio-economic or psychological factors, or simply basic curiosity about the effects of these substances), which is different from asserting that it is the marijuana itself that leads to the use of more dangerous drugs.

Sometimes it isn't clear exactly which version of the false cause fallacy applies. An advertisement for Eukanuba dog food implies that Utah, a 17-year-old dog, has lived for 30% longer than his expected lifespan because he has been fed this brand. There is no indication that any kind of substantial study has been done to illustrate that Eukanuba dog food causally contributes to a dog's increased lifespan, and so, as it stands, the ad commits the false cause fallacy. If what the advertisers mean to say is that the causal connection exists because eating the food precedes the dog's increased lifespan, then this is a *post hoc ergo propter hoc* fallacy. If what they mean to say is that the two (the dog's diet and his increased lifespan) occur simultaneously and therefore a causal connection can be inferred from this alone, then the ad commits the *cum hoc ergo propter hoc* fallacy. In addition, the ad may be ignoring that there could be a common cause that explains both the dog's diet and his longer lifespan – perhaps the dog has the kind of owners who are particularly mindful about their dog's health and this contributes both to buying expensive food for him and also to ensuring his health in other ways. In any case, there is no reason to believe from this ad alone that this particular brand of dog food itself has a direct causal connection to Utah's increased lifespan.

In 2009, the Kellogg Company settled against charges that its advertisements for Frosted Mini-Wheats were deceptive. The ad claimed that the cereal was "clinically shown to improve kids' attentiveness by nearly 20%" (Federal Trade Commission 2009). What it neglected to mention is that the study compared children who had eaten the cereal to children who hadn't eaten any breakfast at all. The study, therefore, did not show that Frosted Mini-Wheats itself causes better attentiveness but rather simply eating *something* for breakfast increases attentiveness. The commercial exploited the false cause fallacy (in particular the *post hoc ergo propter hoc*) to get consumers to buy its product. This fallacy is also present in many of the arguments concerning the alleged connection between vaccines and autism despite the plethora of evidence otherwise. These examples, among many others, highlight the importance of familiarity with fallacious reasoning – the consequences of not being able to distinguish good reasoning from bad reasoning extend outside the classroom and into the depths of society.

For further reading, Tyler Vigen's (2015) website *Spurious Correlations* is a humorous illustration showing that correlative events are not necessarily causal ones, as he presents various graphs of two events that have a correlative, but clearly non-causal, relationship. For example the "number of people who drowned by falling into a swimming-pool correlates with [the] number of films Nicolas Cage appeared in [... the] per capital cheese consumption correlates with [the] number of people who died by becoming tangled in their bedsheets." Martin Myers and Diego Pineda's (2008) book *Do Vaccines Cause That?!* offers excellent data concerning the efficacy of vaccines and highlights how the false cause fallacy is committed by anti-vaccination advocates when trying to connect autism with vaccinations. The website logicalfallacies.info is an excellent compilation of various informal and formal fallacies, including the different variations of the false cause fallacy.

References

Federal Trade Commission. 2009. "Kellogg Settles FTC Charges that Ads for Frosted Mini-Wheats Were False." Federal Trade Commission, December 15. https://www.ftc.gov/news-events/press-releases/2009/04/kellogg-settles-ftc-charges-ads-frosted-mini-wheats-were-false (accessed October 3, 2017).

Hurley, Patrick. 2015. *A Concise Introduction to Logic*. Stamford, CT: Cengage Learning.

Jacobson, S.W., and J.L. Jacobson. 2002. "Breastfeeding and IQ: Evaluation of the Socio-Environmental Confounders." *Acta Pediatric* (91): 258–266.

McKay Illari, Phyllis, Frederica Russo, and Jon Williams. 2011. *Causality in the Sciences*. Oxford: Oxford University Press.

Morton, Sheila. 2014. *Navigating Argument: A Guidebook to Academic Writing*. Greeneville, TN: Tusculum College.

Myers, Martin, and Diego Pineda. 2008. *Do Vaccines Cause That?!: A Guide for Evaluating Vaccine Safety Concerns*. Galveston, TX: Immunizations for Public Health.

Vigen, Tyler. 2015. "Spurious Correlations." http://www.tylervigen.com/spurious-correlations (accessed October 3, 2017).

80

False Cause: *Post Hoc Ergo Propter Hoc*

Bertha Alvarez Manninen

> HOMER: Not a bear in sight. The Bear Patrol must be working like a charm.
> LISA: That's specious reasoning, Dad. By your logic, I could claim that this rock keeps tigers away.
> HOMER: Oh, how does it work?
> LISA: It doesn't work. It's just a stupid rock. But I don't see any tigers around, do you?
> HOMER: Lisa, I want to buy your rock.
>
> *The Simpsons*, "Much Apu About Nothing"

In general, the false cause fallacy occurs when the "link between premises and conclusion depends on some imagined causal connection that probably does not exist" (Hurley 2015, 149). This is certainly the case when it comes to Lisa's rock – there was no evidence that the rock itself was keeping tigers away from Springfield. By the same logic, it could have been her beaded necklace or Bart's skateboard that was keeping the tigers away.

There are three different ways an argument can commit the false cause fallacy: *post hoc ergo propter hoc*; *cum hoc ergo propter hoc*; and ignoring common cause. We'll deal with *post hoc ergo propter hoc* here. Also see the chapters for *cum hoc ergo propter hoc* (Chapter 78); and ignoring common cause (Chapter 79).

Consider Sheldon's words from an episode of *The Big Bang Theory* titled "The Electric Can Opener Fluctuation": "No, Mother, I could not feel your

Bad Arguments: 100 of the Most Important Fallacies in Western Philosophy, First Edition.
Edited by Robert Arp, Steven Barbone, and Michael Bruce.
© 2019 John Wiley & Sons Ltd. Published 2019 by John Wiley & Sons Ltd.

church group praying for my safety. The fact that I am home safe does not prove that it worked, that logic is *post hoc ergo propter hoc.*" This Latin phrase literally translates to "after this, therefore because of this." It is committed when one argues that a causal relationship exists between A and B mainly because A happened before B. On *The Big Bang Theory*, Sheldon notes that his mother commits the *post hoc ergo propter hoc* fallacy when she attributes his safe return from an expedition to the prayers of her church group, for it is not the case that Sheldon's returning from his expedition safely is sufficient evidence for establishing that the prayers worked. Athletes also often commit the same fallacy when they attribute winning an event to an article of clothing that they wore during the event; the flaw in reasoning becomes obvious when one notes that that, by the same logic, the athlete could have attributed her win to the particular shampoo she used that morning while bathing. Or Sheldon's mother could have attributed his arriving home safely to whatever breakfast food she had that morning. Though, of course, causes do precede their effects, this alone does not suffice to prove that there is a causal connection between two events. What is needed is actual evidence that two events have a causal connection.

Some have argued that the use of marijuana serves as a precursor to the use of other, much stronger, drugs. Consider the words of Nick Kristof – quoted in Szalavitz (2010) – who is largely in favor of the legalization of marijuana: "I have no illusions about drugs. One of my childhood friends in Yamhill, Ore., pretty much squandered his life by dabbling with marijuana in ninth grade and then moving on to stronger stuff. And yes, there's some risk that legalization would make such dabbling more common." Yet many have argued that the notion of marijuana as a "gateway" drug is a result of the *post hoc ergo propter hoc* fallacy. While it may be true that people who are addicted to hardcore drugs at first started with drugs like marijuana, that alone does not suffice to show that the use of marijuana is what *caused* the use of the stronger drugs. Indeed, the Institute of Medicine of the National Academy of Sciences, while recognizing that marijuana use precedes the use of much stronger drugs, refutes any such causal connection.

> In the sense that marijuana use typically precedes rather than follows initiation of other illicit drug use, it is indeed a "gateway" drug. But because underage smoking and alcohol use typically precede marijuana use, marijuana is not the most common, and is rarely the first, "gateway" to illicit drug use. There is no conclusive evidence that the drug effects of marijuana are causally linked to the subsequent abuse of other illicit drugs. (Szalavitz 2010)

The *post hoc ergo propter hoc* makes its appearance often in politics. In 2015, Senator Mitch McConnell attributed the improvement of the US economy to the fact that many Republicans had been voted into their positions during the midterm elections: "After so many years of sluggish growth, we're finally starting to see some economic data that can provide a glimmer of hope; the uptick appears to coincide with the biggest political change of the Obama Administration's long tenure in Washington, the expectation of a new Republican Congress" (Jacobson 2015). McConnell neglects to mention that the economy was already improving before the November elections and that it takes much more than two months after voting a party into office before any noticeable changes in the economy can be seen. In 2011, a Fox Nation headline read, "Stocks Tumble Worldwide after Obama Speech" (Wallace and Nazareth 2011), clearly implying that the president's speech contributed to such a decline. Many individuals attribute the cost of gas prices to whichever president is in charge at the time, blaming his policies when gas prices skyrocket while giving him credit when gas prices are low. However, gas prices respond to a variety of worldwide economic conditions, not simply to the policies of one particular administration.

One example of the *post hoc ergo propter hoc* fallacy that has had a great impact on public health has been the recent fear of childhood vaccines, particularly the MMR (measles, mumps, and rubella) vaccine and the concern it can cause autism. The fear started in 1998 when Dr. Andrew Wakefield and 12 colleagues published an essay in *The Lancet* arguing that a correlation exists between the MMR vaccine and autism; the article was later retracted given that several elements in the study were either dubious or outright incorrect. Yet the public had been scared. Celebrity Jenny McCarthy became a vocal opponent of the MMR vaccine, attributing her son's autism to having received it: "If you ask a parent of an autistic child if they want the measles or autism, we will stand in line for the f***ing measles" (Klugar 2009). As a result of this public fear, there has been a substantial decline in the number of children being vaccinated against diseases like MMR and pertussis and an increase in such diseases within the general population. In 2014, the Center for Disease Control released a study that noted that measles in the United States have reached a 20-year high (Center for Disease Control). This is particularly dangerous not just for unvaccinated children but for individuals who cannot receive vaccinations due to autoimmune disorders and who therefore must rely on herd immunity to keep them healthy.

Because children are often diagnosed with autism in early childhood, typically around the same time that the MMR vaccine is also administered, many people have attributed a child's autism to the MMR vaccine. However, subsequent and repeated studies have shown that there is no causal connection between vaccinations and autism (see, for example, Myers and Pineda 2008). Therefore, this is an example of the *post hoc ergo propter hoc* fallacy because the mere fact that the vaccine is administered closely before autism is diagnosed is taken as evidence that the former caused the latter even though there is simply no actual evidence that this causal connection exists.

References

Center for Disease Control. 2014. "Measles Cases in the United States Reach 20-Year High." http://www.cdc.gov/media/releases/2014/p0529-measles.html (accessed October 3, 2017).

Hurley, Patrick. 2015. *A Concise Introduction to Logic.* Stamford, CT: Cengage Learning.

Jacobson, Louis. 2015. "Mitch McConnell Says Economic Uptick Coincides with Expectation of GOP Senate Takeover." Politifact, January 8. http://www.politifact.com/truth-o-meter/statements/2015/jan/08/mitch-mcconnell/mitch-mcconnell-says-economic-uptick-coincides-exp/(accessed October 3, 2017).

Klugar, Jeffrey. 2009. "Jenny McCarthy on Autism and Vaccines." *Time,* December 15. http://content.time.com/time/health/article/0,8599,1888718,00.html (accessed October 3, 2017).

Myers, Martin, and Diego Pineda. 2008. *Do Vaccines Cause That?!: A Guide for Evaluating Vaccine Safety Concerns.* Galveston, TX: Immunizations for Public Health.

Szalavitz, Maia. 2010. "Marijuana as a Gateway Drug: The Myth that Will Not Die." http://healthland.time.com/2010/10/29/marijuna-as-a-gateway-drug-the-myth-that-will-not-die/(accessed October 3, 2017).

Wallace, Stuart, and Rita Nazareth. 2011. "Stocks Tumble Worldwide after Obama Speech." Fox News, September 9. http://nation.foxnews.com/obama-jobs-plan/2011/09/09/stocks-tumble-worldwide-after-obama-speech (accessed October 3, 2017).

81

False Dilemma

Jennifer Culver

Every nation, in every region, now has a decision to make. Either you are with us, or you are with the terrorists.

George W. Bush

According to Lunsford, Ruskiewicz, and Walters (2015), a false dilemma (FD) tends to "reduce a complicated issue to excessively simple terms" or, when intentionally created, tends to "obscure legitimate alternatives" (74). President Bush's quotation above illustrates the FD by metaphorically drawing a line in the sand and telling all other nations that any lack of support would be perceived as an endorsement of terrorist activity. In reality, how nations respond to an attack on another nation involves more complexity, and certainly neutrality is a third option, but Bush's statement reduces their options to only two: with us or against us.

FD reflects incorrect thinking because it presents a problem or issue as having only two possible solutions when in fact there are more. For example, when (then-Governor) Arnold Schwarzenegger said in 2005, "If we here in this chamber do not work together to reform the government, the people will rise up and reform it themselves. And, you know something, I will join them. And I will fight with them," he posited an FD to gain support for his own proposed actions (Broder 2005). Because he wanted to overhaul redistricting in his state, he tried to make the public believe that

Bad Arguments: 100 of the Most Important Fallacies in Western Philosophy, First Edition.
Edited by Robert Arp, Steven Barbone, and Michael Bruce.
© 2019 John Wiley & Sons Ltd. Published 2019 by John Wiley & Sons Ltd.

prohibiting that redistricting would create civil unrest; the citizens would be ready to rise up and take action to make the government work more efficiently.

Liam Dempsey (2013) noted that shows such as *The Daily Show* and *The Colbert Report* often employed FD in order to highlight the "theatrics" that are found in political events (such as national conventions) or the use of FD by politicians (170). As Steven Colbert used to ask many of his guests: "George W. Bush: great president or the greatest president?" This demonstrates nicely why FDs are fallacies. When his guests would refuse to answer, he'd just say "I'll put you down for *great*." Clearly, his guests didn't agree.

Politics aside, an FD exists anytime an extreme dichotomy of choices appears as the only possible answers. To be clear, not every dilemma is an FD. If there really are only two options, presenting only those two options is not fallacious. "You can have soup or salad with your entrée." But if there are more than two options, presenting only two of them commits the FD fallacy.

For example, a person may believe that going to heaven and going to hell are the only possible things that could happen to a person after death. A coach may believe that any competition boils down only to winners and losers. People may compartmentalize everyone who is not their friend as an enemy. In each of these situations, an individual only sees two possibilities when there are more. It's a kind of black-and-white thinking that creates an FD for anyone who does not easily gravitate to either category.

Finally, advertisers also create an FD when creating a situation with only two outcomes and the only correct or positive outcome leads to their brand. Paper towel and toilet paper commercials, for example, usually only compare the favored brand with one other brand, a brand not as absorbent. The audience views the impressive distance between the two brands, but when that same audience goes to purchase toilet paper or paper towels, a myriad of possibilities exist that the commercial does not accurately convey.

References

Broder, John. 2005. "Schwarzenegger Proposes Overhaul of Redistricting." *New York Times*, January 6. http://www.nytimes.com/2005/01/06/us/schwarzenegger-proposes-overhaul-of-redistricting.html (accessed October 3, 2017).

Dempsey, Liam. 2013. "The Daily Show's Expose of Political Rhetoric." In *The Ultimate Daily Show and Philosophy: More Moments of Zen, More Indecision Theory*, edited by Jason Holt and William Irwin. Hoboken, NJ: Wiley-Blackwell, 167–180.

Lunsford, Andrea A., John J. Ruskiewicz, and Keith Walters. 2015. *Everything's an Argument with Readings*. New York, NY: Bedford Books/St. Martin's Press.

82

Free Speech

Scott Aikin and John Casey

Everyone needs to leave Phil Robertson alone for expressing his beliefs. I think it's so hypocritical how the LGBT community expects every single flippen [*sic*] person to agree with their life style. This flies in the face of what makes America great – people can have their own beliefs and own opinions and their own ways of life.

Bristol Palin

The free speech fallacy (FS) consists in thinking one's political right to freedom of expression includes protection from criticism. Those who commit this fallacy allege that critical scrutiny is either tantamount to censorship or equivalent to the imposition of one's views on others. The error in the fallacy is that the freedom of expression includes critical expressions.

A confusion about the nature of critical exchange lies at the heart of the FS. What the FS does is wrongly accuse others of fallacy or abuse of critical dialogue. It achieves this through two key distortions. The first distortion concerns the logical consequences of criticism. If A criticizes B for view p, it stands to reason that A thinks B should no longer hold p. The rejection of p is a logical consequence of A's view. The FS, however, ignores the reasons given for rejecting p as essential to the exchange, treating them instead as incidental to the exchange. What really matters is that B's view has problems, not that A has problems with B's view.

Bad Arguments: 100 of the Most Important Fallacies in Western Philosophy, First Edition.
Edited by Robert Arp, Steven Barbone, and Michael Bruce.
© 2019 John Wiley & Sons Ltd. Published 2019 by John Wiley & Sons Ltd.

The second distortion confuses logical implications of criticism with the criticism itself. Return again to A and B. If A criticizes B for view p, A likely implies B to have incorrectly believed p. This necessarily implies that B has somehow failed in some cognitive obligation, and so B has been superficial, lazy, or biased in believing p. B may thus feel under personal attack and so stifled or discouraged from speaking. The sting of criticism is very powerful, and *so B takes this sting to be the point of A's criticism*. The FS thus takes the personal implications, necessary though they may be, as the defining features of criticism, when they are merely incidental.

Phil Robertson was a national celebrity in 2013. He was one of the stars of the reality television show *Duck Dynasty*. It came to light that Robertson had strong anti-gay views. In a particular sermon, Robertson said that homosexuals are "full of murder, envy, strife, hatred. They are insolent, arrogant, God-haters" (Nichols 2014). Robertson found himself the target for a good deal of criticism. Bristol Palin, blogger and daughter of the 2008 Republican vice-presidential candidate Sarah Palin, came to Robertson's defense with a version of the FS fallacy. Her case (above) ran that because Robertson is guaranteed the right of free expression, others do not have a right to hold his views to critical scrutiny and express their reasons for rejecting them. The trouble with this argument is that freedom of expression does not mean freedom from criticism.

Kanye West, a popular hip hop artist, has had a longstanding feud with another pop artist, Taylor Swift. In his song "Famous," West muses that "I feel like me and Taylor might still have sex. Why? Because I made that bitch famous." The line is a triple-dip on misogyny. He calls Swift a bitch and implies that having sex with him is her best way to thank him for her fame. And there is the thought that it was his actions that made her famous. West quickly found himself in a swirl of criticism. In reply, he tweeted: "I did not diss Taylor Swift and I've never dissed her. [...] First thing is I'm an artist and as an artist I will express how I feel with no censorship" (Johnson 2016).

He follows by noting that the critics are "trying to criticize the real artist" and "want to control us with money and perception and mute the culture." The error, again, is confusing what effects criticism may have (in that one may feel attacked and threatened) with what its ends are (namely, that of subjecting publicly shared views and actions to rational scrutiny).

It is central to FS that it focus on the personal implications of criticism rather than the criticism. Actor Clint Eastwood provides an interesting case in point. In 2009 he said he firmly believes that making jokes about other races is acceptable: "People have lost their sense of humor. [...] In former times we constantly made jokes about different races. You can only tell them today with one hand over your mouth otherwise you will be insulted as a racist" (Hall 2009).

It is indeed true that accusations of racism are particularly powerful. Their power, however, may distract from the reasons offered for employing them. In this case, Eastwood is a victim of name-calling (*ad hominem*: direct; see Chapter 10) by "humorless killjoys." What is missing, and this is crucial, are the reasons for levying such a charge in the first place. The FS has obscured those.

How does one avoid the FS, and how does one criticize it when others use it? In the first place, it is good to remind everyone in a critical discussion that the point of critical discussion is to sort the good ideas from the bad. In the process, so the hope goes, we correct errors, understand more, and come closer to the truth. But for this to happen, people must be free to say what they think, those who disagree must be free to express their disagreements, and all must be willing to hear out the reasons for and against (Aikin and Talisse 2011). Etiquette often stands in the way of such critical discussions – it's an old rule that it is impolite to discuss politics or religion. But well-run critical discussions need not be impolite so long as all involved don't confuse their rights to say what they believe without coercion with their right to say what they believe without criticism.

References

Aikin, Scott, and Robert Talisse. 2011. "Argument in Mixed Company." *Think* (27): 31–43.

Hall, Alan. 2009. "Clint Eastwood Goes Gunning for PC Killjoys." *Daily Mail*, February 25. http://www.dailymail.co.uk/news/article-1155360/Clint-Eastwood-goes-gunning-PC-killjoys-saying-laugh-race-based-jokes.html. (accessed October 3, 2017).

Johnson, Victoria. 2016. "Kanye Responds to the Life of Pablo Critics." The Boom Box, January 15. http://theboombox.com/kanye-west-responds-to-the-life-of-pablo-critics-on-twitter/(accessed October 3, 2017).

Nichols, James. 2014. "New Anti-Gay Sermon from *Duck Dynasty* Star Leaks." *The Huffington Post*, February 2. http://www.huffingtonpost.com/2014/05/22/phil-robertson-anti-gay-easter-sermon_n_5372678.html (accessed October 3, 2017).

83

Guilt by Association

Leigh Kolb

> This is not a man who sees America as you see America and as I see America. Our opponent is someone who sees America, it seems, as being so imperfect that he's palling around with terrorists who would target their own country. Americans need to know this.
>
> Sarah Palin, 2008 presidential election

The guilt by association fallacy (GBA) is the erroneous logic that just because someone/something A is associated with someone/something B, that someone/something A has or accepts all of the qualities of someone/something B. This fallacy permeates society, from social groups, to political campaigns, to business relationships, to the court system.

On the 2008 presidential campaign trail, vice-presidential candidate Sarah Palin said that Barack Obama was "palling around with terrorists" since in the 1990s he had known and worked on community projects with Bill Ayres, a professor who was involved in the domestic terrorist group the Weather Underground in the 1960s. Mike Huckabee echoed her sentiments: "If you hang out with somebody who has never apologized for bombing the Pentagon and the Capitol and is proud of something he should have been ashamed of, then it calls into question your judgment" (Shipman 2008). The fact that Obama had worked with Ayres was enough for his opponents to call into question his patriotism and his loyalty to America (regardless of

Bad Arguments: 100 of the Most Important Fallacies in Western Philosophy, First Edition.
Edited by Robert Arp, Steven Barbone, and Michael Bruce.
© 2019 John Wiley & Sons Ltd. Published 2019 by John Wiley & Sons Ltd.

Obama's denunciation of the acts). As Robert Gula (2002) has noted, true logic would dictate that "what the person is saying is the issue, not who his associates are" (231).

When politics, social issues, and business collide, GBA enters new realms. Michael Hiltzik (2015), an economics reporter with the *Los Angeles Times*, says, "This is a new advance in 'guilt by association': it's guilt by association with the non-guilty." He goes on to explain that the political ramification of association with a party that is deemed legally not guilty but politically guilty is a GBA

In his article for *The Washington Post* titled "Darren Wilson and Guilt by Association," Jonathan Capehart (2014) featured an interview with law professor and author Alexandra Natapoff. She connects Darren Wilson's shooting of Mike Brown in Ferguson to the GBA's being upheld by the 2000 Supreme Court case Illinois v. Wardlow:

> Police officers have been told by authorities as high as the Supreme Court that they can draw inferences in high crime neighborhoods or low-income or urban neighborhoods. [...] He [Wilson] conflates the community and the residents with so-called gangs. And once he does that it's as if we're being told that his excuse for not treating Michael Brown as a child and a resident and someone who he is paid by the taxpayers to protect and care for instead that he's entitled to conflate Michael Brown because of the color of his [Brown's] skin and the neighborhood in which he lives with known criminals.

GBA is also used when it is found that perpetrators of horrific events belonged to a certain group. The other members of the group, church, mosque, online forum, or those with a similar medical diagnosis that the perpetrator is or has identified with then suffers the consequences of being seen as being guilty. The Southern Poverty Law Center reports, "Immediately after the 9/11 attacks, anti-Muslim hate violence skyrocketed some 1,600%." After the Columbine High School shooting in 1999, immediate connections were drawn to the video games, music, and films that the perpetrators consumed, making the pop culture (and its fans) seem guilty by their association to the killers.

Of course, McCarthyism – which came to a head in the 1950s in America with Senator Joseph McCarthy and J. Edgar Hoover at the helm – targeted individuals who supposedly were involved in anti-American/communist activities. Thousands of people lost their jobs and reputations because of their association with other people who were thought to be communists, their connection to groups that had communist sympathies, or their interest in causes that were seen as communist (labor rights, civil rights, etc.). GBA can have dire consequences.

In a *New York Times* column titled "The Perfect-Victim Pitfall," Charles M. Blow (2014) examines how the GBA arguments against Michael Brown and Eric Garner detracted from the root problems of racism and criminal justice. He says,

> The argument is that this is not a perfect case, because Brown – and, one would assume, now Garner – isn't a perfect victim and the protesters haven't all been perfectly civil, so therefore any movement to counter black oppression that flows from the case is inherently flawed. But this is ridiculous and reductive, because it fails to acknowledge that the whole system is imperfect and rife with flaws. We don't need to identify angels and demons to understand that inequity is hell.

His argument relies on how the complexities of the individuals are mirrored by the complexities of the problems, yet reductive and simplified arguments about the individuals detract from the real argument at hand.

GBA is often a knee-jerk reaction that has deep roots in people's implicit biases and has even been supported consistently by legal precedent. To disrupt the desire to make these immediate and fallacious assumptions, individuals must recognize the consequences of doing so and instead build their arguments on facts and realities. In the examples above, those committing fallacious thought spoke about their "victims" as one-dimensional, simplified caricatures instead of as complex individuals, which is the reality. Avoiding that kind of oversimplification and vilification will result in stronger, more responsible arguments. When who a person "palls around with" (or even has been casually associated with) is the object of the argument, and not the person her/himself, the writer/speaker is committing guilt by association.

References

Blow, Charles. 2014. "The Perfect-Victim Pitfall." *The New York Times*, December 3. https://www.nytimes.com/2014/12/04/opinion/charles-blow-first-michael-brown-now-eric-garner.html (accessed October 3, 2017).

Capehart, Jonathan. 2014. "Darren Wilson and Guilt by Association." *The Washington Post*, December 1. https://www.washingtonpost.com/blogs/post-partisan/wp/2014/12/01/darren-wilson-and-guilt-by-association/?utm_term=.18063bd18210 (accessed October 3, 2017).

Gula, Robert. 2002. *Nonsense: A Handbook of Logical Fallacies*. Mount Jackson, VA: Axios Press.

Hiltzik, Michael. 2015. "Planned Parenthood: A Terrified Business Partner Abandons the Organization." *Los Angeles Times*, August 18. http://www.latimes.com/business/hiltzik/la-fi-mh-a-partner-bails-on-planned-parenthood-20150817-column.html (accessed October 3, 2017).

Shipman, Tim. 2008. "Sarah Palin: Barack Obama 'Palling around with Terrorists'." *The Telegraph*, October 4. http://www.telegraph.co.uk/news/worldnews/sarah-palin/3137197/Sarah-Palin-accuses-Barack-Obama-of-terrorist-links.html (accessed October 3, 2017).

84

Hasty Generalization

Michael J. Muniz

> When Mexico sends its people, they're not sending their best. They're not sending you. They're sending people that have lots of problems, and they're bringing those problems to us. They're bringing drugs. They're bringing crime. They're rapists. And some, I assume, are good people.
>
> Donald Trump

The fallacy of hasty generalization (HG) is one that can disrupt inductive reasoning. Before discussing the nature of HG, there needs to be a clear understanding of what defines a proper generalization.

According to Patrick Hurley (2008), a generalization is an "argument that proceeds from the knowledge of a selected sample to some claim about the whole group" (37). For example, after a teacher has graded 10 quizzes from a class of 25 and observes that each of them have gotten, say, question number 8 wrong with the same mistake, she can then argue that the remainder of the class will have probably gotten the same question wrong with the same or a similar mistake. Her generalization is justified because the sample is representative of the whole group. Given that she knows what was taught and how students learned the lesson that preceded the quiz, she induces that question number 8 must have been written in a way that was confusing for students. Additionally, she notes that 10 students in a class of 25 is a reasonable number from which to make such a generalization.

Bad Arguments: 100 of the Most Important Fallacies in Western Philosophy, First Edition.
Edited by Robert Arp, Steven Barbone, and Michael Bruce.
© 2019 John Wiley & Sons Ltd. Published 2019 by John Wiley & Sons Ltd.

Regarding sampling, according to Michael Blastland and Andrew Dilnot (2008) in *The Tiger That Isn't*, "samples have to be large enough to be plausibly representative of the rest of the population" (125). So, for the above example, 10 students are a plausible sample for a proper generalization about a group of 25.

Now, HG is committed when some aspect of the definition of the proper generalization is violated. In other words, the "hasty" aspect of this fallacy is triggered either (1) when there is a lack of knowledge of the selected sample or (2) when the selected sample is not representative of the whole group, or when both (1) and (2) are true.

To demonstrate the first trigger of the hasty part of HG, consider the example of a teacher who has a lack of knowledge of her students' personal circumstances: "Johnny has been failing my quizzes this week. Therefore, Johnny is not capable of grasping my lesson." The fallacy is committed in this case because the teacher failed to consider any possible factors inside and/or outside the classroom that may have contributed to Johnny's failing the quizzes this week. Perhaps a close relative of Johnny might have passed away recently, causing him to not be focused, or perhaps Johnny is distracted in class by the pretty girl who sits next him.

The second trigger of the hasty part of HG is the most popular under-standing of the definition of this fallacy. It suggests that the sampling size is insufficient to represent the whole group. To demonstrate, suppose our teacher is grading a stack of 100 quizzes. By quiz 22, she observes that no student has gotten higher than a D on her quiz. Therefore, she believes that no student will receive at least a B on her quiz. But 22 quizzes are not a sufficient sample to generalize about a group of 100. Like this fictional teacher who does not utilize a large enough sample size, often in reality, we hold certain "truths" about some group or another based on either so-called scientific studies and/or polls that rely on small sample sizes.

To avoid committing this fallacy, the arguer should take into consideration the amount of justifiable knowledge she might have on a particular subject and whether the selected sample being used in the case is justifiably representative of the group in question. This means, the arguer should avoid stereotypes, typecasting, labels, and so on.

We see HG committed just about every day in politics and the media. Moreover, these instances of HG are employed intentionally to convey a specific point to the audience. In politics, HGs are used to emphasize the extremes of a particular viewpoint. Consider the views of Donald Trump expressed in the epigraph and in the following quotation:

> What can be simpler or more accurately stated? The Mexican Government is forcing their most unwanted people into the United States. They are, in many cases, criminals, drug dealers, rapists, etc.

Besides providing great sound bites and material for journalists and social critics to comment on, Mr. Trump's remarks can also be quite entertaining. Concurrently, HG is used quite often by advertisers to promote a particular product. A common usage can be found in medical product commercials:

> Nine out of 10 doctors recommend Advil to treat headaches. Therefore, it must be good.

Furthermore, these commercials are often not creating a stereotype for a product but are working with those already established by society. There is a popular "Guys Love Bacon" commercial by Taco Bell that works because of HG. In the commercial, one young lady has the newly developed bacon taco in her purse while her friend comments that it will not attract other men. Soon after, three men approach the young lady with the bacon taco in her purse. The commercial is suggesting that all men love bacon, and if a women smells like bacon, men will be attracted to her, which is simply not true.

References

Blastland, Michael, and A.W. Dilnot. 2008. *The Tiger That Isn't: Seeing through a World of Numbers*. London: Profile.

Hurley, Patrick. 2008. *A Concise Introduction to Logic*, 10th edition. Belmont, CA: Wadsworth Cengage Learning.

85

Intentional Fallacy

Nicolas Michaud

> Art is not a handicraft, it is the transmission of feeling the artist has experienced.
>
> Leo Tolstoy

The intentional fallacy (IF) is an odd kind of fallacy. Rather than being a fallacy focused on logic and argumentation, it is a fallacy that focuses on art, relating to how we judge art and engage in literary criticism. The IF focuses on the fact that we often think that there is one right interpretation of a work of art – the artist's intention. In other words, when we try to figure out what a work is about, we think of it as trying to figure out the artist's mind. If the artist agrees, "Yes, that is what I was trying to say," then we feel like we were right. It is that belief that it is the artist's intention that reigns supreme in art interpretation that is the fallacy.

According to David Fenner (2003), the IF "states that we do not need to know, nor can we on most occasions, what was in the mind of the artist in order to interpret the art work" (155). So, logically speaking, it seems unreasonable to use the artist's intention as the most important way to understand a work of art as the artist's intention is often unavailable. Most artists of famous works of art are dead. We cannot ask them what they intended. So it seems irrational to make their interpretation more important than anyone else's.

Bad Arguments: 100 of the Most Important Fallacies in Western Philosophy, First Edition. Edited by Robert Arp, Steven Barbone, and Michael Bruce.
© 2019 John Wiley & Sons Ltd. Published 2019 by John Wiley & Sons Ltd.

It's arguable that one often makes a grave logical error when interpreting art. Take, for example, poetry. Let's say you read a poem by John Donne. You sit down, analyze it, and decide that it is a love poem. You have good evidence. Specific passages in the poem seem to mention love and romance, and the work creates a general feeling of longing for someone else. So you go to your friend and say, "I think this poem is about love for these reasons …" If your friend replies, "Well let's do some research to find out what Donne said about his poem. That way we can know if it is *really* about love," then your friend has committed the IF. Your friend has assumed that even though you have given good evidence for your interpretation, the author's intention is the "real" meaning of the work.

Take the example a step further and consider that you and your friend do some research and find commentary by John Donne on that particular poem. You are surprised to see that Donne stated something like, "The poem is really about hate. I don't know why. I just felt a lot of hate when I wrote it." If your friend states, "Oh well, there you go. The poem is about hate," then she has committed the IF. Notice, in the example, there is no instance of Donne's giving *reasons* for his interpretation. He just states that he intended to share a particular feeling, and so our tendency is to say, "Oh well, that is what the work really means because the author intended it." That reply, though, doesn't make much sense. Just because the author intended the work to mean something doesn't mean the work expresses that thing. It just has that feeling or meaning for the author. Whether the artwork communicates that thought or feeling is an entirely different issue.

The problem is that the IF flies in the face of some of our most dearly beloved beliefs about art. Consider the quotation from Tolstoy above. We have this idea that art somehow magically transmits the artist's emotions. We like to think that if *we* create a work of art, the true meaning is whatever we intended. Consider, though, that I draw what I believe to be a tree. Everyone else who sees it says, "What an amazing pig you've drawn!" Should I reply to them, "You are wrong! It is a tree!" Maybe I intended to draw a tree. From the standpoint of the viewers, though, regardless of my intent, it is a pig. Perhaps I could, by pointing out certain aspects and facets of the work, show viewers that my work can *also* be experienced as a tree if you look at it a particular way. However, then, it isn't the fact that I intended it that makes it a tree but, instead, the fact that I can show viewers a way to look at it so that they too will see a tree. Really, that is what good art critics do. They show us ways to look at and listen to art that help us get *more* meaning from art, not less.

From a purely logical perspective, ignoring the argument about whether art can or cannot transmit feelings from the artist to the audience, the IF is a problem because of the inaccessibility to many artists' minds. Many artists are dead, many are unwilling to tell us what the work "means," and many do not know themselves what they intended. The popularity of psychotherapy suggests that we do not always know our own minds, thoughts, and feelings, and so how can we expect an artist always to be able to clarify the "true" meaning of a work of art by referring to her own intentions? Sometimes the artists just don't know. So it makes art interpretation much more difficult if we assume there must be some "correct" meaning that the artist was trying to convey. Sometimes, in fact, an artist may create a work thinking one thing and then be surprised himself when viewers point out it could mean something else. "Hmm, I never thought of that, but my painting really does seem to say that." When we commit the IF, we make it impossible for artists themselves to learn from their own work and see it in many different ways.

The one thing that is available to everyone, including the artist, is the work of art itself. When we say the "real" meaning is the artist's intention, we favor the interpretations of those who can talk to and ask the author what she meant. The rest of the viewers are left only with the work itself to interpret. When we think about it, though, we realize that what really works in art interpretation is evidence. If we can give good reasons and explanations for the meaning of a work of art, and viewers respond, "Oh, wow. Yes, I can see that. Your interpretation makes sense," then why would we treat that interpretation as lesser than the artist's intention? After all, if the artist did a good job, then without his help we can figure out what he meant.

The IF, then, is an error in art interpretation that causes us to realize two important things about art: (1) When trying to judge if an artist effectively accomplished *her* goal, it is helpful to *her* if we or she knows her intention. As an artist, she is struggling if she is trying to draw trees and everyone else is seeing pigs; (2) The intention of the artist is not as important as the *reasons* we can give for interpreting a work a certain way. Otherwise, we make a hero out of the artist and end up forgetting the work itself. Whatever he intended, the work should be able to stand on its own, and we shouldn't limit ourselves to the "true" meaning the artist intended. We can get much more out of art if we consider what good reasons we can come up with for different ways of understanding the work in front of us.

Reference

Fenner, David E.W. 2003. *Introducing Aesthetics*. Westport, CT: Praeger.

86

Is/Ought Fallacy

Mark T. Nelson

> When considering what we *ought to do*, our reflections lead us eventually to a consideration of what we *in fact do*; this is inescapable, for a catalogue of our considered intuitive judgments on what we ought to do is both a compendium of what we do think, and a shining example (by our lights – what else?) of how we ought to think.
>
> Daniel Dennett, *The Intentional Stance*

Some people think that Daniel Dennett must be wrong here because no good arguments exist that lead from factual premises to moral conclusions. This is the doctrine of the is/ought fallacy (IOF), summed up in the slogan, "You can't get an 'ought' from an 'is'," meaning that any attempt to infer a normative conclusion about what we *ought* to do from descriptive premises about what *is* the case must go wrong somehow.

This issue matters for two opposing reasons. First, it is natural to think that our moral beliefs need to be based on facts if they are to be more than mere prejudices or moves in a power game. If we can't infer "ought" from "is," it is difficult to see how ethics can have this factual basis. Second, certain kinds of is-to-ought arguments can be used to support the status quo in objectionable ways: "This is the way things have always been; therefore this is the way things ought to be."

Some philosophers think that no good arguments exist that lead from "is" to "ought" because no logically valid inferences exist from descriptive

Bad Arguments: 100 of the Most Important Fallacies in Western Philosophy, First Edition. Edited by Robert Arp, Steven Barbone, and Michael Bruce.
© 2019 John Wiley & Sons Ltd. Published 2019 by John Wiley & Sons Ltd.

propositions to normative propositions, an idea they trace back to David Hume's (1978) remark that:

> In every system of morality, which I have hitherto met with, I have always remark'd, that the author proceeds for some time in the ordinary way of reasoning, and establishes the being of a God, or makes observations concerning human affairs; when of a sudden I am surpriz'd to find, that instead of the usual copulations of propositions, *is* and *is not*, I meet with no proposition that is not connected with an *ought*, or an *ought not*. This change is imperceptible; but is, however, of the last consequence. For as this *ought* or *ought not*, expresses some new relation or affirmation, 'tis necessary that it should be observ'd and explain'd; and at the same time that a reason should be given, for what seems altogether inconceivable, how this new relation be a deduction from others, which are entirely different from it. (469)

Others dispute this reading of Hume, noting that he does not actually say that it is *impossible* to make such deductions, only that it seems inconceivable unless we can give an explanation of how we can make them (which they say, he goes on to give). Still others note that even if Hume *is* claiming here that there can be no logically valid inferences from descriptive premises to normative conclusions, it is not clear what his argument for this claim is or that he argues for it at all. Indeed, the doctrine of the IOF is rarely argued for; it is usually just asserted without argumentation.

Charles Pigden (1991) argues for the illegitimacy of the move from is to ought, saying that we should understand Hume as pointing to the conservativeness of logic. According to Pigden, logic is conservative in that "the conclusions of a valid inference are contained within the premises. You don't get out what you haven't put in" (423). The implication for morality is this: logically valid arguments will not yield moral propositions as their conclusions if they do not already contain at last one moral proposition among their premises. This raises the question: What is it to be a moral (or other normative) proposition?

If being a moral proposition is just a matter of containing moral words such as "right," "wrong," or "ought," then valid inferences need not be conservative, as the following example from Arthur Prior (1960) shows:

(1) Tea-drinking is common in England.
(2) Therefore, tea-drinking is common in England or all New Zealanders ought to be shot.

In this argument, the premise does not contain any moral words, the conclusion does contain a moral word, and the argument is valid because it is an instance of the "disjunction introduction" rule of inference. Even so, most people feel that it cannot be so easy to get a real "ought" from an "is."

Because the conclusion is a disjunction, we could substitute any arbitrary proposition for the right-hand disjunct – the moral part of it – without affecting the validity of the argument. This suggests that its conclusion is not a genuine moral proposition at all. Pigden (1991) calls propositions like this "vacuously" moral and qualifies his principle accordingly: "The conservativeness of logic becomes the claim that no (non-logical) expression can occur non-vacuously in the conclusion of a valid inference unless it appears in the premises [...]. The autonomy of ethics is simply the moral incarnation of this claim – no non-vacuous 'ought' from 'is'" (424).

What is it to be a moral proposition, then, if it is not just a matter of containing moral words? Stephen Maitzen (1998) and Mark Nelson (1995) have defined genuine moral propositions as all and only those that carry moral commitment, that is, that entail that some particular person is virtuous or vicious, or some particular action is right or wrong, or some particular type of action is required or forbidden. This enables us to explain why Prior's argument is not a counter-example to the doctrine of the IOF. Because it is a disjunction, the conclusion of Prior's argument carries no moral commitment, which implies that it is not a moral proposition at all. Given their definition, however, it is still possible to formulate other counter-examples to the doctrine of the IOF:

(1)   "Bertie morally ought to marry Madeline" is one of Aunt Dahlia's beliefs.
(2)   All of Aunt Dahlia's beliefs are true.
(3)   Therefore, Bertie morally ought to marry Madeline.

Both premises in this argument are descriptive: (1) is a proposition about what some person believes, and (2) is a proposition about the truth-value of that person's beliefs. The conclusion is a moral proposition, entailing that a particular person has a particular moral obligation. The argument is valid according to the standard definition of logical validity: necessarily, if its premises are true, then its conclusion is true. It is also compatible with the conservativeness of logic since no terms appear in the conclusion that do not also appear in the premises. An "ought" appears in premise (1), but that is not enough to make it a normative premise since the word is mentioned in a report of someone's belief and is not used in a normative proposition as such. The truth or falsity of the premises is irrelevant since that does not affect the validity of the argument, and we are currently considering the doctrine of the IOF as a claim about logical validity.

Faced with such counter-examples, some philosophers conclude that the IOF is not a logical problem but an epistemological one, meaning that even if inferences like this one are logically valid, they cannot be used epistemologically to warrant anyone's real-life moral beliefs. Arguments do not warrant their conclusions unless the premises of those arguments are themselves warranted, and in the real world, they say, no one would ever be warranted in believing premise (2). Other critics argue that one might conceivably be warranted in believing (2), but only if one were already warranted in believing the conclusion: one could never be warranted in believing that all of Aunt Dahlia's beliefs were true unless one had checked every one of her beliefs including her belief that Bertie ought to marry Madeline. The obvious reply to this last criticism is that propositions such as (2) may be inductively warranted: one might amass substantial evidence that Aunt Dahlia was infallible without having to check all of her beliefs. In any case, such considerations suggest that the doctrine of the IOF, if it is a fallacy at all, is best understood as a point about epistemology and not about logic.

References

Dennett, Daniel. 1987. *The Intentional Stance*. Cambridge, MA: MIT Press.

Hume, David. 1978. *A Treatise of Human Nature*, edited by L.A. Selby-Bigge. Oxford: Clarendon Press.

Maitzen, Stephen. 1998. "Closing the 'Is'-'Ought' Gap." *Canadian Journal of Philosophy* (28): 349–366.

Nelson, Mark T. 1995: "Is it Always Fallacious to Derive Values from Facts?" *Argumentation* (9): 553–562.

Pigden, Charles R. 1991: "Naturalism" in *A Companion to Ethics*, edited by Peter Singer. Oxford: Blackwell, 421–431.

Prior, A.N. 1960: "The Autonomy of Ethics," *Australasian Journal of Philosophy* (38): 199–206.

87

Masked Man

Charles Taliaferro

> Don't you know that a midnight hour comes when everyone has to take off his mask? Do you think life always lets itself be trifled with? Do you think you can sneak off a little before midnight to escape this?"
>
> Søren Kierkegaard

The masked man fallacy (MM) occurs due to our finite, limited knowledge of reality. It would not occur if we were to think in a Kierkegaardian fashion of a God who is omniscient and can knowingly grasp all truths. I return to this point after explaining the fallacy.

MM involves drawing unjustified conclusions about what is true based on intentional attitudes such as beliefs and desires. The fallacy gets its name from this example:

(1) Joe believes that a masked man robbed the bank.
(2) <u>Joe does not believe his father robbed the bank.</u>
(3) Therefore, the masked man is not Joe's father.

The inference is a fallacy because, unbeknown to Joe, his father might have donned a mask and robbed the bank.

MM is based on a failure to apply fully the principle of the indiscernibility of identicals. According to this principle, if A is identical with B, everything

Bad Arguments: 100 of the Most Important Fallacies in Western Philosophy, First Edition.
Edited by Robert Arp, Steven Barbone, and Michael Bruce.
© 2019 John Wiley & Sons Ltd. Published 2019 by John Wiley & Sons Ltd.

true of A is true of B. So, if water is H_2O, everything true of water is true of H_2O. Given this principle, if the masked man is Joe's father, then everything true of the masked man is true of Joe's father. In a case in which the masked man and Joe's father are one and the same person (Fred), then it is true of Fred that Joe believes both that he, Fred (under the description of 'the masked man'), robbed the bank and that Fred (under the description 'my father') did not rob the bank.

The problem in this case is that Joe is not in a position where his beliefs are fully, as it were, transparent, so that he would realize that he was attributing incompatible properties to Fred (that he did and did not robe the bank). In this context, Joe's beliefs may be described as *opaque* as opposed to *transparent*.

While the case of the masked man seems to be a clear fallacy, the case can be redescribed to offer a non-fallacious inference. Imagine Joe justifiably believes many things about the masked man (he is over 6 feet tall, speaks German, and is right-handed) and that he justifiably believes these things are not true of his father (he is 4 feet tall, cannot speak German, and lacks a right hand). From such a vantage point, Joe would justifiably believe that the masked man is not his father. Another caveat is in order about Joe's being able to draw a conclusion about the world from his different beliefs: Joe is justified in believing that the properties of *being a masked man* and *being his (or a) father* are distinct. This proves to be interesting in the following controversial case.

A controversial philosophical argument that involves the MM is in the philosophy of mind. Some philosophers have maintained that there are some things true of the mental (e.g., we have immediate, experiential access to our mental states) that are not true of the physical (e.g., we do not have immediate, experiential access to our neurological states). In reply, it has been argued that we cannot, given this apparent disparity, conclude that the mental is distinct from the physical because, unknown to us, it might turn out that the mental is the physical or, more particularly, the mental is brain activity. This objection, however, is not as clear as the case of the masked man. First, the data would seem to support what is often called property dualism, the thesis that the property of *being immediately, experientially accessible to a person* is distinct from the property of *not being immediately, experientially accessible to a person*. Second, the data might still be problematic to an identity theory (identifying the mental and physical) and not easily disposed of based on a masked man objection insofar as one has reason to believe that everything true of the physical would not include the mental, for example, one has reason to believe that one can exhaustively and sufficiently describe (in the language of physics, chemistry, biology) all the facts about the physical world without describing (or knowing about) the mental. Based on the indiscernibility of identicals, this data would provide some reason for thinking that the physical is not the same as the mental.

Back to our opening remark about Kierkegaard: MM occurs due to our non-God's-eye view of reality. For a God that knows everything (God knows of all truths that they are true and of all falsehoods that they are false), everything would be transparent. But, for us, our knowledge is typically imperfect and we need to be careful about when to draw conclusions in light of our limitations.

This fallacy may be avoided to the extent that we cultivate what many refer to today as *epistemic humility*. We need to be aware of when our beliefs reflect our proper access to some state of affairs and when our beliefs are mediated through different lenses. For example, you may know that you see Boris entering a hotel in Istanbul and not know that you are seeing the tallest Russian spy entering a hotel in Istanbul. Only infer that Boris is not the tallest Russian spy if you know a great deal more, for example, you happen to know that while Boris is entering that hotel, the reason you do not know that the tallest Russian spy is entering the hotel is because you actually have reliable information that she is under surveillance at the Russian embassy. We need to know our limitations when we make inferences based on partial information.

88

Middle Ground

Grant Sterling

The middle ground fallacy (MG) is committed under the following circumstances:

(A) Two (or more) people have presented conflicting views on some subject.
(B) A third party assumes – without offering reasons – the truth regarding the subject must lie between the extremes presented by the conflicting views.

This fallacy is also called, among other things, the fallacy of/to moderation (*argumentum ad temperantiam*), false compromise, the golden mean fallacy, or the gray fallacy.

Like almost all fallacies, MG is prevalent because it closely resembles a non-fallacious way of reasoning. In many disputes, especially when there is a spectrum of opinions, the truth often lies somewhere in between the most extreme views on either side. But although this is often the case, it is by no means *always* the case, so one cannot simply assume without evidence that the "middle ground" is always correct. Consider the following example:

EXTREME BELIEVER: Many people are abducted by aliens every day.
SKEPTIC: There are no alien abductions at all.
FALLACIOUS REASONER: Obviously, there must be a few alien abductions every day.

Bad Arguments: 100 of the Most Important Fallacies in Western Philosophy, First Edition.
Edited by Robert Arp, Steven Barbone, and Michael Bruce.
© 2019 John Wiley & Sons Ltd. Published 2019 by John Wiley & Sons Ltd.

The mere fact that there are two views on this matter doesn't prove that the truth is in between. If there is no evidence for alien abductions, we shouldn't believe that a few occur merely because someone claims that many occur. Or if there is strong evidence that many occur, we shouldn't believe that there are only a few just because someone denies the evidence. The middle ground view is only reasonable if we have evidence for some abductions but not as many as "Extreme Believer" asserts.

Even worse than this, sometimes the "middle ground" is far less plausible than *either* extreme. For example, if one person claims that all whales are fish and the other claims that all whales are mammals, it would be absurd to suppose that half of all whales are fish and the other half mammals (or that whales are half fish, half mammal)! Sometimes a middle ground isn't even possible. If I say that Springfield is the capital of Illinois and you say that it isn't, there's no logical way that the truth can be somewhere in between.

A further danger of the MG is that it encourages arguers to defend radical, extreme views, expecting that the listener will now embrace part of the arguer's claims. Imagine that an unscrupulous arguer has strong evidence that it would be beneficial for the state to increase income tax by 2%. She knows that her opponent will advocate no increase at all. She may fear that if she defends a 2% increase, the listeners will assume that a lesser (perhaps 1%) increase is best, which she knows will be inadequate. Therefore she may be tempted to distort her evidence and pretend to believe that a 4% increase is needed.

Fortunately, this is an easy fallacy to avoid. Simply keep in mind the fact that merely because someone asserts a theory, especially an extreme theory, this does not by itself provide evidence for any conclusion at all. The fallacy is committed by people who don't listen to the reasons that have been offered by each side to defend their theories – they simply assume that the truth is in the middle. The fallacy is the result of intellectual laziness.

Notice that MG has nothing to do with practical questions of compromise. If you are discussing your yearly bonus and your boss offers you nothing while you ask for $500, there's nothing fallacious about negotiating some figure in between. (The most famous practical application of something like the MG fallacy is the famous "judgment of Solomon" (1 Kings 3:16–28) where Solomon appears to "compromise" by cutting a baby in two.)

89

Mind Projection

Charles Taliaferro

> If you are looking down while you are walking, it is better to walk up hill.
> The ground is nearer.
>
> Gertrude Stein

This fallacy occurs when we reason that the world has features that we (wrongly) project on to it or, using Stein's whimsical language, when we do not carefully and humbly observe the world around us. Physicist E.T. Jaynes claimed to identify this fallacy as part of his critique of quantum theory of probability in his work "Clearing up Mysteries – The Original Goal." He claimed that probability theory led to fallacious thinking about the properties of nature. Probability is not an inherent characteristic of anything in nature, but it actually indicates a deficit of facts or knowledge. This involves mind projection insofar as someone takes a property of the mind (probabilistic reasoning) and falsely attributes this to the world (probability as if it were a feature of things independent of mind). "We are all under an ego-driven temptation to project our private thoughts out onto the real world, by supposing that the creations of one's own imagination are real properties of Nature, or that one's own ignorance signifies some kind of indecision on the part of Nature" (Jaynes 1989, 7). He likens the occurrence of this fallacy to the occurrence of a mental disorder: "A standard of logic that would be considered a psychiatric disorder in other fields, is the accepted norm in

Bad Arguments: 100 of the Most Important Fallacies in Western Philosophy, First Edition.
Edited by Robert Arp, Steven Barbone, and Michael Bruce.
© 2019 John Wiley & Sons Ltd. Published 2019 by John Wiley & Sons Ltd.

quantum theory" (7). This concern over the fallacious thinking of probability theorists points to various inconstancies in the standard of argument among various scientific fields.

Going beyond Jaynes's special use of the term in the context of quantum theory, the mind projection fallacy is committed when a person creates and believes without sufficient justification factual claims about the world solely based on his experiences, mental or sensory, of the world. Given that radical skepticism is false and that some of our experiences of the world are indeed justified, this fallacy is restricted to cases in which a person (Joe) falsely attributes to things in the world properties that actually reflect Joe's own judgments and dispositions rather than the properties that are actually in the world. For example, it would be fallacious to conclude from one's tasting the sweetness of sugar that the property of sweetness is itself lodged in the sugar rather than sweetness's being a feature of how sugar tastes when consumed by humans with healthy taste buds. A more disturbing example of this fallacy is when persons wrongly attribute to others harmful stereotypes that reflect bias in the context of race, sexuality, social class, and so on. In outrageous claims that are clearly false as when a United States citizen claims that all immigrants to the USA from Mexico are rapists and criminals, the claim provides us more information about the person making the claim (he is racist) that it does about the people he seeks to identify (the immigrants to the USA from Mexico).

One promising way to avoid this fallacy is through what is frequently referred to today as epistemic humility. Be cautious about when you can infer from your own response to X that X (whatever it is) has a property related to your response. For example, do not infer just because you happen not to be interested in philosophy (i.e., it is a subjective matter of fact that you are not interested in philosophy) that philosophy is itself uninteresting (in the sense that philosophy is not worthy of interest or, indeed, not worthy of passionate, energetic commitment).

Reference

Jaynes, E.T. 1989. "Clearing Up Mysteries – The Original Goal." *Maximum Entropy and Bayesian Methods* (36): 1–27.

90

Moralistic Fallacy

Galen Foresman

> Since we all know that it's wrong, it obviously is wrong.
>
> John Doe

The moralistic fallacy occurs when one concludes that something is a particular way because it should or ought to be that way. Alternatively, this fallacy occurs when one concludes that something cannot be a particular way because it should not or ought not be that way.

Formally:

(1) X is the way things should/ought to be.
(2) Therefore, X is the way things are or are going to be.

Or

(1) X is not the way things should/ought to be.
(2) Therefore, X is not the way things are or are going to be.

The moralistic fallacy is often described as the reverse of the is/ought fallacy, wherein one reasons fallaciously that because things are a particular way, they ought to be that way. For both fallacies, the systematic error in reasoning occurs in assuming a relationship between normative or evaluative

Bad Arguments: 100 of the Most Important Fallacies in Western Philosophy, First Edition.
Edited by Robert Arp, Steven Barbone, and Michael Bruce.
© 2019 John Wiley & Sons Ltd. Published 2019 by John Wiley & Sons Ltd.

claims and reality, such that what is true of the world entirely explains what is good or ought to be, morally speaking (is/ought fallacy), or, alternatively, what is right, wrong, good, or bad in moral terms entirely explains the way the actual world is and will be (moralistic fallacy). While there are relationships between reality and morality, it is fallacious to deduce one simply based on knowledge of the other.

Variations of the moralistic fallacy occur whenever any normative claim is used to justify a factual claim about the world, and so the pattern of fallacious reason central to the moralistic fallacy can also be found in legal reasoning, prudential reasoning, or reasoning regarding proper etiquette, aesthetics, humor, or appropriate emotional responses. For example, in their paper "The Moralistic Fallacy: On the 'Appropriateness' of Emotions," Justin D'Arms and Daniel Jacobson (2000) argue, "to commit the moralistic fallacy is to infer, from the claim that it would be wrong or vicious to feel an emotion, that it is therefore unfitting," because, as they contend, emotions may be fitting in particular situations, even if it is morally wrong or inexpedient to feel them. A racy or distasteful joke may still be funny even if it is morally wrong to find it humorous. And so, to claim that racy or distasteful jokes can never be funny because they are immoral is to commit the moralistic fallacy.

More commonly, the moralistic fallacy occurs in everyday thinking when one assumes that what is right is what will be. If a teacher assumes students won't cheat because it is wrong for them to do so, that teacher commits the moralistic fallacy. Similarly, the moralistic fallacy is committed when one assumes citizens will vote because they have a moral duty to do so. Fortunately, the flawed reasoning found in these examples of the moralistic fallacy is easily avoided. While norms of morality, prudence, or the law do not entirely determine the way things are or will be, they do often give us reasonable expectations for how things are or will be. It would not, for example, commit the moralistic fallacy to assume an honest person is unlikely to lie to you. And when a person promises to meet you for coffee, it isn't fallacious to conclude that he will probably meet you for coffee. In both of these examples, avoiding the fallacy is a simple matter of relaxing the absolute claim that something is or will be the case to a moderate and qualified claim that something is likely to be the case.

Interestingly, many young drivers are taught to avoid a form of the moralistic fallacy when they are taught to drive defensively. When driving, it is easy to jump to the conclusion that other drivers will behave in ways that conform to standard legal norms of the road. Cars next to you on the highway should stay in their respective lanes and should check their blind spots before changing lanes, but all too often this is not the case. And so, learning to drive defensively is largely about assuming that other automobiles on the road will not always act in ways that conform to the norms of good driving.

Reference

D'Arms, Justin, and Daniel Jacobson. 2000. "The Moralistic Fallacy: On the 'Appropriateness' of Emotions." *Philosophy and Phenomenological Research* 61(1): 65–90.

91

No True Scotsman

Tuomas W. Manninen

> Conservatism can never fail; it can only be failed.
>
> Collected from the Internet

The No true Scotsman fallacy (NTS) may at first blush look similar to the fallacy of accident. But while the latter occurs when trying to apply a general claim to an objectively anomalous sample, the NTS fallacy takes a more subjective form. The NTS fallacy changes the definition of what it takes for something to be a member of a group in order to protect a claim from a putative counter-example. The NTS fallacy is frequently found in ideological (political, religious, etc.) debates where it is used in an attempt to make one's claim unfalsifiable. The NTS is a fallacy of presumption: the arguer committing the fallacy presumes to be the authority on determining what it takes to be a member of a certain group.

Both the name for the NTS fallacy and its definition were first coined by Anthony Flew (1977); the following is a close paraphrase of Flew's (1977, 47) original example:

> A nationalist-minded Scot reads about a heinous sex crime in the newspaper. Perturbed by what he is reading, he thinks to himself, "No Scotsman would ever do such a thing." Some time later, our Scot spies a similar headline in the paper, except that this time the perpetrator is identified as

Bad Arguments: 100 of the Most Important Fallacies in Western Philosophy, First Edition.
Edited by Robert Arp, Steven Barbone, and Michael Bruce.
© 2019 John Wiley & Sons Ltd. Published 2019 by John Wiley & Sons Ltd.

a Scotsman. Instead of admitting that even his compatriots are capable of committing depraved acts, our Scot thinks, "No *true* Scotsman would do such a thing!"

The fallacy occurs because the Scot in Flew's example, instead of accepting the seeming counter-example that falsifies the original claim ("No Scotsman would ever do such a thing"), adjusts the definition of what it is to be a Scotsman. Here, the original definition of "Scotsman" is compatible both with a person's being a perpetrator of heinous crimes and with a person's not being a perpetrator of heinous crimes. The feature "being capable of depraved acts" is a contingent one and, as such, it is compatible with the definition of "Scotsman." However, the revision adds the condition "not capable of committing depraved acts" to the original definition by stipulation; as Flew puts it, this "piece of sleight of mind replaces a logically contingent by a logically necessary proposition" (53). Determining whether one is a Scotsman or not is chiefly based on one's nationality or residence, and this does not necessitate having a strong moral character. Yet, the conclusion drawn – "No true Scotsman would ever do such a thing" – alters the conditions for this determination.

For a real-life example of the NTS fallacy, we can look to the lead-up to the 2014 Scottish independence referendum. The author J.K. Rowling, of *Harry Potter* fame, who has resided in Scotland for two decades, has been heralded as "a tremendous ambassador for the country." But after she donated £1 million to the pro-United Kingdom campaign, she was called "a Union cow bag" by various online independence activists (Riley-Smith and Johnson 2014). Although Rowling had previously appeared to be Scottish aplenty for all Scots involved, to some members of the independence movement, all of a sudden, she was not Scottish enough. The barrage of criticism aimed at Rowling shows that living in Scotland may be sufficient to make you Scottish, absent a contentious political issue. After such an issue is introduced, some would also require that one support a specific viewpoint when it comes to the question of Scotland's independence. To put the point slightly differently, the term "Scottish" was initially used with the assumption that everyone agreed to its meaning. However, given the amorphous nature of the term, the uses of it turned out to be incompatible when scrutinized. Or, as Ludwig Wittgenstein (1958) put the point: "none [no boundaries to the use of the term] has so far been drawn. But that never troubled you before when you used the word" (§68).

For another illustration, we turn to contemporary American political discourse, where the pejorative acronyms RINO and DINO (Republican-in-name-only and Democrat-in-name-only, respectively) are commonplace and commonly attached to high-ranking officials of either party by members of that party who view that the official in question has strayed from the ideals.

The actual examples are too numerous to list here, but many can be found using a simple online search for the terms – for example, "Paul Ryan" and "RINO" yields several results. Granted, the term 'Republican' is amorphous (as is the term 'Democrat'): there may be no precise way for defining what it is to be a Republican (or Democrat). However, even if most everyone would agree that the Speaker of the House or the House Majority Leader are Republicans – due to their respective positions, their respective voting record, and the fact that the majority of the party caucus is supporting them – there are some voices that challenge this. In cases such as these, the Republicans challenging the political *bona fides* of these other Republicans may be operating with a different definition of what it is to be a Republican. The criticism seems to stem from the belief (held by the critics) that the ideology – conservatism – is impervious to failure and that it can only be criticized when poorly implemented.

In September 2015, when John Boehner, the US Speaker of the House, announced that he was stepping down from his position, many of his critics were elated as they found him to be not conservative enough. For most observers, however, this criticism can (rightly) seem to be fallacious: one does not advance to the rank of the majority leader of a political party by being lukewarm about one's commitment to the party's ideology. Still, the group most directly responsible for forcing Speaker Boehner to step down (on the pain of being ousted from his position), the House Freedom Caucus (a contingent of ultra-conservative members of the Republican majority), seems to have appointed itself to the role of the kingmaker: without its express approval, no one can be deemed conservative enough. In a curious twist of events, even the members of the House Freedom Caucus have been called RINOs by their constituents after the caucus agreed to support Paul D. Ryan as Boehner's successor (DeBonis 2015).

Further examples of this fallacy can be found in discussions on religion. For example, if we ask the question, "What is it to be a Christian?" (or "Who is a Christian?"), we receive various answers depending on who answers the question. In the broadest use of the term "Christian," it seems that anyone identifying herself as one would count as a Christian. In a more strict sense, anyone adhering to (some of) the central tenets of Christianity (such as creeds, etc.) would likely count as one. Yet, there are plenty of other, even more specific definitions of what it is to be a Christian; these definitions are frequently incompatible with each other, and this provides an incredibly fertile source for instances of the fallacy. This point is thoroughly explored by Martin Thielen (2011) in his book *What's the Least I Can Believe and Still Be a Christian?* and even more poignantly expressed in the comedy routine by the stand-up comedian Emo Phillips. The latter tells a story of a member of the Church of Northern Conservative Fundamentalist Baptists, Great Lakes Region, Council of 1879, who tries to prevent a suicidal man from jumping off a bridge by showing how much there is to live for.

Once the discussion reveals that the would-be-jumper is a member of the Church of Northern Conservative Fundamentalist Baptists, Great Lakes Region, Council of 1912, the punchline is, "I said, 'Die, heretic!' and pushed him off the bridge"; for present purposes, the punchline may just as well have involved the NTS fallacy.

A likely factor that contributes to the NTS fallacy is the arguer's own cognitive bias, specifically the in-group ('us')/out-group ('them') bias: the arguer's in-group is taken to be homogeneous, and when differences of opinion crop up, the offending member is delegated to the out-group (i.e., as one of 'them'). To revisit our first example, the arguer (the nationalist-minded Scot) may first have thought that having an acclaimed author like J.K. Rowling as a member of their group would only serve to accentuate the group's collective accomplishments. However, when Rowling contributed to the cause against the independence movement, she went against the arguer's values, which they had presumed to apply to all members of the group. Similar considerations apply, *mutatis mutandis*, for the other examples.

In order to avoid the NTS fallacy, the arguer needs to be mindful of his own cognitive biases and allow for the fact that in-group disagreements do happen. In a case such as this, here's what might become of the argument in the first example:

> "I am proud to be a Scot, and I think it's great to have an accomplished author such as J.K. Rowling as my compatriot. Even though I don't like her anti-independence sentiments, she still is a Scot inasmuch as I am."

Then again, as reality has shown, reaching such a fantastic level of self-awareness may be impossible to achieve.

References

DeBonis, Mike. 2015. "Fuming over Ryan, Some Conservative Voices Turn on the Freedom Caucus." *Washington Post*, October 25. https://www.washingtonpost.com/politics/fuming-over-ryan-some-conservative-voices-turn-on-the-freedom-caucus/2015/10/25/8194f3ce-7999-11e5-a958-d889faf561dc_story.html (accessed October 4, 2017).

Flew, Anthony. 1977. *Thinking Straight*. Buffalo, NY: Prometheus Books.

Phillips, Emo. 1987. "Golden Gate Bridge" (recorded at Hasty Pudding Theater"). http://www.emophilips.com/video/video/244. (accessed October 9, 2017).

Riley-Smith, Ben, and Simon Johnson. 2014. "JK Rowling Subjected to Cybernat Abuse after £1 M Pro-UK Donation." *The Telegraph*, June 11. http://www.telegraph.co.uk/news/uknews/scottish-independence/10893567/JK-Rowling-subjected-to-Cybernat-abuse-after-1m-pro-UK-donation.html (accessed October 4, 2017).

Thielen, Martin. 2011. *What's the Least I Can Believe and Still Be a Christian?: A Guide to What Matters Most*. Louisville, KY: Westminster John Knox Press.

Wittgenstein, Ludwig. 1958. *Philosophical Investigations*, 3e. Translated by G. E. M. Anscombe. Englewood Cliffs, NJ: Prentice Hall

92

Reification

Robert Sinclair

> Objects derive their influence not from properties inherent in them; but from such as are bestowed upon them by the minds of those who are conversant with or affected by these objects.
>
> John Ruskin, *Modern Painters*

A relative newcomer to the world of logical fallacies, reification is difficult to place and its status as a fallacy not that well understood. In general, reification involves taking something that is abstract, like an idea or concept, and making it concrete, or assigning it a concrete, 'real' existence. The apparent error involves assuming that something with only abstract existence should be seen as having material, physical existence. Examples might include the myriad uses of 'nation,' 'state,' 'nature,' and 'race.' Take the old familiar expression "It's not nice to fool Mother Nature." Here, 'Nature' is an abstraction or abstract concept used to name a sequence of natural events. But the expression assigns a material human character to this concept, which as an abstraction it cannot have. Put simply, nature is not a human being and cannot then be fooled. When used metaphorically as in this and many other everyday examples, such reifications are relatively harmless. It is when they form part of an argument that they become more problematic. Consider the following short argument:

Bad Arguments: 100 of the Most Important Fallacies in Western Philosophy, First Edition.
Edited by Robert Arp, Steven Barbone, and Michael Bruce.
© 2019 John Wiley & Sons Ltd. Published 2019 by John Wiley & Sons Ltd.

The State controls the business world and has its hand in everyone's pocket. By limiting this governmental pickpocketing, we can prevent such obstructions to our individual rights and freedoms.

Here, the concept of the 'State' has been assigned humanlike traits involving the desire to control and 'pickpocket.' While not explicit, it is further suggested that such desires are wrong and the government is then behaving unethically when it engages in such actions. However, the 'government' or 'State' is not a person, but a legal entity of some kind, or, perhaps, a specific kind of social organization designed to meet the interests of its citizens. It is not a human agent that is capable of possessing these human traits and desires. The State's taxing of individuals and control of the business community may be mistaken but cannot be convincingly shown to be wrong through this flawed (and misleading) attribution or reification of human characteristics. The faulty reasoning of such arguments rests on a specious presumption concerning the assignment of concrete properties, traits, and causal powers to an abstraction (the State) and so fails to offer any support for its conclusion (Dewey 2012, 41–59). Avoiding this type of mistaken reasoning requires that one not make this presumption. Consider this example:

The policies of the current government (an organized group of public officials) seek to control the economic transactions within the business community and use taxation to limit the income of its citizens. Such actions are not in the interest of either the business community or its citizens. The public officials who are implementing such policies do so wrongly. In order to prevent this we must limit such actions by taking the needed step to remove these individuals from public office.

This argument attempts to capture the main criticism of the previous argument but without assigning humanlike causal agency to the state itself. It does so by focusing more carefully on the specific context of this alleged connection between the government and its activities. Here, we can see that while this argument is still somewhat general, it more specifically targets the way public officials are promoting policies that are not in the interest of those individuals they serve. While it remains inconclusive, it has become more convincing precisely because it highlights the problematic consequences of human individual actions that are based on flawed social policies.

The standard analysis of reification then presents it as a fallacy of presumption, which can be avoided by minimizing the assignment of causal agency to the abstractions used in logical reasoning. However, the perhaps deeper and more serious consequences of what has been called "pernicious reification" have been further explored by the pragmatist philosophers

William James and John Dewey (Winther 2014, 9). Both philosophers emphasize the indispensable value found through the use of abstract thought (Dewey 1920, 86–87; James 1997, 246–247; also see Quine 2015, 17–19). But they further warn us of the ways in which our aptitude for abstraction and classification can be misused. Take, for example, abstract concepts such as 'elasticity' or 'voluminousness,' which can be partially but incompletely applied to any physical body, or the further judgment that someone is a 'drunkard,' which can result in an overly universal and fixed claim about someone's basic identity. Dewey and James take such examples to show that abstractions, including concepts and judgments, are purpose-driven and, while only providing partial descriptions of things, remain useful for understanding, inference-making, and within our various interventions with the environment (James 1997, 246–250; Winther 2014, 1). However, most philosophers have missed these salient facts about abstractions, forgetting the context in which they are used. This results in mistakenly using them in ways that are too rigid, too universal, and too ontologically determinate. In such cases, we forget the specific functions assigned to a given abstraction and in the process run the risk of impairing epistemic and moral reasoning in everyday affairs, science, and philosophy (Winther 2014, 9–17).

James describes such mistakes as examples of 'vicious abstractionism,' when the attempt to classify things yields the belief that the abstracted elements of a situation provide a complete and accurate description of the phenomena in question (James 1997, 249; Winther 2014, 10–11). The person who kills someone is wholly and exclusively classified as a 'murderer' without any reference to any other features of that person (such as his being a father or policeman). This oversimplification is obviously limiting, since other concepts (denoting other features) may be connected to the feature picked out by the concept being used. These further connections might then prove useful for different explanatory aims and in different contexts. The error here involves forgetting the specific function of the concept in focusing on only one or perhaps several properties and how these properties are further connected to a fallible network of other concepts (James 1997, 249–250; Winther 2014, 11). This important local and specific function of concepts is ignored, resulting in classifications that are at once both too narrow and too universal. Dewey more generally labels this mistake the *philosophic fallacy*, where the failure to note function and context leads philosophers to convert "eventual functions into antecedent existence" (1929, 29; also see Pappas 2008, 26–29). All attempts at reasoning and explanation must be selective, but when such decisions are disregarded, the selected abstraction (the possible eventual function) is replaced in thought as a finished reality that preceded it (antecedent existence), resulting in an overly generous and unnecessary reification of that prior decision. Dewey argues that the empirical method used in modern science helps to keep focus on this initial decision and thus keeps us on guard against these abstractive reifications. This perspective is seen with Dewey's criticism of psychological descriptions of human reflexes in terms of a 'reflex arc,' where a firm distinction is drawn between stimulus and response. Dewey contends that rather than denoting a fixed 'antecedent' reality, this distinction is a functional one that points to the way behavior is integrated and continuous with its environment (Winther 2014, 15). By taking the distinction between stimulus and response as a fixed reality, we fail to recognize that the proper unit of psychological analysis is located in the organized functional coordination of sensations and responses.

Within the rarified air of philosophical theory, the failures of abstraction that lead to pernicious reification might be of little consequence. But abstract reasoning plays a fundamental role in both science and everyday reasoning, and so its abuses can lead to inaccurate scientific explanations and further damaging social consequences (Duster 2005). For example, it has been recently argued that the biological data used to support various positions on the biological reality of 'race' fail to distinguish competing claims about racial classification (Kaplan and Winther 2013, 410). The social backdrop to such debates concerning the reality of socially identified races involves the way differences in human welfare (including life expectancy, standards of living, and overall quality of life) are often linked to racial classifications. Pernicious reification in the biological sciences might contribute to mistaken views of such differences, blinding us to the social circumstances that can play a significant role in accounting for the existence of these variations in human well-being across socially recognized racial groups.

References

Dewey, John. 1920. *Reconstruction in Philosophy*. New York, NY: Dover Publications.

Dewey, John. 1929. *Experience and Nature*. New York, NY: Dover Publications.

Dewey, John. 2012. *The Public and its Problems*, edited by Melvin Rodgers. University Park, PA: Pennsylvania State University Press.

Duster, Troy. 2005. "Race and Reification in Science." *Science* (307): 1050–1051.

James, William. 1997. *The Meaning of Truth*. Amherst, NY: Prometheus Books.

Kaplan, Jonathan, and Rasmus Grønfeldt Winther. 2013. "Prisoners of Abstraction? The Theory and Measure of Genetic Variation, and the Very Concept of 'Race'." *Biological Theory* (7): 401–412.

Pappas, Gregory. 2008. *John Dewey's Ethics: Democracy as Experience*. Bloomington, IA: Indiana University Press.

Quine, W.V. 2015. "Levels of Abstraction." In *Quine and his Place in History*, edited by Frederique Janssen-Lauret and Gary Kemp. Basingstoke: Palgrave Macmillan, 12–20.

Winther, Rasmus Grønfeldt. 2014. "James and Dewey on Abstraction." *The Pluralist* (9): 1–28.

93

Representative Heuristic

David Kyle Johnson

> DNA from Genetically Modified Crops Can Be Transferred into Humans Who Eat Them
>
> Headline from *CollectiveEvolution.com*

A heuristic is a shortcut rule, or guide, by which one tries to organize one's understanding of the world. The representative heuristic is the rule that suggests we should associate things that are alike, grouping them together, usually invoking "the principle that members of a category should resemble a prototype" (Schick and Vaughn 2014, 33). Now clearly this rule can sometimes be useful and generate true conclusions in a much needed and timely manner. If you see a violently barking dog foaming at the mouth, it would be rational to avoid it. If the dog matches the prototype of a rabid dog, it is likely rabid. But such reasoning can often lead us astray.

The harder-to-understand version of this mistake involves unjustifiably grouping similar things together – thinking that like goes with like. The easiest way to understand this mistake is to consider how it contributes the conjunction fallacy (see Chapter 74). As a quick reminder of this fallacy, suppose a guy named Chris lives in Alabama, owns lots of guns, and loves to go hunting. Given that, which of these statements is more likely?

Bad Arguments: 100 of the Most Important Fallacies in Western Philosophy, First Edition.
Edited by Robert Arp, Steven Barbone, and Michael Bruce.
© 2019 John Wiley & Sons Ltd. Published 2019 by John Wiley & Sons Ltd.

(a)   Chris voted for Obama in 2012; or

(b)   Chris voted for Obama in 2012 and is a member of the National Rifle Association (NRA).

The intuitive answer is (B), but the right answer is (A). Now choice (A) is the right answer because the probability of two events being true together can never be greater than the probability of either one of them being true by itself. But what's more relevant for our purposes is this question: Why does (B) *seem* to be the right answer to most people?

It's because we tend to group things that are alike together. A prototype NRA member is imagined to be a southern gun-owning hunter. Since (B) mentions the NRA, we tend to think that (B) "represents" Chris. And since that is not what we imagine when we think of an Obama voter, we think (A) does not represent Chris. This tendency to group similar things (in this case Chris and option (B)) together as a rule blinds us to the mathematical facts and leads us astray.

The other way the representative heuristic leads us astray is by making us apt to think that causes and their effects must resemble each other – that like causes like. This is most striking in the realm of alternative and "natural" medicine, where certain physical qualities of objects are thought to be transferable to those who ingest them. According to Schick and Vaughn (2014, 133), some Chinese ingest ground-up bats as a treatment for vision problems because it is (incorrectly) assumed that bats have good vision, some Europeans treat asthma with fox lungs, and some Americans treat mental disorders with raw brains. As we saw in the opening quote, some even erroneously believe that eating genetically modified foods can genetically modify humans. In Vietnam, people grind up rhino horn as a male aphrodisiac. The logic literally is "since rhino horns are long and hard, ingesting them will make me long and hard." Like causes like. Unfortunately, this fallacious logic is helping to drive the rhino to extinction.

Interestingly, this mistake in reasoning also drives conspiracy theories. "Big events," like presidential assassinations and terrorist attacks, "can't have simple small explanations," it is thought. No! Big events need big causes. JFK wasn't shot by Oswald – it was the CIA working in conjunction the Mafia and the Kremlin. The 9/11 attacks weren't pulled off by 19 hijackers – it was really Bush and the US government. As (fictional) President Bush admitted to the boys on *South Park*:

> Quite simple to pull off, really. All I had to do was have explosives planted in the base of the towers. Then on 9/11 we pretended like four planes were being hijacked, when really we just rerouted them to Pennsylvania, then flew two military jets into the World Trade Center filled with more explosives, [and] then shot down all the witnesses of Flight 93 with an F-15 after blowing up

the Pentagon with a Cruise missile. It was only the world's most intricate and flawlessly executed plan ever, ever. (Parker and Smith 2006)

The fallaciousness of such reasoning was demonstrated in a study by Patrick Leman (2003), when he had subjects read one of four different (fictional but convincing) newspaper accounts of a foreign president's assassination. In one, the assassin was successful. In a second, he merely wounded the president. In another, the president was wounded but later died for another reason. In the last, the assassin missed completely. The subjects were much more likely to invoke a conspiracy to explain the first story than the others. But what rational reason could someone have for doing that? In the first story, the assassin's gun was aimed correctly – in the others, his aim was slightly off. But if a conspiracy is not needed to explain how an assassin could manage to get a shot off that grazes or misses the target, why would one be needed to explain how the assassin's aim was actually true? The difference between the stories is literally just a few centimeters, if even that.

Ever wonder why there was a movie made about the conspiracy theories surrounding JFK but you've likely never even heard of a Regan assassination attempt conspiracy theory? It's because of the representative heuristic. Mere attempts aren't that big of a deal, so we aren't apt to demand a big explanation. But such a demand is irrational. So the next time you are inclined to group similar things together or to link similar events and causes, think twice. Sometimes you'll be right, but more often than not, you're being misled by the representative heuristic.

References

Leman, Patrick. 2003. "Who Shot the President? A Possible Explanation for Conspiracy Theories." *Economist* (20): 74.

Parker, Trey, and Matt Smith. 2006. *South Park*, "Mystery of the Urinal Deuce." Comedy Central, October 11.

Schick, Theodore, and Lewis Vaughn. 2014. *How to Think about Weird Things: Critical Thinking for a New Age.* New York, NY: McGraw-Hill.

94

Slippery Slope

Michael J. Muniz

According to Patrick Hurley in *A Concise Introduction to Logic* (2012), "the fallacy of slippery slope is a variety of the false cause fallacy. It occurs when the conclusion of an argument rests on an alleged chain reaction and there is not sufficient reason to think that the chain reaction will actually take place" (135). The key term here is "chain reaction." The arguer is attempting to justify her conclusion by drawing a very weak connection among premises.

The DirectTV ad above is a perfect example of how the conclusion (one should upgrade to DirectTV) is weakly supported by the various unlikely chain reaction circumstances that are triggered by the initial premise (getting angry because your current cable company put you on hold).

Bad Arguments: 100 of the Most Important Fallacies in Western Philosophy, First Edition. Edited by Robert Arp, Steven Barbone, and Michael Bruce.
© 2019 John Wiley & Sons Ltd. Published 2019 by John Wiley & Sons Ltd.

In recent news, the slippery slope fallacy has been popularized as a subject of interest, especially among cable news outlets with regard to the topic of same-sex marriage. The blogosphere, digital media websites, and so on have in some way commented on both sides of the issue while committing the slippery slope fallacy. The American Society for the Defense of Tradition, Family and Property Students Action website lists 10 reasons "Why Homosexual 'Marriage' Is Harmful and Must Be Opposed" (2016). Reason #9 says:

> If homosexual "marriage" is universally accepted as the present step in sexual "freedom," what logical arguments can be used to stop the next steps of incest, pedophilia, bestiality, and other forms of unnatural behavior? Indeed, radical elements of certain "avant garde" subcultures are already advocating such aberrations. The railroading of same-sex "marriage" on the American people makes increasingly clear what homosexual activist Paul Varnell wrote in the Chicago Free Press: "The gay movement, whether we acknowledge it or not, is not a civil rights movement, not even a sexual liberation movement, but a moral revolution aimed at changing people's view of homosexuality."

The "slip" that is committed here is that the initial action of ruling in favor of same-sex marriage will ultimately result in cases where the courts will rule in favor of incest, pedophilia, bestiality, and so on. There is no strong justification to suggest a direct link between the initial premise and the resulting consequences that follow.

On the other hand, proponents of the same-sex marriage issue have also committed the slippery slope fallacy. On the popular ProCon.org website (a platform to explore both sides of controversial issues) the following case was made in favor of gay marriage:

> Denying some people the option to marry is discriminatory and creates a second class of citizens. On July 25, 2014 Miami-Dade County Circuit Court Judge Sarah Zabel ruled Florida's gay marriage ban unconstitutional and stated that the ban "serves only to hurt, to discriminate, to deprive same-sex couples and their families of equal dignity, to label and treat them as second-class citizens, and to deem them unworthy of participation in one of the fundamental institutions of our society."

Judge Zabel, in this case, is asserting that the "denial" itself will result in labeling same-sex couples as second-class citizens.

However, it's difficult to decide when the fallacy has occurred if we're uncertain that the chain of events will come about. Hurley (2012) notes that "many slippery slopes rest on a mere emotional conviction on the part of the arguer that a certain action or policy is bad, and the arguer attempts to trump up support for his position by citing all sorts of dire consequences that will result if the action is taken or the policy followed (147).

So, if Hurley is right, then maybe the DirectTV ad is accurate if it can be proven true that one does blow off steam when getting angry. And, in that process of blowing off steam, the "angry" person (in this case, he is playing indoor racquetball) gets injured in the eye, resulting in getting an eye patch put on by a doctor. This in turn is followed by showing evidence that when one wears an eye patch, it suggests a degree of "toughness" that triggers other people's interests (in this case, the "other" people are a group hoodlums interested in a confrontation). Finally, then it must be demonstrated that these particular hoodlums presented are the type to pick a fight with our "angry" person resulting in his lying semi-conscious in a roadside ditch. If all of these events in the chain reaction can be justified, then the slippery slope is not committed. But the nuances and intricate improbable connections between each event still make it difficult to support the ultimate conclusion, which is to get rid of cable.

There are two simple techniques to consider in order to avoid committing the slippery slope fallacy. First, the argument at hand must be examined thoroughly for any sequence of reasoning (or chain of events) that put forth an outcome. Consider the formula: If X, then Y, and if Y, then Z... When implanting this formula, the arguer must ensure that the connections between each proposition are reasonable.

The second technique to consider is to reflect on the reverse connection. In this way, the arguer can posit the conclusion (final outcome) first, then the initial premise can be stated later. In other words, the arguer can present his case backwards to ensure there are no lapses in reasoning or false entailments.

References

Hurley, Patrick. 2012. *A Concise Introduction to Logic.* Belmont, CA: Wadsworth.

Pro.Con.org. 2017. "Should Gay Marriage be Legal?" July 24. https://gaymarriage.procon.org/?print=true (accessed October 4, 2017).

TFP Student Action. 2016. "10 Reasons Why Homosexual 'Marriage' Is Harmful and Must Be Opposed." August 1. http://www.tfpstudentaction.org/politically-incorrect/homosexuality/10-reasons-why-homosexual-marriage-is-harmful-and-must-be-opposed.html (accessed October 4, 2017).

95

Stolen Concept

Rory E. Kraft, Jr.

> God works in ways which are mysterious to us. We cannot understand His plan.
>
> Variation of Isaiah 55:8–9

The fallacy of the stolen concept – sometimes referred to as stealing the concept – is most closely associated with the works of novelist Ayn Rand and those who find her philosophy persuasive. The fullest description of the fallacy occurs in an article by Nathanial Branden in *The Objectivist* newsletter, which expands on an idea Rand put forward in *Atlas Shrugged* (1957).

The defining characteristic of the fallacy is "the act of using a concept while ignoring, contradicting or denying the validity of the concepts on which it logically and genetically depends" (Branden 1963, 4). This means that when one uses some higher-order concept – one derived from a simpler concept – to refute a lower-order concept, one is using the concept while denying it. This is not merely a contradiction, because the connection between the two concepts may not be immediately apparent, but is instead its own fallacy.

Branden's example throughout his article is Pierre-Joseph Proudhon's "All property is theft." The phrase derives from Proudhon's 1840 essay, translated in 1874, as "What Is Property?" and is more accurately translated as "Property – it is robbery!" To objectivists like Rand and Branden, theft is a derivative concept that only makes sense in the context of property.

Bad Arguments: 100 of the Most Important Fallacies in Western Philosophy, First Edition.
Edited by Robert Arp, Steven Barbone, and Michael Bruce.
© 2019 John Wiley & Sons Ltd. Published 2019 by John Wiley & Sons Ltd.

This is to say that without having the existing concept of property, it would not make sense to understand the unethical or unlawful taking of something belonging to another. Thus, to proclaim that all property is an unethical taking of property is to desire proper ownership (i.e., non-theft) while decrying all ownership itself.

In *Atlas Shrugged*, Rand has the character John Galt give a speech explaining his theory or morality. Throughout the speech there are several moments that imply the move that Branden would later call stealing the concept. Of these, this passage perhaps shows the reliance upon a lower-order belief:

> "We know that we know nothing," they chatter, blanking out the fact that they are claiming knowledge. "There are no absolutes," they chatter, blanking out the fact that they are uttering an absolute. "You cannot *prove* that you exist or that you're conscious," they chatter, blanking out the fact that *proof* presupposes existences, consciousness and a complex chain of knowledge: the existence of something to know, of a consciousness able to know it, and of a knowledge that has learned to distinguish between such concepts as the proved and the unproved. (965)

Here we see the difference between the first two "chattering" claims, which are more clearly contradictions, and the third (proof of existence), which attempts to steal the concept. For Rand, proof is something that is only possible from the vantage point of an existant. Non-existing objects cannot act (put another way, verbs always require nouns), thus the claim that existence cannot be proven is to steal the existence one needs to exist in order to prove (or claim) existence or non-existence. Rand here is relying upon a line of reasoning quite similar to Descartes's *cogito* but does so here by asserting physical existence, not merely Descartes's mental existence.

Other examples of stolen concepts would be in play when encountering arguments for the existence of a creator (god) because of the rational order of the world. Rationality is a marker of what is understandable by reason and logic. To utilize rationality to assert the existence of some thing or entity that is not understandable is to utilize reason to defend the unreasonable. Perhaps ironically, defenses of a deity's existence that rely upon our lack of ability to reason (i.e., "God works in ways which are mysterious to us. We cannot understand His plan.") also steal the concept of rationality by asking us to accept as reasonable that some things are beyond reason.

In his review of Rupert Sheldrake's *The Science Delusion*, John Greenback (2012) accuses Sheldrake of stealing concepts from science while arguing against them, specifically by borrowing higher-order science concepts to refute the notion of a scientific worldview itself: "Sheldrake makes an irrational conceptual leap to an alternative outlook by stealing the concepts 'morphic' and 'resonance' from their legitimate backgrounds, in biology and physics respectively" (41).

It should be noted that just as Rand's objectivism is not widely accepted in academia, the observation of the fallacy's occurring is not common in academic texts. One of the rare exceptions is Risto Pitkanen's (1976) critique of David Wiggins in his article titled, "Content Identity." Pitkanen accuses Wiggins of stealing the concept of *colour-spot-moment* in his discussion of merelogical entities. Wiggins's supposed theft here involves taking the concepts in order to prove them, which may be more of a circularity than the fallacy normally indicates.

To the extent that one could be said to use a fallacy intentionally, it is more likely to occur when there is a failed attempt to point to a contradiction. The more subtle forms of the fallacy occur at a level that is not as blatant, such as an attempt to use advanced mathematics to "disprove" basic addition. In the failed-contradiction approach, the aim is to display that a concept is flawed, and through the basic law of contradiction, anything could be proven. For example:

(1)   Bobby plays song X every Sunday as an encore.
(2)   The encore on April 2, 2017, (a Sunday) was song Y.
(3)   The encore on April 2, 2017, was both X and Y.

Here, perhaps P1 is a hasty generalization, but it establishes that a particular song is at the same time two different songs. From this, anything can be proven:

(4)   Either the moon is made of green cheese or Bobby played song X.
(5)   Bobby played song Y. (see Premise 2)
(6)   The moon is made of green cheese.
(7)   Either the moon is made of green cheese or Bobby played song Y.
(8)   Bobby played song X. (see Premise 1, Conclusion)
(9)   The moon is made of green cheese.

This is an appropriate manner of arguing, but it is distinct from the stolen concept:

(1)   All property is theft.
(2)   Theft is taking something from an owner without permission.
(3)   All property is taking something from an owner without permission.
(4)   Property is possible only because of ownership.
(5)   All ownership is taking something from an owner without permission.

The second conclusion here can be restated as "All ownership is non-ownership." This is both a contradiction, which seems to be the intent of the method, and also the stealing of the concept.

The easiest way to avoid stealing concepts is to ensure that contradictions are instituted at the same conceptual level or utilizing a lower-order concept to contradict a higher-order one. When higher-order concepts are used to refute the truth of a lower-order concept, we have the fallacy.

References

Branden, Nathaniel. 1963. "The Stolen Concept." *Objectivist Newsletter* (2): 1–4.

Greenback, John. 2012. *Review of Rupert Sheldrake's* The Science Delusion. *Philosophy Now* (93): 40–42.

Pitkanen, Risto. 1976. "Content Identity." *Mind* (85): 262–268.

Proudhon, Pierre-Joseph. 1874. *What Is Property: An Inquiry into the Principle of Right and of Government*, translated by Benjamin R. Tucker. Princeton, NJ: Tucker Publishing.

Rand, Ayn. 1957. *Atlas Shrugged*. New York, NY: Random House.

96

Subjective Validation

David Kyle Johnson

> The year that Saturn and Mars are equal fiery,
> The air very dry parched long meteor:
> Through secret fires a great place blazing from burning heat,
> Little rain, warm wind, wars, incursions.
>
> Nostradamus, Century IV, Quatrain 67

An objective validation of a statement can be accomplished by showing that the statement actually matches up to the way the world is; this can be done by comparing the statement to the world itself. For example, if you say that dropped objects accelerate at a speed of 9.9 m/s/s, I can validate that objectively by dropping objects myself and seeing how fast they accelerate. On the other hand, a subjective validation of a statement's accuracy or meaning occurs when one evaluates its truth or meaning based on one's personal reaction to that statement – based on how one feels about it, or how it seems. Subjective validation is something that occurs often in humans and consistently leads us astray.

One way we consistently (and inaccurately) validate statements subjectively is by concluding that they apply to us personally. This was first demonstrated by Bertram Forer in 1948. In his now infamous study (see Carroll 2015), he gave the exact same generic, general, and vague personality description to all his students, which read in part:

Bad Arguments: 100 of the Most Important Fallacies in Western Philosophy, First Edition.
Edited by Robert Arp, Steven Barbone, and Michael Bruce.
© 2019 John Wiley & Sons Ltd. Published 2019 by John Wiley & Sons Ltd.

You have a need for other people to like and admire you, and yet you tend to be critical of yourself. While you have some personality weaknesses you are generally able to compensate for them. You have considerable unused capacity that you have not turned to your advantage. Disciplined and self-controlled on the outside, you tend to be worrisome and insecure on the inside.

He then asked them how accurately they thought the description they had received described them specifically and personally. (Each student thought he was receiving a unique description.) Most thought it was dead on; the class ranked its accuracy as 4.26 out of 5, and those results have been repeated with essentially the same results countless times. (The overall average is around 4.2.) Clearly, we like to make things about ourselves. Even if they are generic and vague, we like to think they are about us specifically. This is now known as the Forer effect (see Carroll 2015).

Clearly this kind of subjective validation can lead us astray. The Forer effect plays a huge role in making people think that their astrological horoscope and tarot card readings are accurate. Combined with other mistakes, like confirmation bias and availability error, subjective validation can fool people into thinking that psychics can read their minds, predict the future, or even communicate with the dead.

It is a key component of cold reading, a technique used by psychics to fool people they have never met into thinking that they have information they don't actually have. (They read the information off of them "cold," hence "cold reading.") During a cold reading of a crowd of people hoping to communicate with their recently deceased loved ones, you might hear something like this:

MEDIUM:	I'm feeling like there's a name with an S sound, maybe a father figure, possibly from this part of the crowd.
SITTER IN THE AUDIENCE:	My husband Sam just passed. I and his two sons miss him.
MEDIUM:	Yes, Sam is telling me that he too misses you and the boys.

The medium is giving something very general – there are lots of S names, and "father figure" could be someone's husband, someone's father or grandfather, or even a son that is a father – that is bound to apply to someone in the crowd. The medium is counting on the Forer effect – for someone in the crowd to apply that general "S name/father figure" statement to herself or her deceased love one. When she does, the person in the crowd is likely to reveal some specific information – in this case the deceased's name and that he had two boys. The medium then repeats that information back to her, to solidify the notion that the statement did apply to her, thus reinforcing the

Forer effect. (And thanks to the malleability of memory, the sitter will also likely later think the medium knew her husband's name before she said it.) The sitter will likely be amazed and conclude the medium couldn't have known what he seemed to know unless he had the ability to speak to her deceased loved one. (Consequently the sitter will likely spend lots of money on the medium's materials and future psychic readings.)

But we don't just validate statements subjectively by making them about ourselves; we can take anything that is vague and make it apply to what we want. The clearest example of this comes from the (supposed) prophet Michel Nostradamus, who made predictions that he himself admitted were intentionally vague. People love to read these things and think that Nostradamus was predicting the future, but the only way you can think this is if you subjectively validate the statements as accurate after the fact – that is, if you make them about what you want them to be about.

Take the quotation that begins this chapter. I found an internet meme that claims it is about 1986 – because of a February 18 Saturn/Mars conjunction, Haley's comet on April 11, and the Chernobyl nuclear disaster on April 26. But I could just as easily make this about 2016. In 2016, Mars's closest approach to Earth and that of Saturn were only four days apart, there was major drought in California, there were two major meteors seen in North America alone (on May 17 and June 2), for unknown reasons ("secret fires") a giant wildfire broke out in Fort McMurray (in Alberta, Canada), and there was little rain, warm wind, wars and incursions in the Middle East (as there usually is). And with about 10 minute's internet research, you could make this "prediction" apply to just about any year you wanted.

But it's not just "internet scholars" who have this problem with Nostradamus's predictions. The "experts" do too. Take this passage:

> From the Orient shall emerge the African heart
> to trouble Hardie and the heirs of Romulus
> along with the Libyan fleet
> the temples of Malta and nearby Islands shall be deserted. (Sharma 2001, 39)

Nostradamus scholar Erika Cheetham thinks that "Hardie" in lines 1–2 "refers to Henry IV. The man who troubles him from East [the Orient] is the Duke of Parma. Lines 3–4 refer to the siege of Malta." Nostradamus scholar Henry Roberts, on the other hand, thinks this is a "remarkably prophetic description of the role of Emperor Haile Selassie, in World War II, who reconquered Ethiopia, in East Africa and sent an expedition to aid the Allied Cause, eventually defeating the Fascists of Italy, self-styled 'Heirs of Romulus'" (see Schick and Vaughn 2014, 123).

Which is it? It's neither. It's so vague, you could make it about almost anything at all. If it was a real prediction, you could tell what event it was about before the event happened. If you can only tell what event a statement was predicting after an event happens, then it didn't really predict the event. That's retro-diction, not prediction. The passage isn't really about anything – it's just vague.

Although the subjective validation of Nostradamus's "predictions" doesn't fuel much else besides silly beliefs in the paranormal, falling prey to subjective validation can be much more costly. The same subjective validation "retro-diction" techniques are also used to interpret the prophecies of the Bible, like those that are supposedly in the Book of Revelation. And when Harold Camping convinced people, based on such readings of scripture, that the end of the world was going to occur in 2011, many people literally spent their life savings to help him spread the message (see Seidl 2011).

Wasting your money on psychics is one thing; but what would you do if you sold everything you owned based on someone's subjective reading of scripture, sat and watched the news all day for news of the rapture, and then it didn't happen? So be aware when subjectively evaluating statements for truth or meaning. Although you may occasionally get it right, more often than not you will be led astray by your tendency to read into things. More often than we realize, we apply statements to ourselves and make them say what we want them to say.

References

Carroll, Robert. 2015. "Forer Effect." *The Skeptic's Dictionary*, October 27. http://skepdic.com/forer.html (accessed October 4, 2017).

Schick, Theodore, and Lewis Vaughn. 2014. *How to Think about Weird Things: Critical Thinking for a New Age*. New York, NY: McGraw-Hill.

Seidl, Johnathon. 2011. "'Judgment Day May 21, 2011': Man Spends Life Savings Proclaiming End of Days." *The Blaze*, May 16. http://www.theblaze.com/stories/2011/05/16/judgement-day-may-21-2011-man-spends-life-savings-proclaming-end-of-days/ (accessed October 4, 2017).

Sharma, Ashok. 2001. *Nostradamus and Prophecies of the Next Millennium*. New Delhi: Diamon Pocket Book.

97

Subjectivist Fallacy

Frank Scalambrino

> This question brings us to the heart of the problem of the feeling of reality
> [...] the real, or what is perceived as such, is what resists symbolization
> in language absolutely. Every signification only refers back to another
> signification.
>
> Jacques Lacan

The subjectivist fallacy (SbF) occurs when one concludes that something is
true for one person (a subject) but not true for another person (another
subject), when, in fact, it is true objectively for all persons. SbF is a fallacy of
relativism. Relativism, in general, means the truth-value of a judgment is
neither necessary nor universal; however, there are multiple kinds of relativism.
To hold that the truth of a judgment about some event or thing is relative to
the *subject* making the judgment is to espouse a kind of subjective
relativism.

We say judgments may be characterized as either *objective* or *subjective*.
On the one hand, the truth-value of an objective judgment is understood to
be necessary and universal, that is to say, not relative. For example, the claim
that Immanuel Kant was 5 feet tall is supposed to be objective. On the other
hand, the truth-value of a subjective judgment is understood to be neither
necessary nor universal. For example, the claim that, when walking around
his neighborhood, Kant walked quickly is supposed to be subjective.

Bad Arguments: 100 of the Most Important Fallacies in Western Philosophy, First Edition.
Edited by Robert Arp, Steven Barbone, and Michael Bruce.
© 2019 John Wiley & Sons Ltd. Published 2019 by John Wiley & Sons Ltd.

The truth of the judgment that Kant was "5 feet tall" is supposed to be true for everyone; the judgment that Kant walked "quickly" may be deemed true or false relative to one's own walking pace.

Thus, importantly, not all instances of subjective relativism are logically fallacious. We should ask if that which is being relativized to the subject is objective or subjective; the latter will not be logically fallacious and the former will. However, since the term *objective* may involve some degree of vagueness, the following clarification should render the SbF more distinct in regard to relativism in general and non-fallacious subjective relativism in particular.

The possible vagueness regarding objectivity may be emphasized in the following question. Since it may be objectively true that someone is experiencing some particular subjective state, why must the subjective state be considered "subjective" rather than "objective"? Yet, at the same time, consider how the world, or put more precisely mind-external reality, is independent from whatever we may believe about it. Were this not true, then tree limbs could change into cheeseburgers simply by a hungry person believing that a tree limb is a cheeseburger.

In the *Enchiridion*, Epictetus (c. 50–130 CE) famously espoused, "It is not things that upset people but rather ideas about things" (§5). Again, "Remember that it is not the man who curses you or the man who hits you that insults you, but the idea you have of them as insulting [...] try not to be carried away by impressions" (§20). Referencing such an insight, then, psychologists can legitimately make the claim that one's reaction to an event or thing may be relative to something other than the event or the thing. That is to say, the *impressions* and *ideas* of things and events, because they are mind-internal, are subjective. While at the same time, the event of a person's subjective reaction may be considered an objective event, for example, it may be objectively true that a person is sad or angry in response to some event.

The problem comes when the psychologist attempts to push this insight too far, that is, suggesting the mind-external reality of the thing or event is also relative to the subject. This usually happens in one of two ways. The first is when a psychologist claims a thing or an event cannot be characterized universally and necessarily in language because to use language would only be to talk about our impressions or to characterize our ideas. The second is when a psychologist claims that because we will all have different impressions and ideas regarding some particular mind-external thing or event, the truth of claims made regarding the identity of the thing or the event is subject relative, that is, subjective.

Regarding the Epictetus quotations, then, the truth-value of judgments made regarding the subjective outcomes of objective events is, of course, subjective, that is, relative. However, if we were to direct the judgment espoused in the Epictetus quotation toward objective, rather than subjective, outcomes, we would have a judgment regarding objective outcomes in relation to objective mind-external events, and the truth-value of such a judgment could not be made relative to a subject. For example, it would be fallacious to say of someone who has a physical disease that whether he has the physical disease depends on how he feels or thinks about the disease. Therefore, claims with this latter structure, that is, treating the truth of objective judgments regarding mind-external reality to be relative to subjects, commit SbF.

Moreover, SbF is not only a fallacious depiction of relativity; it is also self-refuting. For if some subject were to claim that the fallacious subjective relativism on which SbF stands were not fallacious, a different subject could simply judge differently and the different judgment would, per the logic of the first subject, necessarily be true. In fact, were subjective relativism capable of being extended to mind-external reality, it would seem to eliminate error altogether. That is to say, a person could only judge incorrectly by judging that she had judged incorrectly; suddenly all humans would be on the verge of infallibility.

To avoid this fallacy, one needs to ground arguments with claims that are objective or that hold universally. When the claims on which an argument is based are objectively verifiable or pertain to a set of individuals universally, then the logical necessity of the argument's conclusion may be determined. Thus, the argument would not be subjectively relative.

98

Suppressed Evidence

David Kyle Johnson

> Did you know that disco record sales were up 400% for the year ending 1976? If these trends continue ... AAY!
>
> Disco Stu, *The Simpsons*, "The Twisted World of Marge Simpson"

The fallacy of suppressed evidence is as simple as it seems: one commits the fallacy when one presents evidence or an argument for a position but leaves out (or suppresses) relevant evidence that would weaken or show false one's conclusion. In the quotation that opens this chapter, Disco Stu (a classic *Simpsons* character) is arguing that now is a good time to invest in Disco. Stu, however, leaves out a large portion of important evidence that would refute his hypothesis: years of slumping disco sales since 1976.

Now, of course, it's not always fallacious to suppress evidence. If some piece of information is irrelevant to your conclusion, you probably should leave it out. Or if it helps your case, but it would probably lead to an unwanted distracting discussion, it's probably acceptable not to bring it up. But when you intentionally leave out evidence that would hurt your case, that's suppressing the evidence. And this fallacy is important to understand because of how common it is and all the different forms it can take.

The name of this fallacy might make you think of when, in a courtroom, a lawyer for the prosecution suppresses evidence of the defendant's innocence – and that is one example. But it is perhaps most common as a tactic

Bad Arguments: 100 of the Most Important Fallacies in Western Philosophy, First Edition.
Edited by Robert Arp, Steven Barbone, and Michael Bruce.
© 2019 John Wiley & Sons Ltd. Published 2019 by John Wiley & Sons Ltd.

in misleading advertising. In 2009, Olay suppressed the fact that, in ads for their wrinkle-eliminating eye cream, images of their spokesperson (the 62-year-old actress Twiggy) had been retouched. That same year, Kellogg's suppressed the fact that the studies showing Frosted Mini-Wheats could boost attention in kids by 20% were highly dubious. The herbal supplement Airborne had to pay $23.3 million when it was shown that there was no evidence of its immune-boosting properties. The list goes on and on: Sketchers Shape-Ups don't tone your ass; Activia doesn't make you poop; and Extenze doesn't extend (Weinmann and Bhasin 2011).

But, of course, scientific evidence is not the only kind of evidence that one can suppress. Sometimes the relevant evidence is simply context; without it, information or quotations can be highly misleading. Take quotation mining, for example. Modern Christian opponents of homosexuality often quote Leviticus 20:13, "If a man lies with a male as with a woman, both of them have committed an abomination." But this verse lies in the middle of a huge list of Old Testament laws and commands, most of which modern Christians largely ignore – like those that forbid eating pork and shellfish (11:4–12), sex during a woman's period (18:19), mixing fabrics (19:19), trimming one's beard (19:27), getting a tattoo (19:28), and charging interest on loans to the poor (35:37). Of course, one might reply that since God's prescribed punishment for homosexuality is more severe than the punishment for these others, we should still take this law seriously today (unlike the others). But notice that this reply also involves suppressing evidence. The prescribed punishment is death, yet few modern Christians suggest the death penalty for homosexuals. Touting the first half of a verse, while ignoring the second, is a textbook example of quotation mining.

But, of course, scripture is not the only thing that is quotation mined; so too are politicians. Take this quote from President Obama's 2012 campaign: "If you've got a business – you didn't build that. Somebody else made that happen." His opponents repeated this, *ad nauseum*, as proof that Obama thought business owners deserved no credit for their accomplishments because they didn't actually build their own business. But, in context, the quotation takes on a whole new meaning:

> If you were successful, somebody along the line gave you some help. There was a great teacher somewhere in your life. Somebody helped to create this unbelievable American system that we have that allowed you to thrive. Somebody invested in roads and bridges. If you've got a business – you didn't build that. Somebody else made that happen. The Internet didn't get invented on its own. Government research created the Internet so that all the companies could make money off the Internet. The point is, is that when we succeed, we succeed because of our individual initiative, but also because we do things together. (Blake 2012)

In context, it's quite clear Obama's "that" – in "you didn't build that" – referred to roads and bridges, not businesses. *That* is what business owners didn't build.

Suppression of evidence is also commonly found in the (mis)presentation of statistics. For example, in 2012, when the Bush tax cuts were set to expire, a cable news outlet presented a graph which suggested that the result would entail a fivefold increase in the top tax rate. But the graph started at 34%. If it had started at 0, the increase wouldn't have seemed so dramatic. Essentially, the (original) graph suppressed the evidence by suppressing the rest of the graph. In fact, it also suppressed some historical evidence as well. The highest marginal tax rate was around 90% after World War II; include that fact and letting the Bush tax cuts expire would seem inconsequential.

Scientific evidence can also be suppressed. Sometimes a scientific fact can seem to be good evidence for a claim when the "full story" reveals it's obviously not. For example, as John Rennie points out, those who deny anthropomorphic climate change often point out that natural processes produce more CO_2 than humans ever could; indeed, it's true that 95% of the CO_2 released into the atmosphere each year is from natural processes. Sounds convincing, right? How could humans possibly be responsible for global warming in light of this evidence?

What the deniers don't realize (or fail to mention) is that natural processes also subtract CO_2 from the atmosphere – so much so that their net effect is zero. Humans, on the other hand, add tons of CO_2 without taking it out – which means that, each year, we *add* far more than natural processes do. This is (one of the many reasons) why climate scientists think humans are responsible for levels of CO_2 in the atmosphere rising to their highest point in millions of years (388 parts per million compared to the typical 284).

Suppression of evidence is perhaps most common among conspiracy theorists. For example it's true that, when shot, JFK's head moved "back and to the left" – that is, *toward* the point that Oswald's bullet would have entered Kennedy's head, not *away*. (Oswald's sniper point was behind Kennedy.) Does this mean there was a second shooter that shot Kennedy from the front right? Is that what made his head move back and to the left? No. Kennedy's head moving back and to the left is actually what you would expect if Oswald was the lone shooter and shot Kennedy in the head from behind. Bullets don't create a lot of resistance when they hit the surface of an object; they just pass though that surface. What creates motion is the explosion bullets cause. In Kennedy's case, the front right of his head exploded – which pushed his head back and to the left. Don't let what getting shot looks like on TV fool you.

The fallacy of suppressing the evidence can come from left, right, or center. According to *The Skeptics Dictionary*, scientists sometimes do it, reporters do it, and pretty much everybody does it now and again. And that shouldn't be too surprising; it's an extremely effective (although under-handed) way to make one's argument appear stronger than it is. But those interested in the truth should always present all the evidence they can, regardless of whether it hurts or hinders what they want to believe.

References

Blake, Aaron. 2012. "Obama's 'You Didn't Build That' Problem." *The Washington Post*, July 18. https://www.washingtonpost.com/blogs/the-fix/post/obamas-you-didnt-build-that-problem/2012/07/18/gJQAJxyotW_blog.html (accessed October 4, 2017).

Weinmann, Karlee, and Kim Bhasin. 2011. "14 False Advertising Scandals That Cost Brands Millions." Business Insider, September 16. http://www.businessinsider.com/false-advertising-scandals-2011-9?op=1 (accessed October 4, 2017).

99
Unfalsifiability

Jack Bowen

> Horoscopes correctly predict the future: you just need to know how to interpret them. For example, if a horoscope predicted Bill would have a good day, but then that day Bill got fired from his job, his girlfriend broke up with him unexpectedly, and his car broke down, Bill could conclude that he now has the opportunity to look for a new and better job and girlfriend, and start walking more. That's all good. See: horoscopes always get it right.
>
> Example of the fallacy

The unfalsifiability fallacy occurs when someone makes a claim that is impossible to prove false. In our example, no possible evidence or outcomes could falsify the claim, "Horoscopes correctly predict the future." In this case, they have counted as "good" things we typically consider *not good*, such as getting fired, being left by a loved one, and having one's car break down. If *these* count as "good," then, it seems, no possible state of affairs could be considered not good. That being the case, the claim is unfalsifiable and becomes essentially meaningless.

Falsifiability – the *ability* to be falsified or proven wrong – is considered a key criterion for deeming a hypothesis scientific. As philosopher of science Karl Popper reflects, "A theory which is not refutable by any conceivable event is nonscientific. Irrefutability is not a virtue of a theory (as people often think) but a vice" (Popper 2014, n.p.). That is to say, while it may initially seem a strength for a theory to have no way of being proven false,

Bad Arguments: 100 of the Most Important Fallacies in Western Philosophy, First Edition.
Edited by Robert Arp, Steven Barbone, and Michael Bruce.
© 2019 John Wiley & Sons Ltd. Published 2019 by John Wiley & Sons Ltd.

it turns out to render the theory useless and, thus, relying on such a theory to determine future conclusions is fallacious. With the impossibility of false-hood goes the loss of predictive and explanatory power (see also Chapter 40).

It often helps to think of the fallacy in terms of predictability. Viewing this particular horoscope in the manner considered provides no predictive power. In predicting you will have a "good" day, it includes such antithetical results as having a successful day at your job *and* getting fired; going on a great date with your girlfriend *and* being dumped; having your car run smoothly *and* your car breaking down. Given that, then, the horoscope's prediction provides no insight as to what will actually happen and thus the statement, "Horoscopes correctly predict the future," loses meaning. Just so, an unfalsifi-able claim can't explain why one event occurred and not its opposite.

It's important to recognize that, as with most fallacious statements, committing the unfalsifiability fallacy does not necessarily prove a state-ment is false, just that no possible result or observation could demonstrate its falsehood. This is one reason such thinking can be so seductive. Conspiracy theories often rely on unfalsifiable claims in which the theorist ardently defends a theory despite any facts that disprove it, suggesting only, "Well, it's a conspiracy. It's impossible to disprove." Understanding the unfalsifiability fallacy helps to highlight where this sort of approach goes awry.

One can implement various strategies to combat committing this fallacy. First, clear conditions must be established as to how a proposed statement or claim could be falsified. For example, when the geocentric theory was posited, there were *possible* results from various tests regarding the bending of light, effects of gravity, and so on, which made the theory falsifiable. As we now know, the geocentric theory was, in fact, falsified and now the helio-centric theory has taken its place, itself another falsifiable, testable theory.

Second, we should be aware of how we consider our acceptance of various beliefs. Humans are naturally inclined toward confirmation: confirming our beliefs provides comfort, feels good, and yet can lead us to (wrongly) assum-ing a particular belief holds true. This confirmation bias happens in the case of those defending paranormal, pseudoscientific theories: they seek only to confirm and never to disconfirm. As George Bernard Shaw once wrote, "The moment we want to believe something, we suddenly see all the arguments for it, and become blind to the arguments against it" (Shaw 1928, 460).

This feature of human nature makes us vulnerable to deception. Horoscopes, for example, often make contradictory claims about a reader's life, knowing the reader will seek to confirm the horoscope's prediction no matter what happens, and hence conclude, "Horoscopes correctly predict the future." As an example of how a horoscope does this, consider these unfalsifiable predictions: "You will create your own success, or may just have success come to you given your affable personality," and, "Your rela-tionship will continue to bring great joy unless it has run its course, in which case you will encounter great despair." These statements are both excessively general, such that they're true about nearly everyone, and they also allow readers to choose what fits their own lives, either "creating success" or "having success come to them," and also having a relationship bring both "joy" and "despair" – whichever they see themselves experiencing.

And so, instead of seeking to confirm a specific claim, one should consider what possible state of affairs would render it false. One should seek to *dis*-confirm it. While confirming instances of a claim can add some credibility to it, a single disconfirming instance renders it falsified. Every white swan we encounter is evidence all swans are white, but one black swan proves that the general claim is untrue.

Once the criterion of falsifiability has been established, it is important to examine a statement or theory more critically. The defense of horoscopes not only involves an unfalsifiable claim but can also involve anecdotes. As it turns out, when tested objectively, claims made by horoscopes (and other pseudoscientific approaches) tend to be false considerably more often than many people recognize. Because of the bias toward confirmation and the vagueness and unfalsifiability of such claims, people often recognize only the "hits" – the times their hypothesis was proven correct – and they ignore the "misses" – the various times it was falsified. Rigorous, objective analysis constitutes an antidote to this sort of poor thinking.

Studies repeatedly show that people accept conclusions that conform to their current beliefs and reject those that do not. For example, when a subject who opposes same-sex marriage is shown statistics that are unfavorable regarding same-sex marriage and child rearing, he tends to accept the findings; yet when such subjects are shown statistics favoring same-sex marriage and child rearing, they reject the data and instead chose some other form of defense, typically on moral grounds, instead of relying on statistics and data. Likewise, those defending the other position tend to accept data that favors their position and reject other data, offering, instead, some sort of *post hoc* reasoning such that their position remains intact. Because so many of our beliefs are rooted in emotion, it is often difficult to "think slowly" and work through the logic and factual claims that may uproot this belief so emotionally entrenched in our ideological framework.

As with most of our philosophical reasoning, one of the big takeaway points and strategies for avoiding committing fallacies such as this involves keeping an open mind. Recognize you may be wrong and may not have all the relevant information needed to develop a sound conclusion. In addition, it is helpful to follow Plato's dictum, "Know thyself." Understand we are all subject to relying on and creating unfalsifiable statements because they help confirm what we already believe. In recognizing this in ourselves and also seeking to disconfirm our previously held beliefs, we can better avoid making fallacious arguments and, thus, be more likely to develop conclusions that are true.

References

Popper, Karl. 2014. *Conjectures and Refutations: The Growth of Scientific Knowledge*. New York, NY: Routledge.

Shaw, George Bernard. 1928. *The Intelligent Woman's Guide to Socialism and Capitalism*. New York, NY: Transaction.

100

Unwarranted Assumption

Kimberly Baltzer-Jaray

BLIND MAN:	I am healed! The Master has healed me!
BRIAN:	I didn't touch him!
BLIND MAN:	I was blind and now I can see. Arrgghh. [whump]
FOLLOWERS:	A miracle! A miracle! A miracle!
SIMON:	Tell them to stop it. I hadn't said a word for eighteen years till he came along.
FOLLOWERS:	A miracle! He is the Messiah!
SIMON:	Well, he hurt my foot!
FOLLOWERS:	Hurt my foot, Lord! Hurt my foot. Hurt mine.
ARTHUR:	Hail Messiah!
BRIAN:	I'm not the Messiah!
ARTHUR:	I say You are, Lord, and I should know. I've followed a few.
FOLLOWERS:	Hail Messiah!
BRIAN:	I'm not the Messiah! Will you please listen? I am not the Messiah, do you understand?! Honestly!
GIRL:	Only the true Messiah denies His divinity.

Monty Python, *Life of Brian*

The Monty Python Film *Life of Brian* is built entirely on one unwarranted assumption: that Brian is the Messiah. Brian was born on the same day as Jesus and right next door to him; the three wise men accidentally visit and temporarily mistake him for Christ. As a young man, he attends Jesus's Sermon on the Mount, and later when he lands in a line-up of would-be

Bad Arguments: 100 of the Most Important Fallacies in Western Philosophy, First Edition.
Edited by Robert Arp, Steven Barbone, and Michael Bruce.
© 2019 John Wiley & Sons Ltd. Published 2019 by John Wiley & Sons Ltd.

mystics and prophets who spout off speeches to the passing crowd in the plaza, he utters something he heard Jesus say. This inadvertently leads to Brian's developing a following, and any time something unusual happens, it is hailed as a miracle and the crowd of loyal worshipers grows. No matter how hard he tries, or his mother tries for that matter, to prove to the followers that he is not the Messiah, their belief increases and strengthens – in their firmly made-up minds he IS the Messiah. While this movie takes unwarranted assumptions to a ridiculous end, it was able to make a solid point about the dangers of being too willing to believe things without evidence and also to make some sharp satirical digs at trade unionists, left-wing politics, guerrilla organizations, religion, and revolutionary groups. So, what have those bloody Romans done for us anyway? Oh, sanitation, education, medicine, wine, public order, roads, fresh water, public health, just about everything!

Unwarranted assumptions are claims or beliefs that possess little to no supporting evidence, things we might take for granted as true, or just completely false ideas we inherited without reflection. When we reason using implicit assumptions or further propositions whose truth is uncertain or implausible, we commit the fallacy of unwarranted assumption and the truth of our conclusions is grossly affected. Prejudices and stereotypes are some common ways in which we make unwarranted assumptions. For example, all Irish are alcoholic bar-fighting people; the only food in America is McDonald's; or all Canadians drink maple syrup instead of water.

There are several kinds of fallacies that involve or rely on unwarranted assumptions. Begging the question (see Chapter 70), loaded question, false dilemma (see Chapter 81), fallacy of accident (see Chapter 67), and false cause (see chapters 78–80) are just some examples. In the case of a loaded question, the fallacy involves a question that has a presupposition built in, often implying something questionable: "Have you stopped beating your children?" The question assumes already that the person it is directed at abuses her children, and for that person to answer this question is a real catch-22 since if she says "yes," then that entails she used to beat her children, and if she says "no," then she is still beating them. Concerning the fallacy of accident, when a statement that is generally true is misapplied or is used in an atypical way, such as "Since women earn less than men for doing the same work, that means Ellen Degeneres makes less than all the other male talk-show hosts," the problem lies in mistaking this general rule to be a true universal premise, which is true for all cases (no exceptions!). In these cases, the assumptions implicitly or explicitly found in the premises prevent one from establishing the conclusion as true.

The key to preventing this fallacy is evidence: warranted assumptions have evidence and ways of demonstrating their truth with certainty. It's best to not hold something as true or applicable without proof that it is true and applicable. This implies that we need to make sure our biases, prejudices, generalizations, and stereotypes don't find their way into our arguments – we need to assess our ways of thinking and belief formation critically. The old saying, "When you assume, you make and ass out of U and Me," speaks volumes about the cost of such faulty, uncertain reasoning. But preventing this fallacy isn't only about yourself; the task extends to others: you must be ready to recognize and call out when others use arguments that contain unwarranted assumptions. This requires educating yourself on the issues or details before passing judgment or adding your voice to the argument.

Index

Note: Page numbers in **bold** refer to diagrams, page numbers in *italics* refer to information contained in tables.

9/11 "Truthers" 290–1, 319
  see also September 11 attacks

abortion 256, 262–3, 285, 294–5, 310
abstract existence 378–81
abstraction 380–1
accent 27, 241–5
accident
  converse 330–1
  fallacy of 145, 299–300, 374, 408
Activia 400
ad hominem 25, 232, 313
  ad hominem: bias 71–6
  ad hominem: circumstantial
    77–82, 90
  ad hominem: direct 3–7, 83–7, 91,
    93, 118, 350
  ad hominem: *tu quoque* 88–93, 232
  and appeal to ridicule 118
  and the complex question
    fallacy 316
  see also poisoning the well; *reductio
    ad Hitlerum*
ad infinitum see argument by
  repetition
ad nauseam see argument by repetition
ad populum 155
addiction 79
adverse consequences 94–7

advertising
  and the false cause fallacy 335–6,
    339–40
  and hasty generalization 356
  and the slippery slope fallacy
    385, 387
  and the suppressed evidence
    fallacy 400
affirming the consequent 20–1, 42–5,
  125–6
affirming a disjunct 39–41
African Americans 215–16
agency
  ascribing human-like 305–6
  causal 379
Airborne 400
al Qaeda 319
alcohol consumption 146–7
Aldrich, Henry 52, 64
Alexander of Aphrodisias 51–3, 64–5
aliens
  and the middle ground fallacy
    367–8
  and the mystery, therefore magic
    fallacy 190
  see also unidentified flying objects
all or nothing 301–4
Almossawi, Ali 264
alternative medicine 154–5, 383

Bad Arguments: 100 of the Most Important Fallacies in Western Philosophy, First Edition.
Edited by Robert Arp, Steven Barbone, and Michael Bruce.
© 2019 John Wiley & Sons Ltd. Published 2019 by John Wiley & Sons Ltd.

ambiguity
  and the existential fallacy 333
  and the fallacy of four terms 57–8
  linguistic 40, 57–8
  see also fallacies of ambiguity
American Civil Liberties Union 225
American Philosophical Association 282
American Society for the Defense of
  Tradition, Family and Property
  Students Action 386
amphiboly 27, 246–9
analogy
  strong arguments from 236–7
  weak 234–7
ancient Egyptian pyramids 190
and statements 44
animals 236–7, 305–6, 339–40
  welfare 123
Anscombe, Elizabeth 282, 283, 284–5
antecedents 42–3
  denying the 46–7
anthropomorphic bias 305–7
anti-gay views 348, 349
anti-Muslim sentiment 352
anti-Semitism 197, 217
anti-vaccination advocates 340, 344
appeal to authority 291
  inappropriate 25, 31, 168–71, 203
appeal to emotion 118, 203, 278
  appeal to emotion: force of fear
    98–101
  appeal to emotion: pity 102–5
appeal to force 25
appeal to ignorance 106–10, 191
  burden of proof model 107–8, 138
  interrogative form 107, 109
appeal to the masses *see* appeal to the
  people
appeal to the people 25, 26, 112–14
  argument from popularity
    version 112
  bandwagon version 113
  disjunctive type 113
  emotive form 113
  negative form 113
appeal to the person *see ad hominem*
appeal to personal incredulity 115–16

appeal to ridicule 118–20
appeal to tradition 121–4
Aquinas, Thomas 202
  natural law theory 194–5
Archaeopteryx 186
argument by repetition 215–18
argument from fallacy 125–7
argument to logic *see* argument from
  fallacy
arguments 6–11, **8**, 29–34
  and accent 242
  and *ad hominem*: bias 71–6
  and *ad hominem*: circumstantial
    77–82
  and *ad hominem*: direct 83–7
  and adverse consequences 94–7
  and the all or nothing fallacy 302–3
  from analogy 234–7
  and the anthropomorphic bias 307
  and appeal to emotion: force of fear
    98–101
  and appeal to emotion: pity 102–5
  and appeal to ignorance 106–10
  and appeal to the people 112–14
  and appeal to ridicule 118–20
  and appeal to tradition 123
  bad 29–33, **33**
  and base rates 135–6
  and begging the question 308–10
  and burden of proof 138
  chain 213
  circular 308
  and claims 7–9, **8**
  cogent 31, **32**
  and the complex question 314–16
  and composition 250–1
  and confusing an explanation for an
    excuse 253, 254
  content 21
  and countless counterfeits 141, 143
  deductive 13–14, 17, 29–30,
    31–2, 34
  and the definist fallacy 256
  and equivocation 26–7, 261–4
  and the etymological fallacy 268
  as evidence 3–4
  ex silentio (from silence) 110

arguments (*cont'd*)
  and the existential fallacy 332
  and fallacies of ambiguity 260
  and the fallacy of accident 299
  and the false cause fallacy 335,
    338, 340
  and formal fallacies 20, 26–7
  and the genetic fallacy 161, 162
  good 29–33, **32**, 34
  and inappropriate appeal to
    authority 170, 171
  inductive 13, 17–18, 29–32, 34
  and informal fallacies 25, 26–7
  invalid 30, 32, **33**, 43–5, 47, 250–1
  and irrelevant conclusions 172–3
  and the is/ought fallacy 360–3
  and kettle logic 174–6
  and the masked man fallacy 365
  moral 103–4
  and persuasion 9–11
  and proof by verbosity 289–92
  and proving too much 201–3
  and red herrings 208–9
  and reification 378–9
  and the sorites fallacy 294
  sound 30, 31–2, **32**, 203
  and special pleading 220–2
  and the straw man fallacy 223–5
  strong 30–1, **32**, **33**
  structure/form 20–1, 28–9, 30,
    34, 45
  testing the form of 45
  truth 203
  uncogent 31, 32, **33**
  unsound 30, 32, **33**
  validity 30, 32, **32**, **33**, 42–4, 47,
    203, 362
  weak 30–1, 32, **33**
  see also claims; premises; syllogism
argumentum ad ignorantiam see appeal
    to ignorance
argumentum ad logicam see argument
    from fallacy
argumentum ad populum see appeal to
    the people
argumentum ad temperantiam see
    middle ground

argumentum verbosium see proof by
    verbosity
Aristotle 195, 202, 206
  function argument 194
  logic 14–16, 51, 55–6, 58, 60–2, 333
  means between the extremes 180
  Nicomachean Ethics 146, 194
  Prior Analytics 14–15, 51–3, 55–6,
    60, 64, 309
  Sophistical Refutations 51
  on syllogism 15, 52, 54, 55–6, 60
  Topics 309
Arkowitz, Hal 143
Arp, Rob 55
art, and the intentional fallacy 357–9
artificial intelligence 307
ASCC 96–7
assumptions 251
  unwarranted 407–9
  warranted 408–9
astrologers 129
  see also horoscopes
atomic weapons 164
attentiveness 340, 400
attraction, law of 199
audiences, ignorance 225
authority, inappropriate appeal
    to 168–71
autism 155, 340, 344
autokinetic effect 327
availability error 128–31, 152–3,
    320, 393
Ayres, Bill 351

back masking 328
bank robbery 232
Barack, Obama 39, 41
Barfield, Owen 311, 312, 313
Baronett, Stan 98, 118
base rate 133–6
Bayes' Theorem 134
BBC News 243
Beatles 328
Beckwith, Francis 263
begging the question 23–4, 27, 202,
    274, 308–10, 316, 408
Behe, Michael 116, 190

beliefs 33
  contradictory 174–6
  opaque 365, 366
  testing 320
  transparent 365, 366
  and unwarranted assumptions 408
Ben-Zvi, Yitzhak 145
Bennett, Bo 277
Berra, Yogi 174, 175
bias 377
  ad hominem 71–6
  anthropomorphic 305–7
  confirmation 128, 152, 317–20, 393,
    404–5
  in-group/out-group 377
  liberal mainstream media bias
    frame 197
  linguistic 221
Bible 309, 395
  see also Old Testament
Biblical literalism 302
Big Bang Theory, The (TV show) 342–3
Bigfoot 190, 191, 202, 203
Billig, Michael 205–6
bin Laden, Osama 319
biological sciences 381
Birmingham Six 94
blame, assignment 146
Blastland, Michael 355
Blondlot, René 153
Blow, Charles M. 352–3
Boehner, John 376
Book of Revelation 395
Boole, George 333
Boolean logic 61
Boudry, Maarten 138, 139
Bowser (Super Mario character) 185
brain
  and constructions of reality 325, 327
  and the homunculus fallacy 165,
    166–7
  right hemisphere 325–6
Branden, Nathaniel 388
breastfeeding 339
Brown, Darin 152, 155
Brown, Mike 352–3
Buckingham, Bill 115–16

burden of proof 137–9, 191
Bureau of Justice Statistics 133
Buridan, John 54, 64
Burley, Walter 54
Bush, George W. 183, 246, 248, 287,
    314, 346, 347, 383, 401
Bush administration 256, 319

calculus 230
Callicles 114
Calrissian, Lando 185
Cameron, Kirk 235
Camping, Harold 319, 395
Camus, Albert, *The Stranger* 252–3
cancer 96–6
capacity, diminished 147
Capehart, Jonathan 352
carbon dioxide emissions 401
card games 158
Carlin, George 270
carnivorism 235
Carson, Ben 223–4
Cartesian theater 166, 167
Cartesian worldview 213
categorical claims 14–16, *14–15*
categorical logic 14–16, 49–65, 333
  exclusive premises 51–4
  four terms 55–9
  illicit major and minor terms 60–2
  undistributed middle 63–5
categorical syllogism 51, 60
categories of things 14, 16, *55*
  vagueness 295
Catholic Church 263
Catholics 170
causal agency 379
causation, mistaking the relevance of
    proximate 181–3
cause and effect 287–8, 383
causes
  fallacy of the single cause 287
  intermediate 182
  jointly sufficient 287, 288
  proximate 182
  sufficient 287–8
  ultimate 182
  see also false causes

Center for Disease Control 344
Central Intelligence Agency (CIA) 383
"chain reactions" 385, 386, 387
chance 158
    see also gambler's fallacy
change
    ignoring the evidence for 121
    resistance to 121
character
    and *ad hominem*: circumstantial
        77–81, 90–1
    and *ad hominem*: direct 83, 84, 85,
        86–7, 91
    and *ad hominem*: *tu quoque* 88–9,
        90, 91–2
    and the *ad hominem* argument: bias
        71–6
    and essentializing 149, 151
cheating 220, 232, 300
Cheetham, Erika 394
Cheney, Dick 175, 197, 199
Chernobyl nuclear disaster 394
Chesterton, G.K. 313
child poverty 338–9
child psychology 205–6
choice 146–8
Christian law 284
Christians 115–16, 119, 197, 318, 319,
        376–7, 400
chronological snobbery 311–13
Chrysippus 16–17, 21
Church 200
    see also Catholic Church
Church of Northern Conservative
        Fundamentalist Baptists, Great
        Lakes Region, Council of 1879
        376–7
Churchill, Winston 299
CIA see Central Intelligence Agency
circular arguments 308
circular reasoning 24
    see also begging the question
claims 1–2, 21, 34
    ambiguous 275
    and arguments 7–9, 8
    categorical 14–16, *14–15*
    and composition 251

and conclusions 7–9, 11, 13
evidence for 2–5, 11
false 2, 4–5, 10, 17, 125–6, 198,
        276, 405
and inferences 6–7, 8
lack of evidence regarding
        106–10
naturalistic 195
normative 195, 371–2
and premises 7–9, 11, 13
prescriptive 10–11
and propositional logic 16
and reasoning 16
true 2, 4, 6, 9, 10–11, 13–14, 17,
        125–6, 198
truth 2–3, 11, 397
truth-value 160–2, 212–13, 333
unfalsifiable 374, 403
universal 333
and unwarranted assumptions 408
weakened 274–5
Clark, Jeff 95
Clark, Theo 95
classification 55, 382–3
Clifford, W.K. 95
climate change 286–7
    anthropogenic 116, 401
Clinton, Bill 169–70
Clinton, Hillary 209, 223, 318
Clue (film, 1985) 210
Coast to Coast AM with George Noory
        (radio show) 25
cocaine 339
Code of Hammurabi 231, 232
coffee 339
Cohen, Carl 108
Cohen, Elliot D. 44
coin flipping 157–8, 159
Colbert, Stephen 216, 314, 347
cold reading techniques 393–4
CollectiveEvolution.com 382
Collins, Robin 190
color perception 325
Columbine High School shooting
        1999 352
Columbus, Christopher 153
commas 241, 242–4

common consent arguments 114
communists 106, 352
compensation 231, 232
competence, perceived 169
complex question 23, 314–16
  explicit form 314–15
  implicit form 314, 315
complexity, and proof by verbosity
    289–90
composition 27, 250–1
compromise 368
Conan Doyle, Sir Arthur 210
concepts
  higher-order 388, 389, 391
  lower-order 388, 389, 391
  moral 284
  stolen 388–91
conclusions 7–9, 8, 11–14, 19–20,
    28–9, 34
  and *ad hominem*:
    circumstantial 79–81
  and *ad hominem*: direct 85, 87
  and adverse consequences 95–7
  and affirming the consequent 42, 43,
    44–5
  and appeal to emotion: force of fear
    98–100
  and appeal to emotion: pity 102–5
  and argument from fallacy 125–7
  and begging the question 308
  and the complex question
    fallacy 316
  and composition 250
  and denying the antecedent 47
  and the exclusive premises fallacy 54
  and the existential fallacy 332
  and the fallacy of four terms 57, 58
  and the fallacy of illicit major and
    minor terms 61
  false 29, 44–5, 47, 125–6, 174, 202,
    208–10
  and the false cause fallacy 335,
    338, 342
  and the genetic fallacy 160
  and good arguments 30–2, 34
  and inductive reasoning 17–18
  and informal fallacies 21, 22, 23, 26

  and the irrelevant conclusion fallacy
    172–3
  and the is/ought fallacy 361–3
  and kettle logic 174, 175
  and the masked man fallacy 364,
    365, 366
  and *modus tollens* 47
  negative 58–9
  particular 332
  and proving too much 202–3
  and red herrings 208–10
  and the slippery slope fallacy 385
  and the straw man 225
  and syllogisms 15
  true 47, 203, 308, 362
  truth 43
  unjustified 364
Concorde fallacy *see* sunk cost fallacy
conditional statements 42–4, 46–7
conditionals 44
confabulation 130, 131
confirmation bias 128, 152, 317–20,
    393, 404–5
conflict, inflation of 280–1
confounders 336, 339
confusing an explanation for an
    excuse 252–4
conjunctions 44, 321–3, 382
consciousness 204
consensus, contradiction 152–6
consensus gentium (common consent)
    arguments 114
consequences, adverse 94–7
consequentialism 162
consequents 47
  denying the consequent 46
conservatism 153, 154
conspiracy theorists
  and evidence denial 319–20
  and moving the goalposts 187
  and proof by verbosity 290–1
  and the representative heuristic
    383–4
  and suppression of evidence 401
constructive nature of perception
    324–8
context 245

continuums 293–5
contradictories 108
contradictory beliefs 174–6
converse accident 330–1
Copi 99–100
Copi, Irving M. 108
coronary heart disease 336, 339
counter-evidence 273–6
counter-examples 331, 362, 374
countless counterfeits fallacy 140–3
courts of law 2–3
    and *ad hominem*: direct 86–7
    and appeal to emotion: pity 104–5
    and attribution of guilt 138
    and the suppressed evidence
        fallacy 399
Covert, Bryce 135
Cowan, Tom 245
Craig, William Lane 190
Craske-Trump Theorem 290
creation mythology 235–6, 389
creationists 244–5, 280, 302
credibility 73, 76–81, 83–4, 86, 175
crimes of passion 98
criminal justice system 353
criminality 149–50, 215–16
criticism 348–9
cryptozoology 25–6
cum hoc ergo propter hoc 335–6, 340
Cuonzo, Margaret 180

Damer, Edward 105, 168
D'Arms, Justin 372
Darwin, Charles 115–16, 186, 234
    On the Origin of Species 186, 244–5
Darwinian evolution 115–16, 186,
    244–5, 264
death penalty 231, 400
deception 277, 404
    intention to deceive 19
deduction/deductive reasoning 12–17,
    29–32, **32–3**, 34
    and *ad hominem*: bias 74
    and *ad hominem*: circumstantial 80
    and *ad hominem*: direct 85
    and affirming the consequent 125
    and categorical logic 14–16

and the fallacy of four terms 56–8
and formal fallacies 19–21
and the is/ought fallacy 360–1
and *modus ponens* 21, 42–5, 74,
    80, 85
and propositional logic 14, 16–17
see also categorical logic
deductive arguments, and countless
    counterfeits 143
definist fallacy 255–8, 278–9
Degeneres, Ellen 408
demarcation problem 198
Demby, Gene 217
Democrat-in-name-only (DINO) 375–6
Democritus 311
Dempsey, Liam 347
Dennett, Daniel 360
Denning, Lord 94, 97
denying the antecedent 46–7, 46–7
denying the consequent 46
deoxyribonucleic acid (DNA) 150, 151
"depth of search premise" 110
Descartes, René 213, 389
    Third Meditation 109
design argument *see* teleological
    argument
detensification 274
determinism 150
Deuteronomy 231
Devil 199, 200
Dewey, John 164, 380–1
Dick, Philip K., "Minority Report"
    133–4
dictum de omni 333
diet 96–7
differential treatment 219–22
Digby (blogger) 374
Dilnot, Andrew 355
diminished capacity 147
diminished responsibility 145–8
DINO (Democrat-in-name-only) 375–6
dinosaurs 186
DirectTV 385, 387
disjunctions 41, 44, 361–2
distribution 61–2, 63–5
divine design 190
divine intervention 190

divine judgment 199
division 27, 259–60
DNA *see* deoxyribonucleic acid
doctors, authority of 170
Donne, John 358
Doody, Ryan 227–8
double entendres 247
double standards 220
double talk 277
Dowden, Bradley 303
"Dr. Phil" effect 169
dream world logic 175
dreams 130, 175
"dressgate" 325
driving, defensive 372
drug abuse 339, 343
drugs tests 135
dualism 95, 199, 365
Duyser, Diana 324

Earth, age of the 280, 281
Eastwood, Clint 349–50
economic depression 291
economy 343–4
Eichmann, Adolf 145–6
Einstein, Albert 152, 153, 154
emotion
    and the appeal to the people 113
    and the moralistic fallacy 372
    see also appeal to emotion
Empire Strikes Back, The (film,
    1980) 185
empirical method 380–1
Engel, Morris 220
Enlightenment 311
enthymemes 315
environmental factors 150
environmentalism 74–5
Epictetus 397–8
epistemic humility 366, 370
epistemological problems 362, 363
equivocation 26–7, 261–4
"error destroys action" maxim 282
Esquire (magazine) 267
essence 151
essentializing 149–51
ethics 193, 284

etymological fallacy 266–8
etymons 266–8
Eukanuba 339–40
euphemism 270–2, 278
evidence 2–5, 8, 11, 34
    arguments as 3–4
    and authoritative explanations 3
    and the availability error 128–31
    and confirmation bias 319–20
    counterfeit 140–3
    forms of 3–4
    historical 10
    and informal fallacies 25
    lack of 106–10, 191
    legitimate 140
    logical/mathematical entailment 3, 5
    negative 110
    and *reductio ad absurdum* 119–20
    sense evidence of spatiotemporal
        entities 3, 4, 5
    suppressed 23, 153, 399–402
    and the testimony of trusted
        others 3, 4
    and unwarranted assumptions
        408–9
    weak 143
    see also counter-evidence
evidence denial 319–20
evil, problem of 110
evolution, theory of 115–16, 186,
    244–5, 264
ex silentio (from silence)
    arguments 110
exclusive premises 51–4
excuses, confusing explanations
    for 252–4
executions 183, 400
existence
    abstract 378–81
    "existence precedes essence" 151
    and the existential fallacy 333
    of God 23–4, 109, 114, 137, 143,
        235, 309, 333
    proof of 389
existential fallacy 332–4
Exodus 231
expectations, and perception 326

experience
  first-person 204–6
  religious 199
expert opinions 3, 4, 115
  backhanded undermining of 116
  and inflation of conflict 280–1
Extenze 400
extremist views 367–8
eyewitness testimony 86–7
  unreliability of 25, 131, 143
  see also leading the witness

fairness, principle of 219–20, 222
fallacies 18–29
  definition 19, 125
  as errors in reasoning 125
  reasons to be concerned about 27–33
  see also formal fallacies; informal
    fallacies; *specific fallacies*
fallacies of ambiguity 25, 26–7, 239–95
  accent 27, 241–5
  amphiboly 27, 246–9
  composition 27, 250–1
  confusing an explanation for an
    excuse 252–4
  definist fallacy 255–8, 278–9
  division 27, 259–60
  equivocation 261–4
  etymological fallacy 266–8
  euphemism 270–2, 278
  hedging 273–6
  if by whiskey 277–9
  inflation of conflict 280–1
  legalistic mistake 282–5
  oversimplification 286–8
  proof by verbosity 289–92
  sorites fallacy 180, 293–5
fallacies of personal incredulity 115–16
fallacies of presumption 22–5,
    297–409
  accident 145, 299–300, 374, 408
  all or nothing 301–4
  anthropomorphic bias 305–7
  begging the question 23–4, 27, 202,
    274, 308–10, 316, 408
  chronological snobbery 311–13

complex question 23, 314–16
confirmation bias 317–20
conjunction 44, 321–3, 382
constructive nature of perception
    324–8
converse accident 330–1
existential fallacy 332–4
false cause 22–3, 335–6, 385, 408
false cause: *cum hoc ergo propter hoc*
    335–6, 340
false cause: ignoring common cause
    338–40
false cause: *post hoc ergo propter hoc*
    126–7, 340, 342–4
false dilemma 23, 178–9, 202–3,
    346–7, 408
free speech 348–50
guilt by association 351–3
hasty generalization 354–6
intentional fallacy 357–8
is/ought fallacy 360–3, 371
masked man 364–6
middle ground 367–8
mind projection 369–70
moralistic fallacy 371–2
no true Scotsman 374–7
reification 378–81
representative heuristic 382–4
slippery slope 126, 178, 274, 385–7
stolen concept 388–91
subjective validation 392–5
subjectivist fallacy 396–8
suppressed evidence 23, 153,
    399–402
unfalsifiability 403–5
unwarranted assumptions 407–9
fallacies of relativism
  psychologist's fallacy 204–6
  subjectivist fallacy 396–8
fallacies of relevance 25, 69–237
  ad hominem 25, 118, 232, 313, 316
  ad hominem: bias 71–6
  ad hominem: circumstantial 77–82
  ad hominem: direct 3–7, 83–7, 91,
    93, 118, 350
  ad hominem: *tu quoque* 88–93, 232

adverse consequences 94–7
appeal to emotion 118, 203, 278
appeal to emotion: force of fear 98–101
appeal to emotion: pity 102–5
appeal to force 25
appeal to ignorance 106–10, 191
appeal to inappropriate authority 25, 31, 168–71, 203
appeal to the people 25, 26, 112–14
appeal to ridicule 118–20
appeal to tradition 121–4
argument by repetition 215–18
argument from fallacy 125–7
availability error 128–31, 152–3, 320, 393
base rate 133–6
burden of proof 137–9, 191
countless counterfeits 140–3
diminished responsibility 145–8
essentializing 149–51
Galileo gambit 152–6
gambler's fallacy 157–9
genetic fallacy 160–2
historian's fallacy 163–4
homunculus 165–7
irrelevant conclusion 172–3
kettle logic 174–6
line drawing fallacy 177–80
mistaking the relevance of proximate causation 181–3
moving the goalposts 185–8
mystery, therefore magic fallacy 189–91, 306
naturalistic fallacy 193–5
poisoning the well 196–200
proving too much, fallacy 201–3
psychologist's fallacy 204–6
red herrings 208–10, 232, 316
reductio ad Hitlerum 212–14
special pleading 219–22
straw man 178, 179, 223–5, 274
sunk cost 227–8
two wrongs make a right 230–3
weak analogy 234–7

fallacist's fallacy *see* argument from fallacy
fallacy of accident 145, 299–300, 374, 408
fallacy fallacy *see* argument from fallacy
fallacy of the maturity of chances *see* gambler's fallacy
fallacy of/to moderation *see* middle ground
false causes 22–3, 335–6, 385
    false cause: *cum hoc ergo propter hoc* 335–6, 340
    false cause: ignoring common cause 338–40
    false cause: *post hoc ergo propter hoc* 126–7, 340, 342–4
    and unwarranted assumptions 408
    see also slippery slope
false compromise *see* middle ground
false dichotomy 316
false dilemma 23, 178–9, 202–3, 346–7, 408
    see also all or nothing
false negatives 134
false positives 134
falsifiability 198, 199, 403–5
fear 98
    appeal to emotion: force of fear 98–101
Feinberg, Joel 282, 283–5
Fenner, David 357
fetus 256, 262–3, 285, 294–5
Fields, W.C. 289
financial crash 2008 183
First World War 288
first-person point of view 204–6
Fleischmann, Martin 153
Flew, Antony 374–5
"flim-flam" 140, 141, 142, 143
Fogelin, Robert 119
folk concepts 180
Fool Us (TV show) 189
Foot, Philippa 194
Forer, Bertram 392–3
Forer effect 393–4
forgetting 130–1

formal fallacies 19–21, 28, 32, 34,
    35–65
  affirming the consequent 20–1,
    42–5, 125–6
  affirming a disjunct 39–41
  and categorical logic 49–65
  denying the antecedent 46–7
  distinction from informal 26–7
  exclusive premises 51–4
  existential fallacy 332–4
  fallacy of the undistributed middle
    28, 63–5
  four terms 55–9
  illicit major and minor terms 60–2
  and invalid arguments 30
  and propositional logic 20, 37–47
  undistributed middle 63–5
fossil record 186–7
Foucault, Michel 161
four terms, fallacy of 55–9
Fox Nation 344
Fox News 318
Frankena, William 255
Franz Ferdinand, Archduke 288
free speech 348–50
Freud, Sigmund 160, 161, 174, 175–6
Freudian psychoanalysis 198
Frosted Mini-Wheats 340, 400
fruitfulness 154
Fulton 153

Galen, *De Captionibus (On Fallacies)* 51
Galileo Galilei 152
Galileo gambit fallacy 152–6
gambler's fallacy 157–9
Garner, Eric 353
Geis, Irving 157
generalization
  and converse accident 330
  definition 354–5
  and the fallacy of accident 299–300
  and the irrelevant conclusion fallacy
    172–3
  proper 354–5
  see also hasty generalization
genetic fallacy 149, 160–2, 203, 313
genetically modified food 75–6

geocentrism 312, 404
Germany 302
Gervais, Ricky 165, 167
Ghost Hunters (TV show) 328
ghosts
  and the anthropomorphic bias 306
  and burden of proof 138
  and the constructive nature of
    perception 326, 328
  and countless counterfeits 140,
    141–2
  and the mystery, therefore magic
    fallacy 190
Gilliam, Franklin D. 216
global warming 280, 401
God 277, 302, 400
  belief in 162, 201, 202
  as creator 235–6
  existence of 23–4, 109, 114, 137,
    143, 235, 309, 333
  omniscient 364, 366
  and the problem of evil 110
  and the supernatural 190
  creator 389
gods 160, 202, 306
Goddard, Ives 266
Goebbels, Joseph 217
Goldbach's Conjecture 108
golden mean fallacy *see* middle ground
Golden Rule 299
Goldstein, Rebecca 143
good 194–5
Google 41
government 379
Grant, John 290
gravity, theory of 154
gray fallacy *see* middle ground
Great Depression 291
Greenback, John 389
guilt
  attribution 138
  by association 313, 351–3
Gula, Robert 268, 352
gun regulation 302–3
Gustafson, Kaaryn 216
Gustave, Eiffel 3
Guthrie, Stewart 306

Haile Selassie 394
Haley's comet 394
hallucinations 326
    mass/collective 25–6
Ham, Ken 280
Hamad bin Isa Al Khalifa, king of
    Bahrain 270
Hanson, Victor Davis 223
happiness 112, 113, 193, 194
Hart, Herbert 283–4
Hartmann, Betsy 212
Harwood, William 183
hasty generalization 23, 24–5, 27, 129,
    354–6
    and chronological snobbery 313
    and converse accident 330
    and essentializing 150
    and inflation of conflict 280
    and stolen concepts 390
Hawking, Stephen 169, 170, 171
health-related behaviors 95
hearing 327–8
Hebraic law 230, 231, 232
hedging 273–6
Hegel, Georg Wilhelm Friedrich 232
Heidegger, Martin 91–3, 213–14
Henry IV 394
heroin 339
heuristic, representative 382–4
Hiltzik, Michael 352
hindsight 163–4
hippocampus 166
Hirst, W. 131
historian's fallacy 163–4
historical fallacy 164
Hitchens, Christopher 311
Hitler, Adolf 163–4, 212, 213, 214, 302
    Big Lie technique 217
    Mein Kampf 302
    Hitler, Adolf, Big Lie technique 217
Hitler regime 282
HIV denial 155
Holmes, Baxter 267
Holmes, Sherlock 210
Holocaust 213, 217
homeopathy 142
Homer 202

homosexuality 348, 349, 386, 400
homunculus fallacy 165–7
Honoré, Tony 283–4
Hoover, J. Edgar 352
hormone replacement therapy (HRT)
    336, 339
horoscopes 403, 404–5
    see also astrologers
hot hand fallacy 158
House Freedom Caucus 376
Huckabee, Mike 351
Huff, Darrell 157
Huffington Post 209
Huggett, Nick 202
human beings 262–3
Hume, David 198, 235–6, 320, 361
humility
    epistemic 366, 370
    intellectual 120
hunter-gatherers 306
Hurley, Patrick 71, 74, 81, 234, 261,
    354, 385–7
Husserl, Edmund 205, 213
hyperbole 178
hypotheses 198
    and confirmation bias 318
    falsifiability 403–4
    formulation 150

ideas 397
if by whiskey 277–9
"if-then" statements 42, 44, 74, 80, 85
    converse 42
ignorance
    appeal to 106–10, 138, 191
    audience 225
illicit major and minor terms, fallacy of
    60–2
illusions 326–7
imagination 369
imitation 169
immigration 286
impressions 397
in-group/out-group bias 377
inappropriate appeal to authority 25,
    31, 168–71, 203
inconsistency 77–9, 80–1, 90, 220

incredulity, appeal to personal 115–16
indeterminacy 273
indiscernibility of identicals
    principle 364–5
induction/inductive reasoning 13,
    17–18, 21–7, 29–32, **32–3**, 34
  and *ad hominem*: bias 74
  and *ad hominem*: direct 85
  and the appeal to ignorance 109
  and appeal to the people 113–14
  and the is/ought fallacy 363
  problem of 198
inductive arguments, and countless
    counterfeits 143
inferences 6–9, 6–7, 8, 11–12
  and categorical logic 14
  disjunction introduction rule of
    inference 361–2
  from a part to a whole 251
  and the is/ought fallacy 360–1
  and the masked man fallacy 364,
    365, 366
  and mind projection 370
inflation of conflict 280–1
infomercials 22
informal fallacies 19, 21–7, **24**, 32, 34,
    67–409
  distinction from formal 26–7
  fallacies of ambiguity 25, 26–7,
    239–95
  fallacies of presumption 22–5,
    297–409
  fallacies of relevance 25, 69–237
  and weak arguments 31
Inhofe, James 286–7
Inquisition 199
insanity, as legal defence 161
Institute of Medicine of the National
    Academy of Sciences 343
intelligence quotient (IQ) 95, 339
intentional fallacy 357–8
intentionality, of inanimate objects 198
intermediate causes 182
interpretation 241–5, 246–7
  art 357–9
"interrogator's fallacy" 314
IQ *see* intelligence quotient

Iraq 175
  weapons of mass destruction 291–2
Iraq War 183, 228, 319
irrationality 220
irreducible complexities 190
irrelevant conclusion (*ignoratio
    elenchi*) 172–3
is/ought fallacy 360–3, 371
ISIS 183
Islamophobia 224
Israel 232–3
Israel, John 135

Jacobson, Daniel 372
James, William 204–5, 380
Japan 164
Jarus, Owen 190
Jason 274
Jastrow, Robert 234, 235
Jaynes, R.T. 369–70
Jefferson, Thomas 212, 302
Jesus 302, 319
Jews 92, 123, 197
  International Jewry 217
Jillette, Penn 39, 41
John Paul II, Pope 263
jointly sufficient causes 287, 288
Jordan, Michael 169, 171
judgments
  moral 171
  objective 396–8
  subjective 206, 396–8
jurors 143, 147
justice
  and cultural difference 245
  and law 112
  restorative 232
  retributive 231–2

Kaczor, Christopher 263
Kahneman, Daniel 321, 323
Kant, Immanuel 109, 332, 333, 396–7
karma 198
Kellogg's 340, 400
Kelly, Thomas 114
Kennedy, John F. 232, 261, 383–4, 401
Kenny, Anthony 166

kettle logic fallacy 174–6
Kierkegaard, Søren 364, 366
Kneale, Martha 63–4
Kneale, William 63–4
knowledge
  lack of 107, 108, 110
  progress and 311–13
Kreeft, Peter 140, 141
Kremlin 383
Kristof, Nick 343
Krugman, Paul 216
Kurtz, Howard 118

labelling 151
Lacan, Jacques 205–6, 396
Lacanian psychoanalysis 205–6
Lancet, The (journal) 344
language
  amphiboly 246–9
  direct 272
  and informal fallacies 21–2
  meaning 241–5
  offensive 267–8
  see also linguistics
Lasky, Victor 232
latency 274
law 283, 302–3
  Christian 284
  divine 285
  Hebraic 230, 231, 232
  and justice 112
  moral 283
  natural 285
law of attraction 199
law of excluded middle 52
law of identity 52
law of non-contradiction 52
Le Verrier, Urbain Jean Joseph 153
leading questions 143
leading the witness 315
Left, The 224
"legal-like" concepts 283–5
legalistic mistake 282–5
Leman, Patrick 384
Levin, Josh 217
Leviticus 231, 400
Lewis, C.S. 311, 312, 313

lex talionis 231
lexical stress 241
liberal mainstream media bias
  frame 197
Life of Brian (film, 1979) 407–8
Lilienfeld, Scott O. 143
Limbaugh, Rush 291
Linda problem 321–2
line drawing fallacy 177–80
linguistics
  linguistic ambiguity 293–4
  linguistic bias 221
  and syntax 246
  see also language
loaded questions 314, 315, 408
lobbyists 99–100
Loch Ness monster 25, 141, 190
logic 301
  conservativeness of 361–2
  dream world 175
  modern 51–2
  semantic 333, 333
  see also categorical logic;
    propositional logic
Los Angeles Times (newspaper) 209, 352
lunatic fallacy *see* genetic fallacy
lung cancer 336, 339
Lunsford, Andrea A. 346
lying 232

Mafia 383
magic, mystery, therefore magic fallacy
  189–91, 306
magicians 142
Maier, D.S. 289–90
Maitzen, Stephen 362
major terms, fallacy of illicit major and
  minor terms 60–2
Mandela, Nelson 241
marijuana, as gateway drug 339, 343
Mario (Super Mario character) 185
marriage, same-sex 310, 386, 405
Marx, Groucho 247
Mary, Mother of God 324, 327
masked man fallacy 364–6
Mathias, Charles, Jr. 121
McCarthy, Jenny 344

McCarthy, Joseph 106, 352
McCarthyism 352
McCartney, Paul 328
McConnell, Mitch 343–4
McCoy, Glenn 197
McMahon, Kenneth 108
McRaney, David 228
meaning
　ambiguous words 276
　double 246–9
　and language 241–5
　and syntax 246
　unintended 248
"means and ends" reasoning 162
measles, mumps, and rubella (MMR)
　　vaccination 344
mediums 129, 142
memory
　and the availability error 129–30
　flashbulb 131
　unreliability of 130–1, 143
mens rea 282–3
mental capacity 147
mental disorders 369–70
mental existence 389
mental illness 253
Merchant, Stephen 165
Mercury 154
middle ground 367–8
middle terms 53, 56
　fallacy of the undistributed
　　middle 28, 63–5
Mill, John Stuart 112, 113, 114, 193,
　　194, 287
Miller, Michael 146, 147
mimicry 169
mind projection 369–70
mind-body dualism 199
mind-external reality, independence
　　from belief 397–8
mind-internal 397
minds
　open 405
　other 307
　philosophy of mind 265
minor terms, fallacy of illicit major and
　　minor terms 60–2

"mirror stage" 205
misogyny 349
mistaking the relevance of proximate
　　causation 181–3
MMR (measles, mumps, and rubella)
　　vaccination 344
modern logic 51–2
modus ponens ("method of
　　affirming") 21, 42–5, 74, 80, 85
modus tollens ("the mode of
　　taking") 47, 110
Monsanto 75–6
Monte Carlo fallacy *see* gambler's fallacy
Monty Python 407–8
Moore, G.E. 193–4, 195, 255
morality
　of abortion 256
　of the appeal to tradition 122,
　　123, 124
　and the is/ought fallacy 360–2
　moral arguments 103–4
　moral concepts 284
　moral judgments 171
　moral law 283
　moral properties 193–4
　moral responsibility 146–8
　moral standards 164
　moralistic fallacy 371–2
　and the naturalistic fallacy 193–4
　and *reductio ad Hitlerum* 213
Morton, Sheila 338
moving the goalposts 185–8
MSNBC 318
murder 252–3, 282–3, 285
Murdock, Casey 330
Muslims 224
Myers, Martin 340
mystery, therefore magic fallacy
　　189–91, 306

narrative scripts 216, 217
Natapoff, Alexandra 352
National Crime Victimization
　　Survey 133
National Football League (NFL) 187
National Geographic's Is It Real?
　　(show) 141

National Review 224
National Rifle Association (NRA) 181, 182, 225, 383
Native Americans 266, 267–8
natural law theory 194–5
natural properties 193–5
natural selection 116, 190, 244–5
naturalistic fallacy 193–5, 255
nature 160, 378, 401
  properties of 369–70
Nazi Party 213–14
Nazis 91–3, 171, 213–14, 233
near-death experiences 199
necessary causes 287, 288
necessary conditions 44, 47
Neil, Samuel 51, 52, 54
neuroscience 166
New York Times, The (newspaper) 216, 267, 352–3
Newton, Isaac 3, 154
NFL *see* National Football League
NGRI *see* not guilty by reason of insanity
Nielsen, Eric 228
Nieman Reports 216
Nintendo 185
Nixon, Richard 83, 232
no true Scotsman 374–7
"non-syllogistic" 51, 53
Norenzayan, A. 306
normative claims 371–2
normative properties 194–5
"noseeum" principle 110
Nostradamus, Michel 392, 394–5
not guilty by reason of insanity (NGRI) 161
Novella, Steven 325
NRA *see* National Rifle Association
Nuremberg Principles 146
Nye, Bill 280
Nyhan, Brendan 319

Obama, Barack 183, 187, 209, 351–2, 400–1
Obama Administration 344
objective judgments 396–8
objective validation 392

Ogelsby, Pat 278
Olay 400
Old Testament 400
omniscience 364, 366
ontology 333
open minds 405
oppression 122
Oprah effect 169
or statements 44
  ambiguity of 40–1
  exclusive 40–1
  inclusive 40–1
orders, following 145–6
O'Reilly, Bill 189, 190
Ortega, Tony 140–1
Oswald, Lee Harvey 383, 401
other minds 307
overinflation 183
oversimplification 286–8
overstatement 274

pain, animals and 236–7
paleontology 186–7
Palestinians 233
Palin, Bristol 348, 349
Palin, Sarah 349, 351
paradoxes 180
  and the sorites fallacy 293–4
  Zeno's 178, 202
paranormal 140, 141, 142
  and the anthropomorphic bias 306
  and confirmation bias 404
  and subjective validation 395
  see also ghosts; supernatural
paranormal, the 138, 139
pareidolia 327, 328
Paris terrorist attacks 2016 330
Park, Robert L. 156
parsimony 154
partiality 220
Pascal, Blaise 201
Pascal's wager 201–3
past, romanticizing the 122
Pasteur, Louis 152
patterns 327
Pauley, William 234
Pearl Harbor 163

Pelosi, Nancy 74–5
Penn & Teller 189
Penn & Teller: Bullshit! (TV show)
    129, 305
Pentagon 271
Pentateuch 232
perception
    constructive nature of 324–8
    perceptual constancy 326–7
    unreliable nature of 143
perfectionist fallacy 303
perjury 86–7, 94, 97
personal circumstances, and
        ad hominem 77–82
persuasion
    and appeal to emotion: force of fear 99
    and arguments 9–11
persuasive definition *see* definist fallacy
Petraeus, General David 84–6
pets 305–6, 339–40
Pew Research 268
Phillips, Emo 376–7
philosophic fallacy 380
philosophy, religious 312–13
philosophy of mind 265
physical existence 378–81, 389
physicalism 95
Piercy, Joseph 241
Pigden, Charles 361, 362
Pigliucci, Massimo 138, 139
Pilkington, Karl 165, 167
Pineda, Diego 340
pitch 19
Pitkanen, Risto 390
pity, appeal to emotion: pity 102–5
placebo effect 142
plane crashes 128–9
Plato 98, 114, 405
    Republic 282
poetry 358
poisoning the well 196–200, 313
police homicide rates 133, 135–6
political correctness 270
politicians 19
    and *ad hominem*: bias 71, 74–5
    and *ad hominem*: *tu quoque* 88–9
    and the all or nothing fallacy 302

and appeal to the people 113
and the appeal to personal
    incredulity 116
and the appeal to tradition 121
and argument by repetition 216, 217
and begging the question 310
and false dilemmas 346–7
and guilt by association 351–2
and hasty generalization 354, 355–6
and the no true Scotsman fallacy
    375–6
and *post hoc ergo propter hoc* 343–4
and red herrings 209–10
and *reductio ad Hitlerum* 213
and reification 379
and suppression of evidence 401
and two wrongs make a right 232
Pons, Stanley 153
Ponzo illusion 327
Pope, the 170
Popper, Karl 198, 199, 403–4
positivism, wicked 282, 283
post hoc ergo propter hoc 126–7, 340,
    342–4
Postman, Neil 313
poverty 338–9
Praeger, Dennis 224
pragmatic arguments 96
pragmatics 241–2
    fallacies of *see* accents
prayers, answered/unanswered 199
predictability 404
prediction 393, 394–5, 403, 404–5
pregnancy, unwanted 236
prejudice 24–5, 72, 408, 409
premises 7–9, 8, 11–14, 17, 19–20,
    28–9, 34
    and *ad hominem*: bias 74
    and *ad hominem*: direct 85
    and affirming the consequent 42, 43,
        44–5, 125
    assessing the truth of 29
    and begging the question 308
    and the complex question fallacy 314
    and composition 250
    contradictory 174
    and denying the antecedent 47

"depth of search premise" 110
and the exclusive premises fallacy
51–4
and the existential fallacy 332–3
and the fallacy of accent 241–5
and the fallacy of four terms 57–9
and the fallacy of illicit major and
minor terms 61
and the fallacy of the undistributed
middle 63–5
false 29, 30, 31, 32
and the false cause fallacy 335, 338, 342
and good arguments 30, 31, 32, **32**, 34
and informal fallacies 21, 22, 23,
25, 26
and the irrelevant conclusion
fallacy 172–3
and the is/ought fallacy 361–3
and kettle logic 174, 175–6
major 42
minor 42, 46
and *modus tollens* 47
negative 52–4, 58–9
and proving too much 202–3
and the slippery slope fallacy 385
and syllogisms 15
true 30–1, 32, **32**, 34, 44–5, 47, 202,
203, 362
truth 43
universal 332–3
premonitions 130
presentism 164
Princess Peach (Super Mario
character) 185
principle of explosion 154
Prior, Arthur 361, 362
pro-life position 256, 263, 270, 285
probabilistic reasoning 133–4, 369
probability theory
and the conjunction fallacy 321–3
misapplication of the rules of
probability 321–3
quantum theory of 369–70
and the representative heuristic 383
problem of induction 198
ProCon.org 386
progress 311–13

prohibition 278
Project Mogul 150
proof 107, 109, 110, 389
burden of 107–8
negative 109–10
proof by verbosity 289–92
see also proving too much
propaganda 215, 216, 218, 302
properties of nature 369–70
property, as theft 388–9, 390
property dualism 365
prophecy 393, 394–5
propositional logic 14, 16–17, 20, 37–47
affirming the consequent 20–1, 42–5
affirming a disjunct 39–41
denying the antecedent 46–7
propositional syllogism 42, 46
propositions
descriptive 360–1, 362
false 301
and the is/ought fallacy 360–3
moral 361
normative 361
true 301
prosodic stress 241–2, 243
Proudhon, Pierre-Joseph 388
Proverbs 286
proving too much 201–3
proximate cause 182
pseudoscience 198–9
psychics 129, 393–4
psychoanalysis 161, 198, 205–6
Psychological Review, The 164
psychologism 204, 205
psychologist's fallacy 204–6
psychologizing 205
punctuation 241, 242–4
pyramids 190

qualification 274–5
quantum theory, of probability 369–70
questions
complex 23, 314–16
leading 315
loaded 314, 315, 408
open-ended 315
Socratic 316

Quine, W.V. 380
quotation mining 400

racial groups 381
racism 95, 150, 172, 224, 286,
    349–50, 353
radical skepticism 370
radical views 367–8
Ramachandran, V.S. 325
Rand, Ayn 388, 389, 390
Randi, James 140
rapid eye movement (REM) sleep 130
rapture 319, 395
rationality 389
Ray, Gene 289, 290
Reagan, Ronald 215, 384
Reagan era 339
reality
    mind-external 397–8
    and morality 372
reasoning 11–18, 34
    and the anthropomorphic bias 306–7
    circular 24
    errors in *see* fallacies
    "means and ends" 162
    and the moralistic fallacy 371–2
    probabilistic 133–4, 369
    two-step process 28–9
    see also deduction/deductive
        reasoning; induction/inductive
        reasoning
recall 130
red herring 208–10, 232, 316
redskins 266, 267, 268
reductio ad absurdum (reduction to
    absurdity) 4, 119–20
reductio ad Hitlerum 212–14
reflexes 381
Reich, William 153
Reichenbach 202
reification 378–81
    pernicious 37–80, 381
Reifler, Jason 319
reincarnation 199
relativism 396–7
    fallacies of 204–6, 396–8
    multiple kinds of 396
relativity 295, 398

relativity theory 152, 154
relevance *see* fallacies of relevance
religion 161, 311
    and confirmation bias 318
    and the no true Scotsman fallacy 376
    and the supernatural 190
religious experience 199
religious philosophy 312–13
REM (rapid eye movement) sleep 130
Rennie, John 401
repetition, argument by 215–18
representative heuristic 382–4
Republican-in-name-only (RINO)
    375–6
Republicans 224, 343–4
respect 120
responsibility
    diminished 145–8
    moral 146–8
Ricoeur, Paul 161
ridicule, appeal to 118–20
RINO (Republican-in-name-only)
    375–6
Roberts, Henry 394
Robertson, Phil 348, 349
Robison, Richard 107, 108
Rockmore, Tom 213
Roman law 231, 232
Ronson, Jon 317
Roudinesco, Elizabeth 205
Rowe, William 120
Rowling, J.K. 375, 377
Rumsfeld, Donald 291–2
Ruskiewicz, John J. 346
Ruskin, John 378
Ryan, Paul D. 376

Sacks, Oliver 326
Sagan, Carl 153
Salem witch trials 199
same-sex marriage 310, 386, 405
sample size 354–5
Sartre, Jean Paul 151
Schick, Theodore 130, 154, 319, 326,
    327, 383
Schultz, Debbie Wasserman 224
Schwarzenegger, Arnold 346–7
science 198–9

scientific consensus, contradiction
152–6
scientific evidence, suppression 401
scientific research 110
scientific theory, proving true 198
scope 154
Scottish independence referendum 2014
375, 377
search engines 40–1
Second World War 164, 302
self-fulfilling explanations 197,
199–200
self-interest 109
semantic logic 333
senses
misleading nature of 324–8
sense evidence of spatiotemporal
entities 3, 4, 5
sentential logic *see* propositional logic
sentimentality 121, 124
September 11 attacks (9/11) 131, 187,
233, 254, 287, 352, 383
see also 9/11 "Truthers"
sexism 123
sexual assault 146–7
shares 344
Shaw, George Bernard 404
Sheidlower, Jesse 267–8
Sheldrake, Rupert 155, 389
Shermer, Michael 156
Shredded Wheat 335–6
simplicity 154
Simpson, O.J. 172
Simpsons, The (TV show) 315,
342, 399
sin, original 277
Singer, Peter 236–7
Singer, S. Fred 280
single cause, fallacy of the 287
Sinnott-Armstrong, Walter 119–20
Skeptic Magazine 140–1
skepticism, radical 370
Sketchers 400
slavery 122
slippery slope 126, 178, 274,
385–7
smoking 79–80, 336, 339
social cognitive theory 169

socioeconomic position 336
Socratic questions 316
soldiers 170–1
Solly, Thomas 52
Solomon, judgment of 368
Sorensen, Roy 178
sorites fallacy 180, 293–5
South Park (TV show) 208, 383–4
Southern Law Poverty Center 352
space 202
special pleading 219–22
Spielberg, Steven 133
State 379
statistics, (mis)representation 401
stealing the concept *see* stolen concept
Stein, Gertrude 369
stereotypes
and argument by repetition 217
and essentializing 149, 150
and hasty generalization 355, 356
and mind projection 370
and unwarranted assumptions
408, 409
Stoics 16
stolen concept 388–91
straw man 178, 179, 223–5, 274
hollow man version 224
representational 223–4
selectional (the weak man) 224
stroke patients 325–6
Strongman, L. 307
subjective judgments 206, 396–8
subjective validation 392–5
subjectivist fallacy 396–8
subjectivity 374
substance 64–5
substitution 275
sufficient causes 287–8
sufficient conditions 43–4, 47
sunk cost fallacy 227–8
Super Mario Bros 185
supernatural 190, 198–9, 306
see also ghosts; paranormal
superstition 22–3
suppressed evidence 23, 153,
399–402
Swanson, David 175
Sweat, Noah S. "Soggy", Jr. 277–8

Swift, Taylor 349
syllogism 15, 60–1
    categorical 51, 60
    disjunctive 41
    and the existential fallacy 332
    and the fallacy of exclusive premises
        51–4
    and the fallacy of four terms 56–8
    and the fallacy of illicit major and
        minor terms 61–2
    and impossible situations 64–5
    incomplete (enthymemes) 315
    major term 53, 56, 58
    middle term 53, 56, 57–8, 59
    minor term 53, 56, 58
    propositional 42, 46
    valid 55–8, 61, 65
    Whately's sixth rule of 58
syllogistic logic *see* categorical logic
syntax, fallacies of 246–9
Syrian refugees 330
Szalavitz, Maia 343
Szasz, Thomas 230

Taco Bell 356
taxation 257, 401
Taylor, Linda 217
teachers' pay 73–4
technological advances 312
Ted 2 (film) 179
teleology 198, 235
Temporary Assistance for Needful
    Families (TANF) 135
terrorism 254, 287, 330, 351–2
    see also September 11 attacks
Tesfaye, Sophia 223–4
testability 127, 154
testimony of trusted others 3, 4
testing 243
theft, property as 388–9, 390
theodicy 198
theories 264
Thielen, Martin 376
Thomas, Dave 150
Thomson, Judith Jarvis 236
Thrasymachus 282
tides 190

time 202
Time Cube (2015) 290
Toad (Super Mario character) 185
Tolstoy, Leo 4, 357, 358
Townsend, Tim 141
traditional logic *see* categorical logic
traffic accidents 129
transitivity 3
true positives 134
Trump, Donald 118, 209–10, 223–4,
    318, 354–6
truth, and confirmation bias 317
truth tables
    and affirming the consequent 45
    and denying the antecedent 47
    and *modus ponens* 44, 45
    and propositional logic 44–5
truth-values 397–8
    claims 160–2, 212–13, 333
    necessary 396–7
    objective judgments 396–7
    subjective judgments 396–7
    universal 396–7
truthiness 216
tu quoque fallacy 88–93, 232
Turing Test 307
Turner, Brock 146–7
Turner, Dan 146–7
Tversky, Amos 321, 323
Twain, Mark 241
Twelve Tables 232
two wrongs make a right 230–3

UFOS *see* unidentified flying objects
ultimate cause 182
understatement 273–5
undistributed middle, fallacy of the 63–5
unfair play 220
unfalsifiability 199, 403–5
unidentified flying objects (UFOs)
    140–1, 142, 155, 190, 327
    see also aliens
United States 228, 233
    Constitution 187
    presidential election 2016 209–10
United States Sentencing Commission
    146–7

universe
  complexity of the 235
  creation 235–6
untestability 127
unwarranted assumptions 407–9
US Census Bureau 135–6
Ustinov, Peter 241
utilitarianism 112

vaccinations 155, 340, 344
Vader, Darth 185, 187
vagueness 19, 26, 177–8, 271, 274, 295
validation, subjective 392–5
variables, confounding 336, 339
Varnell, Paul 386
Vaughn, Lewis 130, 154, 319, 326,
  327, 383
Venn diagrams 322
Venus 141
Vietnam war 228
Vigen, Tyler 340
virtues 120
vision, constructive nature 324, 326–7

Wakefield, Andrew 155, 344
Wallon, Henri 205
Walters, Keith 346
Walton, Douglas 72–3, 77, 79, 83,
  88–9, 99–100, 102–3, 106–10,
  112–13, 137–8
Warren, Ed 141
Warren, Lorraine 141
Warren, Mary Anne 262–3
Washington Post, The (newspaper) 352
Washington Redskins 266, 267, 268
weak analogy 234–7

weapons 182–3, 223–4
weasel words 271–2
Wegener, Alfred 152
welfare 338–9
"Welfare Queen' myth 215–16, 217
West, Kanye 349
Whately, Richard 52, 58–9, 64
White House Task Force Report 338–9
Whittington, Harry 197
Wiggins, David 390
Wikiquote 248
Wilkinson, Michael 290
Willard, A.K. 306
William of Sherwood 51–2, 54, 58
Wilson, Darren 352
Wimpy 187–8
Winters, Shelley 219
wiretapping 232
witchcraft 199–200
Wittgenstein, Ludwig 166, 204,
  206, 375
Woods, John 106–8, 112, 113
words
  with ambiguous meaning 276
  and the etymological fallacy 266–8
  weasel 271–2
worldviews 318, 325–6
Wreen, Michael 109, 113
Wright brothers 153
Wykstra, Stephen 110

Zabel, Judge Sarah 386
Zagzebski, Linda 114
Zeno's paradoxes 178, 202
Zeus 306
Zucchino, David 216